CLINICAL NEGLIGENCE

Third Edition

GW00717022

General Editor:

Laura Begley, Barrister.

Founding Editor:

Grahame Aldous, Queen's Counsel.

Contributing Authors:

John Foy, Queen's Counsel.
Giles Eyre, Barrister.
Christopher Wilson, Barrister.
Jeremy Crowther, Barrister.
Christopher Stephenson, Barrister.
Giles Mooney, Barrister.
Perrin Gibbons, Barrister.
Adam Dawson, Barrister.
Shahram Sharghy, Barrister.
Robert McAllister, Barrister.
Esther Pounder, Barrister.
Oliver Millington, Barrister.
Emily Verity, Barrister.
Edward Lamb, Barrister.
Ben Rodgers, Barrister.
Kate Lamont, Barrister.
William Dean, Barrister.
Laura Hibberd, Barrister.

Published by Chambers of Andrew Ritchie QC, 9 Gough Square, London.

Published in July 2015 by the Chambers of Andrew Ritchie, QC, 9 Gough Square, London, EC4A 3DG. Tel. 0207 832 0500, fax: 0207 353 1344, email: clerks@9goughsquare.co.uk.

www.9goughsquare.co.uk

ISBN 978-0-9555197–8-9

A Cataloguing-in-Publication record is available for this book from the British Library.

EDITORIAL TEAM

The general editor, founding editor and contributing authors are all barristers who have extensive experience of clinical negligence claims and are members of the clinical negligence team within the Chambers of Andrew Ritchie QC, 9 Gough Square, London.

ACKNOWLEDGEMENTS

The editors and authors would like to thank Cheryl Prophett for her helpful suggestions and invaluable proof reading and formatting skills.

Any mistakes that remain in the text are entirely the fault of the editors. We have tried to state the law as we understand it as at May 2015.

TABLE OF CONTENTS

TABLE OF CASES

TABLE OF STATUTES AND STATUTORY INSTRUMENTS

Chapter 1

HEALTHCARE BODIES

1   NATIONAL HEALTH SERVICE AND RELATED BODIES

1.1   National Health Service (NHS)

The NHS is the publicly funded healthcare system for England and Wales. It is controlled by the Department of Health, headed by the Secretary of State for Health. It is funded centrally through national taxation. The NHS provides free healthcare to those normally resident in England and Wales, although there are charges associated with some services, including eye tests, some prescriptions and dental care. (Websites: www.nhs.uk; www.gov.uk/government/organisations/department-of-health.)

1.2   Health and Social Care Act 2012

Until 31st March 2013, the NHS was structured around ten Strategic Health Authorities (SHAs) and Primary Care Trusts (PCTs). On 1st April 2013, SHAs and PCTs were abolished by the Health and Social Care Act 2012 and replaced by Clinical Commissioning Groups (CCGs), commissioning consortia led by general practitioners.

Some of the property owned by SHAs and PCTs was transferred to the commissioning consortia. All remaining property is held by NHS Property Services Ltd, a limited company owned by the Department of Health. (Website: www.nhs.uk/NHSEngland/ thenhs/about/Pages/nhsstructure.aspx.)

1.2.1   Before 1st April 2013

The Department of Health controlled ten SHAs, which oversaw all NHS activities in England and managed the local NHS on behalf of the Secretary of State. Each SHA was responsible for enacting directives and implementing fiscal policy at a regional level. Each SHA area contained various NHS trusts which were responsible for local NHS services.

There were numerous NHS trusts within each SHA area. PCTs controlled 80% of the NHS budget and were responsible for all primary care in their area. (Primary care involves care provided by the professionals one would normally see when a health problem arises, like a GP, dentist or optician.) PCTs also dealt with vaccinations and the control of epidemics. They had their own budgets and priorities and were able to control these within the overriding parameters set by the SHAs and Department of Health.

The National Patient Safety Agency (NPSA) was established in 2001 with a mandate to identify patient safety issues and find appropriate solutions to them. It was divided into three divisions: the Patient Safety Division, to collect and analyse patient safety incident information, respond to incidents (and to develop responses); the National

Clinical Assessment Division, to provide confidential advice and support to the NHS when the performance of doctors or dentists was giving cause for concern; and the National Research Ethics Service, to maintain a UK-wide system of ethical review. The NPSA was also responsible for commissioning and monitoring confidential enquiries into suicide and homicide, maternal and child health and patient outcome and death. On 1st June 2012, the NPSA's functions were transferred to the NHS Commissioning Board Special Health Authority (now NHS England).

1.2.2   From 1st April 2013

NHS England (formerly the NHS Commissioning Board Special Health Authority) exists to provide national leadership for improving the quality of care. It is independent of the government. Its other functions are overseeing and allocating resources to CCGs and commissioning primary care and specialist services. It also received most of the functions of the NPSA (para. 1.2.1 above) and the Health Protection Agency (para. 3.3 below). (Website: www.england.nhs.uk.)

CCGs, which replaced PCTs, have the function of arranging for the provision of healthcare services. They now commission most health services including emergency and out-of-hours care, hospital care, community-based and rehabilitative care and services in the areas of mental health and learning disabilities. As of October 2014, 80% of CCG chairpersons were general practitioners. One of the most controversial changes under the 2012 Act was that CCGs may commission services from any provider which meets specified standards and costs, taking into account NICE guidelines and data from the Care Quality Commission. Such providers may include NHS hospitals, private providers and charities.

Public Health England (PHE) is an executive agency sponsored by the Department of Health. It was established on 1st April 2013 with a view to coordinate public health specialists (mostly scientists, researchers and public health professionals) from over 70 organisations into a single public health service. It has a number of functions in relation to supporting and coordinating public health services. It assists in the collation of research and has a role in preparation for public health emergencies. (Website: www.gov.uk/government/organisations/public-health-england.)

Health and Wellbeing Boards (HWBs) were also established under the 2012 Act. There is one for every top tier and unitary local authority. Each HWB is considered a forum for local NHS, social care and public health commissioners. The intentions are to encourage integrated commissioning and to strengthen working relationships between health and social care.

1.3   Patient Advice and Liaison Services (PALS)

PALS is a body created to provide confidential advice, assistance and support to patients, families and their carers, as well as information on the NHS, its complaints procedures and other health-related matters. PALS will refer patients and families to local or national-based support agencies, as appropriate. Feedback received from patients is used to inform service developments and PALS also reports on trends and gaps in services. (Website: www.nhs.uk/chq/pages/1082.aspx?CategoryID=68.)

1.4 Special Health Authorities

Special Health Authorities provide a health service to the whole of England, not just a local community. They are independent, but can be subject to ministerial direction in the same way as other NHS bodies. The National Blood Authority is an example of such a body as is the NHS Litigation Authority. The remaining organisations listed below in this section are all special health authorities.

1.5 National Health Service Litigation Authority (NHSLA)

NHSLA handles, on behalf of the NHS, all clinical negligence claims against it, as well as claims relating to non-clinical risks. It provides indemnity cover for legal claims against the NHS and provides legal and professional services for its members. It determines whether to admit or deny liability for an accident on behalf of the NHS. It is a not for profit organisation. It also has a risk management programme intended to help raise the standards of care within the NHS and reduce the number of accidents within its premises and care remit. It is responsible for handling family health service appeals and coordinating equal pay claims. (Website: www.nhsla.com.)

1.6 The National Institute for Health and Clinical Excellence (NICE)

NICE is responsible for providing guidance, setting quality standards and managing a national database intended to improve people's health and prevent and treat ill health, with a strong focus on evidence-based treatment. It makes recommendations to the NHS regarding new and existing medicines, treatments and procedures, treating specific conditions, improving health and preventing illness. All recommendations and services are developed in consultation with independent committees and experts, who can include health experts, academics, patients and members of the public with a background or interest in the area. (Website: www.nice.org.uk.)

2 HEALTHCARE REGULATORS AND PROFESSIONAL ORGANISATIONS

2.1 General Medical Council (GMC)

The GMC is an organisation independent from government that registers doctors to practise medicine in the UK, and is an independent regulator of them. It sets standards for medical schools and postgraduate education and training. It deals with doctors whose fitness to practise is in doubt, and has the power to remove doctors from its register and take away their right to practise medicine if necessary. It keeps an up-to-date register of qualified doctors and aims to foster good medical practice and promote high standards. Its job is to protect the public, the needs of the medical profession being protected by the BMA (see para. 2.3 below). (Website: www.gmc-uk.org.)

2.2 Other Regulatory Bodies

Numerous other bodies regulate practitioners other than doctors and carry out similar functions to the GMC. These include the Health Professions Council (regulates other health professions in the UK), the Nursing and Midwifery Council (regulates nurses and midwives), the General Optical Council, General Dental Council, General Chiropractic Council, General Osteopathic Council and the General Pharmaceutical

Council. Further details about these bodies can be found at the relevant websites listed below. (Websites: www.hpc-uk.org; www.nmc-uk.org; www.optical.org; www.gdc-uk.org; www.gcc-uk.org; www.osteopathy.org.uk; www.pharmacyregulation.org.). See also Chapter 2 which deals with Healthcare Regulatory Law.

2.3   British Medical Association (BMA)

The BMA is the doctors' professional organisation that looks after the professional and personal needs of its doctor members. It represents doctors in all branches of medicine all over the UK in its capacity as a trade union. It keeps its members up to date with clinical and other medical issues through the *British Medical Journal*. Approximately two-thirds of practising UK doctors are members. It is not responsible for registering or disciplining doctors (for this, see GMC, para. 2.1 above). (Website: www.bma.org.uk.)

3   PUBLIC HEALTHCARE ORGANISATIONS

3.1   Healthwatch (replacing LINks)

Local Involvement Networks (LINks) were launched in 2008, replacing the Commission for Patient and Public Involvement in Health and PPI Forums. LINks existed in every local authority area with a responsibility for social services. There were 151 in total. They were independent, comprising individuals and community groups who worked together with the intention of improving local health and social care services. They could request that health and social care commissioners provide information, issue reports or make recommendations about a service, refer matters to the local council and enter the premises of certain services and view the care provided.

As a result of the reforms under the Health and Social Care Act 2012, LINks were abolished and Healthwatch was created in their place. Healthwatch is an independent 'consumer champion' set up to collate and represent public opinion on health and social care in England. National policy is considered by Healthwatch England. Local matters are dealt with by Local Healthwatch, which has a branch for each local authority. (Website: www.nhs.uk/NHSEngland/thenhs/healthregulators/Pages/healthwatch-england.aspx.)

3.2   Care Quality Commission (CQC)

The CQC is the independent regulator of all healthcare and adult social care in England. It regulates care provided by the NHS, local authorities, private companies and voluntary organisations. It looks at care provided in hospitals, care homes and people's own homes. It replaced the Healthcare Commission, Commission for Social Care Inspection and the Mental Health Act Commission, all of which ceased to exist on 31st March 2009. It registers providers of health and social care, monitors compliance with standards, investigates areas of concern, has enforcement powers if services drop below essential standards, including the power to close a service down, acts to protect patients whose rights are restricted under the Mental Health Act, and gives the public information about the work done. (Website: www.cqc.org.uk.)

3.3   Health Protection Agency (HPA)

Before 2013, the HPA was an independent organisation set up by the government to protect the community against infectious diseases and other dangers to health. The HPA detected and responded to hazards caused by infectious diseases, hazardous chemicals, poisons or radiation and prepared for new and emerging threats such as bio-terrorist attacks or virulent new strains of disease. It became part of Public Health England (para. 1.2.2 above) in 2013.

3.4   The Health Service Ombudsman (HSO)

The office of the HSO carries out independent investigations into complaints about UK government departments and their agencies, as well as the NHS, in order to improve public services. This includes complaints about services provided by hospitals, health authorities, trusts, GPs, dentists, pharmacists, opticians and other healthcare practitioners. It also investigates complaints against private health providers if the treatment was funded by the NHS. The Ombudsman combines the two statutory roles of Parliamentary Commissioner for Administration (the Parliamentary Ombudsman) and Health Service Commissioner for England (Health Service Ombudsman), whose powers are set out in the Parliamentary Commissioner Act 1967 and the Health Service Commissioners Act 1993 respectively. The current Parliamentary and Health Service Ombudsman for England is Dame Julie Mellor. (Websites: www.ombudsman.org.uk; www.ombudsman-wales.org.uk.)

3.5   Independent Complaints Advocacy Service (ICAS)

ICAS provides advocacy support to patients and their carers wishing to pursue a complaint regarding their NHS treatment or care through the NHS complaint procedure. The service is independent, free and confidential. ICAS will explore the options available to patients at every stage of the complaints procedure, provide assistance by writing letters and preparing for meetings, attend meetings with patients if necessary and, upon instruction, liaise with third parties on a patient's behalf. ICAS does not advise, encourage complaints, offer legal or medical advice, take meeting minutes (the advocate may take file notes though), deal with private treatment/nursing homes (unless funded by the NHS), support clients once legal proceedings have been initiated or investigate complaints. Each region of the country has its own ICAS office. (Websites: www.nhscomplaintsadvocacy.org; see also: www.pohwer.net; www.seap.org.uk/icas.)

3.6   Medicines and Healthcare Products Regulatory Agency (MHRA)

MHRA is an executive agency of the Department of Health, responsible for ensuring that medicines and medical devices work and are acceptably safe. It assesses medicines and authorises the sale or supply of medicines in the UK for human use. It oversees the auditors of medical device manufacturers. It regulates clinical trials and ensures compliance with statutory obligations. MHRA is also responsible for regulating blood establishments and hospital blood banks. It oversees the use of Advanced Therapy Medicinal Products (ATMPs) (medicinal products which are prepared industrially or manufactured by a method involving an industrial process). It provides information to the public designed to enable informed decisions about treatment choices. (Website:

www.gov.uk/government/organisations/medicines-and-healthcare-products-regulatory-agency.)

4 CLINICAL NEGLIGENCE GROUPS AND SCHEMES

4.1 Action against Medical Accidents (AvMA)

AvMA is an independent charity that aims to promote better patient safety and justice for people who have been affected by a medical accident. It seeks to find an explanation, support and compensation in appropriate cases for those who have been involved in such accidents. It also considers what steps could be taken to prevent similar accidents recurring. Within the clinical negligence field, it accredits solicitors for its own specialist panel of claimant solicitors and is active in lobbying in policy areas. (Website: www.avma.org.uk.)

4.2 Clinical Negligence Accreditation Scheme (CNAS)

The Law Society operates a number of accreditation schemes, including one for clinical negligence. These schemes are intended to promote high standards in legal service provision, help consumers make informed choices, and ensure that scheme members maintain relevant standards of competency and expertise. It puts members of the public in contact with legal practitioners who can provide advice and assistance in claims arising from medical or dental negligence matters. The Scheme only accredits claimant solicitors and legal executives. If lawyers do both claimant and defence work they must demonstrate that they can properly conduct cases on behalf of victims. Both solicitors and legal executives are permitted to join the Scheme, and details on how to join can be found at the address below. (Website: www.lawsociety.org.uk/support-services/accreditation/clinical-negligence.)

4.3 Clinical Disputes Forum (CDF)

The CDF works to try and improve procedures in the field of clinical negligence litigation and reduce the number of patients who have to resort to legal proceedings to resolve their disputes with healthcare providers. It is registered as a charitable company. Its members include claimant and defendant solicitors, barristers, judges, medical personnel, NHS and private health sector managers, the Deputy Health Service Ombudsman and patient representatives, together with officials from the Departments of Health and Constitutional Affairs, the National Health Service Litigation Authority, the Legal Services Commission and other regulatory bodies. Its projects have included the pre-action protocol. (Website: www.clinical-disputes-forum.org.uk.)

4.4 The Expert Witness Institute (EWI)

EWI provides support to experts of all professional disciplines and other occupations requiring skills and judgment. It engages in the training of experts to ensure competency and an understanding of responsibilities. It works with other professional bodies and associations, as well as making representations to them when appropriate. It also communicates with the government and media. It actively encourages lawyers to make use of experts wherever specialised knowledge is required. It publishes regular newsletters, free to members, with recent cases and useful information. It also runs an expert referral service. It is a non-profit making company. (Website: www.ewi.org.uk.)

4.5   Medical Protection Society (MPS)/Medical Defence Union (MDU)

These are medical defence organisations. They offer services to members including legal and ethical help over a range of areas: clinical negligence actions and related claims handling; general complaints; representation at inquests and fatal accident enquiries; GMC conduct issues; court martial and criminal investigations. The services indemnify members for the costs of being involved in such actions. The organisations are not insurance companies (see *MDU v. Dept of Trade*[1]); the services they offer are provided at the discretion of the organisation. (Websites: www.medicalprotection.org/uk/about-mps; www.themdu.com.)

---

1 [1980] Ch 82.

Chapter 2

HEALTHCARE REGULATORY LAW

1   INTRODUCTION

Whilst this work is mainly concerned with civil actions for compensation by patients against healthcare professionals, some consideration must be given to the linked and often overlapping area of regulation and discipline of the healthcare profession.

There are 12 healthcare regulators whose role it is to regulate and discipline professionals working within the various areas of medical practice:

- The General Medical Council;
- The General Dental Council;
- The Nursing and Midwifery Council;
- The General Pharmaceutical Council;
- The Pharmaceutical Society of Northern Ireland;
- The General Optical Council;
- The General Osteopathic Council;
- The General Chiropractic Council;
- The Health Professions Council;
- Care Council for Wales;
- Scottish Social Services Council;
- Northern Ireland Social Care Council.

In April 2003, the Council for the Regulation of Health Care Professionals was created with the aim of overseeing the bodies and promoting best practice and consistency across the Councils. Each of the bodies has its own procedures and rules and this chapter will take an overview of the common themes in healthcare regulation, but with greater emphasis on the General Medical Council (GMC) and its workings.

That said, all disciplinary procedures by the various bodies follow the same three-stage approach. Firstly, the regulatory body will investigate a complaint which has been made. This investigation includes dealing with matters of jurisdiction and whether the complaint crosses the relevant seriousness threshold as well as obtaining further information. The second stage involves adjudicating on the complaint while the third stage is the appeal process.

2   COMPLAINT

The procedures leading to disciplinary proceedings are engaged by the various regulators upon receipt of information about a practitioner which raises issues about his fitness to practise. There is no limit on who can provide information to the relevant Council. Any member of the public can make a complaint and there is no requirement that the particular complainant was a "victim" of any alleged mistreatment by the healthcare professional. Accordingly information may be provided by the relatives of patients or even somebody unconnected and merely acting in the public interest.

The principles of public interest are invoked in cases where police investigations reveal matters that the police may decide to pass onto the regulatory body. Indeed even in cases where charges are not laid, the public interest considerations will override considerations of confidentiality that might otherwise be owed by the police to the person under investigation should the police decide that information should be referred to the regulator.

3   THE NEW REGIME

As a result of a number of high profile cases and inquiries, culminating in the Fifth Shipman Inquiry Report of December 2004, healthcare regulation has undergone a large scale overhaul and the historical categorisation of allegations facing practitioners has changed. These changes affected the whole approach to regulation and are reflected in the amendments to primary legislation governing the regulatory bodies.

The change of emphasis is illustrated in the current approach to disciplinary proceedings. Historically a practitioner would have faced an allegation under one of four categories:

(a) serious professional misconduct/misconduct (depending on the regulatory body);
(b) conviction of a criminal offence;
(c) impairment by ill health;
(d) allegations relating to performance or competence.

This compartmentalisation of allegations was reflected in the make-up of the GMC. Disciplinary proceedings were conducted by three separate committees (Professional, Conduct, Health and Performance) to deal with the various types of allegation. These three committees have been replaced with a single Fitness to Practise Panel which illustrates the new approach being taken. Under s. 35C(1) of the Medical Act 1983 (which came into force on 1st November 2004) the question for the single panel is whether a practitioner's fitness to practise is "impaired".

4 IMPAIRED FITNESS TO PRACTISE

The rather vague concept of impaired fitness to practise is given some clarification by s. 35C(2). This provides that fitness to practise should be regarded as impaired by reason only of the following:

- misconduct;
- deficient professional performance;
- a conviction or caution in the British Islands for a criminal offence, or a conviction elsewhere for an offence which, if committed in England and Wales, would constitute a criminal offence;
- adverse physical or mental health;
- a determination by a body in the UK responsible under any enactment for the regulation of a health or social care profession to the effect that the practitioner's fitness to practise as a member of that profession is impaired, or a determination by a regulatory body elsewhere to the same effect.

The other bodies have or are in the process of adopting similar schemes and the list of actions that could amount to impairment of fitness to practise found in the various schemes, whilst slightly different in terminology, are largely the same in effect. The most significant difference in terminology which does lead to some divergence in effect is that certain regulatory bodies substitute deficient professional performance with deficient professional conduct. The relevance of this is discussed below.

Although it is clear from statutory law that only actions falling within one or more of the five categories can amount to impairment of fitness to practise the term itself is not defined. The difficulty of defining the term was considered by Dame Janet Smith in the *Fifth Shipman Inquiry Report*.

Dame Janet suggested that at the investigation stage of the process the following questions should be considered:

> "1.　*Is there one or more than one allegation of misconduct, deficient professional performance or adverse health and/ or one or more report of a conviction, caution or determination which, if proved or admitted, might show that the doctor:*
> > a.　*has in the past acted and/ or is liable in the future to act so as to put a patient or patients at unwarranted risk of harm; and/ or*
> > b.　*has in the past brought and/ or is liable in the future to bring the medical profession into disrepute; and/ or*
> > c.　*has in the past committed a breach (other than one which is trivial) of one of the tenets of the medical profession and/ or is liable to do so in the future; and/ or*
> > d.　*has in the past acted dishonestly and/ or is liable to do so in the future.*
>
> *If so:*
>
> 2.　*Is the available evidence such that there is a realistic prospect of proving the allegation.*"

At the adjudication stage the relevant questions were:

> *"Do our findings of fact in respect of the doctor's misconduct, deficient professional performance, adverse health, conviction, caution or determination show that his/her fitness to practise is impaired in the sense that s/he:*
>
> a. *in the past acted and/ or is liable in the future to act so as to put a patient or patients at unwarranted risk of harm; and/ or*
>
> b. *has in the past brought and/ or is liable in the future to bring the medical profession into disrepute; and/ or*
>
> c. *has in the past committed a breach (other than one which is trivial) of one of the tenets of the medical profession and/ or is liable to do so in the future; and/ or*
>
> d. *has in the past acted dishonestly and/ or is liable to do so in the future."*

Dame Janet expressed the view that her proposed tests should be enshrined in legislation.

Although all questions will be looked at in the framework of whether the allegations amount to an impairment of fitness to practise, a closer look is necessary in relation to misconduct and deficient professional performance and competence.

5   MISCONDUCT

In the majority of regulatory schemes misconduct is not defined. The most helpful definition comes from case law prior to the changes of November 2004 in *Roylance v. General Medical Council (No 2)*.[1] This remains the test that is generally applied:

> *"Misconduct is a word of general effect, involving some act or omission which falls short of what would be proper in the circumstances. The standard of propriety may often be found by reference to the rules and standards ordinarily required to be followed by a medical practitioner in the particular circumstances."*

Prior to the 2004 changes many of the regulatory bodies including the GMC and the General Dental Council required "serious professional misconduct". Whether the omission of the words serious and professional has greatly changed the type or nature of the conduct for a finding to be made against the practitioner, remains debatable. This is because the overriding test must be whether the misconduct is such as to impair the practitioner's fitness to practise and hence misconduct will have to be at a level to reach this threshold. It may be that the regulatory bodies will be more willing to look at conduct not directly linked to the professional's practice.

Whilst clinical negligence can constitute misconduct, the conduct must be gross negligence as opposed to simple professional negligence. In *Preiss v. General Dental Council*[2] Lord Cooke noted *"something more is required than a degree of negligence enough*

---

1 [2000] 1 AC 311.
2 [2001] 1 WLR 1926.

to give rise to civil liability but not calling for the opprobrium that inevitably attached to a disciplinary offence".

6 DEFICIENT PROFESSIONAL PERFORMANCE AND LACK OF COMPETENCE

Unfortunately the regulatory bodies have taken two different paths when considering the performance jurisdiction. The GMC, as can be seen above, has focussed on performance. This lead has been followed by other bodies, but not all. The General Chiropractic Council, the General Osteopathic Council and the Nursing and Midwifery Council preferred to use competence. The difference was looked at in the *Fifth Shipman Inquiry Report* and has been highlighted in GMC cases. In short, competence describes a practitioner's knowledge and skills whilst performance describes what a practitioner actually does in practice. Professional performance has a wider application as it can include matters such as poor record keeping, failure to keep confidentiality, or even deficiencies in consideration and courtesy towards patients. As a general rule performance and competence-related complaints will be less serious than misconduct.

6.1 The Investigation Stage

Once a complaint has been made or information has been received, the regulatory body will consider whether the matter should be considered in a full hearing. In the case of the GMC this will be a decision by the Investigation Committee as to whether the matter should be considered by the Fitness to Practise Panel. The Investigation Committee (formerly known as the Preliminary Proceedings Committee or the PPC) is a statutory committee of the GMC which at the end of an initial investigation into concerns about a doctor considers those cases where case examiners are unable to agree on what should happen next, or considers that a warning is appropriate but the doctor has disputed the facts or requested a hearing of the Investigation Committee. It is important that this filtering system occurs to prevent practitioners facing disciplinary hearings for vexatious or frivolous complaints against them.

The test applied by the GMC has evolved as a result of voluminous case law and is now seen as being a "realistic prospect test". As a result of confusion and disagreement between members, senior Counsel was asked to draft an aide-memoire for the then PPC (now the Investigation Committee) to apply when considering whether a complaint should go before the Fitness to Practise Panel. Even though the aide-memoire pre-dates the 2004 changes the new legislation remains as vague as that which it replaces and hence it remains a useful tool. (References to the PPC below should be understood as relating now to the Investigation Committee.)

> *"AIDE-MEMOIRE GUIDANCE*
>
> 1. *In conduct cases the PPC's task is to decide whether, in its opinion, there is a real prospect of serious professional misconduct being established. Serious professional misconduct may be considered in the context of conduct so grave as potentially to call into question a*

practitioner's registration whether indefinitely, temporarily or conditionally.

2.   *The 'real prospect' test applies to both the factual allegations and the question of whether, if established, the facts would amount to serious professional misconduct. It reflects not a probability but rather a genuine (not remote or fanciful) possibility. It is in no-one's interest for cases to be referred to the PPC when they are bound to fail, and the PPC may properly decline to refer such cases. On the other hand, cases which raise a genuine issue of serious professional misconduct are for the PPC to decide.*

3.   *The following does not purport to be an exhaustive list, but in performing the task the PPC:*

    (i)   *should bear in mind that the standard of proof before the PPC will be the criminal standard (beyond a reasonable doubt);*

    (ii)   *is entitled to assess the weight of the evidence;*

    (iii)   *should not, however, normally seek to resolve substantial conflicts of evidence;*

    (iv)   *should proceed with caution;*

    (v)   *should proceed with particular caution in reaching a decision to halt a complaint when the decision may be perceived as inconsistent with a decision made by another public body with medical personnel or input (for example, a NHS body, a Coroner or an Ombudsman) in relation to the same or substantially the same facts and, if it does reach such a decision, should give reasons for the apparent inconsistency;*

    (vi)   *should be slower to halt a complaint against a practitioner who continues to practise than against one who does not;*

    (vii)   *if in doubt, should consider invoking Rule 13 of the Procedure Rules [ie the power to cause further investigations to be made before reaching a decision] and in any event should lean in favour of allowing the complaint to proceed to the PPC; and*

    (viii)   *should bear in mind that, whilst there is a public interest in medical practitioners not being harassed by unfounded complaints, there is also a public interest in the ventilation before the PPC in public of complaints which do have a real prospect of establishing serious professional misconduct."*

Despite the frustrating lack of statutory guidance the existence of the aide-memoire as well as the proposals from the *Fifth Shipman Inquiry Report* (see above) means that there should be some certainty as to the role of the sifting process at the investigation stage. See Annex B of the guidance for decision-makers on the GMC's website www.gmc-uk.org/concerns/the_investigation_process/decision_makers.asp for further detail. Other more general guidance for decision-makers is also available on the GMC's website and updated periodically.

6.2   The Charge

Although the terminology of the charge will rather depend on the particular regulatory body, the rules of drafting the charge (or allegation) are relevant across the bodies. The charge will usually contain all the allegations against the practitioner in the form of particulars. In this regard the charge resembles the particulars of negligence in a civil pleading. It is important to note that there is nothing duplicitous about this approach as the charge is the unit of accusation and determination. In other words a practitioner is being accused of having impaired fitness to practise by reason of a number of factual allegations. The charge will also include the conclusions to be drawn from the alleged facts.

6.3   The Hearing

All the healthcare regulatory bodies are public bodies and hence, since the Human Rights Act 1998 came into force in 2000, they have been compelled to provide "a fair and public hearing". Generally the criminal rules of evidence apply. The panel or committee hearing the matter will be assisted by a legal assessor. The legal assessor performs a task akin to the role of the clerk of the court in the Magistrates' Court in that his role is to advise the panel, upon request, on matters of law, to inform the panel of any irregularity in the conduct of the proceedings and to advise the panel, on his own motion, to prevent a mistake of law being made. The panel has a duty to provide adequate and sufficient reasons for its decisions.

One area which requires further consideration is the standard of proof to be applied when making findings against a practitioner. There is no assistance in governing legislation for the various regulatory bodies as to the standard of proof to be applied. This has led to inconsistency between the regulatory bodies and even within the same regulatory body. Historically the GMC applied the criminal standard to serious professional misconduct matters where cases commenced before 31st May 2008. The position now is that a civil burden of proof is applied. Even on the civil standard the evidence required to prove an allegation must be in keeping with the severity of the allegation and inherent likelihoods are a factor for the tribunal to take into account, but that does not mean that there is a higher standard for more serious allegations.[3] The General Chiropractic Council and General Osteopathic Council both employ the civil standard to all hearings. Dame Janet in the *Fifth Shipman Inquiry Report* suggested that the civil standard should be applied to all hearings and this may be a change across the board which will be seen in the future.

6.4   Sanctions

In ascending order of seriousness, a Fitness to Practise Panel may:

- give a formal warning that will last for 5 years;
- impose conditions on the practitioner's registration;
- suspend the practitioner for a maximum of 12 months;
- erase the practitioner's name from the register.

In GMC proceedings, s. 35D(3) allows the panel to warn the practitioner even where they have found that fitness to practise is not impaired. Whilst a warning would not affect a practitioner's registration it is disclosable if anyone enquires about the practitioner's fitness to practise history. For further details (revised periodically in respect of sanctions imposed by the GMC) see www.gmc-uk.org/Indicative_Sanctions _Guidance_April_2009.pdf_28443340.pdf. Conditions imposed usually relate to further training to be undertaken by the practitioner within a specified period of time. Some other disciplinary panels may still be able to reprimand or admonish a practitioner.

---

3 See *Inayatullah v. GMC* [2014] EWHC 3751 (Admin) a decision of Dove J.

6.5   Appeals

Under the primary legislation in relation to each of the healthcare regulators a practitioner has a right to appeal most categories of decisions made in the course of disciplinary proceedings. Appeals from all of the regulatory bodies' committees lie to the High Court and are governed by Part 52 of the Civil Procedure Rules. There is no requirement for permission to appeal. The appeal process is initiated by a Notice to Appeal which has to be filed within 28 days of the decision which is to be appealed. Under Part 52 the hearing is a review of the panel or committee's decision and an appeal will only be allowed where the decision of the panel or committee was wrong or unjust as a result of serious procedural or other irregularity in the proceedings in the panel or committee.4 Practice Direction 52(D) refers. Permission is required to appeal a High Court decision to the Court of Appeal.

If it considers that the decision should not have been made or a sanction is unduly lenient the Health & Care Professionals Council (previously known as the Council for the Regulation of Health Care Professionals) may refer the matter to the High Court pursuant to s. 29 of the National Health Service Reform and Health Care Professions Act 2002. The s. 29 referral is akin to Attorney-General's References in criminal proceedings.

---

4 *Meadow v. GMC* [2006] EWCA Civ 1390.

Chapter 3

FUNDING OF CLINICAL NEGLIGENCE CLAIMS

1   INTRODUCTION

Since the second edition of this book, there have been further developments which affect the funding of clinical negligence claims in a major way. Following Lord Justice (Sir Rupert) Jackson's *Review of Civil Litigation Costs: Final Report* (published 14th January 2010) (hereafter "Final Report"), discussed in the second edition, came the Legal Aid, Sentencing and Punishment of Offenders Act 2012 (hereafter "LASPO") which implemented many of Sir Rupert's recommendations, save for his recommendation to preserve legal aid for clinical negligence claims. Instead, it has been scrapped save for in a very limited number of claims.

1.1   Summary of Changes

In summary, LASPO and post-Jackson changes to the CPR provide for:

- very limited recourse to legal aid for clinical negligence work, restricted to neurological injuries caused during pregnancy, at birth or within the first 8 weeks of life, as defined;
- a fundamentally different CFA regime:
  o with success fees limited to 25% of a successful claimant's damages (excluding those for future care and expenses), net of any CRU recovery, taken from those damages. Appeals are treated differently;
  o success fees being irrecoverable from the defendant;
  o much reduced scope for adverse costs orders against unsuccessful claimants ("QOCS");
  o reduced need for (and recoverability of) ATE premiums, with limited exceptions for clinical negligence cases where ATE insurance covers the cost of certain expert reports;
- scope for damages based agreements (or contingency fees), again capped at 25% of damages for past losses;
- 10% uplift on general damages where there is no success fee claimed from the defendant;
- up to 10% increase upon damages where claimants beat their own Part 36 offer;
- a very different approach to costs generally, including:
  - an express requirement of the overriding objective is to deal with cases justly and at proportionate cost;
  - a new definition of proportionality, which "trumps" reasonableness;
  - costs management at the commencement of multi-track cases, resulting in approved costs budgets for the litigation;

- a revised CPR, r. 3.9 for relief from sanctions, strictly interpreted in *Mitchell v. News Group Newspapers*[1] concerning the late filing of a costs budget;
- a new form N260 for summary assessment containing more detail;
- there are also a number of fixed costs regimes within the CPR. The NHSLA has published a pilot fixed costs regime for certain clinical negligence claims up to £25,000.00.

1.2   Philosophy behind the Changes

It is worth reproducing some of Lord Justice Jackson's response to the consultation process that followed the Final Report here as a summary of the views of one of the most influential judicial thinkers in this area and as an explanation for the reforms that underpin LASPO and the changes to the CPR. Under the heading of "Complex personal injury or clinical negligence claims" Lord Justice Jackson said:

"2.10 Many complex personal injury claims present little or no risk on liability, so there is no need for a success fee at all in such cases. So far as quantum is concerned, there is no reason why the Part 36 risk should be borne by the defendant. On any view, that should be a matter between the claimant and his own solicitors. Where there is genuine need for a CFA, I adhere to the view that a scheme whereby (a) general damages are increased, (b) the rewards for effective claimant offers are increased and (c) the client has a limited liability to pay a success fee out of damages is the best way forward. Another option for complex personal injury or clinical negligence cases will be contingency fees, as discussed in [the Final Report's] chapter 12. I do not accept that these arrangements will either (a) deny access to justice for claimants who have strong claims or (b) make it uneconomic for solicitors to act in such cases.

2.11 An argument which has been urged at many meetings over the last year is that solicitors will stop taking on 'risky' cases. I view this argument with scepticism because (with certain honourable exceptions) claimants with risky cases are already unable to find CFA solicitors. Indeed one of the arguments which is repeatedly urged in support of the present regime is that ATE insurers see to it that only very strong cases are pursued on CFAs. One substantial claimant clinical negligence firm examined its records over the period April 2004 to June 2009 for the purposes of the Costs Review. It found that there was not a single CFA case which had been lost at trial or dropped at a late stage. When one looks at the various statistics, it can be seen that the vast majority of claims recorded as 'unsuccessful' are dropped at a very early stage.

2.12 Traditionally, the more risky clinical negligence cases have been supported by legal aid. According to the NHSLA statistics, cases supported by legal aid have a lower success rate than those funded by any other means. The question whether legal aid should be retained for clinical negligence is the subject of a separate consultation, upon which it is not my function to comment in this paper."

1.3   Scope of this Chapter

Despite the wide-ranging reform, this chapter will still start with a consideration of the retainer (from which, traditionally at least, any claim for costs arises) and entitlement to costs, before considering the new landscape for each of public funding and CFAs.

---

1 [2013] EWCA Civ 1526.

There is also a section on legal expense insurance and the chapter ends by considering various statutory cancellation and "cooling off" periods, which may be relevant to the entering into of many retainers.

Damages-based agreements are not dealt with in any detail as it is understood that there is little uptake at the present time.

This chapter can be no more than a general guide to key areas of costs and funding as they relate to clinical negligence claims. This is no substitute for specialist texts on the subject of costs and a good knowledge of LASPO and the CPR. Please note that the funding of inquests is covered in Chapter 14 which deals with inquests generally.

2   THE RETAINER, THE INDEMNITY PRINCIPLE AND COSTS

In short, costs are the client's costs and not the solicitor's. The order for costs in a party's favour is by way of an indemnity for the costs that the party has incurred. If there is no legal liability for costs between the solicitor and client there is nothing to indemnify and no costs will be recoverable from the third party. This is why it is fundamentally important to get the retainer right, particularly with high value (or high value of costs) cases. Whether 100% of costs incurred (or more, where there are pre-LASPO success fees) will be recovered depends largely on the soundness of the retainer between the solicitor and client and on the CPR and related case law about the recoverability of costs (see below at para. 2.2).

Whilst calls for the indemnity principle to be abolished have not yet been acceded to, there have been significant inroads into the principle in recent years, for example: s. 194 of the Legal Services Act 2007, in respect of pro bono cases, CFAs "lite" (as to which see the second edition of this work); and, by way of background, the increasing number of fixed costs regimes in the CPR.

2.1   The Traditional Retainer: Privately Funding Clients

A solicitor's right to be paid arises from the retainer, which is a contract, governed by the ordinary law of contract, but subject to statutory provisions and rules of professional conduct. At least some of the retainer must be in writing (the name and status of the person dealing with the matter), but it is certainly good practice for the entire retainer to be set out in writing. See further the various regulations discussed in Section 7 below.

A traditional retainer (with a client paying privately) commonly includes provision for interim fees to be paid and for money to be paid on account, particularly in respect of disbursements. This is, of course, good practice when contemplating a private retainer in a clinical negligence case even if it is viewed as a short-term source of funding and as a stepping stone to entering into a CFA once the merits are clearer.

Practitioners should be open with clients about the likely costs of each stage of a claim (and cost/benefit) and be clear about what any private fees will be used for (expert reports, preliminary advice or obtaining counsel's view) and when the position will be reviewed. If the plan is for a CFA to be entered into in due course, then much of the investigation will be aimed at satisfying an after the event insurer to insure the CFA.

In all cases the Solicitors' Code of Conduct 2011 should be borne in mind, and in particular outcomes 1.6 and 1.14, which provide:

> "...only enter into fee agreements with your clients that are legal, and which you consider are suitable for the client's needs and take account of the client's best interests;
>
> clients are informed of their right to challenge or complain about your bill and the circumstances in which they may be liable to pay interest on an unpaid bill;"

Further, the following "Indicative Behaviours" relate to fees:

> "Fee arrangements with your client
>
> IB(1.13) discussing whether the potential outcomes of the client's matter are likely to justify the expense or risk involved, including any risk of having to pay someone else's legal fees;
>
> IB(1.14) clearly explaining your fees and if and when they are likely to change;
>
> IB(1.15) warning about any other payments for which the client may be responsible;
>
> IB(1.16) discussing how the client will pay, including whether public funding may be available, whether the client has insurance that might cover the fees, and whether the fees may be paid by someone else such as a trade union;
>
> IB(1.17) where you are acting for a client under a fee arrangement governed by statute, such as a conditional fee agreement, giving the client all relevant information relating to that arrangement;
>
> IB(1.18) where you are acting for a publicly funded client, explaining how their publicly funded status affects the costs;
>
> IB(1.19) providing the information in a clear and accessible form which is appropriate to the needs and circumstances of the client;
>
> IB(1.20) where you receive a financial benefit as a result of acting for a client, either:
> paying it to the client; (b) offsetting it against your fees; or (c) keeping it only where you can justify keeping it, you have told the client the amount of the benefit (or an approximation if you do not know the exact amount) and the client has agreed that you can keep it;
>
> IB(1.21) ensuring that disbursements included in your bill reflect the actual amount spent or to be spent on behalf of the client;"

The code is a reminder that there may be other sources of funding, not discussed in detail in this chapter, such as employer or trade union funding.

2.2 Recovery of Costs – a Summary

As costs and funding are so interrelated, a very brief reminder of how costs recovery works in practice is useful. This section also introduces significant post-LASPO changes.

Traditionally, in civil litigation "the general rule" was *"that the unsuccessful party will be ordered to pay the costs of the successful party"* in addition to any damages award. A major change has now taken place, with "Qualified one-way costs shifting" or "QOCS" for clinical negligence and personal injury litigation, discussed below. This is closely tied to success fees and ATE insurance premiums not generally being recoverable from the paying party post-LASPO, save for limited exceptions in clinical negligence.

As well as being able to control costs at the end of litigation (by means of issue-based costs orders and, traditionally, through the assessment process) the court has for some time been able to make a costs capping order *"limiting the amount of future costs (including disbursements) which a party may recover pursuant to an order for costs subsequently made"* and costs estimates have long been relevant to the assessment process.

There are various reasons why only a proportion of costs might be recovered on assessment or in costs negotiations. This may be because costs have been unreasonable in amount or unreasonably incurred or, if the overall bill is disproportionate (in either its old or new meaning – see below) or unnecessarily incurred. Failure to beat Part 36 (or other) offers may mean that full costs are not recovered.

Post-LASPO/Jackson, costs budgets have been introduced for multi-track cases (see below) so that there will be no recovery of costs outwith pre-approved budgets.

Post-LASPO there is a revision of what is meant by proportionality and changes to Part 36, intended to make the rules fairer; to give claimant offers more bite; and to mitigate there being the recovery of CFA success fees from claimants.

2.3 Overriding Objective and Proportionality

It is now part of the overriding objective of the civil courts (CPR, r. 1) to deal with cases justly and at proportionate cost.

The definition of proportionality has been amended and is found in CPR, r. 44.3(5):

> *"Costs incurred are proportionate if they bear a reasonable relationship to –*
> *(a)   the sums in issue in the proceedings;*
> *(b)   the value of any non-monetary relief in issue in the proceedings;*
> *(c)   the complexity of the litigation;*
> *(d)   any additional work generated by the conduct of the paying party; and*
> *(e)   any wider factors involved in the proceedings, such as reputation or public importance."*

Further, CPR, r. 44.3(2) provides:

> *"Where the amount of costs is to be assessed on the standard basis, the court will –*

> *(a)   only allow costs which are proportionate to the matters in issue. Costs which are disproportionate in amount may be disallowed or reduced even if they were reasonably or necessarily incurred; and*
>
> *(b)   resolve any doubt which it may have as to whether costs were reasonably and proportionately incurred or were reasonable and proportionate in amount in favour of the paying party. "*

Taken together, the proportionality (rather than the reasonableness) of costs as they relate to the issues in the case ought to be at the forefront of the court's and practitioner's minds given that most assessments are carried out on the standard basis. The court is encouraged to stand back, having looked at reasonableness first, and make a global assessment based on proportionality, making a further reduction if necessary.

2.4   Costs Management Orders and "Costs Budgets" (CPR, rr. 3.12–3.18)

In multi-track cases issued after 1st April 2013, the court requires costs budgets to be filed and exchanged in a standard form "Precedent H", within 28 days of the date specified in the court notice or no later than 7 days before the first case management conference or as otherwise directed: see CPR, r. 3.13. This excludes cases where a claimant expects damages to exceed £10 million. Litigants in person are also exempt. If estimated costs do not exceed £25,000.00 then only the first two of the nine pages of Precedent H need to be completed.

Any party who fails to file a budget when required to do so will be treated as having filed a budget comprising of only the applicable court fees (CPR, r. 3.14). It was failure to file a budget in time that caused the claimant such problems in *Mitchell v. Newsgroup Newspapers*[2] in which the Court of Appeal upheld Master McCloud's decision not to grant relief from sanctions under the revised CPR, r. 3.9 and, in effect, endorses a strict approach to procedural rules even where the consequences are as profound as nearly all costs being irrecoverable. In clinical negligence cases this is likely to be a far bigger issue for claimants than defendants, given both QOCS (such that defendants will probably not expect to recover costs in the majority of cases) and the need to do the running on the claim.

Following the filing of Precedent Hs the first CMC, now known as a Costs and Case Management Conference ("CCMC") then deals with both the procedural steps to be taken and revisions to the parties' proposed costs budgets. This does not involve assessment or approval of costs already incurred, save for their relevance to future work that needs to be done. Further, if parties agree budgets or certain issues the court will not be able to interfere. The court will then make a Costs Management Order which will approve the revised budgets and note those areas of agreement. The approved budget is for the total sum in respect of each phase, although it may be based on each constituent part. When making Case Management Orders the court will have regard to available budgets and the costs involved in the procedural step. There is scope for revision of budgets upwards or downwards during the course of litigation if there is a significant development in the course of litigation (PD3E para 2.6).

Broadly speaking, the idea is that parties will be kept to their last approved budget come assessment on the standard basis, unless there is a good reason to depart: see CPR, r. 3.18 and the judgment of Moore Bick LJ in *Henry v. News Group Newspapers*

---

2 [2013] EWCA Civ 1526.

Limited.[3] For an example of a costs order being made within minutes of judgment being given where costs expenditure was within budget see *Safetynet Security Ltd v. Coppage*.[4]

The procedure for assessing costs is set out in CPR, r. 44.6. Summary assessment remains the general rule for fast track claims or hearings lasting less than a day. See the Guide to Summary Assessment of Costs, para. 48 and subsections 8 and 9 of PD44. Detailed assessment is dealt with at CPR, r. 47 and it is beyond the scope of this work to comment further in this respect. It should be noted that "unless there is good reason not to do so", the court will order a party to make a payment on account before assessment takes place in accordance with CPR, r. 44.2(8). This may result in a payment in the region of 60% of the likely assessed costs absent any particular conduct issues.

3   PUBLIC FUNDING OF CLINICAL NEGLIGENCE CASES

Following LASPO, legal aid is limited to clinical negligence in the case of neurological injury to infants suffered in-utero, during birth or, in effect, within the first 8 weeks of life: see para. 23 of Sch. 1 to LASPO.

There is a new Funding Checklist, although this does not apply where the likely final costs exceed £25,000.00 where a Very High Costs Contract will be entered into.

There have also been cuts to expert fees generally.

Reference should be made to specialist texts in the event that public funding is being considered for a clinical negligence claim.

3.1   A Footnote or Two on Public Funding

Lord Justice Jackson's comments at para. 3.3 of chapter 7 of his Final Report are now a footnote in the history of civil funding and costs:

> *"Legal aid is still available for some key areas of litigation, in particular clinical negligence, housing cases and judicial review. It is vital that legal aid remains in these areas ... I place on record my firm view that it would be quite wrong to tighten the eligibility criteria further, so that an even larger percentage of the population falls outside the legal aid net."*

Of interest, it appears that the retention of legal aid for expert fees in clinical negligence cases generally would have cost less to the public purse than the exception, discussed below, which allows an ATE premium to be recoverable in respect of the same fees: see the first Implementation Lecture, Cambridge, 5th September 2011.

4   CONDITIONAL FEE AGREEMENTS

The pre-LASPO CFA regime was discussed at length in the second edition of this work and the reader is referred to that edition and specialist texts on costs for issues that specifically relate to

---

3 [2013] EWCA Civ 19.
4 [2012] EWHC B11 (Mercantile).

pre-1st April 2013 CFAs. Some of the general principles underpinning CFAs are retained here where potentially relevant to the post-LASPO regime.

4.1   Introduction

Funding for clinical negligence cases can usually be provided by means of a conditional fee agreement (CFA). It must be remembered that costs are those of the client, not the solicitor, and this principle has lain at the root of the enormous amount of satellite litigation which has grown up around CFAs in the past. It is important therefore that necessary formalities are complied with in order for a CFA to be effective.

At common law a receiving party cannot receive more costs from the paying party than he is actually liable to pay his own lawyers. They are not a punishment to the paying party for losing the case, nor are they a bonus to the receiving party for winning it – *Gundry v. Sainsbury*.[5]

If the client does not have an obligation to pay his own lawyers he has no need for any costs from the other side and will not recover any – he is only entitled to be indemnified against his own liability to his lawyers – this is the indemnity principle which lies behind applications for and assessments of costs.

If a client is supported by a trade union or other organisation, the member claimant remains liable for his lawyers' costs but will be entitled to be indemnified by the trade union or organisation. Because, however, he is primarily liable to his solicitors he is able to recover costs from the unsuccessful party – *Adams v. London Improved Motor Coaches Builders Ltd*.[6]

A CFA which complies with the relevant statutory requirements is enforceable against the client and costs can be recovered from the other side by virtue of it. Historically base fees or profit costs could be increased by up to 100% if the case was successful. Success fees are now, post-LASPO, recoverable from a client and not the other side and these are capped at 25% of past loss.

Trade unions and other organisations, which were prescribed pursuant to s. 30 of the Access to Justice Act 1999, who are mass providers and purchasers of legal services may enter into a single *collective conditional fee agreement* with solicitors and this will govern the way in which cases for its members will be conducted and funded. Pre-LASPO success fees could be recovered in much the same way as CFAs. Post-LASPO, success fees are recoverable from the client's damages rather than the other side and, importantly, the date the CFA was entered into (pre or post-1st April 2013) is determinative of whether LASPO applies.

4.2   ATE Insurance and CFAs

When CFAs were made enforceable in October 1993, they were sometimes advertised as "no win no fee", but generally in the early days this description was untrue because the losing client still had a liability for his opponent's costs and, if he used the growing market for after the event ("ATE") insurance, he had to pay the insurance premium.

---

5 [1910] 1 KB 654.
6 [1921] 1 KB 495.

ATE is so named because it is insurance which is taken after the event which gave rise to the cause of action and is intended to protect a litigant against the risk of having to pay the other side's costs.

One of the main planks of the post-Jackson/LASPO regime is that the cost of ATE insurance entered into by a winning claimant cannot be recovered from a losing defendant where that policy is taken out after 1st April 2013, save for a limited extent in clinical negligence cases: see s. 46 of LASPO. The other side of this coin is that claimants will not normally face a claim for costs from a winning defendant under QOCS – see below. There is a potential mismatch in cases with a recoverable ATE premium that also benefits from QOCS.

Section 47 of LASPO provides that trade union etc. insurance premium equivalents cease to be recoverable where the undertaking to meet adverse costs liabilities is after 1st April 2013.

4.3 Exception for Clinical Negligence Cases

In respect of clinical negligence claims only, some recoverability of ATE premiums remains by virtue of the Recovery of Costs Insurance Premiums in Clinical Negligence Proceedings (No 2) Regulations 2013. Regulation 3 provides:

> *"(1) A costs order made in favour of a party to clinical negligence proceedings who has taken out a costs insurance policy may include provision requiring the payment of an amount in respect of all or part of the premium of that policy if—*
> *(a) the financial value of the claim for damages in respect of clinical negligence is more than £1,000; and*
> *(b) the costs insurance policy insures against the risk of incurring a liability to pay for an expert report or reports relating to liability or causation in respect of clinical negligence (or against that risk and other risks).*
> *(2) The amount of the premium that may be required to be paid under the costs order shall not exceed that part of the premium which relates to the risk of incurring liability to pay for an expert report or reports relating to liability or causation in respect of clinical negligence in connection with the proceedings."*

Clinical negligence claimants can, therefore, recover the cost of an ATE policy which insures against the risk of incurring a liability to pay for an expert report or reports relating *to liability or causation* (NB not quantum). If the ATE policy covers other issues, only the costs in respect of those expert reports will be recoverable.

4.4 Issues Arising Where a New CFA is Required

There are as yet unresolved issues over factors which might terminate a pre-LASPO CFA and/or necessitate a new post-LASPO CFA such as child claimants gaining their majority, clients moving firms and death of a claimant. It seems likely that anything that might be construed as a "new CFA" (to include, potentially, purported assignment) runs the risk of being a post-LASPO CFA with success fees being recoverable from a client and not the defendant.

4.5   Naming the Defendant

There is no need to name a defendant in a CFA. Where an opponent *is* named, the answer as to whether this covers the putative paying party is one of contractual interpretation. There are two relevant cases, decided in opposing directions: *Law v. (1) Liverpool City Council and (2) Berrybridge Housing Association*[7] and *Brierley v. Prescott*.[8]

4.6   Retrospectivity

It seems that retrospective CFAs are permissible, i.e. agreements which provide that work already done before the agreement was entered into may be included in the agreement. However, there must be express provision for this in the agreement and the date on the agreement should not be backdated – see *Holmes v. Alfred McAlpine Homes (Yorkshire) Ltd*.[9] This case proceeded on the basis that there was an ordinary retainer prior to the date of the agreement and the position is less clear if there was some other form of funding arrangement in place then. There remains some doubt over whether any success fee can be recovered for work done before the CFA was entered into – see *King v. Telegraph Group Ltd*.[10] However, in *Birmingham City Council v. Rose Forde*,[11] Christopher Clarke J, 13th January 2009, it was held that a retrospective success fee in a retrospective CFA was not contrary to public policy, disapproving *King v. Telegraph Group Ltd*. The court had the ability to disallow or reduce retrospective fees that were unreasonable. If that was wrong, there was no reason why the court could not delete the success fee leaving the obligation to pay unaffected. However, permission to appeal was given by the Court of Appeal in relation to the recoverability of the retrospective success fee but a compromise was reached and the appeal was withdrawn.

The above issues may well be revisited in the post-LASPO world, given that costs will be recoverable from one person (the losing party in litigation) and the success fees will be recoverable from the person entering into the CFA. It is tolerably clear that any authorities on backdated or retrospective CFAs would not be able to make a post-1st April 2013 CFA a pre-1st April 2013 CFA.

4.7   The Success Fee

Pre-LASPO the success fee was limited to 100% of base costs. Disbursements were not subject to a success fee, however funded, although counsel might also have entered into a CFA so that, in effect, there was a success fee on that disbursement. The principle (at least pre-Jackson) was that winning cases should pay for losing ones – see *Callery v. Gray*[12] – but the success fee was subject to assessment in the same way as other costs. The success fee is, however, irrelevant to the question of whether the costs claimed are disproportionate. In *Callery v. Gray*, Lord Woolf recommended a two-stage uplift and it was certainly easier to justify a 100% uplift at trial or if the case settled near to trial if the agreement provided for a two- or three-staged uplift, i.e. a success fee which increased if the case went to trial. It was made clear, however, in *U v. Liverpool City*

---

7 HHJ Stewart QC, 10 May 2005.
8 31st March 2006, Sup Ct Costs Office, Master Gordon-Saker.
9 [2006] All ER 9 (D) 68 (Feb).
10 SCCO Ref: PTH 0408205 and 0408206: 2nd December 2005.
11 [2009] EWHC 12 (QB) (Birmingham).
12 [2001] 1 WLR 2112.

Council[13] that a costs judge has no power to direct that a success fee is recoverable at different rates for different periods of the proceedings and so the costs judge could not vary the success fee for the period when the risk changed. Once the appropriate uplift was determined in accordance with a two- or three-stage CFA, that uplift was to be applied throughout.

Costs judges carrying out an assessment of costs including a success fee cannot use hindsight. The court must make an assessment of the risk as it appeared at the time when the CFA was entered into. Relevant factors to be taken into account include the risk that no costs will be recovered (usually because the case may be lost but also that a Part 36 offer will not be beaten), the legal representatives liability for disbursements and what other methods of financing the costs were available to the receiving party.

The amount of the success fee allowed will, in a clinical negligence case, vary according to the facts of the case. In *Bensusan v. Freedman*,[14] a single stage success fee of 20% was assessed in a straightforward modest value clinical negligence claim. In a single stage uplift the following formula can be applied: if the probability of success is x%, the conditional fee should be 100 divided by x multiplied by the basic fee. So, for example, if the probability of success is 50% the calculation is 100 divided by 50, which equals twice the normal fee, i.e. an uplift of 100%. This, however, compensates solely for the uncertainty of outcome. It does not compensate for the outlay of any disbursements which the solicitor may fund, nor for delay in remuneration. An increase in the uplift is appropriate to take account of these factors, but the paying party will not have to pay any proportion of the increase that is attributable to the delay in payment.

5   CONDITIONAL FEE AGREEMENTS – POST-LASPO

Lord Justice Jackson's primary recommendations on the reform of CFAs in the Final Report were that the recoverability of success fees and ATE insurance premiums from the losing party should be abolished. In addition, to help protect claimants from the consequences of this major change, he recommended: (i) a 10% increase in general damages to assist the claimant in paying for success fees, (ii) the amount of success fees which lawyers may deduct be capped at 25% of damages, excluding any damages referable to future care or future losses, and (iii) a regime of QOCS as an alternative to ATE insurance to protect the most vulnerable from adverse costs orders whilst negating the need for ATE.

Abolishing recoverability means reverting, to an extent, to the CFA arrangements which existed prior to the Access to Justice Act 1999 changes. They were intended to deal with concerns around high costs arising out of 100% success fees and ATE insurance premiums while preserving access to justice for claimants. Lord Justice Jackson was convinced that if recoverability were abolished then success fees and ATE insurance premiums would become subject to market forces; claimants would shop around for lower success fees and ATE insurance premiums.

Of note, is that Lord Justice Jackson said (at paras 4.10–4.11 of his Response), in justifying a 10% increase as sufficient:

---

13 [2005] 1 WLR 2657.
14 SCCO 20th August 2001.

"4.10 There are many clinical negligence cases in which, despite their complexity, the claimant has a good case on liability. Solicitors conducting such cases will (under my proposals) be able to deduct from damages success fees of up to 25% of general damages + past special damages. I do not accept that this regime (a) makes it uneconomic for solicitors to conduct such cases or (b) would be unacceptable to claimants. This was precisely the regime that prevailed before April 2000 and was regarded as satisfactory for non-legally aided cases. This has been confirmed by well-informed claimant representatives.

4.11 Success fees will be highest in those few cases which proceed to trial. In those cases, however, the claimant can dramatically improve his position by making a Part 36 offer, reflecting the true value of his claim. If the defendant does not accept that offer, the claimant will make a substantially enhanced recovery and will be well placed to pay the success fee."

5.1 Qualified One-way Costs Shifting ("QOCS")

Lord Justice Jackson believed that in personal injury litigation (including clinical negligence) in particular, claimants required protection against adverse costs orders. Under one way costs shifting, losing claimants are only liable to pay their own legal costs including any success fee, and not the winner's costs if the case is lost. Losing defendants would continue to be liable to pay both their own and the claimant's costs in the normal way. With QOCS, a losing defendant would continue to pay a winning claimant's costs, but a losing claimant would pay a winning defendant's costs only where – and to the extent that – in all the circumstances it is reasonable to do so.

The aim of QOCS is to reduce the financial risk of litigation for the claimant and hence the need for ATE insurance. The retention of the recoverability of ATE insurance premiums relating to insuring the costs of liability and causation expert reports makes some inroads into this notion. The interrelation between ATE, QOCS and, in particular, Part 36 offers is yet to be fully understood.

5.2 Disbursements

A question arises as to how disbursements would be funded under the new arrangements. Disbursement costs include, for example, medical and other experts' reports, counsel's fees, court fees, photocopying costs, etc. Disbursement costs can vary considerably depending on the nature and complexity of the claim. Under pre-LASPO arrangements a losing claimant's ATE insurance covered the costs of disbursements as well as the defendant's costs. If the claimant wins, disbursement costs are paid by the defendant. Lord Justice Jackson considered that there was no justification for requiring defendants either collectively or individually to pay claimants' disbursements in cases which the claimants lose, as defendants will be making a sufficient contribution in these cases by bearing their own costs. The government's thinking was that, provided ATE insurance products remained available, claimants should be able to continue to insure against the risk of having to meet their disbursement costs in cases in which they are unsuccessful, but would have to pay the premium themselves. Alternatively, claimants may choose to meet the disbursement costs themselves if they can afford to do so or the claimant's solicitor might agree to fund disbursements in exchange for an increased success fee, provided this would not take the success fee above the proposed 25% damages cap in personal injury cases. At least in clinical negligence claims, ATE costs relating to liability and causation reports remain recoverable.

5.3   Increase on general damages

The 10% increase in general damages in personal injury and clinical negligence claims was explored by the Court of Appeal in *Simmons v. Castle*.[15] The result is that the 10% uplift applies where no success fee is being claimed from the paying party.

A further 10% is available to claimants who match or beat their own Part 36 offers – see below.

Together, these are meant to help claimants who may well now being paying their legal advisers uplifts on costs from their damages.

5.4   Changes to Part 36 – Increased Incentives to Settle and Reversal of *Carver v. BAA*

Lord Justice Jackson thought that the pre-LASPO Part 36 did *"not go far enough in terms of incentivising defendants to accept offers made by claimants"*. He recommended, therefore, that where a defendant fails to beat a claimant's offer, the claimant's recovery should be enhanced by 10%, i.e. 10% of: (a) any financial sum awarded; and (b) the best assessment that the judge can make of the financial value of any non-monetary relief granted, such as an injunction or vindication of reputation.

Section 55 of LASPO and the Offers to Settle in Civil Proceedings Order 2013 provides that in money-only claims there shall be the following percentage uplifts for those claimants who successfully matched or beat their own Part 36 offer:

In claims for monetary awards only:

Amount awarded by the court as damages	Percentage increase on damages
Up to £500,000	10%
Over £500,000 up to £1 million	£50,000 (i.e. 10% of the first £500,000) + 5% of excess over £500,000
Above £1 million	£75,000 (i.e. those sums set out above) with a further 0.001% over £1 million

In non-monetary claims there is an uplift on *costs* and not damages along similar lines, capped at £75,000.00. In claims where there is a mix between monetary and non-monetary benefits, there is an uplift on *damages* at those percentages capped at £75,000.00.

It is clear that the *Simmons v. Castle* 10% uplift would be in addition to enhanced interest on damages under CPR, r. 36.14(3)(a). Footnote 144 on page 426 of the Final Report notes that:

> *"The claimant receives (i) a 10% increase in general damages in all cases, as proposed in chapter 10 above; (ii) a 10% increase in all damages (both general*

---

15 [2012] EWCA Civ 1039.

> *and special damages) as a reward for having made an adequate offer; and (iii) enhanced interest on damages under CPR rule 36.14(3)(a)."*

Lord Justice Jackson's Final Report suggested that these potential extra funds should be sufficient to meet success fees taken from claimant's damages (capped at 25% of damages (excluding damages referable to future loss)) and provides a potentially greater success fee for lawyers.

Lord Justice Jackson's Final Report recommended reversal of the case of *Carver v. BAA plc*,[16] so that it was made clear that in any purely monetary case "more advantageous" means better in financial terms by any amount, however small, thereby removing an unwelcome degree of uncertainty into the Part 36 regime. This was done from 1st October 2011 within CPR, r. 36.14(1A).

6   CLINICAL NEGLIGENCE CLAIMS SUPPORTED BY BTE INSURANCE

Clients may have relevant BTE insurance by way of a stand-alone legal expenses insurance ("LEI") policy or as part of household or motor insurance. The relevant policy is most likely to be that covering the period when the injury occurred, although this may not be straightforward where, for example, clinical negligence may have occurred over one of a number of stages of treatment.

Of utmost importance are the questions of whether the policy covers the type of claim being made, whether the policy covers the claimant (e.g. in a policy covering multiple members of a family), whether the claim has been notified within the time period and manner provided for by the policy and whether the indemnity is of a sufficient amount to cover the likely costs.

Many insurers encourage or require the client to use one of its panel solicitors. The Ombudsman has, however, made it clear that clients should be able to choose their solicitor in serious cases, at least when proceedings are to be commenced.

In theory, the policy indemnifies the client in respect of his liability for his solicitor's costs. It may well be that the insurer seeks to limit hourly rates or to refuse (full) indemnity if there is no recovery of costs from the other side. Prior authority may well be required for the instruction of experts and counsel.

It may be that the policy can be used for initial investigation, with alternative funding when the limit of indemnity is reached.

In most cases, the retainer should provide for the client to be primarily liable for the solicitor's fees both to protect the solicitor and to ensure recovery of costs.

Early liaison with the insurer is essential, as is a full explanation to the client of the obligations and costs position. Policies of insurance bring with them general obligations as well as those specific to the policy itself. There is a duty of utmost good faith and the need to disclose full facts, breach of which may lead to the policy being avoided. The solicitor may well, as the client's agent, have duties to disclose and it is advisable to secure waiver of privilege and authorisation of disclosure to the insurer at the outset.

---

16 [2008] EWCA Civ 412; [2009] 1 WLR 113.

In Lord Justice Jackson's Final Report, he formed the view that clinical negligence claims funded by BTE insurance have a reasonable success rate and that costs in those cases are significantly lower than in clinical negligence claims supported by CFAs. He is, however, alive to concerns about: (i) the insured having no say in the terms of the contract between the insurer and the panel solicitor and therefore having less influence in the handling of the case than a client who does not have the benefit of BTE; (ii) the lack of freedom of choice of a client's own solicitor; (iii) the definition of proceedings in reg. 6 of the Insurance Companies (Legal Expenses Insurance) Regulations 1990 (SI 1990/1159) and how this is interpreted.

The Report considers that the above concerns would all be met if reg. 6 of the 1990 Regulations were amended to provide that the insured's right to choose a lawyer arises when a letter of claim is sent on his behalf to the opposing party. This is not made a formal recommendation as Lord Justice Jackson says that, before any such amendment of reg. 6 is considered, the effect upon BTE insurance premiums must first be considered but places on record his support for making such an amendment if the impact of such an amendment on premiums turns out to be modest.

The government says (para. 266 of the Jackson Consultation) that it *"supports Sir Rupert's view on BTE insurance and would welcome a change in culture so that there is a greater use of existing BTE insurance policies and the development of the market to expand BTE insurance coverage"*.

7   RETAINERS ENTERED INTO AT A CLIENT'S HOME, ETC.

The Cancellation of Contracts made in a Consumer's Home or Place of Work Regulations 2008 (SI 2008/1816) apply to contracts made between 1st October 2008 and 12th June 2014. In short, they provide a cancellation period of 7 days to clients who enter into a wide variety of contracts (including retainers and CFAs, but probably not ATE insurance policies) at their or another person's home or at work. Many serious clinical injury cases might potentially fall within the Regulations since it is common in such cases for a retainer to be entered into during a home visit. For contracts concluded on or after 13th June 2014, the Consumer Contracts (Information, Cancellation and Additional Charges) Regulations 2013 (SI 2013/3134) apply, offering more consumer protection and giving a 14 day cancellation period in wider circumstances.

Regulation 5 of the 2008 regulations provides for the scope of application:

> *"These Regulations apply to a contract, including a consumer credit agreement, between a consumer and a trader which is for the supply of goods or services to the consumer by a trader and which is made—*
> *(a)   during a visit by the trader to the consumer's home or place of work, or to the home of another individual;*
> *(b)   during an excursion organised by the trader away from his business premises; or*
> *(c)   after an offer made by the consumer during such a visit or excursion."*

The solicitor (or an agent) is the trader. Regulation 6 provides for exceptions, and Sch. 3 lists excepted contracts, none of which appear to apply to solicitors or legal services.

Insurance contracts (therefore ATE) are excepted as are contracts under which the total payments to be made by the consumer do not exceed £35.00. The latter exception seems unlikely to exempt "no win, no fee" agreements as there is usually some liability of the client for costs.

Regulation 7 gives the consumer the right to cancel and details the obligations on the trader:

> *"(1) A consumer has the right to cancel a contract to which these Regulations apply within the cancellation period.*
> *(2) The trader must give the consumer a written notice of his right to cancel the contract and such notice must be given at the time the contract is made except in the case of a contract to which regulation 5(c) applies in which case the notice must be given at the time the offer is made by the consumer.*
> *(3) The notice must—*
> *(a)   be dated;*
> *(b)   indicate the right of the consumer to cancel the contract within the cancellation period;*
> *(c)   be easily legible;*
> *(d)   contain—*
> > *(i)   the information set out in Part I of Schedule 4; and*
> > *(ii)   a cancellation form in the form set out in Part II of that Schedule provided as a detachable slip and completed by or on behalf of the trader in accordance with the notes; and*
> *(e)   indicate if applicable—*
> > *(i)   that the consumer may be required to pay for the goods or services supplied if the performance of the contract has begun with his written agreement before the end of the cancellation period;*
> > *(ii)   that a related credit agreement will be automatically cancelled if the contract for goods or services is cancelled.*
> *(4) Where the contract is wholly or partly in writing the notice must be incorporated in the same document.*
> *(5) If incorporated in the contract or another document the notice of the right to cancel must—*
> *(a)   be set out in a separate box with the heading 'Notice of the Right to Cancel'; and*
> *(b)   have as much prominence as any other information in the contract or document apart from the heading and the names of the parties to the contract and any information inserted in handwriting.*
> *(6) A contract to which these Regulations apply shall not be enforceable against the consumer unless the trader has given the consumer a notice of the right to cancel and the information required in accordance with this regulation."*

Part 1 of Sch. 4 of the Regulations indicates what needs to be contained within the Notice of the Right to Cancel:

> *"1.   The identity of the trader including trading name if any.*
> *2.   The trader's reference number, code or other details to enable the contract or offer to be identified.*
> *3.   A statement that the consumer has a right to cancel the contract if he wishes and that this right can be exercised by delivering, or sending (including by electronic mail) a cancellation notice to the person mentioned in the next*

paragraph at any time within the period of 7 days starting with the day of receipt of a notice in writing of the right to cancel the contract.
4.   The name and address, (including any electronic mail address as well as the postal address), of a person to whom a cancellation notice may be given.
5.   A statement that notice of cancellation is deemed to be served as soon as it is posted or sent to a trader or in the case of an electronic communication from the day it is sent to the trader.
6.   A statement that the consumer can use the cancellation form provided if he wishes."

Part II provides for the terms of the cancellation notice that is to be included in Notice of the Right to Cancel, and provides a form of words for inclusion:

"If you wish to cancel the contract you MUST DO SO IN WRITING and deliver personally or send (which may be by electronic mail) this to the person named below. You may use this form if you want to but you do not have to.

(Complete, detach and return this form ONLY IF YOU WISH TO CANCEL THE CONTRACT.)
To: .... [trader to insert name and address of person to whom notice may be given.]
I/We (delete as appropriate) hereby give notice that I/we (delete as appropriate) wish to cancel my/our (delete as appropriate) contract .... [trader to insert reference number, code or other details to enable the contract or offer to be identified. He may also insert the name and address of the consumer.]
Signed
Name and Address
Date"

Regulation 8 provides for the mechanism by which the consumer can cancel:

"(1) If the consumer serves a cancellation notice within the cancellation period then the contract is cancelled.
(2) A contract which is cancelled shall be treated as if it had never been entered into by the consumer except where these Regulations provide otherwise.
(3) The cancellation notice must indicate the intention of the consumer to cancel the contract and does not need to follow the form of cancellation notice set out in Part II of Schedule 4.
(4) The cancellation notice must be served on the trader or another person specified in the notice of the right to cancel as a person to whom the cancellation notice may be given.
(5) A cancellation notice sent by post is taken to have been served at the time of posting, whether or not it is actually received.
(6) Where a cancellation notice is sent by electronic mail it is taken to have been served on the day on which it is sent."

Particular note should be taken of reg. 8(5). There will be a risk of a client having cancelled a retainer within the 7-day cancellation period prescribed by para. 3 of Part 1 of Sch. 4 of the Regulations and the trader not being aware.
Whilst reference to the Regulations in full is advised, the following further points are of particular importance:

- The provisions cannot be contracted out of; such a term would be void. See reg. 15.
- Criminal liability arises for failure to give a consumer notice of the right to cancel in accordance with reg. 7. The offence is summary only and the maximum penalty is a fine of level 5 (£5,000). There is a defence of due diligence. See further regs 17 and 18. There is a form of accessory liability contained in reg. 19 and reg. 20 provides for offences by bodies corporate and their officers. There are various powers of investigation and seizure of documents within reg. 22.
- If work needs to be commenced within the cancellation period, reg. 9 provides that this is possible only where the consumer requests this in writing. Absent the consumer being informed in writing that he may be required to pay for work done in this period, there will be no right for the solicitor (trader) to charge.

A paying party in litigation will probably be able to avoid paying costs in the event that the retainer is unenforceable, due to the indemnity principle. See *Dimond v. Lovell*[17] and *Hollins v. Russell*[18] in respect of different regulations. Whilst the consequences of both of those cases have been reversed by legislation, the principle remains.

The 2008 Regulations revoked and replaced the Consumer Protection (Cancellation of Contracts Concluded away from Business Premises) Regulations 1987 (SI 1987/2117). The 1987 Regulations still apply to contracts made between 1st July 1998 and 1st October 2008. It is arguable that those Regulations and the (applicable before 13th June 2014) Consumer Protection (Distance Selling) Regulations 2000 (SI 2000/2334) apply to solicitor-client retainers in certain circumstances (broadly speaking, unsolicited visits to the client's home for the 1987 Regulations and contracts made over the phone in respect of the 2000 Regulations) so that the retainers might be (respectively) unenforceable or liable to be cancelled by the client for a longer period if certain rights of cancellation were not expressly brought to the client's attention. The Electronic Commerce (EC Directive) Regulations 2002 also impose specific technical information to be given to clients where services are sold by email or on the internet. These may have some relevance as failure gives rise to a right by the client to rescind the contract. Specialist advice should be taken where these issues appear relevant.

In respect of contracts concluded on or after 13th June 2014 the Consumer Contracts (Information, Cancellation and Additional Charges) Regulations 2013 apply in place of the 2000 and 2008 regulations. Schedule 1 to the 2013 regulations lists the information to be provided for on-premises contracts (as defined). Schedule 2 lists the information to be provided for distance and off-premises contracts (as defined). Where cancellation rights exist, all distance and off-premises sellers covered by the regulations will need to provide the cancellation form set out in Schedule 3 to the regulations. The cancellation period is normally 14 days, but can be up to 12 months where insufficient information is given. Services are not to be provided within the cancellation period unless expressly requested by the consumer "on a durable medium". The regulations do not apply to insurance contracts, but the same might be ancillary contracts and also liable to cancellation. Again, specialist advice should be sought to ensure that retainers are compliant.

---

17 [2002] 1 AC 384, HL.
18 [2000] 2 All ER 897, HL.

Chapter 4

COMPLAINTS, NHS REDRESS AND PRE-ACTION PROTOCOL

1   THE NHS COMPLAINTS PROCEDURE

1.1   Summary

A patient who has experienced errors in diagnosis, poor communication from medical professionals, avoidable delay, misleading advice or any other form of poor treatment or even lack of treatment may decide to pursue a number of courses of action. If financial compensation is sought then he will need to seek the advice of a solicitor. In a rare case where public funding may still be available (see Chapter 3 generally and s. 23, Sch. 1 of LASPO specifically), then the solicitor will need to be a member of the Law Society's clinical negligence panel or the AvMA panel and hold a franchise from the Legal Services Commission to carry out clinical negligence work.

Following Lord Justice Jackson's review of civil litigation costs, it is likely that the NHS complaints procedure will be elevated in importance. In any event quite frequently, patients desire an explanation for what went wrong and the poor treatment they have received, an apology or reassurance that such mistakes will not be repeated. In fact this is often considered to be more important to patients than any compensation which may be awarded.

Should the patient decide to make a complaint the starting point is the NHS complaints procedure. Public funding may be denied if the complaints procedure has not been used first without good reason. This internal complaints procedure covers complaints made in relation to services provided by or paid for by NHS organisations or primary care practitioners, i.e. GPs, dentists, opticians and pharmacists. There are two stages to the procedure; local resolution followed by referral to the Parliamentary and Health Service Ombudsman who is independent of the NHS and government.

1.2   Local Resolution

This part of the process is relatively straightforward and simply requires patients who wish to complain to first contact the manager at the organisation where the care was received, i.e. the hospital, general practice, dental practice, pharmacy or optician. Alternatively the complainant can raise the matter with the relevant commissioning body such as NHS England or the local Clinical Commissioning Group.

Complaints can be raised orally or in writing by any person who is affected by, is likely to be affected by or is aware of an action, omission or decision of NHS England, or a service commissioned by NHS England. There are circumstances in which another may act on the patient's behalf, for example where the patient is a child/has died/lacks capacity.

Complaints should be made within 12 months from the date on which the matter that is the subject of the complaint came to notice of the complainant. If there are good reasons for not having made the complaint by the first anniversary then if it is still possible to investigate the complaint effectively and fairly, NHS England may still consider the complaint.

All complaints will be acknowledged within 3 working days and an offer made to discuss with the complainant timescales for responding (amongst other things). If the complainant does not accept the offer to discuss the complaint, then the Case Officer will determine the response period and notify the complainant in writing. After completing the investigation, a formal response in writing will be sent to the complainant.

1.3   The Parliamentary and Health Service Ombudsman

If a patient remains unhappy with the way in which the complaint has been dealt with, he can then contact the Parliamentary and Health Service Ombudsman. This is the final rung in the complaints process. The contact details for the Ombudsman can be found at www.ombudsman.org.uk.

The Parliamentary and Health Service Ombudsman is independent from the NHS and the government and carries out investigations into complaints made about the service a patient has received from the NHS in England. The Ombudsman covers NHS hospitals, trusts and health authorities, GPs, dentists, opticians, pharmacists and other providers (including private healthcare) where the service is paid for by the NHS. Patients in Wales or Scotland should contact the Public Service Ombudsman for Wales and the Scottish Public Services Ombudsman respectively.

The Ombudsman aims to treat everyone fairly and impartially and is confidential and free. However, complaints can take a long time to investigate. Most of the complaints received involve clinical matters. Unsurprisingly the two main categories of complaint concern in-patient hospital treatment and treatment by GPs. In addition, the Ombudsman can deal with complaints about being struck off a GP's list and complaints about payment for continuing care in nursing homes.

The patient must bring the complaint to the Ombudsman's attention within one year of becoming aware of the cause of the complaint. If the NHS complaints procedure has taken longer than it should have done to resolve the time limit for making a complaint to the Ombudsman can be extended.

Complaints should generally be made in writing, whether by letter or email. Should they wish, patients can also make a complaint over the phone (the helpline number is available on the website). Any complaint should include details about the problem, how the patient has suffered personal hardship or injustice and be accompanied by as much evidence as possible. Complaints will be acknowledged within 2 working days. The first step will be for the Ombudsman to decide if he will investigate.

It is worth noting that fewer than half of the complaints made to the Ombudsman are accepted, usually because complaints are referred prematurely to the Ombudsman prior to the local complaints procedure having been tried. Many complaints which are accepted are resolved by the Ombudsman at an early stage, either because the patient has already received an apology or explanation via the NHS complaints procedure and the Ombudsman has no further recommendation to make, or because the local NHS body agrees a particular remedy. The Ombudsman cannot investigate complaints from patients who have indicated an intention to commence legal proceedings.

Once a complaint is accepted for full investigation the body complained about is sent a copy of the complaint and the patient is contacted. In some cases the patient is informally interviewed by someone from the Ombudsman's office to discuss his desired outcome. Upon the investigation being concluded the Ombudsman sends a report setting out the recommended remedies to the patient and body complained of. The possible remedies include: an apology, an explanation of what went wrong, a change of decision, repayment of costs incurred by the patient as a result of the mistake, a change in procedure, improvement of facilities and the provision of consolatory payments in respect of distress or inconvenience.

Although the Ombudsman can also recommend that financial recompense is made to cover expenses that the patient has incurred as a result of the faults found he does not award financial compensation. Ideally patients should get independent advice before pursuing a complaint through the NHS complaints procedure and with the Ombudsman. If financial compensation is likely to be needed to provide ongoing care, legal proceedings will need to be commenced.

1.4   Ombudsman Reports

Annual reports are published by the Ombudsman giving an overview of the cases handled that year. The reports name health authorities and trusts involved in the complaints reported but do not name individual general practitioners. Special reports are also published highlighting particular issues of widespread concern and advisers are encouraged to put cases forward to the Ombudsman where they represent a general problem which needs investigation.

1.5   Joint Investigations

The Regulatory Reform Order 2007 (SI 2007/1889) which came into force on 1st August 2007 amended the Parliamentary Commissioner Act 1967, the Local Government Act 1974 and the Health Service Commissioners Act 1993. The Order enables the Parliamentary Ombudsman, the Local Government Ombudsman for England and the Health Service Ombudsman for England to work together collaboratively on cases and issues relevant to more than one of their individual jurisdictions.

1.6   Relevant Legislation

The legislation governing NHS complaints procedure is the Local Authority Social Services and National Health Service Complaints (England) Regulations 2009 (SI 2009/309 as amended by SI 2009/1768). The 2009 Regulations were enacted pursuant to the Health and Social Care (Community Health and Standards) Act 2003. The Regulations set out the various obligations on NHS bodies, GPs and other primary care providers, and independent providers of NHS care and adult social care in relation to the handling of complaints. The two-stage complaints system described above was introduced in April 2009. Formerly there was an intermediate stage where the Healthcare Commission would conduct an independent review into the case concerned. The Healthcare Commission was abolished in April 2009 and although some of its functions were taken on by the Care Quality Commission, the new body did not take over the role of reviewing individual cases.

1.7   General Advice for Patients

A patient who wishes to bring a complaint can seek advice and guidance from various organisations. The Citizens Advice Bureau is often the first port of call. They are likely to point the patient in the direction of AvMA (see Chapter 1 for further details) or an independent advocacy service (which since 1st April 2013 all local authorities have a statutory duty to commission to provide support for people making, or thinking of making, a complaint about their NHS care or treatment). A patient can also speak to the Patient Advice and Liaison Service (PALS) based in the trust he is intending to complain about. PALS will be able to advise about the complaints procedure and may be able to deal with the complaint quickly and confidentially without the need to take any further steps.

1.8   Private Patients

The complaints procedure outlined above applies only to patients in receipt of treatment carried out or paid for by the NHS and does not apply to private treatment. Similarly, patients who have paid for treatment from a consultant provided in a NHS hospital's private pay bed will not be covered by the procedure even though treatment was provided on NHS premises. Private patients will need to take up complaints with the consultant direct and/or contact the General Medical Council.

The NHS complaints procedure will however cover any complaint made about the hospital's staff (other than the consultant) or facilities relating to the care in its private pay beds.

2   NHS REDRESS SCHEME

2.1   Origins

For many years both the NHS and the legal system has been criticised for the manner in which patient's complaints or claims for clinical negligence have been dealt with. The processes have been long considered complex, costly and slow. The consultation process to consider alternative solutions began in 2000 and in June 2003 the Chief Medical Officer published his consultation document "Making Amends" which sets out his proposals for an alternative system of redress for patients who have suffered injury as a result of clinical negligence. A scheme was envisaged whereby an NHS panel would decide if redress should be offered and to what extent (i.e. what rehabilitation services and/or whether and how much compensation should be offered).

2.2   The NHS Redress Act 2006

When the NHS Redress Act 2006 received royal assent on 8th November 2006 it appeared to be the final step in a drawn out process to improve the efficiency of the handling of clinical negligence complaints and claims against the NHS. The regulations to enact the scheme however have not been brought into effect in England. The Redress Act imposes a general duty on those involved in the scheme to promote the resolution of claims, having particular regard to the desirability of redress being provided without resorting to civil proceedings.

The Redress Act gives the Secretary of State the power to establish a scheme of redress through enacting regulations. The details of the scheme will be contained in secondary legislation, and the Act merely sets the framework within which the scheme will operate. By enacting the scheme through secondary legislation, the Department of Health hopes that it will be flexible and easy to amend as circumstances change. Some guidance can be found in the explanatory notes to the Redress Act. However, given that the devil is going to be in the detail, the consideration below of how the scheme will work in practice is as yet untested.

2.3   Scheme Members

The Department for Health envisages that all providers of hospital services will be required to be members of the scheme and the Redress Act provides for members to have roles in the mechanics of the scheme.

2.4   Scheme Authority

The Redress Act stipulates that a specified Special Health Authority must be provided to have such functions in connection with the scheme as the Secretary of State thinks fit. The appointed authority will deal with questions of liability and quantum and will oversee the scheme generally and monitor consistency. Although the Act does not specify who the Scheme Authority will be, the Department of Health has stated in numerous papers that the National Health Service Litigation Authority (NHSLA) is the intended authority.

The NHSLA currently handles all clinical negligence claims made against the NHS and is presently the body which determines whether to admit or deny liability for an incident on behalf of the NHS. This body has thus far therefore played a very one-sided role in clinical negligence litigation. There is obviously a very real concern that the NHSLA will lack independence, either perceived or actual. This could undermine public confidence in the scheme or at worse lead to insufficient offers of compensation being offered or failures to accept liability.

2.5   What Acts Will the Scheme Apply to?

The scheme will apply to any "qualifying liability in tort" (i.e. any breach of duty of care owed to a person in connection with the diagnosis of illness, of care or treatment of any patient), on the part of a body or other person arising in connection with the provision, as part of the health services in England, of "qualifying services". The *Bolam* and *Bolitho* tests will apply; see Chapter 5.

2.6   Which Services Are Covered?

The scheme will cover "qualifying services" which are those provided in a hospital or otherwise as directed by the Secretary of State. Treatment given by primary carers and other medical staff who work outside hospitals will not be covered by the scheme. Specifically, primary medical services, dental services, general ophthalmic and local pharmaceutical services are not covered by the scheme. The Department of Health takes the view that many primary carers do not have the appropriate relationship with the NHSLA for the system to work and due to the lower incidents of clinical negligence cases occurring in primary care settings such claims would incur disproportionately high administrative costs.

2.7   Who may Claim under the Scheme?

It is envisaged that the scheme will not be restricted to claims by patients but will also deal with claims resulting from the death of a patient under the Law Reform (Miscellaneous Provisions) Act 1934 and claims by dependants of the deceased under the Fatal Accidents Act 1976.

2.8   Remedies Available under the Scheme

The Redress Act provides that the scheme may make *"such provision as the Secretary of State thinks fit"*. However, the scheme must provide for a complainant to receive one or a combination of the following: compensation, an explanation, an apology and a report setting out action taken or to be taken. An investigation will be proportionate to the type and seriousness of the injury. Compensation may not be merely financial. It may take the form of care and treatment.

2.9   Financial Compensation

Where financial compensation is awarded it is suggested that damages will be assessed in accordance with existing legal principles. The Redress Act specifies that the scheme may set an upper limit for the amount of financial compensation to be offered, or an amount specifically for pain, suffering and loss of amenity. It is currently the Department of Health's intention to set the upper limit at £20,000. Any necessary remedial care will be provided over and above any financial offer and the limit will not include the cost of that care. If the offer of compensation is accepted the complainant will be prevented from bringing civil proceedings in respect of the liability concerned. Proceedings under the scheme will be terminated if liability to which the proceedings relate become the subject of a civil claim. Although not provided for by the Redress Act it is envisaged by the Department of Health that all offers of settlement under the scheme would be made without prejudice and will not be capable of being considered an admission of liability in a later court action.

2.10   Commencing the Application

The Redress Act does not provide for how an application will be commenced under the scheme. It is presently intended that the scheme will be triggered by an initial report being sent from a scheme member to a scheme authority. A patient or dependant may be able to apply to the scheme but largely it depends on the hospital reporting itself. At this stage it is difficult to predict how much the bodies will be held to account without a patient taking steps to initiate proceedings.

2.11   Procedure under the Scheme

The detail of how the scheme will run is also unknown at present. The Redress Act merely states that the scheme may make provision for the investigation of cases, the making of decisions about the application of the scheme, time limits in relation to acceptance of an offer, the form and contents of settlement agreements and the termination of proceedings under the scheme. It is envisaged that the court's approval will be required for cases involving children and mentally incapacitated people.

The Department of Health states that the scheme member (hospital) will be required to provide a full investigation report to the scheme authority who will then determine liability and quantum. It is assumed that the applicant will be allowed to submit evidence. The hospital will then make the offer of redress. The Redress Act provides that the report need not be disclosed until an offer is made under the scheme or proceedings are terminated. There is no formal appeal procedure against the decision of the authority, presumably because if the offer is unacceptable the applicant can reject the offer and seek compensation through the courts.

Furthermore, the scheme will not be retrospective. Only those cases relating to incidents that occurred on or after the date of the scheme's implementation will be eligible.

Presently it appears that the individual will have little information about the investigation as it is being carried out and will sometimes not be able to view the report it results in. There is therefore a real concern that patients will be shut out of the process and there will be an imbalance in the equality of arms between the authority and individuals involved in the scheme.

2.12   Instruction of Experts under the Scheme

The Department of Health has stressed that the final decision as to the liability of the NHS for clinical negligence will rest with the scheme authority and that in some cases, to avoid unnecessary expense independent, medical opinion will not be sought. An individual will have the option of funding an independent medical expert himself if the scheme member decides it is not appropriate for them to do so. To that extent the scheme must make provision for the medical experts to be jointly instructed by the scheme authority and the individual seeking redress.

There may be some negative implications for the patient in that there will be no conferences held between the expert and the patient and his advisers so there is risk that experts will not be properly focused on the issues in question and applications will not be properly investigated.

2.13   Suspension of Limitation Period

The Redress Act requires that the period of time when a case is subject to the scheme should not be included in any calculation of a limitation period in civil proceedings under the Limitation Act 1980 or any other enactment. The explanatory notes suggest that the period of time to be disregarded will begin when the scheme member commences proceedings and will end at the end of the fixed period of time that the patient is allowed to consider the offer or redress or when the patient chooses to reject the offer.

The suspension of the limitation period offers a significant protection to patients' rights and ensures that patients will not be under time pressure to go to court if the mechanics of the scheme are not running as smoothly as they should.

2.14 Access to Assistance and Legal Advice

The Act provides that it is the duty of the Secretary of State to arrange, to the extent he considers necessary, to meet all reasonable requirements for the provision of assistance. The Department for Health states that the type of assistance envisaged is similar to that currently given to patients who are moving through the NHS complaints service, from PALS.

The scheme must also make provision for patients to have access to free legal advice in relation to any offer made or settlement that is arrived at. The explanatory notes state that it is envisaged that such legal advice will be for the purpose of assessing whether or not an offer under the scheme is reasonable and equivalent to what the patient would have received through the courts.

The explanatory notes indicate that it is envisaged that a body such as the Legal Services Commission will compile and maintain a list of independent providers of legal advice, with whom the scheme authority will have made arrangements for the provision of such advice at a flat rate. This approach raises questions about whether the rate will take into account the complexity of issues and the required preparation time which will vary from case to case. The obvious concern is what effect this will have on the quality of advice patients will receive if the flat rate is insufficient remuneration for the more involved cases. One can easily envisage a situation arising whereby work requiring the expertise of senior lawyers is carried out by junior solicitors sometimes to the patient's detriment.

2.15 Complaints about the Scheme

The Department of Health envisages that most complaints about the scheme can be dealt with locally and informally. However, the Secretary of State may by regulations make provision about the handling and consideration of complaints of maladministration by any body or other person in the exercise of functions under the scheme or in connection with any agreement entered into under the scheme. The complaints will be considered by the scheme authority or a member of the scheme.

The Redress Act also provides that such regulations may also stipulate who can bring a complaint, which complaints will be considered, the time frame for bringing such complaints, the procedures to be followed in making a complaint and the action taken as a result of a complaint. For forward-looking solicitors, however, the scheme may provide an opportunity to attract clients whose complaints will turn into significant litigation.

Unfortunately, no progress has been made with respect to the implementation of the scheme since the first edition of this publication.

3 PRE-ACTION PROTOCOL

3.1 Summary

If a patient does decide to seek financial redress by initiating legal proceedings any claim for financial compensation must be brought in compliance with the Pre-Action Protocol for the Resolution of Clinical Disputes which came into force on 26th April 1999.

The Protocol was the first major initiative of the Clinical Disputes Forum, the multi-disciplinary body formed in 1997 as a result of Lord Woolf's "Access to Justice" inquiry. It was designed to encourage a climate of openness when something has "gone wrong" with a patient's treatment or the patient is dissatisfied with that treatment and/or the outcome, and recommend a timed sequence of steps for patients and healthcare providers, and their advisers, to follow when a dispute arises, to speed up the exchange of relevant information and increase the prospects of dispute resolution without resorting to legal action.

The Protocol sets out a "code of good practice" which parties should follow when litigation might be a possibility. It applies to all aspects of the health service, primary and secondary and both public and private. The introductory sections of the Protocol, which should not be overlooked, set out why it was established and its aims and objectives. The steps of the Protocol have been kept deliberately simple.

The 53rd Update to the Civil Procedure Rules introduced changes in a number of areas including two significant amendments to the Pre-Action Protocol for the Resolution of Clinical Negligence Disputes. These came into force on 1st October 2010 and are identified below.

3.2 Obtaining Medical Records

Any request for a patient's medical records should specify as far as possible the records which are required and provide sufficient information to alert the healthcare provider where an adverse outcome has been serious or had serious consequences.

Any request should be made on the Law Society and Department of Health approved standard forms as in Annex B to the Protocol.

A copy of the records should be provided within 40 days of the request and for a cost not exceeding the charges permissible under the Access to Health Records Act 1990 (currently a maximum of £10 plus photocopying and postage).

In the rare circumstances that the healthcare provider is in difficulty in complying with the request within 40 days, the problem should be explained quickly and details given of what is being done to resolve it. If the healthcare provider fails to provide the records within 40 days, the patient or their adviser can apply to the court for an order for pre-action disclosure.

Third party record holders are expected to cooperate with the request. The Protocol provides that if either the patient or the healthcare provider considers additional health records are required from a third party, in the first instance these should be requested by or through the patient. The Civil Procedure Rules enable patients and healthcare providers to apply to the court for pre-action disclosure by third parties (CPR, r. 31.17).

3.3   Letter of Claim

Following receipt of the medical records, if upon analysis the patient or his adviser considers there are grounds for a claim, a letter should be sent as soon as practicable to the potential defendant. This letter should contain a clear summary of the facts on which the claim is based, including the alleged adverse outcome, and the main allegations of negligence. It should also describe the patient's injuries, present condition and prognosis. The financial loss incurred by the claimant should be outlined with an indication of the heads of damage to be claimed and the scale of the loss, unless this is impracticable. A template for such a letter is provided at Annex C1 to the Protocol.

In more complex cases a chronology of the relevant events should be provided, particularly if the patient has been treated by a number of different healthcare providers.

The letter of claim should refer to any relevant documents, including health records, and if possible enclose copies of any of those which will not already be in the potential defendant's possession, e.g. any relevant general practitioner records if the claimant's claim is against a hospital. Sufficient information must be given to enable the healthcare provider defendant to commence investigations and to put an initial valuation on the claim.

Letters of claim are not intended to have the same formal status as a pleading, nor should any sanctions necessarily apply if the letter of claim and any subsequent statement of claim in the proceedings differ. Care does need to be taken however, as if there is a difference in accounts then it may affect the credibility of evidence at trial.

Proceedings should not be issued until after 4 months from the letter of claim, unless there is a limitation problem and/or the patient's position needs to be protected by early issue.

The patient or their adviser may want to make an offer to settle the claim at this early stage by putting forward an amount of compensation which would be satisfactory (possibly including any costs incurred to date). If an offer to settle is made, generally this should be supported by a medical report which deals with the injuries, condition and prognosis, and by a schedule of loss and supporting documentation. The level of detail necessary will depend on the value of the claim. Medical reports may not be necessary where there is no significant continuing injury, and a detailed schedule may not be necessary in a low value case. The Civil Procedure Rules (CPR, r. 36) set out the legal and procedural requirements for making offers to settle and should be followed with respect to offers made in clinical negligence claims.

Since 1st October 2010 the amendments to the Protocol introduced a provision that any letter of claim sent to an NHS Trust or Independent Sector Treatment Centre is to be copied to the NHSLA.

Previously letters of claim were required to be reported to the NHSLA within 24 hours of receipt. The requirement that letters of claim are copied to the NHSLA was designed to assist with the frequent difficulties Trusts experience in complying with this tight deadline.

3.4   Response

The healthcare provider should acknowledge the letter of claim within 14 days of receipt and should identify who will be dealing with the matter and, within 4 months of the letter of claim, provide a reasoned answer.

The second of the two aforementioned amendments to the Protocol implemented since 1st October 2010 is an extension of the time to respond from 3 to 4 months. No doubt this is a welcome extension enabling respondents an extra month to collate records and contact clinicians in order to prepare the response.

If the claim is admitted the healthcare provider should say so in clear terms; if only part of the claim is admitted the healthcare provider should make clear which issues of breach of duty and/or causation are admitted and which are denied and why. If it is intended that any admissions will be binding and if the claim is denied, this should include specific comments on the allegations of negligence, and if a synopsis or chronology of relevant events has been provided and is disputed, the healthcare provider's version of those events.

If the patient has made an offer to settle, the healthcare provider should respond to that offer in the response letter, preferably with reasons. The provider may make its own offer to settle at this stage, either as a counter-offer to the patient's, or of its own accord, but should accompany any offer with any supporting medical evidence, and/or any other evidence in relation to the value of the claim which is in the healthcare provider's possession.

Where additional documents are relied upon, e.g. an internal protocol, copies should be provided. If the parties reach agreement on liability, but time is needed to resolve the value of the claim, they should aim to agree a reasonable period.

A template for the suggested contents of the letter of response can be found at Annex C2 to the Protocol.

3.5   Experts

The Protocol is not prescriptive about the process with respect to the instruction of experts. It merely provides that in clinical negligence disputes the parties and their advisers will require flexibility in their approach to expert evidence. Decisions on whether experts might be instructed jointly, and on whether reports might be disclosed sequentially or by exchange, should rest with the parties and their advisers. Sharing expert evidence may be appropriate on issues relating to quantum.

Obtaining expert evidence will often be an expensive step and may take time, especially in specialised areas of medicine where there are limited numbers of suitable experts. Patients and healthcare providers, and their advisers, will therefore need to consider carefully how best to obtain any necessary expert help quickly and cost-effectively. The NHSLA has accepted the recommendation of Lord Justice Jackson that where it does not accept liability it will obtain independent expert advice at the protocol stage in an effort to prevent it denying liability in cases that later turn out to be indefensible. The subject of experts is dealt with in more detail in Chapter 11.

3.6 Alternative Dispute Resolution (ADR)

The Protocol also stipulates that the parties should consider whether some form of ADR procedure would be more suitable than litigation, and if so, endeavour to agree which form to adopt. Both claimants and defendants may be required by the court to provide evidence that alternative means of resolving their dispute were considered. The courts take the view that litigation should be a last resort, and that claims should not be issued prematurely when a settlement is still actively being explored.

Mediation is suggested as one such means of ADR although it is expressly recognised that no party can or should be forced to mediate or enter into any form of ADR. ADR is considered in greater detail in Chapter 12.

3.7 Failure to Comply with the Protocol

The Protocol specifically warns parties if it is not followed then the court can have regard to such conduct when determining costs. The Civil Procedure Rules enable the court to take into account compliance or non-compliance with an applicable protocol when giving directions for the management of proceedings (see CPR, r. 3.1(4) and (5)) and when making orders for costs (see CPR, r. 44.4(3)(a)).

The Practice Direction to the Protocols stipulates that the court will expect all parties to have complied in substance with the terms of an approved protocol. If it is considered that non-compliance has led to the unnecessary commencement of proceedings, or has led to costs being incurred in the proceedings that might otherwise not have been incurred, the court may order that the party at fault pay the costs of the proceedings, or part of those costs, of the other party or parties, for example the court may impose costs sanctions against a healthcare provider for unreasonable delay in providing health records.

Chapter 5
DUTY OF CARE

1   THE GENERAL DUTY

A doctor's duty towards his patient is a fundamental one, established on the basic principle of a doctor/patient relationship. The duty can be expressed as to take all reasonable care of the patient, and involves not merely the duty to take care once a course of treatment is commenced, but also a duty to investigate and initiate action in order to take all reasonable steps to procure the health of the patient. In terms of a duty that is actionable in negligence, however, the duty of a doctor is not an absolute one. The test is generally referred to as the *Bolam* test, *Bolam v. Friern Hospital Management Committee*,[1] which provides that a doctor is not negligent if *"he has acted in accordance with a practice accepted as proper by a responsible body of medical men skilled in that particular art"*.

This chapter will investigate the failure to act in accordance with this relationship and the relevant standard of care required to succeed in a clinical negligence claim as it has developed under the common law, a failed attempt to legislate as to the test to be applied and then consider the impact on that development of the Human Rights Act 1998.

2   ESTABLISHING NEGLIGENCE

The first question the claimant must ask is: was there an act or omission which amounted to a breach of the duty owed to him. It is important to understand that negligence is never freestanding, it has to be fact specific to the case. The basis of this duty was succinctly set out in the House of Lords by Lord MacMillan in the landmark case of *Donoghue v. Stevenson*[2] where he stated:

> *"The law takes no cognisance of carelessness in the abstract. It concerns itself with carelessness only where failure in that duty has caused damage. In such circumstances careless assumes the legal quality of negligence and entails the consequences in the law of negligence...The cardinal principle of liability is that the party complained of should owe to the party complaining a duty to take care, and that the party complaining should be able to prove that he has suffered damage in consequence of a breach of that duty."*

Historically negligence has been defined by reference to Alderson B in *Blyth v. Birmingham Waterworks Co*,[3] where he states:

> *"Negligence is the omission to do something which a reasonable man, guided upon those considerations which ordinarily regulate the conduct of human affairs, would do, or doing something which a prudent and reasonable man would not do."*

---

1 [1957] 2 All ER 118, 121.
2 [1932] AC 562 at 618–619.
3 (1856) 11 Ex Ch 781 at 784.

This would appear to be using the word negligence in "layman's terms" as opposed to applying the duty of care. In terms of a clinical negligence claim the clinician is viewed within the context of their clinical field and experience.

In breaking down this test, there are two key elements. First, the appropriate standard of care must be determined; secondly, the claimant must establish that the conduct in question fell below that standard.

Unlike a breach of contract, the tort of negligence is not complete as a cause of action without establishing that some loss has been caused. The concept of causation will be discussed later in this book, but it is important to note at this stage that causation of injury is a matter that the claimant is to prove in addition to breach of duty in order to succeed. This has a significant impact on risk assessment of potential claims. Before significant expense is incurred in investigating breach of duty it will be necessary to consider whether causation is likely to be capable of being proved.

3   PRE-BOLAM

In the early part of the 20th century, prior to the decision in *Bolam v. Friern Hospital Management Committee*, the test in clinical negligence claims had been expressed in several ways.

In *R v. Bateman*[4] a physician was described as owing a duty to the patient:

> *"to use diligence, care, knowledge, skill and caution in administering the treatment. No contractual relation is necessary, nor is it necessary that the service be rendered for reward...The law requires a fair and reasonable standard of care and competence."*

And in *Marshall v. Lindsey County Court*,[5] and approved by the House of Lords in *Whiteford v. Hunter*,[6] it was held that a defendant who is charged with negligence can clear himself if he shows that he acted in accordance with general and approved practice.

4   THE "BOLAM TEST"

The case of John Bolam (*Bolam v. Friern Hospital Management Committee*) was to provide authority for all future clinical negligence claims. In the summer of 1954 John Bolam was a patient at the Friern Hospital. He was admitted suffering from a mental illness and was advised by a consultant that he should undergo electro-convulsive therapy. The therapy was relatively new in 1954 and involved passing an electric current through the patient's brain. Some physicians recommended relaxation medication and restraining the patient, whereas others did not. Mr Bolam was not restrained and sustained serious physical injuries including dislocation of both hip joints and fractures to both sides of his pelvis. He sued the hospital in negligence putting forward the case

---

4 (1925) 94 LJKB 791.
5 [1935] 1 KB 516.
6 [1950] WN 553.

that the physician who treated him had been negligent in the way that the treatment was carried out.

In directing the jury McNair J set out a useful summary of a legal definition of negligence stating at 121D:

> "In the ordinary case which does not involve any special skill, negligence in law means this: some failure to do some act which a reasonable man in the circumstances would do, or doing some act which a reasonable man in the circumstances would not do; and if that failure or doing that act results in injury, then there is a cause of action. How do you test whether this act or failure is negligent? In an ordinary case it is generally said, that you judge that by the action of the man in the street. He is the ordinary man. In one case it has been said that you judge it by the conduct of the man on the top of a Clapham omnibus. He is the ordinary man. **But where you get a situation which involves the use of some special skill or competence, then the test whether there has been negligence or not is not the test of the man on the top of the Clapham omnibus, because he has not got this special skill. The test is the standard of the ordinary skilled man exercising and professing to have that special skill**." (emphasis added)

McNair J goes on to say that:

> "A man need not possess the highest expert skill at the risk of being found negligent. It is well established law that it is sufficient if he exercises the ordinary skill of an ordinary competent man exercising that particular art."

In directing the jury in *Bolam* he neatly summarised the legal test at 122B as:

> "A doctor is not guilty of negligence if he has acted in accordance with a practice accepted as proper by a responsible body of medical men skilled in that particular art...Putting it the other way round, a doctor is not negligent, if he is acting in accordance with such a practice, merely because there is a body of opinion that takes a contrary view."

The "Bolam test" has been applied as the correct test in professional negligence claims for half a century and even with the regular scrutiny by the courts over that period of time there has been virtually no addition or subtraction to McNair J's formulation.

5   DEVELOPING BOLAM

Some tinkering with the wording came from the House of Lords in the matter of *Sidaway v. Board of Governors of the Bethlem Royal Hospital and Maudsley Hospital*[7] where Lord Bridge endorsed the Court of Appeal dicta that:

> "the practice accepted as proper by a responsible body of medical men must be 'rightly' so accepted."

As per *Maynard v. West Midlands Regional Health Authority*[8] it appears that the word "responsible" is interchangeable with the word "respectable".

---

7 [1985] 2 WLR 480.
8 [1984] 1 WLR 634.

In essence Lord Bridge placed the responsibility on a defendant relying on an expert's body of opinion to show that the responsible body of opinion was indeed responsible. It would prevent defendants from placing experts in front of the court purporting to represent a "body of opinion" who were in effect just representing "an opinion".

In *Meiklejohn v. (1) St George's Healthcare NHS Trust (2) Homerton University Hospital NHS Foundation Trust*[9] the appellant appealed a decision to dismiss his claim for damages arising out of the mis-diagnosis of a rare genetic disorder. The Court of Appeal reiterated that the regardless of the type of clinician involved, the duty to advise and warn about diagnosis, treatment and possible side-effects was to be assessed in accordance with the practice of a "reasonable body of doctors". Therefore *Bolam* still applied.

Reflecting changing society since the early 1980s when *Sidaway* was determined, the Supreme Court earlier this year overturned its ratio in an 'informed consent' case the matter of *Montgomery v. Lanarkshire Health Board.*[10] Montgomery (M) was a pregnant woman who was diabetic when she came under the care of the defendant's hospital. Due to the diabetes M was likely to have a large baby. As such the risk of shoulder dystocia was in the region of 9-10% and risk of catastrophic injury of less than 0.1%. The defendants did not however advise M of either risk. During the delivery, shoulder dystocia occurred leading to the baby being deprived of oxygen and being born with severe disabilities. M's case was that she should have been advised of the risk of shoulder dystocia, and the possibility that a Caesarean section would be a delivery option for her. She stated that had this been explained to her she would have opted for a Caesarean section.

The Court of Session rejected that argument and followed the precedent set in *Sidaway* namely that the question of whether a doctor's omission to advise a patient of risks involved in treatment amounted to a breach of duty of care should be decided on the *Bolam* basis.

However the Supreme Court overturned the decision in *Sidaway* using as their starting point, Lord Justice Scarman's dissenting judgment in *Sidaway* that it is the patient's basic human right to make his own decision and that if a patient suffered damage as a result of an undisclosed risk which would have been disclosed by a doctor exercising reasonable care to respect the patient's right to decide whether to incur the risk, and the patient would have avoided the injury if the risk had been disclosed, then the patient would have a cause of action in negligence. This approach having been advocated by Lord Walker in *Chester v. Afshar*[11] who observed (in 2004) that in the previous 20 years since Sidaway "*the importance of personal autonomy had been more widely recognised, and that, in making a decision which might have a profound effect on her health and wellbeing, a patient was entitled to information and advice about possible alternative or variant treatments*". This approach had been adopted by the Department of Health and GMC which treated *Chester* as a leading authority.

On that basis the Supreme Court held in *Montgomery* that *Sidaway* was no longer satisfactory and that an adult person of sound mind was entitled to decide which, if any, of the available forms of treatment to undergo, and her consent had to be obtained

---

9 [2014] EWCA Civ 2010.
10 [2015] UKSC 11.
11 [2004] UKHL 41, [2005] 1 AC 134.

before treatment interfering with her bodily integrity was undertaken. Doctors were under a duty to take reasonable care to ensure that patients were aware of any material risks involved in any recommended treatment, and of any reasonable alternative or variant treatments. The Supreme Court (ironically) accepted the doctor's evidence that had M known of the risks she would have opted for a Caesarean section (the court at first instance not having been convinced of her evidence) and consequently her case succeeded on breach and causation.

Importantly, the Supreme Court in *Montgomery* makes it clear that the *Bolam* test is no longer applicable in what may be termed "informed consent" cases.[12] The test to be applied in such cases is dealt with in greater detail below.

6   LEVEL OF SKILL REQUIRED

In prosecuting clinical negligence claims it is vital, per *Bolam*, that the specialist who is being proceeded against is tested against the standard of care of the reasonably competent specialists practising in that field. Lord Bridge in his judgment in *Sidaway* states at 502B that the:

> "*language of the Bolam test clearly requires a different degree of skill from a specialist in his own special field than from a general practitioner. In the field of neuro-surgery it would be necessary to substitute for Lord Clyde's phrase 'no doctor of ordinary skill', the phrase 'no neuro-surgeon of ordinary skill'. All this is elementary...and firmly established law.*"

It is good law that the more skills a person in a specialist field possesses, the higher the standard of skill expected of him. However, he is not required to attain the highest degree of skill and competence, merely a reasonable level of skill within the field (see *Ashcroft v. Mersey Regional Health Authority*[13]).

It of course remains open for a claimant to argue that whilst they accept that the treating registrar for example carried out his diagnosis and/or treatment within the scope of a reasonable body of registrars, he failed to refer the case up to a consultant, which whilst the other "reasonable" registrars may have treated in the same way, the reasonable act would be to refer the patient higher up the specialist tree.

In *Wilsher v. Essex Area Health Authority*[14] a junior doctor who was on placement training within an intensive care neonatal unit wrongly inserted a catheter into a vein as opposed to an artery. The registrar failed to check what the junior doctor had done and the result was that the infant patient sustained serious personal injury. The majority of the Court of Appeal held that in analysing the appropriate standard of care, the law required that a trainee or learner should be judged by the same standards of care of his more experienced colleagues. This was expressed by Mustill LJ at 813:

> "*To my mind, this notion of a duty tailored to the actor, rather than to the act which he elects to perform, has no place in the law of tort. Indeed, the defendants did not contend that it could be justified by any reported authority on the general law of tort. Instead, it was suggested that the medical profession is a special case.*"

---

12 Lords Kerr and Reed at para 86.
13 [1983] 2 All ER 245; affd [1985] 2 All ER 96, CA.
14 [1986] 3 All ER 801.

> *Public hospital medicine has always been organised so that young doctors and nurses learn on the job. If the hospitals abstained from using inexperienced people, they could not staff their wards and theatres, and the junior staff could never learn. The longer term interests of patients as a whole are best served by maintaining the present system, even though this may diminish the legal rights of the individual patient for, after all, medicine is about curing, not litigation. I acknowledge the appeal of this argument...Nevertheless, I cannot accept that there should be a special rule for doctors in public hospitals...To my mind, it would be a false step to subordinate the legitimate expectation of the patient that he will receive from each person concerned with his care a degree of skill appropriate to the task which he undertakes to an understandable wish to minimise the psychological and financial pressures of the hard-pressed young doctors."*

This test invariably places the claimant under a significant burden to prove their case; it is not simply the case that the defendant can absolve responsibility (and ultimately liability) by parading in front of the court an expert or experts to state that they are from the same body of opinion as the defendant.

The test of reasonableness is an objective test and for the court to determine on balance whether they are satisfied that the expert evidence they have in essence amounts to a defence. Whilst rare, the courts have shown a willingness to step in and dismiss a "body of expert evidence" if they consider that it is manifestly wrong.

7   BOLITHO

The leading case which develops the *Bolam* test is that of *Bolitho v. City and Hackney Health Authority*.[15]

In Bolitho a 2-year-old boy was admitted to the defendant's hospital suffering from respiratory problems. The day after he was admitted he suffered two short episodes of further respiratory problems. On each of these occasions a doctor was called but failed to attend. After the first episode it appeared that boy had recovered. Initially after the second attack it also appeared as though the boy had recovered however half an hour after the attack the boy collapsed owing to failure of his respiratory system, and suffered a cardiac arrest as a result of which he suffered severe brain damage. Tragically the boy died some time after the proceedings were issued.

The medical evidence agreed that had the boy been intubated after the respiratory problems the cardiac arrest would have been prevented. The defendants accepted that there was a breach of duty on their part, but contended that even if a doctor had attended she would not have arranged for the child to be intubated. On that basis they argued, and at first instance the judge accepted, that there would have been no injury or damage arising out of the accepted breach of duty.

The claimant alleged that the failure to intubate was negligent in any event. The judge heard expert evidence on behalf of the defendant to the effect that intubation would not have been appropriate, and held (applying the *Bolam* test) that a decision not to intubate would have been in accordance with a body of responsible professional opinion. It followed that causation had not been proved.

---

15 [1993] 4 Med LR 381, CA; affd [1997] 4 All ER 771, HL.

The claimant appealed to the Court of Appeal and the House of Lords but failed at each stage.

In terms of the development of the *Bolam* test however, Lord Browne-Wilkinson, whilst agreeing that the authority of *Bolam* applied to causation as well as liability, stated at 778d–g:

> *"in my view the court is not bound to hold that a defendant doctor escapes liability for negligent treatment or diagnosis just because he leads evidence from a number of medical experts who are genuinely of the opinion that the defendant's treatment or diagnosis accorded with sound medical practice. In Bolam's case McNair J stated that the defendant had to have acted in accordance with a practice accepted as proper by a 'responsible body of medical men'. Later he referred to a 'standard of practice recognised as proper by a competent reasonable body of opinion'. Again in the passage cited from Maynard's case, Lord Scarman refers to a 'respectable' body of professional opinion. The use of these adjectives – responsible, reasonable and respectable – all show that the court has to be satisfied that the exponents of the body of opinion relied on can demonstrate that such opinion has a logical basis. In particular in cases involving, as they so often do, the weighing of risks against benefits, the judges before accepting a body of opinion as being responsible, reasonable or respectable, will need to be satisfied that, in forming their views, the experts have directed their minds to the question of comparative risks and benefits and have reached a defensible conclusion on the matter."*

This extended the test in *Bolam* to the extent that the defendant would have to show that the body of responsible, reasonable or respectable medical opinion for which they were relying could be demonstrated to be such. Lord Browne-Wilkinson does within his judgment express the view that in the vast majority of cases the expert will be able to satisfy the court that his opinion is a reasonable medical opinion but opens the door for the defendants to fail where it can "*in rare cases*" be "*demonstrated that the professional opinion is not capable of withstanding logical analysis, the judge is entitled to hold that the body of opinion is not reasonable or responsible*" (at 779g).

It is fair to say that Lord Bridge proffered the view that it would be rare for the judge to take that position and that the trial judge must guard against applying this test as a way of stating that he prefers one expert's opinion to the other. It must be emphasised that *Bolitho* merely offers trial judges the option for such disregard of defendant's experts as opposed to encouraging judges to take sides in terms of expert evidence.

Within this it is of course open to the judge, with reasons, to find that the defence expert evidence is simply wrong. This may be on the basis that the expert is in fact speaking solely for himself as opposed to a "reasonable body of opinion" or that the expert may not have considered all of the factors in any given case and/or simply be wrong.

In practice, leading a judge to this conclusion will normally be as a result of cross-examination which probes into the purported reliability of the defendant's expert case.

Following *Bolitho* courts applied a logical analysis to the issue of whether the body of opinion was reasonable. In recent times the court considered the issue in *Marriott v.*

West Midlands Regional Health Authority[16] where the GP left a patient at home, despite the fact that he knew the patient had a history of head injury and was showing signs of drowsiness and headaches. The trial judge concluded that if the defence expert's evidence did in fact establish that there was a body of GPs who, on the patient presenting as he did, would not have referred the patient to hospital then such approach was *"not reasonably prudent"*. The Court of Appeal upheld the first instance decision, commenting that it was open for the trial judge to *"subject a body of opinion to analysis to see whether it could be properly regarded as reasonable"*.

A more recent example of the practical application is by Reddihough J, sitting in the High Court in the matter of *Ecclestone v. Medway NHS Foundation Trust*[17] where the claimant presented with a history of knee problems. It was decided to perform a "lateral retinacular release" on the knee. Post-operatively the claimant developed further pain and swelling in his knee and alleged that this was as a result of poorly undertaken surgery. The issue for the court was whether it was negligent of the surgeon to use a percutaneous technique to perform the release as opposed to undertaking an arthroscopic approach. Whilst in hindsight an arthroscopic approach may have been preferable, the judge was satisfied that *"Both [techniques] were recognised and acceptable surgical techniques logically supported by a responsible body of opinion"*. As such the claim for negligence failed.

8   HOW IT WAS BEFORE *BOLITHO*

In order to fully appreciate the significance of *Bolitho*, it is of interest to note how the law was before *Bolitho*. In *Clarke v. Adams*[18] the claimant was severely burned during a course of heat treatment applied by a physiotherapist. The determined facts of the case were that the claimant had been warned of the risk of danger occurring following the treatment. This warning had been given in accordance with standards for giving warnings approved by the Chartered Society of Physiotherapists. Nevertheless, the court was prepared to find that the warning was inadequate properly to safeguard the patient.

A further example of this arose in the case of *Hucks v. Cole*[19] a 1968 case where a doctor failed to treat a patient with penicillin. Even though responsible doctors testified that they would have acted in the same way that the defendant did in not administering penicillin, Sachs LJ held that:

> *"if the court was satisfied that a lacuna existed in professional practice whereby the patient was exposed to unnecessary risks, the court would so declare and would expect the professional practice to be altered accordingly."*

Sachs LJ was of the opinion that the evidence as to whether other practitioners would have acted as the defendant did was not conclusive and was not satisfied that the experts' reasons for agreeing with the defendant stood up to proper judicial scrutiny.

This can of course be contrasted with the position that just because an expert states that they would not have (and a body of medical opinion) would not have acted in the way

16 [1999] Lloyd's Rep Med 23.
17 [2013] EWHC 790 (QB).
18 (1950) 94 Sol Jo 599.
19 [1993] 4 Med LR 393.

of the defendant, the court is still able to hold that in their opinion the expert faced with the same factual situation as presented to the clinician at the time, would have acted in the same or similar way and thus the case, under application of the *Bolam* test, would fail.

9   THE LEGAL BURDEN

In terms of the legal burden of establishing clinical negligence, the test is the standard test applied to all civil cases, that of proof on the balance of probabilities. The burden is, of course, on the claimant to prove their case.

It should be noted however that whilst the test is that of balance of probabilities the practical application of the test demonstrates that the more serious the allegation the stronger must be the evidence. This is a matter of common sense.

In *Audrey Burnett v. Lynch*[20] Rafferty LJ relied on the dictum of Lord Carswell in *Re D*[21] to re-state the law in respect of the burden of proof in the context of a clinical negligence case.

> *"27. Richards LJ expressed the proposition neatly in R (N) v Mental Health Review Tribunal (Northern Region) [2005] EWCA Civ 1605,[2006] QB 468, 497-8, para 62, where he said: '62. Although there is a single civil Standard of proof on the balance of probabilities, it is flexible in its application. In particular, the more serious the allegation or the more serious the consequences if the allegation is proved, the stronger must be the evidence before a court will find the allegation proved on the balance of probabilities. Thus the flexibility of the standard lies not in any adjustment to the degree of probability required for an allegation to be proved (such that a more serious allegation has to be proved to a higher degree of probability), but in the strength or quality of the evidence that will in practice be required for an allegation to be proved on the balance of probabilities.'*
>
> *In my opinion this paragraph effectively states in concise terms the proper state of the law on this topic I would add one small qualification which may be no more than an explanation of what Richards LJ meant about the seriousness of the consequences. That factor is relevant to the likelihood or unlikelihood of the allegation being unfounded as I explain below.*
>
> *28. It is recognised by these statements that a possible source of confusion is the failure to bear in mind with sufficient clarity the fact that in some contexts a court or tribunal has to look at the facts more critically or more anxiously than in others before it can be satisfied to the requisite standard. The standard itself is, however, finite and unvarying. Situations which make such heightened examination necessary may be the inherent unlikelihood of the occurrence taking place (Lord Hoffmann's example of the animal seen in Regent's Park), the seriousness of the allegation to be proved or, in some cases, the consequences which could follow from acceptance of proof of the relevant fact. The seriousness of the allegation requires no elaboration: a tribunal of fact will look closely into the facts grounding an allegation of fraud before accepting that it has been established. The seriousness of consequences is another facet of the same proposition: if it is alleged that a bank manager has committed a minor speculation, that could entail very serious consequences for his career, so making it the less likely that he would risk doing such a thing. These are all matters of ordinary experience, requiring the*

---

20 [2012] EWCA Civ347.
21 [2008] UKHL 33, [2008] 1 WLR 1499.

application of good sense on the part of those who have to decide such issues. They do not require a different standard of proof or a specially cogent standard of evidence, merely appropriately careful consideration by the tribunal before it is satisfied of the matter which has to be established."

10   *BOLAM* NOT APPLICABLE

The principles in *Bolam* cannot be applied to questions of fact, hypothetical or otherwise. So, where for example there is an issue of causation, such as whether treatment which was not given would have cured the patient or otherwise avoided injury, a dispute between the experts does not attract a *Bolam* analysis and the court must simply determine which evidence on balance it prefers.

In cases of informed consent (i.e. where the issue is the omission of a doctor to warn or advise in respect of risks and alternatives), *Bolam* does not apply, but the test in *Montgomery v Lanarkshire Health Board*[22] does. This may be stated as follows: *"The doctor is … under a duty to take reasonable care to ensure that the patient is aware of any material risks involved in any recommended treatment, and of any reasonable alternative or variant treatments. The test of materiality is whether, in the circumstances of the particular case, a reasonable person in the patient's position would be likely to attach significance to the risk, or the doctor is or should reasonably be aware that the particular patient would be likely to attach significance to it."*

For further details on consent see Chapter 7 below.

11   THE MEDICAL INNOVATION BILL

In January 2015 Lord Saatchi proposed the Medical Innovation Bill to the House of Commons. The object of the Bill was said to be to encourage responsible innovation in medical treatment (and accordingly to deter innovation which is not responsible). The thinking behind the Bill appears to have been that innovation had been stifled by the current system and the application of the Bolam test in negligence and that doctors would and could responsibly innovate especially in cancer or other very serious cases of illness where the prognosis was poor and where relatively untried or untested treatments might possibly assist the patient. However, the means by which innovation was promoted in the Bill was effectively by seeking to reduce or remove the threat of medical negligence litigation against doctors who innovate. In summary, the requirements which a doctor had to meet under the Bill, in order to avoid a finding of negligence, included a requirement that he should obtain an opinion about the proposed treatment from an appropriately qualified doctor and take that opinion into account in a way in which any responsible doctor would do and also to comply with any professional requirement to register the treatment (although there is in fact no such professional requirement). If the doctor had complied with these two requirements he would make out what was dubbed by the press to be the "Saatchi Defence" and could not be found to be negligent.[23]

The Bill did not seek to make inroads on the law of consent. Nor did it address regulations governing the trial and introduction of new treatments, nor the funding of research or the commissioning of new treatments by the NHS. The Bill was publically

---

22 [2015] UKSC 11 considered in detail in Chapter 7.
23 Section 1(3).

opposed by the MDU, the MPS, the BMA, the Academy of Royal Medical Colleges, Cancer Research UK, the Medical Research Council, the Wellcome Trust, Parkinson's UK, the Lancet Oncology and the British Heart Foundation. The thrust of the objections was obvious. The operation of the law as it stands per Bolam is that those who have suffered harm as a consequence of treatment which would not have been supported by a responsible body of medical opinion can obtain redress from that doctor or his insurer. The Bill would have removed the right of redress if the doctor behaved in a "responsible" manner by providing innovative treatment even when no other doctor would support the treatment actually given. The Bill came before the House of Commons for its second reading on 6th March 2015. Not one MP moved for the Bill which may now effectively be consigned to history. The Bolam test still stands – unaltered.

12   ORGANISATIONAL FAULT

From time to time a case will hinge not on the negligence of a particular clinician but on the management or organisation of a hospital or surgery. In such cases liability may be difficult to establish. In *Wilsher v. Essex AHA*[24] (a case primarily concerned with causation), Mustill LJ considered the possibility that the *"Health authority owed a duty to ensure that the special baby care unit functioned according to the standard reasonably expected of such a unit. This approach would not require any consideration of the extent to which the individual doctors measured up to the standards demanded of them as individuals, but would focus attention on the performance of the unit as a whole."* In *Godden v. Kent & Medway SHA*[25] Gray J held that it was not unarguable that the health authority had a duty at common law to proceed against a GP with a known propensity to improper behaviour towards patients, in refusing a strike out application. He considered this was a developing area of law whilst doubting that the claimant would pass the threshold to establish a common law duty pursuant to *Caparo Industries plc v. Dickman and others.*[26] In *Robertson v. Nottingham HA*[27] negligence was established where there was a lack of proper communication between clinicians resulting in the delay of a Caesarean, although that case failed on causation. An organisation may be under a duty to provide treatment and liable in negligence if it does not do so.[28] In *Collins v. Mid-Western Health Board*[29] the defendant was liable for a failure to have sufficient equipment on hand to deal with emergencies. They also failed to have made adequate arrangements for the diagnosis of patients arriving in casualty and to have adequate coordination of facilities and clinicians. That said the court will not be blind to budgetary considerations. See, for example, *Ball v. Wirral HA*[30] where the hospital had four ventilators but not one was available to a baby who needed one. This was adjudged not negligent.

---

24 [1987] 1 QB 730 at 747 and also Browne-Wilkinson LJ at 778.
25 [2004] EWHC 1629 (QB), [2004] Lloyds Rep Med 521.
26 [1990] 2 AC 605, [1990] 2 WLR 358.
27 [1997] 8 Med LR 1.
28 In *Steele v. Home Office* [2010] EWCA Civ 724, (2010) 115 BMLR 218 the claimant (a prisoner) was denied access to a dentist for 7 months and the Home Office thereafter failed to offer an alternative dentist in circumstances where the dentist had refused to treat the claimant save in an emergency and the claimant had refused to be seen by that dentist. Some attempt at alternative provision ought to have been made.
29 [2000] 1 IR 154.
30 [2003] Lloyds Rep Med 165.

13   VICARIOUS LIABILITY FOR INDEPENDENT CONTRACTORS

In the majority of cases it will be clear that the doctor or clinician concerned was employed by the hospital or clinic and that the hospital or clinic will be vicariously liable to the claimant for any negligence on the part of the clinician. The Court of Appeal in *Cassidy v. Ministry of Health and others*[31] made it clear that a hospital authority was liable for the negligence or professional medical staff whether employed under contracts of services, or contracts for service. Delegation of the performance of the duty of care to give proper treatment did not remove its liability for that treatment. The reasoning behind this is that the central function of a hospital or health authority is to provide healthcare to patients. The decision of the Supreme Court in *Woodland v. Swimming Teachers Association*[32] provides an emphatic endorsement of this approach (albeit it was in the context of the duty owed by a local authority to a child). The claimant was a school pupil and attended a swimming lesson in school hours as part of the then national curriculum. In the course of the lesson she was found "hanging vertically in the water". She was resuscitated but had suffered severe brain damage. The lesson was conducted by a teacher and lifeguard who were employed by an independent contractor with whom the local authority had a contract. The claimant sued the local authority. The case had been struck out at first instance on the basis that the defendant did not owe a non-delegable duty of care. By a majority the Court of Appeal had agreed. On appeal to the Supreme Court (Hale, Clark, Wilson, Sumption, Toulson JSCs) the appeal was allowed. In the lead judgment, Lord Sumption set out the principles applicable in such cases and it is clear that the reasoning applies to hospitals and doctors because it is the nature of the relationship and the assumption of responsibility that counts.

> *"23. In my view, the time has come to recognise that Lord Greene in Gold and Denning LJ in Cassidy were correct in identifying the underlying principle, and while I would not necessarily subscribe to every dictum in the Australian cases, in my opinion they are broadly correct in their analysis of the factors that have given rise to non-delegable duties of care. If the highway and hazard cases are put to one side, the remaining cases are characterised by the following defining features:*
>
> *(1) The claimant is a patient or a child, or for some other reason is especially vulnerable or dependent on the protection of the defendant against the risk of injury. Other examples are likely to be prisoners and residents in care homes.*
>
> *(2) There is an antecedent relationship between the claimant and the defendant, independent of the negligent act or omission itself, (i) which places the claimant in the actual custody, charge or care of the defendant, and (ii) from which it is possible to impute to the defendant the assumption of a positive duty to protect the claimant from harm, and not just a duty to refrain from conduct which will foreseeably damage the claimant. It is characteristic of such relationships that they involve an element of control over the claimant, which varies in intensity from one situation to another, but is clearly very substantial in the case of schoolchildren.*
>
> *(3) The claimant has no control over how the defendant chooses to perform those obligations, i.e. whether personally or through employees or through third parties.*
>
> *(4) The defendant has delegated to a third party some function which is an integral part of the positive duty which he has assumed towards the claimant; and the third*

---

31 [1951] 2 KB 343.
32 [2013] UKSC 66.

> *party is exercising, for the purpose of the function thus delegated to him, the defendant's custody or care of the claimant and the element of control that goes with it.*
>
> *(5) The third party has been negligent not in some collateral respect but in the performance of the very function assumed by the defendant and delegated by the defendant to him."*

Per Lady Hale at para. 39: *"The boundaries of what the hospital or school has undertaken to provide may not always be as clear cut as in this case and in Gold[33] and Cassidy but will have to be worked out on a case by case basis as they arise."* She also made the point that it is worth remembering that before the advent of outsourcing most public authorities would have been vicariously liable to claimants who were harmed in this case.

It is worthy of note per Lord Sumption in *Woodland*[34] in expressly approving the decision in *Faaraj v. King's Healthcare Independent Trust*,[35] that liability will not attach in circumstances where the contractor is not providing the actual care of the individual. In that case the defendant was an independent analytical laboratory performing analysis of a tissue sample for a person who was not being treated by the hospital and not in its custody or care. Similarly, merely arranging for another to provide healthcare will not attract a non-delegable duty. As to which see *A v. Ministry of Defence*[36] where the MOD was not liable for the failings of the negligence of a hospital subcontracted to treat service families. This is explained on the basis that one of the essential elements is not so much control of the environment where the claimant is injured but control over the claimant for the purpose of performing the function. In addition and importantly, there was no delegation of any function which the MOD had assumed personal responsibility to carry out and no delegation of any custody exercised by the MOD over soldiers and their families.[37] A distinction may also be made where the claimant has a substantial say in the selection of the subcontractor.[38]

In *Whetstone v. Medical Protection Society Limited*[39] Mr Whetstone had been a sole principal of a dental practice and had engaged a Mr Sudworth as an associate dentist. Mr Whetstone started to receive complaints about Mr Sudworth's work and terminated the contract which they had entered. A number of the claimants in the dental negligence claims had proceeded against Mr Whetstone on the basis that he was vicariously liable for the negligence of Mr Sudworth.

Mr Whetstone sought an indemnity from the MPS (the judgment contains a useful detailed analysis of the legal basis of discretionary cover by medical defence organisations). The court closely scrutinised the contract between the claimant and Mr Sudworth and found that the contract was *"akin to a contract of employment"*.[40] The judge held that Mr Whetstone was vicariously liable for Mr Sudworth but that the MPS was entitled to refuse an indemnity for his liability and for the costs of remedying the effect of the negligence because of the nature of the contract of insurance. Permission to appeal from this decision was declined.[41]

---

33 *Gold v. Essex County Council* [1942] 2 KB 293,301.
34 Paragraph 24 of the judgment.
35 [2009] EWCA Civ 1203, [2010] 1 WLR 2139.
36 [2004] EWCA Civ 641, [2005] QB 183.
37 Paragraph 24 of the judgment of Lord Sumption in *Woodlands*.
38 Paragraph 23 of the judgment of Lord Sumption in *Woodlands* above.
39 [2014] EWHC 1024 (QB).
40 Paragraph 123 of the judgment.
41 [2015] EWCA Civ 127.

The contractual relationship in this case was one in which the principal regulated the conduct of the associate in an unusually tight manner. It is perhaps clear that on these facts and the application of the principles in *Cassidy* and *Woodland* that liability would be made out (although neither case features in the judgment, rather the judge relied other cases[42]). If Mr Sudworth had simply been renting accommodation within Mr Whetstone's practice and was the patient's chosen dentist, it is less clear that Mr Whetstone would have been vicariously liable.

14   HUMAN RIGHTS ACT AND DUTIES OF CARE

In May 2000, just 5 months before the European Convention on Human Rights was to be incorporated into UK law under the Human Rights Act 1998, Lord Justice Mance was heard to say in the course of argument in *Re S*[43] that after the 2nd October 2000 the *Bolam* test would be dead so far as public authorities were concerned. In the event, however, the judgment of the Court of Appeal (Butler-Sloss P, Thorpe and Mance LJ) in *Re S*, a case involving the sterilisation of a psychiatric patient lacking capacity, did not bear out the threatened demise of the *Bolam* test. Instead *Bolam* was said to be the starting point of any medical decision but that in considering what could lawfully be done to someone unable to consent the court was concerned with their "best interests" and could incorporate broader ethical, social, moral and welfare considerations.

Just after the Human Rights Act came into force an opportunity arose to abolish the *Bolam* test in *NHS Trust A v. Mrs M and NHS Trust B v. Mrs H*.[44] There were two applications for declarations to enable hospitals to withdraw treatment from patients in a persistent vegetative state. It was held that the right to life under Article 2 contained a negative obligation on the state to refrain from taking life intentionally. That did not prevent the withdrawal of treatment, however, where the court determined that it was in a patient's "best interests". The court held that though Article 2 imposed a positive obligation on the state to take adequate and appropriate steps to safeguard life, where a responsible clinical decision to withhold treatment was in accordance with a respectable body of medical opinion, the state's obligation was discharged.

These two cases were the latest shots in a battle that had been raging for some time over the approach the court should take to applications for declarations that it would be lawful to treat someone who is not competent to give consent for their own treatment. The two sides to the battle have generally been lawyers and judges from a family background versus those from a common law background in clinical negligence. The family lawyers, rooted in the concept of wardship, have favoured a best interests of the patient test akin to the notion of *parens patriae*. The common lawyers have tried to apply the *Bolam* test.

It was clear that Butler-Sloss P, from a family background, wanted to bring the best interests test to the fore, despite the success of the *Bolam* test on the issue of informed consent in the House of Lords in *Sidaway v. Board of Governors of the Royal Bethlem Hospital and the Maudsley Hospital*.[45] She did so. But what was of interest was the manner in which she did it. She could have achieved her end by saying that *Bolam* was

---

42 *E v. English Province of Our Lady of Charity* [2013] QB 722 and *Cox v. Ministry of Justice* [2014] EWCA Civ 132.
43 [2001] Fam 15.
44 [2001] 2 WLR 942.
45 [1985] AC 871.

now out of the running after the Human Rights Act. She did not do so, instead she recognised the continued validity of the *Bolam* test, despite Article 2, but held that the best interest test had to be overlaid by the court.

The Human Rights Act has affected the language used in determining issues such as disclosure and equality of arms in use of experts, but the effect goes further than that. Although the extent of its effect is as yet unclear, the language of breach of duty has also been affected by the Act.

In *Van Colle v. Chief Constable of Hertfordshire* and *Smith v. Chief Constable of Sussex Police*[46] the House of Lords had to consider how the right to life impacted on claims for damages arising out of the failure by police officers to protect members of the public. They decided the cases on the narrow grounds of policy applicable to such claims and upheld the test set out in *Osman v. United Kingdom*[47] that the positive obligation to protect life under Article 2 was only breached if, following a close examination of the facts, it could be said that the authorities knew or ought to have known at the time that a threat to life was both real and immediate. In *Michael & Ors v. Chief Constable of South Wales & Anor*[48] by a majority (Lady Hale and Lord Kerr dissenting) the Supreme Court followed the decision of the House of Lords in *Van Colle* and concluded that the development of a private duty of care was not necessary for compliance with Article 2 or Article 3 and that there was no basis for creating a wider duty in negligence than would arise either under common law principles or under the ECHR.

The analysis of the problem on the way to the House of Lords in *Van Colle* threw up some very interesting propositions; with the potential to affect the way the duty owed by public health authorities is expressed. Although overturned on the narrow ground of public policy applicable to police omissions, the Court of Appeal in *Van Colle*[49] had upheld an award by Cox J of damages under s. 7 of the Human Rights Act to the parents of a prosecution witness who had been killed by the accused in a forthcoming criminal trial, following threats to his life. Cox J held that the negligent failure of the police to take steps to protect the deceased amounted to a breach of the positive obligation to protect life under Article 2, and that there was a real chance (i.e. a loss of chance test) that action by the police might have prevented the death. At para. 56 of her judgment, recited at para. 75 of the Court of Appeal judgment, Cox J distilled the following principles:

(i)   The positive obligation to protect life in Article 2 is unqualified and self-evidently fundamental, so that any alleged breach or potential breach of that obligation by the state authorities requires the most anxious scrutiny by the court. The right to life in Article 2 is in that sense different in nature from the qualified rights, for example, in Articles 8 to 11, which enable the state in certain circumstances to justify an interference with the right requiring the court to conduct a balancing exercise between the individual's right and the public interest.

(ii)   Nevertheless, Article 2 is not to be interpreted so as to impose an impossible or disproportionate burden on the state authorities. This reflects the need for a fair balance between the rights of the individual

46 [2008] UKHL 50.
47 (1998) 29 EHRR 245.
48 [2015] 2 WLR 343.
49 [2007] EWCA Civ 325.

and the general interests of the community recognised to be inherent in the whole of the Convention: see e.g. *Goodwin v. UK*[50] and *Brown v. Stott*[51] per Lord Bingham at 704F.

(iii)   The state's positive obligation to protect life includes a positive obligation in certain circumstances to take preventive, operational measures to protect an identified individual whose life is at risk as a result of the criminal acts of a third party. That obligation arises where it is established that the state authorities knew or ought to have known at the time of the existence of a real and immediate risk to the life of that individual and yet failed to take such measures within the scope of their powers which, judged reasonably, might have been expected to avoid that risk.

(iv)   To determine, where it is so established, whether there was a breach of that obligation it is not necessary for the claimant to establish that the failure to perceive the risk to life in the circumstances known at the time or the failure to take preventive measures to avoid that risk, amounted to gross negligence or to a wilful disregard of the duty to protect life. It is sufficient to show that the authorities did not do all that could be expected of them to avoid a real and immediate risk to life, of which they had or ought to have had knowledge. The answer to this question will always depend upon the individual facts of the case.

(v)   Where it is the conduct of the state authorities which has itself exposed an individual to the risk to his life, including for example where the individual is in a special category of vulnerable persons, or of persons required by the state to perform certain duties on its behalf which may expose them to risk, and who is therefore entitled to expect a reasonable level of protection as a result, the Osman threshold of a real and immediate risk is too high. If there is a risk on the facts, then it is a real risk, and "immediate" can mean just that the risk is present and continuing at the material time, depending on the circumstances. If a risk to the life of an individual is established, the court should therefore apply principles of common sense and common humanity in determining whether, in the particular circumstances of each case, the threshold of risk has been crossed for the positive obligation in Article 2 to protect life to be engaged.

(vi)   Whether the obligation arose in any particular case and whether the state authorities were in breach of that obligation will therefore depend not only upon the nature of the threat and the degree of risk to the individual, of which the authorities knew or ought to have known, but also upon the extent to which there were appropriate measures, reasonably available to the authorities, to alleviate or obviate that risk. The greater the failure to take such measures as were reasonably open to them to alleviate a risk to human life, the greater the likelihood that the authorities will be held to have failed to comply with their Article 2 obligation.

---

50 (2002) 35 EHRR 18.
51 [2003] 1 AC 681.

The Court of Appeal upheld the decision of Cox J and expressly found the above propositions to be supported by authority. They approved the loss of chance formulation, although they protectively also determined that the judge had found causation even on the "but for" test (at para. 98).

The approval of the "simple" negligence requirement is difficult to reconcile with the Court of Appeal's approval in *R (Takoushis) v. Inner London Coroner*,[52] at para. 95, of the proposition of Richards J that:

> *"Simple negligence in the care and treatment of a patient in hospital, resulting in the patient's death, is not sufficient in itself to amount to a breach of the state's positive obligations under article 2 to protect life. This is clearly stated in the Powell case 30 EHRR CD 362."*

The Court of Appeal in *Van Colle* must have been aware of the *Takoushis* decision, although it was not mentioned in the judgment, as it was the Master of the Rolls, Sir Anthony Clarke, who gave the judgment in both cases. Takoushis was dealing with the sort of investigation that had to be undertaken into the death of someone who was not detained in hospital, either as a prisoner or under s. 3 of the Mental Heath Act 1983, and the Court of Appeal added this rider:

> *"We add only this. We do not accept [the] submission that the principles in the custody cases...apply here because Mr Takoushis would have been detained if the hospital had been aware that he was about to leave the hospital. In our opinion there is an important distinction between those who are detained by the state and those who are not. Mr Takoushis was not."*

In *Savage v. South Essex Partnership NHS Foundation Trust*[53] Swift J considered the first instance decision in *Van Colle* in the context of allegations of clinical negligence and followed the Court of Appeal view in *Takoushis* that gross negligence was required to create a cause of action under the Human Rights Act. The case concerned the death by suicide of a patient who absconded from hospital where she had been detained under s. 3 of the Mental Health Act 1983. *Savage* came before the Court of Appeal, the Master of the Rolls, Waller and Sedley LJJ in October 2007, after the Court of Appeal's judgment, but before the House of Lords speeches, in *Van Colle*. Although it provided the opportunity for the court to clarify the effect of *Van Colle*, when judgment was given on 20th December 2007 no such clarification was given. *Takoushis* was considered in detail, but not *Van Colle*. The court overturned the judgment of Swift J and ruled that the position of a detained patient was akin to that of the prisoner rather than an ordinary patient and that for a detained patient or their relatives to establish a breach of Article 2 all that needed to be shown was that at the material time the Trust knew or ought to have known the existence of a real and immediate risk to life from self-harm and that it failed to take measures within the scope of their powers which, judged reasonably, might have been expected to avoid that risk. There was no requirement to establish gross negligence. The court resisted the temptation to call the test "simple negligence", however, and it may be that it will be necessary to stop importing such common law terms.

---

52 [2006] 1 WLR 461.
53 [2006] EWHC 3562.

The Court of Appeal distinguished between detained and voluntary patients on the basis that detained patients, like prisoners, are particularly vulnerable whilst stating that they understood the submission, which found favour with Swift J, that there was no distinction between the duty owed to a detained patient and to a patient who is not detained. The Trust appealed to the House of Lords which upheld the Court of Appeal's decision in 2008.[54] The House of Lords (Scott, Rodger, Walker, Hale and Neuberger LJJ) considered that the health authority owed two duties pursuant to Article 2. The first was an overarching obligation to protect the lives of patients in their hospitals (whether by employing competent staff and adopting appropriate systems of work (para. 45 of the judgment of Lord Rodger), the second was an "operational" obligation which arose only if a member of staff knew or ought to have known, that a particular patient presented a real and immediate risk of suicide. The operational obligation meant simply that in the critical circumstances of the real and immediate risk of a patient committing suicide, priority had to be given to saving the patient's life. The position in respect of the duty of health authorities pursuant to Article 2 and the interface between this and negligence is explained and summarised in the judgment of Lord Rodger at para. 68:

> *"In terms of article 2, health authorities are under an over-arching obligation to protect the lives of patients in their hospitals. In order to fulfil that obligation, and depending on the circumstances, they may require to fulfil a number of complimentary obligations.*

> *69. In the first place, the duty to protect the lives of patients requires health authorities to ensure that the hospitals for which they are responsible employ competent staff and that they are trained to a high professional standard. In addition the authorities must ensure that the hospitals adopt systems of work which will protect the lives of patients. Failure to perform these general obligations may result in a violation of article 2. If, for example, a health authority fails to ensure that a hospital puts in place a proper system for supervising mentally ill patients and, as a result a patient is able to commit suicide, the health authority will have violated the patient's right to life under article 2.*

> *70. Even though a health authority employed competent staff and ensured that they were trained to a high professional standard, a doctor, for example might still treat a patient negligently and the patient might die as a result. In that situation there would be no violation of article 2 since the health authority would have done all that the article required of it to protect the patient's life. Nevertheless, the doctor would be personally liable in damages for the death and the health authority would be vicariously liable for her negligence. This is the situation envisaged by Powell.[55]*

> *71. The same approach would apply if a mental hospital had established an appropriate system for supervising patients and all that happened was that, on a particular occasion, a nurse negligently left his post and a patient took the opportunity to commit suicide. There would be no violation of any obligation under article 2, since the health authority would have done all that the article required of it. But again, the nurse would be personally liable in damages for the death and the health authority would be vicariously liable too. Again, this is just an application of Powell.*

> *72. Finally article 2 imposes a further 'operational' obligation on health authorities and their hospital staff. This obligation is distinct from, and additional to, the authorities' more general obligations. The operational obligation arises only if members of staff*

---

54 [2009] 1 AC 681, [2009] 2 WLR 115.
55 *Powell v. United Kingdom* (2000) 30 EHRR CD 362.

> *know or ought to know that a particular patient presents a 'real and immediate' risk of suicide. In these circumstances article 2 requires them to do all that can reasonably be expected to prevent the patient from committing suicide. If they fail to do this, not only will they and the health authorities be liable in negligence, but there will also be a violation of the operational obligation under article 2 to protect the patient's life. This is comparable to the position in Osman[56] and Keenan.[57] As the present case shows, if no other remedy is available, proceedings for an alleged breach of the obligation can be taken under the Human Rights Act 1998."*

Their Lordships considered that *Powell* and *Osman* did not lay down mutually exclusive approaches, but related to different aspects of the Article 2 obligations on health authorities and their staff to protect life. The obligations were complementary.

The House of Lords therefore dismissed the appeal and remitted the matter back to the High Court where in April 2010 Mr Justice Mackay entered judgment for the claimant (Mrs Savage's daughter). In determining whether to award compensation and, if so, the amount, s. 8(4) of the Human Rights Act required the court to take into account the principles applied by the European Court of Human Rights in relation to the awards of compensation under Article 41 of the Convention. Mackay J recognised that *"no award could ever compensate S for the loss of her mother"* but awarded the sum of £10,000 as a symbolic acknowledgement that the trust ought properly to give her some compensation to *"reflect her loss"*.

Although the court in *Savage* drew a distinction between detained and "voluntary" patients, it was not dealing with a voluntary patient, and accordingly it left open the issue of how to approach the case of an ordinary patient. In *Rabone and another v. Pennine Care NHS Foundation Trust*[58] the daughter of the claimants committed suicide having been granted weekend leave from a psychiatric unit in circumstances where she was an informal or "voluntary" patient suffering serious recurrent depression. The claimants brought a claim in negligence which had previously been settled for a modest sum. They also brought a claim pursuant to Article 2 on the basis that this imposed an operational obligation on states to protect mentally ill patients who were not detailed under the Mental Health Act 1983 where there was a real and immediate risk of suicide.

Mr Justice Simon, sitting in the High Court determined that as M was an informal mental patient, not detained under the Mental Health Act 1983, s. 3, the trust did not have an operational obligation to her under Article 2 of the Convention.

The Court of Appeal upheld this decision and in dismissing the appeal held that:

> *"Art. 2 did not impose upon the state an operational obligation towards all persons who were at real and immediate risk of death. There had to be some additional element over and above that risk before state authorities came under the operational obligation. Health trusts did not have an art. 2 obligation to voluntary patients in hospital who were suffering from physical or mental illness, even where there was a real and immediate risk of death. The remedy for clinical negligence, even where a real and immediate risk of death had been disregarded, was an action in negligence. At the relevant time, M was not detained under s. 3 of the*

---

56 *Osman v. United Kingdom* (2000) 29 EHRR 245.
57 *Keenan v. United Kingdom* (2001) 33 EHRR 913.
58 [2012] 2 AC 72, [2012] 2 WLR 381, [2012] Med LR 221.

1983 Act. She was a voluntary patient and was allowed to return to her parental home on the day concerned. The trust therefore did not have an operational obligation to her under art. 2."

Further they set out that:

"A state authority was in breach of the operational obligation if the authority knew or ought to have known of a real and immediate risk to the life of the individual concerned and had failed to do all that could reasonably be expected to avoid that risk."

However, the matter proceeded to the Supreme Court[59] who overturned the High Court and Court of Appeal's decision and found unanimously (5-0) in favour of the claimants. Lord Dyson giving judgment for the court pointed out that the reason she was in hospital in the first place was to protect her from the risk of suicide whereas on the other hand a patient who undergoes surgery will have accepted the risk of death by signing a consent form. He said:

"31. In the Savage case, [2009] AC 681, it was submitted on behalf of the defendant NHS Trust that, in the light of the principle stated in Powell v United Kingdom 30 EHRR CD 362 no operational duty was owed under article 2 to take steps to protect a detained mental patient from a real and immediate risk of suicide. This submission was rejected by the House of Lords. At para 59, Lord Rodger said: 'The circumstances in Powell's case...were quite different from circumstances where a patient presents a real and immediate risk of suicide. Therefore, the decision of the European court, which I respectfully consider was correct, provides no guidance on the problem before the House.'

32. And later he said: '65. Neither Powell's case...nor Dodov's case 47 EHRR 932 provides any basis whatever for the proposition that, as a matter of principle, medical staff in a mental hospital can never be subject to an "operational" duty under article 2 to take steps to prevent a (detained) patient from committing suicide—even if they know or ought to know that there is a real and immediate risk of her doing so. The obvious response to that proposition is: Why ever not?...'

33. As I have said, the ECtHR has not considered whether an operational duty exists to protect against the risk of suicide by informal psychiatric patients. But the Strasbourg jurisprudence shows that there is such a duty to protect persons from a real and immediate risk of suicide at least where they are under the control of the state. By contrast, the ECtHR has stated that in the generality of cases involving medical negligence, there is no operational duty under article 2.

34. So on which side of the line does an informal psychiatric patient such as Melanie fall? I am in no doubt that the trust owed the operational duty to her to take reasonable steps to protect her from the real and immediate risk of suicide."

The Supreme Court found:

    (i)   The NHS has a positive duty to protect the deceased's life under Article 2 of the ECHR against the risk of suicide of psychiatric patients ('the operational duty'). They added that while differences existed between detained and voluntary psychiatric patients, these should not be exaggerated. (The difference in this case was adjudged to be one of

---

59 [2012] UKSC 2 (Lord Walker JSC, Lady Hale JSC, Lord Brown JSC, Lord Mance JSC, Lord Dyson JSC).

form, not substance, para. 34. It was clear on the fact that if the deceased had insisted on leaving hospital the authorities could and should have exercised their powers under the MHA to prevent her from doing so.).

(ii)   That the Trust had assumed responsibility for the deceased and as such she was under its control. By reason of her mental state, the deceased should have been viewed as being extremely vulnerable and the Trust owed an operational duty to take reasonable steps to protect her from the "real and immediate risk of suicide".

(iii)   The risk of suicide was "real and immediate" and satisfied the test for Article 2. Two expert psychiatrists in the clinical negligence action had agreed that it was negligent to allow her home and she required protection from the risk of suicide.

(iv)   The deceased's parents were victims under the ECHR and their victim status was not lost as a result of the settlement of the clinical negligence action. The Fatal Accident Act 1976 did not provide bereavement damages for the parents of an adult child and consequently, their claim under Article 2 had not been satisfied.

As a result the Supreme Court awarded the deceased's parents £5,000 each in recognition of the breach of operation duty under Article 2.

It is clear that the courts wish to take any development of the law in this area in a case-specific, gradual way. It is tempting to think that some of the reasoning of the lower courts in *Van Colle* might still open up whole new avenues of remedy, but the court was careful to state that they were taking a fact-sensitive approach, and there will be judicial reluctance to open the floodgates. It should be borne it mind that under the Human Rights Act:

•   remedies are available only against public authorities;
•   damages are secondary to the finding of breach and are only awarded if needed to provide "just satisfaction"; and
•   the time limit for proceedings is one year, although that can be extended in the discretion of the court.

That said, in claims against health authorities, an Article 2 claim may provide a viable alternative claim for some categories of cases where a claim in negligence may not be viable. In a clinical negligence setting it could be the decision in *Gregg v. Scott*,[60] or the restrictive provisions of the Fatal Accidents Act 1976 and its definition of dependants. In *Savage* the parents were not qualifying dependants pursuant to the FAA but recovered £5,000 each for their Article 2 claims.

The role of the Human Rights Act in terms of shaping common law duties is far from settled. In *Smith v. Chief Constable of Sussex Police*[61] an action at common law against the police for failing to protect a victim of a serious assault who had alerted the police to the risk of assault by a former partner, Pill LJ said:

---

60 [2005] 2 AC 176.
61 [2008] UKHRR 551, [2008] PIQR P12.

> *"I consider it unacceptable that a court, bound by S. 6 of the [HRA] 1998, should judge a case such as the present by different standards depending on whether or not the claim is specifically brought under the Convention. The decision whether a duty of care exists in a particular situation should in a common law claim require a consideration of Article 2 rights."*

It is clear that the extent of that consideration is something that will continue to vex the courts for some time to come.

Chapter 6
CAUSATION AND REMOTENESS

1 INTRODUCTION

Establishing breach of duty by a clinician is only part of the claimant's task. In order to recover substantial damages, the claimant must also prove that he has suffered injury or other loss. Without proof of loss a cause of action does not arise at all in the tort of negligence, because damage is the gist of the action. Damage is not essential to complete a cause of action in contract or in the tort of battery, and nominal damages are therefore recoverable on proof only of breach of duty under those heads but, even then, substantial damages will not be awarded without proof of loss.

Not all provable loss is recoverable, however. The law limits the damage for which the clinician will be liable by two mechanisms: causation and remoteness. The basic rule of causation is the "but for" test but other rules have been developed to deal with specific situations and with the limits of current medical knowledge. In addition, the loss will not have been caused by the breach unless it was within the scope of the defendant's duty. Even if the loss was caused by the breach of duty, damages will not be recovered for that loss if it was not foreseeable, the precise test for which depends on whether the claim is brought in tort or in contract.

2 CAUSATION: THE STANDARD TEST

The standard test for determining whether or not the defendant's breach caused the claimant's loss is the "but for" test: the claimant's loss would not have occurred but for the defendant's breach of duty.

If the claimant's loss would have occurred in any event, irrespective of the breach of duty, the loss does not satisfy the "but for" test. In *Barnett v. Chelsea & Kensington Hospital Management Committee*,[1] a casualty officer was found to have been negligent in failing to examine three night-watchmen who were vomiting after drinking tea, one of whom subsequently died of arsenic poisoning. Since the man would have died in any event, the defendant's negligence did not cause his death and liability to his widow was not established. In *Robinson v. The Post Office*,[2] the claimant was given an anti-tetanus injection after a minor accident at work and developed encephalitis 9 days later, resulting in brain damage and permanent partial disability. The doctor was held negligent in failing to test for an allergic reaction half an hour before the injection but since the first symptoms of the reaction did not appear for at least 3 days after the injection, the doctor's negligence was held not to have been the cause of the claimant's

---

1 [1969] 1 QB 42.
2 [1974] 2 All ER 737.

injury. Instead, the claimant's employer was liable because the condition had been caused by the initial accident.

3 THE SCOPE OF THE DEFENDANT'S DUTY

Damages for injury or loss that satisfies the "but for" test may still be irrecoverable if it is not proved that the injury or loss was within the scope of the clinician's duty. The claimant must prove that the clinician's duty was in respect of the kind of loss which he has suffered.[3] The point is illustrated by Lord Hoffman's example of the "mountaineer's knee":[4]

> *"A mountaineer about to undertake a difficult climb is concerned about the fitness of his knee. He goes to a doctor who negligently makes a superficial examination and pronounces the knee fit. The climber goes on the expedition, which he would not have undertaken if the doctor had told him the true state of his knee. He suffers an injury which is an entirely foreseeable consequence of mountaineering but has nothing to do with his knee."*

On the "but for" test the doctor is responsible for the injury suffered by the mountaineer because the damage suffered would not have occurred if he had been given correct information about his knee: the claimant would not have gone on the expedition and would have suffered no injury. Common sense suggests that the doctor should not be liable because there is no sufficient causal connection with the subject matter of the doctor's duty. The reason that he is not liable is that he was asked for information on only one of the considerations that might affect the safety of the mountaineer on the expedition and there is no reason of policy for transferring to the negligent doctor all the foreseeable risks of the expedition. So, a defendant who is under a duty to take reasonable care to provide information on which the claimant will decide upon a course of action is, if negligent, not generally regarded as responsible for all the consequences of that course of action. He is responsible only for the consequences of the information being wrong. If the duty is to advise whether or not a course of action should be taken, the adviser must take reasonable care to consider all the potential consequences of that course of action. If he is negligent, he will be responsible for all the foreseeable loss that is a consequence of that course of action having been taken.

An example in a clinical negligence context is *R v. Croydon Health Authority*.[5] A nurse applied for a job with the defendant health authority and was required to undergo a medical examination by its staff. The radiologist who reviewed the claimant's chest X-ray negligently failed to report a significant abnormality that would have been diagnosed as primary pulmonary hypertension (PPH), an untreatable condition of the pulmonary aorta which limits life expectancy and is particularly dangerous if the sufferer becomes pregnant. The claimant became pregnant after taking the job and after her condition was diagnosed a healthy daughter was born by Caesarean section. The claimant underwent treatment for PPH, which included a hysterectomy, which made it more difficult for her to bond with and care for her child. She developed reactive depression, was retired on the grounds of ill health and separated from her

---

3 *Caparo Industries plc v. Dickman* [1990] 2 AC 605.
4 *South Australia Asset Management Corporation v. York Montague Ltd (sub nom Banque Bruxelles Lambert SA v. Eagle Star Insurance Co Ltd)* [1997] 1 AC 191, a valuer's negligence case.
5 (1997) 40 BMLR 40.

husband. She brought proceedings in negligence against the health authority for damages, including the cost of bringing up a child that she contended she would not have had if she had been made aware of her condition. The Court of Appeal held that damages for the birth and upbringing of a wanted and healthy child were not recoverable but if they had been, the loss was outside the scope of the radiologist's duty. The relationship between the claimant and the health authority was that of prospective employee and employer, the express obligation assumed by the radiologist did not extend to the claimant's private life and the scope of his duty did not include responsibility for the consequences of the claimant's decision to become pregnant.

4   MATERIAL CAUSE

It is not always necessary for the claimant to prove that the clinician's negligence was the sole or principal cause of the loss. Where medical science cannot establish the extent of the contribution of the tortious conduct to the injury, it is enough if it was a "material" or "effective" cause.

In *Bonnington Castings Ltd v. Wardlaw*,[6] an employee contracted pneumoconiosis after inhaling silica dust from two sources at work. The employer was in breach of duty in respect of only one of those sources and it was likely that the other was the greater source of dust. The medical evidence was that pneumoconiosis is caused by a gradual accumulation of dust inhaled over a period of years, so that if dust came from two sources, the condition could not be wholly attributed to one source or the other. The claimant therefore could not prove that the employer's breach was the sole cause of his injury but the House of Lords held that it was not necessary for him to do so: it was enough that the breach was proved to have materially contributed to his illness. This principle applies only where the disease or condition is "divisible" so that an increased dose of the harmful agent worsens the disease. The claim succeeded because the tortious exposure to silica dust had materially aggravated (to an unknown degree) the pneumoconiosis which the claimant might well have developed in any event as the result of non-tortious exposure to the same type of dust. The tort did not increase the risk of harm; it increased the actual harm.[7]

In *Bailey v. Ministry of Defence*,[8] the claimant was admitted to the defendant's hospital for surgery to treat a gallstone. After the surgery she became extremely weak as a result of two cumulative causes: negligent lack of care after the surgery (in particular, failure to resuscitate) and the development of pancreatitis, which was not attributable to the defendant's negligence. The claimant was transferred to another hospital where she vomited after being given a drink and was unable to clear her throat. She aspirated the vomit causing a cardiac arrest which led her to suffer hypoxic brain damage. On her claim against the managers of both hospitals the judge held that the cardiac arrest had been caused by the claimant's weakness, to which the defendant's negligent lack of care had made an unknown but material contribution, and therefore held the defendant liable. The Court of Appeal confirmed that the *Wardlaw* principle applies in medical negligence cases as it does in other cases and that where medical science cannot establish the probability that "but for" an act of negligence the injury would not

---

6 [1956] AC 613.
7 *B and others v. MoD* [2010] EWCA Civ 1317, at para 150.
8 [2008] EWCA Civ 883.

have happened but can establish that the contribution of the negligent cause was more than negligible, the "but for" test is modified, and the claimant will succeed.

Wardlaw does not apply where the defendant is responsible for one of several potential causes of the injury but it cannot be proved which of them caused or materially contributed to the injury. In *Wilsher v. Essex Health Authority*,[9] the defendant negligently failed to monitor the level of extra oxygen given to a baby born nearly 3 months prematurely and he developed retrolental fibropassias (RLF), resulting in blindness. The Court of Appeal held the defendant liable on the ground that he had created a risk of injury or increased an existing risk of injury to the claimant. The House of Lords held that a number of different factors could have caused RLF, including excessive levels of oxygen, and the defendant's negligence in failing to prevent excess oxygen causing the condition provided no evidence and raised no presumption that it was excess oxygen rather than one of the four other non-tortious factors that caused or contributed to the claimant's condition. The trial judge had not resolved the conflict in the expert evidence as to whether excess oxygen caused or materially contributed to the claimant's condition and that issue had to be remitted for a retrial. The claimant's claim was subsequently settled.

Bailey was distinguished on the facts in *Appleton v. Medway NHS Foundation Trust*,[10] in which an NHS trust breached its duty of care to a patient in delaying treatment for a foot infection. However, the Trust had not caused the initial infection and the claimant failed to prove that the Trust's negligence had been the cause of his subsequent below-knee amputation or had made a material contribution to it. In *ST (a protected party by his mother and litigation friend KT) v. Maidstone & Tunbridge Wells NHS Trust*[11] the infant claimant (who suffered from congenital haematological conditions) suffered seizures and strokes leading to brain damage. He alleged that the strokes were caused as a consequence of the defendant's breach of duty in delaying a blood transfusion, failing to give IV fluids promptly and the administration of frusemide during transfusions. However, the Trust had not caused the initial respiratory infection which was adjudged to be the cause of the focal cerebral arteriopathy leading to the stroke and the secondary case relying on the principles in *Bailey* failed because on a close examination of the medical there was no objective medical evidence that the dehydration, aemolysis and severe anaemia (i.e. the results of the breach) contributed to the arteriopathy that led to the strokes. On the other hand, in *Popple v. Birmingham Women's NHS Foundation Trust*,[12] midwives failed to recognise problems with the unborn claimant's heartbeat or to monitor it, and failed to expedite delivery by performing an episiotomy and/or organising an urgent instrumental delivery, causing intra-partum asphyxia which resulted in severe athetoid cerebral palsy. The principle in *Bailey* was held to apply: although it was not possible to identify exactly when the damage occurred, the lack of monitoring and failure to deliver some 5 minutes earlier either caused the damage in its entirety or made a material and probably preponderant contribution to it. The Court of Appeal dismissed the defendant's appeal on the facts.[13] Plainly reliance on *Bailey* will assist claimants only in cases where the medical evidence supports some probable causal connection between the breach of duty and the injury.

---

9 [1988] AC 1074.
10 [2013] All ER (D) 93 (Nov).
11 [2015] EWHC 51 (QB).
12 [2011] EWHC 2320 (QB).
13 [2012] EWCA Civ 1628.

5 INCREASING THE RISK – A NEW TORT?

The *Wardlaw* principle was applied and extended in *McGhee v. National Coal Board*.[14] The employee, who normally worked in pipe kilns, was required to empty brick kilns in hot and dusty conditions for 4½ days and, since no washing facilities were provided, he had to cycle home each day whilst caked in brick dust. He contracted dermatitis, which was attributed to brick dust particles abrading and injuring his skin. The precise cause of the onset of dermatitis could not be medically established but it was accepted that the longer he was exposed to abrasion the greater his chance of developing the condition, and that immediate washing was a proper precaution. The employer was held not to be in breach of duty in respect of the claimant's working conditions but was in breach in failing to provide washing facilities. The House of Lords held by a majority that the lack of washing facilities materially increased the risk of dermatitis and that there was no difference between this and "making a material contribution" to its occurrence. The minority held that there was a difference and that as a matter of policy the law should fill the gap in the medical evidence as to the precise cause of the disease.

McGhee was relied upon by the House of Lords to deal with the impossibility of proving causation in mesothelioma cases involving more than one employer. The current state of medical knowledge is that mesothelioma (a malignant tumour, usually of the pleura of the lung) is always, or almost always, caused by exposure to asbestos but the precise biological mechanism triggering the condition is not known. It is not now thought that it is caused by inhalation of a single asbestos fibre but the degree of exposure required, and the effect of subsequent exposure on earlier exposure, is still unknown. What is known is that the more fibres that are inhaled, the greater the risk of contracting mesothelioma but that, once contracted, further exposure to asbestos has no effect. Mesothelioma is therefore an indivisible injury, unlike pneumoconiosis or asbestosis, which are divisible and cumulative ("dose-related") injuries. Where an employee is wrongfully exposed to asbestos by more than one employer, or even by only one employer in addition to everyday exposure to asbestos in the atmosphere, there is currently no way of identifying, even on a balance of probabilities, the source of the fibres that initiated the genetic process culminating in the development of the malignant tumour. A claimant who has been exposed to asbestos during different periods of employment with different employers and contracts mesothelioma cannot prove which of his employers exposed him to the relevant fibre and therefore, on the standard tests for causation, cannot establish liability for his loss.

Fairchild v. Glenhaven Funeral Services Ltd[15] concerned three such employees. The Court of Appeal dismissed their claims on the ground that they had failed to establish causation against any of the defendants. The House of Lords concluded that where each relevant employer had been in breach of its duty to protect the claimant from the risk of contracting mesothelioma and where that risk had eventuated but, in current medical knowledge, the onset of the disease could not be attributed to any particular or cumulative wrongful exposure, a modified approach to proof of causation was justified, as had happened in *McGhee*. "*The rule in its current form can be stated as follows: when a victim contracts mesothelioma each person who has, in breach of duty, been responsible for exposing the victim to a significant quantity of asbestos dust and thus creating a 'material increase in risk' of the victim contracting the disease will be held to be jointly and severally*

---

14 [1973] 1 WLR 1.
15 [2003] 1 AC 32.

liable for causing the disease."[16] The House concluded that to hold otherwise would be to make it impossible, with the arbitrary exception of single-employer cases, to enforce the defendants' duty to the claimants, such that the duty effectively did not exist.

Subsequent analysis of the *Fairchild* case suggests that it introduced a new tort of negligently increasing the risk of personal injury.[17]

Fairchild concerned claimants whose total exposure to asbestos was caused by the defendants. In *Barker v. Corus UK Ltd,*[18] the issues were whether the *Fairchild* exception applied where the defendants were responsible for only part of the claimant's exposure and, where a defendant was held liable he had materially increased the risk of contracting the disease, whether he was jointly liable for the whole of the claimant's loss or only severally liable for a proportion of it. On the second issue the House of Lords held that where more than one person was in breach of duty and might have been responsible, liability should be attributed according to the defendant's relative degree of contribution to the risk, so that defendant was only severally liable for a share of the damage. That part of the decision has since been reversed by s. 3 of the Compensation Act 2006, see below. On the first issue, the House held that even if not all the exposures to asbestos which could have caused the claimant's mesothelioma involved breaches of duty by his employers, the *Fairchild* exception would still apply. In *Sienkiewicz v. Greif (UK) Ltd*[19] only one defendant had exposed the claimant to asbestos dust. The Supreme Court upheld a finding that the defendant was liable for the claimant's mesothelioma even though the total tortious exposure to asbestos was modest compared with the total environmental exposure in the area where she lived and had increased the risk due to the environment by only 18%.

6   EPIDEMIOLOGICAL EVIDENCE AND "DOUBLING THE RISK"

Where the *Fairchild* exception does not apply, the courts have been prepared to hold that causation is established where the claimant can prove that the risk from the tortious exposure was at least twice as great as the risk from any other exposure.

Evidence of the relevant risk is usually derived from epidemiological evidence, that is, evidence based on data from the study of the occurrence and distribution of events (such as disease) over human populations which seeks to determine if statistical associations between these events and supposed determinants can be demonstrated.

In the Oral Contraceptive Group Litigation,[20] Mackay J accepted the concession by the claimants that it was necessary for them to prove that the risk of suffering cardio-vascular injury from taking one type of oral contraceptive was at least double the risk from taking another type. The logic behind this was that if factor X increases the risk of condition Y by more than 2 when compared with factor Z, it can then be said, of a group of say 100 with both exposure to factor X and the condition, that as a matter of probability more than 50 would not have suffered condition Y without being exposed to X. If medical science cannot identify the members of the group who would and who

---

16 *Sienkiewicz (Administratrix of the Estate of Enid Costello Deceased) v. Greif (UK) Ltd* [2011] UKSC 10; per Lord Phillips at para. 1. The rule as stated takes account of the effect of s. 3(2) of the Compensation Act 2006.
17 [2011] UKSC 10.
18 [2006] 2 AC 573.
19 [2010] 1 QB 370.
20 *XYZ and others v. Schering Health Care Ltd and others* [2002] EWHC 1420 (QB).

would not have suffered Y, it can nevertheless be said of each member that she was more likely than not to have avoided Y had she not been exposed to X.

Since the oral contraceptive case, this method of proving causation has been applied in cases of lung cancer where the claimant has been tortiously exposed to asbestos and non-tortiously exposed to cigarette smoke, both of which are potent causes of the condition. Expert evidence is received as to the relative risks created by the two forms of exposure and, if, on the individual facts of the case, the risk from the asbestos exposure is more than double the risk from smoking, the claimant succeeds.[21]

This approach has been adopted to establish causation. In *Shortell v. BICAL Construction Ltd*,[22] the evidence was that the claimant had a 10% risk of lung cancer from smoking and a 5% risk from exposure to asbestos but combined together the total risk was 50%. Mackay J held that that the exposure to asbestos had more than doubled the risk from smoking alone and that, but for that exposure, the claimant would not have developed the disease. In *Cookson v. Novartis Grimsby Ltd*,[23] the claimant developed bladder cancer caused by exposure to carcinogenic aromatic amines from dyestuffs in his employer's factory and by amines in cigarette smoke. The expert evidence accepted by the trial judge was that the amines in cigarette smoke act on the body in the same way as the amines in the occupational exposure, that the claimant's cancer had been caused by the additive effects of both the occupational exposure and smoking but that the occupational exposure had accounted for 70% to 75% of the total. The trial judge found for the claimant by applying *Wardlaw* but the Court of Appeal held that it had not been necessary to do so: the natural inference to draw from the finding of fact that the occupational exposure was 70% of the total was that, if it had not been for the occupational exposure, the claimant would not have developed the cancer. In terms of risk, the occupational exposure had more than doubled the risk due to smoking and it must, as a matter of logic, be probable that the disease was caused by the occupational exposure. The "but for" test had therefore been satisfied.

Sienkiewicz v. Greif (UK) Ltd was a mesothelioma case in which the *Fairchild* rule of causation was held to apply even where the contributing causes were confined to a single employer's breach of duty and ordinary atmospheric exposure. In the course of her judgment in the Court of Appeal, however, Smith LJ observed (*obiter*) that, in other types of case in which there were multiple potential causes, a claimant can prove causation by showing that the tortious exposure has at least doubled the risk arising from the non-tortious cause or causes.[24]

On appeal to the Supreme Court, observations were made about this approach, again *obiter*. Lord Philips noted that the Oral Contraceptive Group Litigation had been concerned with a preliminary issue as to the effect of epidemiological evidence and not whether the DVT suffered by the claimants had been caused by the second generation of oral contraceptives that they had taken: therefore the decision was of no direct assistance on the question of whether the "doubles the risk" test is an appropriate test for determining causation in a case of multiple potential causes. He took the view that

---

21 *Sienkiewicz v. Greif (UK) Ltd* [2010] 1 QB 370, per Smith LJ at para. 21. See also *Shortell v. BICAL Construction Ltd* (unreported, 16th May 2008): on evidence that the claimant had a 10% risk of lung cancer from smoking and a 5% risk for exposure to asbestos but combined together the total risk was 50%, Mackay J held that that the exposure to asbestos had quadrupled the risk from smoking alone and that, but for that exposure, the claimant would not have developed the disease.
22 Unreported, Liverpool District Registry, 16th May 2008.
23 [2007] EWCA Civ 1261.
24 [2010] 1 QB 370, at para. 23.

the evidence in *Shortell v. BICAL Construction Ltd* had been enough to satisfy the *Wardlaw* test and questioned the need to establish a doubling of the risk in cases where asbestos and tobacco smoke have combined to cause lung cancer. However, he was prepared to accept that, in terms of risk, if occupational exposure more than doubles the risk due to smoking, it must, as a matter of logic, be probable that the disease was caused by the former.[25] Lord Roger said that, in cases where the state of medical knowledge makes it impossible for a claimant to prove whether a defendant's breach of duty actually caused his disease, there is no reason why a claimant needs to prove anything more than that the defendant's breach of duty materially increased the risk that he would develop the disease.[26]

The Supreme Court in *Sienkiewicz* also debated the question of whether or not causation can be established solely by epidemiological evidence. A majority of the justices doubted that it could but the issue remains to be decided.

7   CAUSATION AND APPORTIONMENT

If the injury caused to the claimant is indivisible, the liability of each defendant responsible for that injury is joint and several. The rule was explained by Devlin LJ in *Dingle v. Associated Newspapers Ltd*:[27]

> "Where injury has been done to the plaintiff and the injury is indivisible, any tortfeasor whose act has been a proximate cause of the injury must compensate for the whole of it. As between the plaintiff and the defendant it is immaterial that there are others whose acts also have been a cause of the injury and it does not matter whether those others have or have not a good defence. These factors would be relevant in a claim between tortfeasors for contribution, but the plaintiff is not concerned with that; he can obtain judgment for total compensation from anyone whose act has been a cause of his injury. If there are more than one of such persons, it is immaterial to the plaintiff whether they are joint tortfeasors or not. If four men, acting severally and not in concert, strike the plaintiff one after another and as a result of his injuries he suffers shock and is detained in hospital and loses a month's wages, each wrongdoer is liable to compensate for the whole loss of earnings. If there were four distinct physical injuries, each man would be liable only for the consequences peculiar to the injury he inflicted, but in the example I have given the loss of earnings is one injury caused in part by all four defendants. It is essential for this purpose that the loss should be one and indivisible; whether it is so or not is a matter of fact and not a matter of law."

An apportionment between the claimant and the defendants is not appropriate where the injury is indivisible. But the claimant may be held to have been contributorily negligent and his damages reduced accordingly: for example, in *Badger v. MoD*,[28] the employer admitted primary liability for exposure to asbestos which caused the development of lung cancer but the claimant's failure to stop smoking once he was aware of the health risks gave rise to a finding of 20% contributory negligence against him. In addition, the award of damages may be reduced to take into account future risks of non-tortious loss.[29]

---

25 At para. 78.
26 At paras 161–162.
27 [1961] 2 QB 162, 188–189.
28 [2006] 3 All ER 173.
29 See the observations of Smith LJ in *Dickins v. O2 plc* [2008] EWCA Civ 1144, at para. 46.

In *Barker v. Corus UK Ltd*,[30] the House of Lords held that since *Fairchild* imposed a new form of liability where more than one person was in breach of duty and might have been responsible for the loss, liability should be attributed according to the defendant's relative degree of contribution to the risk and was several only. Although mesothelioma is an indivisible injury, the risk of causing it is divisible. Parliament has intervened in the case of mesothelioma claims: by s. 3(2) of the Compensation Act 2006 (which, by s. 16(3), is treated as having always had effect) a defendant who is found liable for materially increasing the risk of the claimant contracting the disease is liable for the whole of the claimant's loss (subject to contributory negligence) with a right of contribution against other defendants similarly liable.

Where the injury is divisible, or "dose-related", an apportionment of damages between the tortfeasors will be made so that each will be liable to the claimant only in respect of the part of the damage which his tort caused, assuming that it is possible to separate and quantify the aggravation of damage.[31] In *Wardlaw* and *Bailey*, liability was established under the modified "but for" test because medical science could not determine the extent of the contribution to the harm by the relevant tort, beyond that the contribution was material. It was not suggested that damages should be apportioned as between the effect of the tortious and non-tortious components. If expert evidence had been available to show the effect of the different components, the damages would probably have been apportioned: the claimant would have recovered damages for only the harm caused by the tort. However, if such evidence was available, there would have been no need for any modification of the "but for" rule.[32] Similarly, in *Hotson v. East Berkshire Area Health Authority* (see below) the claim failed because the medical evidence established that there was a 75% chance that the condition would have developed anyway, therefore the "but for" test was not satisfied. Had the medical evidence been unable to assess the extent of the chance of the condition developing without the tortious event, but able to show that the tortious event was a material cause of the condition, the claim would have succeeded.

8   LOSS OF CHANCE

The claimant must prove that it is more likely than not (i.e. a greater than 50% chance) that the defendant's negligence caused him loss. If he cannot prove causation to that standard, the court will not hold the defendant liable for any part of the claimant's injury on the basis of a lost chance.[33]

In *Hotson v. East Berkshire Area Health Authority*,[34] a 13-year-old fell from a tree, fracturing his left femoral epiphysis. At hospital his condition was not diagnosed for 5 days and he developed avascular necrosis, resulting in disability in his hip. The health authority admitted negligence but the trial judge found that there was a high probability, assessed at 75%, that the condition would have developed anyway. He awarded damages on the basis of a 25% chance that the condition would not have developed.

---

30 [2006] 2 AC 573.
31 *Holtby v. Brigham & Cowan (Hull) Ltd* [2000] 3 All ER 421; *Rahman v. Arearose Ltd* [2001] QB 351.
32 See the observations of the Court of Appeal in *AB and others v. Ministry of Defence* [2010] EWCA Civ 1317, at para. 134.
33 *Tahir v. Haringey Health Authority* [1998] Lloyd's Rep Med 104.
34 [1987] AC 750.

The House of Lords reversed the trial judge's conclusion, holding that since, on the balance of probabilities, the condition was bound to develop even with the correct diagnosis and treatment, he had not established causation. Lord Bridge pointed out that principle is the same on the other side of the coin: if the claimant had proved on a balance of probabilities that the health authority's negligent failure to diagnose and treat his injury promptly had materially contributed to the development of avascular necrosis, the defendant would not have been entitled to claim a discount from the full measure of damage to reflect the chance that, even given prompt treatment, the condition might well still have developed. He did, however, leave open the argument that damages for loss of a chance might be awarded in a case where causation is "*so shrouded in mystery*" that the court can only measure statistical chances.

Academic writers have suggested that in cases of clinical negligence, the need to prove causation is too restrictive of liability, and this argument has appealed to judges in the US, New South Wales and Ireland.[35] The House of Lords had the opportunity to reconsider the issue in *Gregg v. Scott.*[36]

In that case the claimant developed non-Hodgkin's lymphoma, a malignant form of cancer, that was negligently diagnosed as benign, thereby delaying treatment for about 9 months during which time the cancer spread. He was initially advised that the delay had deprived him of an early and complete cure and he made a conventional claim on that basis. Before the trial, however, it was discovered that he had a rare type of cancer with a less favourable prognosis and he therefore put forward an alternative claim for damages for the reduction of the chance of a favourable outcome. No claim was made for the more intrusive treatment made necessary as a result of the delay or greater pain and suffering that he experienced as a result. The trial judge found on statistical evidence that the claimant's prospects of recovery (defined as living for more than 10 years) were 42% when his condition was misdiagnosed and had reduced to 25% as a result of the defendant's negligence, but held that since the claimant would on a balance of probability have failed to survive the 10-year period even if treated promptly, he had failed to show that the outcome for him would have been materially different had he been treated earlier. He held that the alternative claim for loss of a chance was bad in law and dismissed the claim. The claimant appealed, arguing that he had suffered at least some injury, because the judge had found that the cancer had spread more quickly as a result of the delay, and that a reduction in his chance of surviving from 42% to 25% was itself a compensatable head of damage because it represented a loss of chance.

The Court of Appeal dismissed Mr Gregg's appeal. By a majority of 3-2 the House of Lords also dismissed his appeal but the majority was not unanimous in its reasons for doing so. Lord Hoffman and Baroness Hale decided the issue on the *Hotson* and *Wilsher* line of authority requiring a claimant to prove that it was more likely than not that the injury had been caused by the relevant negligence and held that an exception would not be made to allow a percentage reduction in the prospects of a favourable outcome as a recoverable head of damage. Lord Hoffman noted that to allow such an exception would require a radical departure from precedent (involving overruling *Hotson* and *Wilsher* and dismantling the careful restrictions applied in arriving at the *Fairchild* exception) and that any artificial method of control the extent of such an exception would be a fertile source of litigation. Baroness Hale observed that the

---

35 *Rufo v. Hosking* [2004] NSWCA 391; *Philp v. Ryan* [2004] IESC 105.
36 [2005] 2 AC 176.

exception would have to cut both ways: almost any claim for personal injuries could be reformulated as a claim for a loss of a chance and a claimant would not therefore recover a full award if his prospects of recovery were less than 100%. The other member of the majority, Lord Phillips, analysed the expert evidence and, noting the way in which the claim had developed and that Mr Gregg had in fact survived for 9 years by the time of the appeal, took the view that that there was a fallacy in the statistical evidence such that it was particularly difficult to draw any quantitative conclusions as to the effect of the delay. He held that the complications in the case made it an unsuitable vehicle for introducing into the law of clinical negligence the right to recover damages for the loss of a chance of a cure, but left the door open to such a claim by stating that where medical treatment has resulted in an adverse outcome and negligence has increased the chance of that outcome, there may be a case for permitting a recovery of damages that is proportionate to the increase in the chance of the adverse outcome.

The minority view was also not unanimous. Lord Nicholls took the view that it was *"irrational and indefensible"* not to recognise that where a patient is suffering from illness or injury where there is a significant degree of medical uncertainty about his prospects of recovery and he suffers a significant diminution of those prospects by reason of medical negligence, that diminution constitutes actionable damage. He rejected the proposition that the spread of the cancer as a result of the delay constituted an actionable injury because a claim on that basis would not provide an answer to the fundamental question of recovery of loss of a chance. Lord Hope considered that the case was in essence a claim for physical injury caused by the enlargement of the tumour due to the delay in diagnosis that caused a reduction in the prospects of a successful outcome. The reduction in the chance of a successful recovery from a disease that the claimant was already suffering is not a separate cause of action as it is where negligence causes him to suffer from a disease that he did not have. The latter type of claim will be dismissed if the claimant cannot prove that he probably would not have developed the disease in any event but the former should be regarded as a loss to be valued whether or not the prospect of a cure was less than 50%.

The majority decision in *Gregg v. Scott* puts the issue of lost opportunity in the case of clinical negligence out of step with the law applied to other professions. A claim against a doctor who has negligently caused a reduction in the prospects of a successful recovery will fail on causation grounds if the claimant cannot prove that on balance of probability that he would have recovered. However, if a solicitor negligently causes a clinical negligence claim to become statute barred by failing to issue proceedings in time, the claimant has a claim for the lost chance of success in the action without proof that he would have succeeded (see *Kitchen v. Royal Air Forces Association*[37] and *Allied Maples Group v. Simmons & Simmons*[38]). The principles relevant to a claim against a solicitor were summarised by Simon Brown LJ in *Mount v. Baker Austin*, as follows:[39]

- The claimant has the legal burden of proving that he has lost something of value, i.e. that his claim had a real and substantial rather than merely a negligible prospect of success.

---

37 [1958] 1 WLR 563, CA.
38 [1995] 1 WLR 1602, CA.
39 Unreported, 18th February 1998.

- The defendant has an evidential burden of establishing that (despite acting for the claimant and charging for the service) the litigation was of no value and he lost nothing of value. The burden is heavier where the solicitors failed to advise that the claim was hopeless and any advice they did give about the merits of the claim is likely to be highly relevant.
- If and to the extent that it is now more difficult to determine the strength of the original claim, that difficulty is held against the solicitor rather than the claimant.
- If the court finds that the claimant's prospects of success in the original action were more than negligible, it will evaluate the loss by making a realistic assessment of what would have been the claimant's prospects of success had the original litigation been fought out. The court will generally tend towards a generous assessment, given that it was the defendant's negligence that lost the claimant the opportunity of succeeding in full or fuller measure.

If the original claim was hopeless, the fact that the solicitors were negligent in failing to pursue it does not cause the claimant any loss because the action had no value.[40] If a claim to be struck out on the ground that long delay caused by the solicitor's negligence results in it being impossible to have a fair trial, the court assessing the value of the original claim will not attempt to try the issues in that claim (because it has already been decided that it would be impossible to do so fairly) but must form a broad view of the merits of the claim on the available information.[41]

A key distinction between cases of medical negligence (which almost always results in personal injury) and cases of other professional negligence (which almost always results in financial loss) is the tendency to apply an "all-or-nothing" approach to damages in personal injury cases. It may be that a principled solution to the problem typified in *Gregg v. Scott* cannot be achieved for as long as this approach is maintained and that the resulting unfairness to claimants or defendants (depending on whether the lost chance exceeds 50%) can only be resolved by statutory intervention, as happened in the case of the common law's insistence on several liability for damages for mesothelioma (see above).

Perhaps unsurprisingly this continues to be a burgeoning area of litigation. In *Wright v. Cambridge Medical* Group,[42] a GP negligently failed to see and to refer an 11 month old with a superinfection to hospital until 2 days after the initial consultation. The hospital failed to diagnose the claimant correctly for a further 3 days, by which time her hip had become infected and she suffered permanent restricted movement. The trial judge dismissed the claim on the ground that if the GP had referred in good time, the claimant would have suffered injury in any event and therefore the GP's negligence caused no loss and she had not lost the opportunity to be treated properly at the hospital. By a majority the Court of Appeal held that this approach was wrong: the hospital delay was not so unusual as to break the causative link. Where a GP's negligence resulted in the patient's lost opportunity to be treated as she should have been at hospital, the GP could not escape liability by establishing the hospital would have negligently failed to treat her even if promptly referred. The Court of Appeal

---

40 E.g. *Hatswell v. Goldbergs* [2002] Lloyd's Rep PN 359.
41 *Sharif v. Garrett* [2002] 1 WLR 3118, CA: cf. *Harrison v. Bloom Camillin* [2000] Lloyd's Rep PN 89, per Neuberger J.
42 [2012] 3 WLR 1124.

specifically declined to extend the principle of awarding damages for loss of chance to clinical negligence cases involving third parties.[43]

In *Oliver v. Williams*,[44] a GP, in breach of his duty, failed to tell Ms Oliver that he was urgently referring her to hospital for further investigations, with the result that when the referral letter was lost, she did not chase up the hospital appointment for some 5½ months and a diagnosis of ovarian cancer and subsequent surgery were delayed. However, the claimant could not establish that the breach had caused a material or measurable difference to her life expectancy and was not able to recover damages for the loss of a chance.

In *JD v. Mather*,[45] on the other hand, a GP admitted breach of duty in failing to diagnose a malignant melanoma in the claimant's groin. The claimant was able to prove damage caused by the 7-month delay in diagnosis: having regard to the predictive factors for the staging of cancer by the American Joint Committee on Cancer, a timely diagnosis would not have increased the chances of disease-free survival, but it would have increased life expectancy by 3 years.[46]

9   FAILURE TO WARN

As discussed in Chapter 7, every individual of adult years and sound mind has a right to decide what may or may not be done with his body. Individuals have a right to make important medical decisions for themselves and to make decisions that doctors would regard as ill-advised. A doctor is usually under a legal duty to a patient to warn him in general terms of possible serious risks involved in a proposed treatment and treatment performed without the consent of the patient is unlawful. Where the surgeon fails to give a warning of a potential risk of complication and the patient consents to the operation which results in that complication developing, the patient is entitled to damages in negligence provided that, on normal principles of causation, he can establish that had he been properly warned he would not have consented to the procedure.[47] A cause of action in trespass does not require proof of loss[48] but a claim for substantial damages will require proof of loss.

Deciding on whether or not the claimant would have consented if he had been properly informed of the risks requires a subjective review of what the particular claimant would have done, albeit that the assessment of the reliability of the claimant's evidence on that issue (given after the event and in the knowledge that the outcome of the claim depends on that evidence) is likely to be weighed by comparing it to what a reasonable patient would have done.[49]

Accordingly, if the evidence is that the claimant probably would have gone ahead with the operation even if warned of the risk, causation of loss is not established.[50] But what if the claimant would not have proceeded on that occasion but probably would have

---

43 Per Lord Neuberger MR at para. 84; Ellias LJ at para. 93.
44 [2013] Med LR 344 (QBD).
45 [2013] Med LR 291 (QBD).
46 See also *Clinical Risk 2013* Vol. 19, no. 6 pp. 130-138: "Proof of Causation: a new approach to cancer cases" 14.3.2014.
47 *Montgomery v Lanarkshire Health Board* [2015] UKSC 11 is the seminal case on failure to warn and informed consent.
48 *Chatterton v. Gerson* [1981] QB 432, Bristow J.
49 See the approach taken in *Smith v. Barking, Havering and Brentwood Health Authority* [1994] 5 Med LR 285, per Hutchinson J.
50 See e.g. *Smith v. Salford Health Authority* [1994] 5 Med LR 321.

undergone the operation subsequently? In *Chester v. Afshar*[51] the House of Lords held by a majority that this did not matter: in order to vindicate the claimant's right of choice and to provide a remedy for the breach in respect of that particular operation by that particular surgeon, a modification of the traditional principles of causation was required.

In that case Ms Chester suffered repeated episodes of back pain caused by the protrusion of discs in her spine. She was referred to Mr Afshar who recommended surgery but neglected to warn her of the small (1%–2%) risk of developing a serious condition known as cauda equine syndrome (ces). The patient developed this syndrome and brought proceedings on the ground that the surgery was performed negligently and on the failure to warn. The trial judge dismissed the complaint about the surgery itself but held that Ms Chester would not have undergone the surgery when she did if Mr Afshar had warned her properly but would have sought a second opinion. He made no finding, however, as to whether or not she would ever have undergone the surgery and the evidence was that the risk was liable to occur at random, irrespective of the degree of care and skill with which the operation was conducted by the surgeon, so that it was difficult to say that the failure to warn was the effective cause of the injury.

Lord Bingham and Lord Hoffmann both applied the traditional "but for" test for causation and would have dismissed the appeal on the ground that no exception to vindicate the claimant's right to consent was called for. Lord Hoffmann recognised that there might be a case for a modest award in such cases but said it would be difficult to fix a suitable figure. The majority (Lords Steyn, Hope and Walker) held that the issue of causation was to be addressed by reference to the scope of the doctor's duty to warn and that this duty was central to her right to exercise an informed choice. Since the injury she sustained was within the scope of the duty and was the result of the risk of which she was entitled to be warned, the injury was to be regarded as having been caused by the defendant's breach of duty. In order to provide a remedy for that breach and to avoid the normal rule of causation from rendering the duty useless, justice required a narrow modification of that rule. The majority observed that the *Fairchild* case showed that a modification of causation principles may be required if justice and policy demand it and took the same course to avoid injustice to Ms Chester. Of interest is that, out of the five members of the committee, the two who were concerned in the *Fairchild* decision formed the minority.

The judges in *Chester v. Afshar* focussed on the issue of causation in negligence and breach of contract but did not re-examine the proposition, first stated in *Chatterton v. Gerson*,[52] that once the patient is informed in broad terms of the nature of the procedure, her consent to it is real and her cause of action for failure to warn is negligence, not trespass. This approach was subsequently approved in the House of Lords.[53] However, a patient's right to be properly informed of the risks of the proposed procedure would more easily be vindicated by an award of damages in trespass, which would not require any change to the principles of causation. As Bristow J observed:

> *"When the claim is based on negligence the plaintiff must prove not only the breach of duty to inform, but that had the duty not been broken she would not have*

---

51 [2005] 1 AC 134.
52 [1981] 1 QB 432.
53 See *Sidaway v. Governors of Bethlem Royal Hospital and the Maudsley Hospital* [1985] 1 AC 871.

chosen to have the operation. Where the claim is based on trespass to the person, once it is shown that the consent is unreal, then what the plaintiff would have decided if she had been given the information which would have prevented vitiation of the reality of her consent is irrelevant."

It might therefore have been better if the House of Lords had been asked to consider vindicating the patient's right to be warned by reference to a claim in trespass, rather than by identifying yet another exception to the general rule of causation in negligence.

In *Birch v. University College London Hospital NHS Foundation Trust*,[54] Cranston J held that there could be circumstances where a duty to inform a patient of the significant risks of a medical procedure would not be discharged unless the patient was also made aware that fewer or no risks were associated with another procedure. It is clear that it is incumbent on a medical practitioner to discuss the pros and cons of each potential option for treatment including the option of no treatment.

10   FAILURE TO ACT

Where a doctor negligently does an act the primary question on causation is usually one of fact: did the wrongful act cause the injury? Where the negligence consists of an omission, it may first be necessary to decide hypothetically what would have happened in order to determine if the omission caused the injury and what would have constituted a continuing exercise of proper care had the initial failure not taken place. The second part of that enquiry will involve consideration of the *Bolam* test for the standard of care required of the doctor, but that test does not otherwise apply in deciding questions of causation.

The point is illustrated by *Bolitho v. City and Hackney Health Authority*,[55] in which nurses called for assistance from a doctor to deal with the claimant, a 2-year-old boy suffering from croup. The doctor failed to attend and the boy suffered brain damage as a result of cardiac arrest caused by a blockage in his respiratory system. The health authority admitted that the doctor was negligent in failing to attend and it was common ground that the only way in which the damage could have been avoided was by intubating the patient and clearing the obstruction. The doctor's evidence was that, had she attended, she would not have intubated anyway, and there was evidence of a body of medical opinion that would have supported her decision. The House of Lords held that the claimant could have established causation either by proving that the doctor would have intubated (even if she would not have been negligent if she had not) or that it would have been negligent not to have intubated and that the second of these issues, but not the first, involves consideration of the *Bolam* test. On the facts the House upheld the judge's decision that the claimant had failed to prove liability by either route.

11   SUCCESSIVE CAUSES

If there are two successive events that are both sufficient to cause the injury suffered by the claimant, liability depends on the nature and order of those events. If both

---

54 [2008] 104 BMLR 168.
55 [1998] AC 232.

events are tortious, the first in time is the causative event and the responsibility of the defendant for the second event is limited to any additional damage occasioned. So if the defendant damages the claimant's car but the car was already damaged in a previous accident, the defendant is not liable for the cost of repairs that were already required.[56] In *Baker v. Willoughby*[57] the unfortunate Mr Baker was knocked down by a car, causing severe damage to his leg. Shortly before the trial, his leg had to be amputated after he was shot during an armed robbery. The Court of Appeal accepted the defendant car driver's contention that the loss caused by his negligence ended with the amputation but the House of Lords was unimpressed, holding instead that the claimant's disability had two causes and since the amputation was merely a concurrent cause of the disability the defendant remained liable for all the effects of the injury he had caused. An important consideration seems to have been the view that the claimant would otherwise not be compensated by anyone for his loss of amenity after the date of the amputation but the prospect of a claim under the Criminal Injuries Compensation Scheme seems to have been overlooked.

Where the second event is not tortious, the result is different. In *Jobling v. Associated Dairies*,[58] the claimant suffered an accident at work, causing him back pain, but later developed myelopathy, an unrelated condition of the back which became totally disabling and which would have developed in any event. Rather than treat the issue as one of causation the House of Lords viewed it as one of quantum of loss and held that an award of damages that ignored a vicissitude of life such as the development of myelopathy would provide excessive compensation. The decision in *Baker v. Willoughby* was criticised but not departed from: it seems, however, that in future the extent of a defendant's liability for damages for personal injury where a second event causes the same or greater injury will be regarded as a question of quantum rather than of causation.

12   INTERVENING ACTS

The causative link between the defendant's negligent act and the claimant's loss may be broken by a supervening event caused by a third party or by the claimant himself. In that event the "chain of causation" is broken by a *novus actus interveniens* and the defendant escapes liability for his negligence. Whether the supervening event has that effect depends on the extent to which it was foreseeable, which in part may depend on whether it was reasonable.

In *Robinson v. The Post Office* (see above) the claimant was injured as a result of his employer's negligence and his subsequent reaction to the anti-tetanus serum administered at hospital was not caused by negligence on the part of the doctor. All of the consequences of his injury were therefore held to have been caused by the employer's negligence. In *Hogan v. Bentinck West Hartley Collieries Ltd*,[59] the House of Lords upheld an arbitrator's decision to refuse compensation to an employee under a statutory scheme on the ground that the pain in his thumb was not caused by the original accident but by the subsequent surgery that had been "ill advised" and which on the unusual facts of the case broke the chain of causation. That does not mean that subsequent medical treatment that is carried out negligently and makes the condition

---

56 *Performance Cars Ltd v. Abraham* [1962] 1 QB 33.
57 [1970] AC 467.
58 [1982] 1 AC 794.
59 [1949] 1 All ER 588.

worse will always break the chain of causation: the question is whether the subsequent treatment is so grossly negligent that its effect is to *"eclipse the original wrongdoing"*[60] and *"extinguish the causative potency of the earlier tort"*.[61]

> *"The law is that every tortfeasor should compensate the injured claimant in respect of that loss and damage for which he is justly held responsible. To make that principle good, it is important that the elusive conception of causation should not be frozen into constricting rules."*[62]

Illustrations of this principle in a medical context may be found in *Prendergast v. Sam & Dee Ltd*,[63] where a doctor negligently wrote a prescription in illegible handwriting. The pharmacist negligently misread it and supplied the wrong drug but that was held not to have broken the chain of causation from the doctor's negligence since it was reasonably foreseeable that the script might be misread. In *Thompson v. Blake-James*,[64] two doctors gave conflicting advice on vaccination for an infant claimant. At the time of the advice of the first doctor it was foreseeable that the second would advise nearer the relevant time. The advice of the second doctor was held to have broken the chain of causation between the parents' decision not to vaccinate and the advice given by the first doctor.

Causation may be affected where the claimant fails to cooperate with the treatment or fails properly to describe his symptoms. Negligence on the part of the claimant in these respects may reduce the damages awarded or, in an extreme case, breach the chain of causation between the doctor's negligence and the injury.

In *McKew v. Holland & Hannen & Cubitts (Scotland) Ltd*[65] an injury to the claimant's leg at work caused it to give way on occasions. Despite this, he tried to walk down a steep staircase unaided and broke his ankle. He was held to have acted unreasonably and to have broken the chain of causation between that injury and the original breach of duty of his employer. The claimant in *Wieland v. Cyril Lord Carpets Ltd*[66] suffered injury to her neck with the result that she had to wear a collar which made looking though her bifocals difficult, causing her to misjudge her footing on a staircase and suffer further injury. Her use of the stairs in these circumstances was not unreasonable and she did not break the chain of causation.

McFarlane v. Tayside Health Board[67] established that while the financial cost of bringing up a child after a negligently unsuccessful sterilisation operation is not recoverable, the pain, suffering and cost of a pregnancy will be. The claimant in *Sabri-Tabrizi v. Lothian Health Board*[68] knew that she remained fertile after an unsuccessful sterilisation operation but took the risk of falling pregnant by neglecting to use contraceptive measures. Her actions were held to have broken the chain of causation between the negligent operation and her losses on the birth of a child. In *Pigeon v. Doncaster Health Authority*,[69] a cervical smear test was negligently reported to be negative. Over subsequent years the claimant was reminded seven times to have further tests but

---

60 *Webb v. Barclays Bank plc* [2002] PIQR P161, CA.

61 *Rahman v. Arearose Ltd* [2001] QB 351, CA, per Laws LJ at para. 29.

62 Ibid.

63 [1989] 1 Med LR 36, CA.

64 [1998] Lloyd's Rep Med 87, CA.

65 [1969] 3 All ER 1621, HL.

66 1969] 3 All ER 1006, per Eveleigh J.

67 [2002] 2 AC 59.

68 1998 SC 373.

69 [2002] Lloyd's Rep Med 130.

refused to do because the original test had been painful and embarrassing. Cervical cancer was later diagnosed and she underwent extensive surgery. The county court judge held that the claimant's failure to take tests did not break the chain of causation from the first test but did amount to two-thirds contributory negligence. The judge distinguished *McKew* and *Sabri-Tabrizi* on the ground that the claimants there knew about their condition, whereas Ms Pigeon did not.[70]

13   SO WHAT IS THE TEST FOR CAUSATION?

It appears now to be generally accepted that while the "but for" test will, in the usual run of cases, produce a just result, it does not provide a comprehensive or exclusive test of causation in the law of tort. Applied simply and mechanically, it can give too expansive an answer, as in the example of the mountaineer's knee. Sometimes, if rarely, it yields too restrictive an answer, as in *Fairchild*. In the "cumulative cause" cases, modifications to the test for causation are required.

The cases establish the following principles.

    (a)   If the evidence demonstrates on a balance of probabilities that "but for" the contribution of the tortious cause the injury would probably not have occurred, the claimant will establish liability, subject always to proving that the injury was within the scope of the defendant's duty.

    (b)   If the evidence demonstrates that the injury would have occurred as a result of a non-tortious cause or causes in any event, the claimant will be unable to establish that the tortious cause contributed (*Hotson*).

    (c)   Where there are multiple, concurrent distinct causes which operate in a different way and might have caused the injury but the inadequacies of medical science make it impossible for the claimant to establish which of them either caused or materially contributed to the injury, liability will not be established where one of the causes was tortious (*Wiltshire*).

    (d)   In a case where medical science cannot establish the probability that "but for" an act of negligence the injury would not have happened, in certain circumstances the "but for" test is modified, and the claimant will succeed.

        (i)   Where the claimant proves that he suffered injury caused by cumulative exposure to a substance known to be hazardous and a single defendant is responsible for both culpable and non-culpable exposure to that substance but it is impossible to prove which of the exposures in fact caused the injury, proof of a material contribution to the cause of the injury by the culpable cause will be enough, even if the non-culpable exposure was greater than the non-culpable exposure (*Wardlaw*).

        (ii)   Where the claimant suffers injury following cumulative exposure to a substance which may be responsible for that injury, although medical science cannot prove the precise mechanism by which the injury was caused, and a single defendant is responsible for both culpable and non-culpable exposure to that substance, proof of a significant increase of the risk of that injury being caused by the culpable exposure will suffice (*McGhee*).

---

70 See also Walker and Charles, "Misguided advice as a novus actus": JPILaw 2014 No. 1, pp. 10-15.

(iii)   Where there is more than one defendant, each of whom is in breach of a duty of care to the claimant by exposing him to the very harm that the duty was designed to prevent, and the mechanism by which the injury was suffered in each case is identical but it is medically impossible to prove which of the defendants in fact caused the harm suffered, proof that each defendant's wrongdoing materially increased the risk of contracting the disease will do (*Fairchild*). At present, this principle is limited to the development of mesothelioma, but may extend to dermatitis,[71] cancer of the bladder,[72] and (possibly) palmer arch disease of the hand[73] and vibration white finger.[74] It does not apply where the causal link can be proved by expert evidence.[75] At common law a defendant is only severally liable for the consequences of his portion of the risk (*Barker*).

(e)   As a matter of logic, if the claimant proves that the defendant is responsible for a tortious exposure that has more than doubled the risk of the claimant's disease, it follows on the balance of probability that he has caused the disease. However, epidemiological evidence by itself is unlikely to be sufficient to establish causation.[76]

(f)   Where the defendant is in breach of his duty to warn the claimant of the risk of an adverse result of medical treatment and the claimant suffers that result but cannot prove that she would never have undergone the treatment if she had been warned of the risk, it is enough if she proves that she would not have consented to that treatment by that doctor at that time (*Chester*).

(g)   If the complaint is that a clinician negligently failed to attend on the patient, liability may be established either by proving on the balance of probabilities that, had she attended, she would have treated the claimant (even if it would not have been negligent not to have done so) or that on the *Bolam* test it would have been negligent not to have treated the claimant (*Bolitho*).

(h)   Where there are successive, tortious, events causing injury by separate defendants, the first in time is the causative event and responsibility for the second event is limited to any additional damage occasioned (*Baker*). If the second event is not tortious, the award of damages against the defendant responsible for the first event will take into account the occurrence and effect of the second event if known (*Jobling*).

(i)   The chain of causation between the defendant's act or omission and the claimant's injury may be broken by the supervening actions of the claimant or of a third party, depending on whether or not those actions were foreseeable.

---

71 *McGhee v. National Coal Board* [1973] 1 WLR 1.

72 See the observations of Smith LJ in *Cookson v. Novartis Grimsby Ltd* [2007] EWCA Civ 1261 at para. 72.

73 *Transco Plc v. Griggs* [2003] EWCA Civ 54: but note the observation by Dame Janet Smith DBE in her article "Causation – The Search For Principle" [2009] JIPL 101 that, on the facts, it was not necessary to use the *Fairchild* exception because the "but for" test would have been satisfied.

74 *Brown v. Chorus (UK) Ltd* [2004] EWCA Civ 374: again, note Dame Janet Smith's analysis in her article mentioned above.

75 *Hull v. Sanderson* [2008] EWCA Civ 1211 (bacterium from turkeys causing infection on entering by mouth: how it had been transferred to the claimant's mouth was not a Fairchild issue).

76 See dicta in *Sienkiewicz v. Greif (UK) Ltd* [2011] UKSC 10; per Lord Roger at para. 163; Lady Hale at para. 170; Lord Kerr at para. 206 and cf. Lord Dyson at para. 222.

In circumstances in which the standard "but for" test will produce unfairness, particularly where it is impossible to satisfy the standard test, the House of Lords has been prepared to substitute a less stringent test of causation. There is nothing new in that.[77] In *Barker*, Lord Hoffmann proposed a list of five criteria to be applied before the standard test for causation should be modified.[78] The range of disagreement in *Gregg v. Scott* about recovery for loss of a chance, and Lord Phillips' observation that there may be a case for permitting such recovery, means that we may yet see more refinements to the standard test for causation.

14   FORESEEABILITY OF HARM

14.1   The Standard Test

The second mechanism by which the law limits the damage for which the clinician will be liable is that the loss must not be too remote. Different tests have developed in tort and contract.

For a claim brought in tort, the test is that the loss was reasonably foreseeable at the date of the breach of duty. For a claim brought in contract, the test is that the loss was reasonably in the contemplation of the parties at the date they entered into the contract as being not unlikely to arise from the breach. In most cases, the end result is the same.

The standard test has been developed so that only the type of harm needs reasonably to have been foreseen, not the precise injury, with the result that a claimant who is affected by the injury in a way that was not itself foreseeable – the claimant with an "eggshell skull" – may recover for the whole of his injury.

14.2   Type of Harm

It is not necessary for the claimant to prove that the extent of the injury actually suffered was foreseeable, only the type of harm. Provided the type of injury was foreseeable, the defendant is liable for all of its consequences. An example is *Smith v. Leech Brain & Co*,[79] where the claimant was splashed by molten metal that burned his lip. The burn promoted the development of a fatal cancer that might otherwise never have developed, although there was a strong likelihood that it would have done so at some stage in his life. The defendants were held liable for his death on the ground that the burn was foreseeable and the cancer was merely an extension of the burn. In *Hepworth v. Kerr*,[80] a thrombosis was a foreseeable consequence of negligent treatment by the defendant but a spinal stroke was not: the defendant was nevertheless found liable for the consequences of the latter because it was within the general category of foreseeable risk.

The relevant consequences may arise from events after the initial incident caused by the breach of duty. In *Robinson v. The Post Office*,[81] the employers were liable for the consequences of the claimant's allergic reaction to the anti-tetanus serum administered

---

77 See *Blatch v. Archer* (1774) 1 Cowp 63 per Lord Mansfield at 65: "*It is certainly a maxim that all evidence is to be weighed according to the proof which it was in the power of one side to have produced, and in the power of the other to have contradicted.*"
78 Paragraph 61.
79 [1962] 2 QB 405.
80 [1995] 6 Med LR 39.
81 See above.

following a minor accident at work because it was reasonably foreseeable that he might require medical treatment for the injury caused by their negligence and, subject to the principle of *novus actus interveniens*, they were liable for the consequences of that treatment, even if they could not reasonably foresee the consequences or that they could be serious.

For this principle to apply, however, the unforeseeable harm must be connected with the breach of duty. Accordingly, where a patient was negligently discharged from hospital with a chest infection, the hospital was not liable for the consequences of the undiagnosed deep vein thrombosis (DVT) from which the patient also suffered, because the DVT would not have been diagnosed any sooner if he had remained in hospital and his discharge did not contribute to its development.[82] As the Court of Appeal put it:[83]

> *"In short it must be shown that the injury suffered by the patient is within the risk from which it was the doctor's duty to protect him. If it is not, the breach is not a relevant breach of duty."*

14.3   Eggshell Skull

It follows that where a claimant has an unforeseeable predisposition to a particular injury or illness, physical or psychological, that is activated by the defendant's breach of duty, the defendant is responsible for the unforeseeable damage attributable to that predisposition, provided that the injury caused by the breach is itself foreseeable. In *Page v. Smith*,[84] the traffic accident for which the defendant was responsible caused an unforeseeable exacerbation of the claimant's underlying condition (variously described as myalgic encephalomyelitis, chronic fatigue syndrome or post viral fatigue syndrome): the defendant was found liable for the effects of that exacerbation because it was foreseeable that the claimant might suffer some form of personal injury.

15   CONCLUSION

This chapter concerns two particular mechanisms by which the law limits the damage for which the clinician will be liable on proof of negligence: causation and remoteness. However, it would be wrong to view these mechanisms and their component parts in isolation. In *Rahman v. Arearose*,[85] Laws LJ in the Court of Appeal commented that the principles such as *novus actus interveniens*, the eggshell skull, and (in the case of multiple torts) the concept of concurrent tortfeasors, are all no more and no less than tools or mechanisms which the law has developed to articulate in practice the extent of any liable defendant's responsibility for the loss and damage which the claimant has suffered. The real question is: "What is the damage for which the defendant under consideration should be held responsible?" That in turn depends on the type of harm against which it is the defendant's duty to guard the claimant.

An example is *Corr v. IBC Vehicles Ltd*,[86] where, as a result of a serious injury at work, the deceased became severely depressed and ultimately committed suicide. The

---

82 *Brown v. Lewisham and North Southwark Health Authority* [1999] Lloyd's Rep Med 110.
83 Ibid.
84 [1996] AC 155.
85 [2001] 1 QB 351, at 361.
86 [2008] 2 WLR 499. Members of 9 Gough Square (John Foy QC, Andrew Ritchie and Robert McAllister) represented the successful claimant.

defendant employer admitted breach of duty and the deceased's wife claimed in damages under the Fatal Accidents Act 1976 arising from his death. The House of Lords upheld her claim, holding that the employer owed his employee a duty to take reasonable care to avoid causing him personal, including psychiatric, injury and that foreseeability of risk of physical injury was sufficient to establish liability. The depressive illness had been the direct and foreseeable consequence of the breach of duty and his suicide, although his own deliberate, conscious act, had been the direct result of that depressive illness at a time when his capacity to make reasoned and informed judgments about his future had been impaired by it. Accordingly, the chain of causal consequences for which the defendant was liable was not broken by the suicide. The case demonstrates how the various mechanisms for determining and limiting liability (including causation and foreseeability) work in arriving at the conclusion that the claimant is entitled to recover in respect of losses for which the defendant is responsible.

Chapter 7
CONSENT

1   INTRODUCTION

Medical treatment almost always involves some form of physical contact with the patient's body. That contact will in law constitute a trespass to the person, specifically the tort of battery, unless the patient has consented to it. The requirement that the patient consents to the treatment carries with it the right of the patient to choose whether or not to accept the treatment and to refuse it even where there are overwhelming medical reasons not to do so.

> *"If the patient is capable of making a decision on whether to permit treatment and decides not to permit it his choice must be obeyed, even if on any objective view it is contrary to his best interests. A doctor has no right to proceed in the face of objections, even if it is plain to all, including the patient, that adverse consequences and even death will or may ensue."1*

In order to avoid liability in trespass, either the patient has to have given voluntary and informed consent to the treatment and had capacity to give that consent, or the treatment must have been carried out in an emergency, such that the principle of necessity applies. The Mental Health Act 1983, as amended by the Mental Health Act 2007, makes provision for the patient's consent to certain forms of medical treatment for a mental disorder from which he is suffering. In respect of other forms of treatment, the Mental Capacity Act 2005 provides a statutory test for capacity and a new procedure for obtaining declarations about the lawfulness or otherwise of any act done, or proposed to be done, in relation to a person who does not have capacity to decide the matter for himself; but the common law still largely applies in relation to persons under the age of 16. In extreme cases, the court will declare it lawful to withdraw treatment from a patient where it is no longer in the patient's interests to continue with that treatment, even where that course will result in the patient's death.

With the exponential growth in medical technology that prolongs life in previously hopeless situations a question of increasing importance is how the courts determine the extent to which life-prolonging treatment is necessary and/or in the patient's bests interests. The Mental Capacity Act 2005, with the establishment of a distinct Court of Protection, has heralded a marked increase in cases dealing with these difficult concepts.

Once the patient is informed in broad terms of the nature of the procedure that is intended, and gives consent, that consent is valid, and the appropriate cause of action for failing to adequately explain the risks and implications of the procedure is in negligence, not trespass.[2] Such cases have been held to give rise to a modification to

---

1 *Airedale NHS Trust v. Bland* [1993] AC 789, per Lord Mustill at 891.
2 *Chatterton v. Gerson* [1981] QB 432.

the general principle of causation of loss.[3] Very recently the law on "informed consent" (an import originally from the United States) has been re-formulated in the Supreme Court's decision in *Montgomery v. Lanarkshire Health Board*.[4] This decision is discussed in detail below.

2 TRESPASS TO THE PERSON

In the law of tort, an assault is an intentional offer of force or violence to the person of another, such as by advancing within striking distance with a clenched fist and with the intention of striking that person immediately, or pointing a weapon at another with the intention of using it. It is not necessary for there to be actual physical contact for an assault to take place. Battery, on the other hand, is an act of the defendant which directly and either intentionally or negligently causes some physical contact with the body of the claimant without his consent. Usually a battery will be part of, and preceded by, an assault, but circumstances could arise in which a battery takes place without an assault (e.g. if A accidentally hits B when intending to hit C). It seems that consent is a true defence to an action for damages for battery and, therefore, the burden of proof where consent is in issue, is on the medical practitioner.[5]

The advantages of an action in battery are that *any* direct contact will be sufficient (other than generally acceptable contact, such as normal jostling in a busy street or touching another person's arm to gain his or her attention). It has been said by the Court of Appeal that the contact must be "hostile" in order to amount to a battery,[6] but this has since been doubted in the House of Lords.[7] In the tort of battery it is unnecessary to prove that the defendant intended to injure the claimant, or that the claimant would not have consented to the treatment if he had been properly informed of the risks, and the exercise of reasonable care is not a defence to liability.

Complete absence of consent will give rise to liability in battery. Similarly, consent that is obtained as a result of fraud will be held to be invalid: in *R v. Tabassum*,[8] the defendant persuaded two women to allow him to examine their breasts on the pretext that he was medically qualified and was conducting a breast cancer survey in order to prepare a database software package. His conviction for indecent assault was upheld on the ground that although the women consented to the touching, it was in the mistaken belief that it was for medical purposes and true consent had therefore not been given. In *Appleton v. Garrett*,[9] a dentist carried out excessive and unnecessary dental treatment for profit, having deliberately withheld from his patients that their teeth were healthy and where they would not have consented if they had known the truth. Dyson J held that the effect of this non-disclosure in bad faith was to invalidate the consents given and that the patients were entitled to aggravated damages for trespass.[10] On the other hand, in *R v. Richardson*,[11] a dentist who carried out dental

---

3 *Chester v. Afshar* [2005] 1 AC 134, HL.

4 *Montgomery v Lanarkshire Health Board* [2015] UKSC 11.

5 See *Collins v. Wilcock* [1984] 3 All ER 374, per Goff LJ at 378, and *Re F (Mental Patient: Sterilisation)* [1990] 2 AC 1, per Neill LJ at 29. In *Freeman v. The Home Office (No. 2)* [1984] QB 524 (below) McCowan J held that the burden of proving absence of consent rested with the claimant.

6 *Wilson v. Pringle* [1987] QB 237, CA.

7 *Re F (Mental Patient: Sterilisation)* [1990] 2 AC 1 at 73, per Lord Goff of Chieveley.

8 [2000] 2 Cr App R 328, CA.

9 [1996] PIQR P1.

10 Aggravated damages at 15% of the sums awarded for pain, suffering and loss of amenity were awarded on the ground that the patients had suffered mental distress and a sense of injury that was heightened by the knowledge that the treatment was unnecessary.

work without telling her patients she had been suspended from practice was not guilty of a criminal assault on the ground that fraud only vitiated consent to an act which would otherwise be an assault where it had induced a mistaken belief as to the identity of the person doing the act or as to the nature or quality of the act. A mistake as to identity did not extend to a belief as to a person's professional qualifications and attributes.

However, the courts in this country have discouraged claims in battery in the context of informed consent. In *Chatterton v. Gerson*,[12] Bristow J considered that *"it would be very much against the interests of justice if actions which are really based on a failure by the doctor to perform his duty adequately to inform were pleaded in trespass"*. In *Hills v. Potter*,[13] Hirst J agreed in deploring reliance on these torts in medical cases, stating that the proper cause of action, if any, is negligence. Lord Scarman took the same view in *Sidaway v. Governors of Bethlem Royal Hospital and the Maudsley Hospital*.[14]

It follows that where (save in an emergency) the patient has not consented to the treatment at all, or their consent has been obtained by means of fraud as to the identity of the person doing the act or as to the nature or quality of the act, the practitioner who undertakes the treatment, is at common law, liable in trespass as well as in negligence, and may be subject to an award of aggravated damages. Where the patient was given inadequate information on which to give informed consent to the proposed act, the practitioner is liable in negligence alone, and the principle of causation of loss altered to vindicate the patient's right to full information.[15]

3   CAPACITY TO CONSENT AND NECESSITY

At common law, a patient has legal capacity to consent to treatment if he has the ability to understand the broad nature of that treatment. If he has capacity to consent, it follows he is entitled not to consent for any reason, and even for no reason at all. However, where he refuses to consent on grounds that appear to be irrational, there is a risk he will be treated by his doctors as lacking the necessary capacity such that his wishes are wrongly overridden.

If the patient lacks capacity to consent, in an emergency the practitioner may lawfully give the necessary treatment. This principle, which is probably based on necessity rather than implied consent, applies where the patient cannot consent because he is unconscious or is otherwise mentally incapable of giving consent and the treatment is in his best interests.[16]

The relevant legal principles on capacity to consent were identified in *Re T (Adult: Refusal of Treatment)*[17] and developed in *Re MB (Medical Treatment)*.[18] In the latter case a baby was found to be in the breech position, resulting in a 50% risk to the child if born naturally but little risk to the mother. A Caesarean section was advised and the mother initially agreed to the procedure but withdrew consent when she was unable to accept

---

11 [1999] QB 444.
12 [1981] QB 432.
13 [1984] 1 WLR 641 (Note).
14 [1985] 1 AC 871 at 883E.
15 See Chapter 6.
16 *Re F (Mental Patient: Sterilisation)* [1990] 2 AC 1.
17 [1993] Fam 95, per Lord Donaldson MR at 115–116.
18 [1997] 2 FLR 426.

an anaesthetic due to extreme needle phobia. The High Court granted a declaration that it would be lawful to carry out the procedure, using such reasonable force as might be necessary, and the Court of Appeal held that the mother's needle phobia had rendered her incompetent so that the principle of necessity applied. In doing so, the court outlined the basic principles at common law to be borne in mind when dealing with the issue of capacity to consent:

> *"(1)   Every person is presumed to have the capacity to consent to or to refuse medical treatment unless and until that presumption is rebutted.*
>
> *(2)   A competent woman who has the capacity to decide may, for religious reasons, other reasons, for rational or irrational reasons or for no reason at all, choose not to have medical intervention, even though the consequence may be the death or serious handicap of the child she bears, or her own death. In that event the courts do not have the jurisdiction to declare medical intervention lawful and the question of her own best interests objectively considered, does not arise.*
>
> *(3)   Irrationality is here used to connote a decision which is so outrageous in its defiance of logic or of accepted moral standards that no sensible person who had applied his mind to the question to be decided could have arrived at it...it might be otherwise if a decision is based on a misperception of reality (e.g. the blood is poisoned because it is red). Such a misperception will be more readily accepted to be a disorder of the mind. Although it might be thought that irrationality sits uneasily with competence to decide, panic, indecisiveness and irrationality in themselves do not as such amount to incompetence, but they may be symptoms or evidence of incompetence. The graver the consequences of the decision, the commensurately greater the level of competence is required to take the decision...*
>
> *(4)   A person lacks capacity if some impairment or disturbance of mental functioning renders the person unable to make a decision whether to consent to or to refuse treatment. That inability to make a decision will occur when:*
>
> *(a)   the patient is unable to comprehend and retain the information which is material to the decision, especially as to the likely consequences of having or not having the treatment in question;*
>
> *(b)   the patient is unable to use the information and weigh it in the balance as part of the process of arriving at the decision. If, as Thorpe J. observed in Re C[19]...a compulsive disorder or phobia from which the patient suffers stifles belief in the information presented to her, then the decision may not be a true one. As Lord Cockburn CJ. put it in Banks v. Goodfellow:[20] '...one object may be so forced upon the attention of the invalid as to shut out all others that might require consideration.'*
>
> *(5)   The 'temporary factors' mentioned by Lord Donaldson MR in Re T (above) (confusion, shock, fatigue, pain or drugs) may completely erode capacity but those concerned must be satisfied that such factors are operating to such a degree that the ability to decide is absent.*

---

19 See below.
20 (1870) LR 5 QB 549 at 569.

> *(6)*   *Another such influence may be panic induced by fear. Again, careful scrutiny of the evidence is necessary because fear of an operation may be a rational reason for refusal to undergo it. Fear may also, however, paralyse the will and thus destroy the capacity to make a decision."*

In *Re C (Adult: Refusal of Medical Treatment),*[21] a chronic paranoid schizophrenic refused to consent to the amputation of his gangrenous foot. The court decided it had not been established that the patient's general capacity was so impaired by schizophrenia to render him incapable of understanding the nature, purpose and effects of the treatment advised and consequently his right of self-determination had not been displaced. The court accordingly granted an injunction restraining the hospital from operating without his written consent. In *Secretary of State for the Home Department v. Robb,*[22] a prisoner had capacity to refuse nutrition and hydration and it was therefore lawful for prison staff to observe his wishes and not to force food and water on him for so long as he retained that capacity. The position was different in *R v. Collins & Ashworth Hospital Authority ex p Brady,*[23] in which Ian Brady was held to have been incapacitated by mental disorder in all his decisions about refusing food and that forcible feeding was therefore lawful.

In *St George's Healthcare NHS Trust v. S,*[24] S, who was 36 weeks pregnant, was diagnosed with pre-eclampsia and advised to have an induced delivery, without which her life and that of her unborn child would be in danger. She understood the risks but rejected the advice since she wanted a natural delivery. Against her will she was admitted to a mental hospital under s. 2 of the Mental Health Act 1983 and a declaration was obtained from the High Court in her absence, dispensing with her consent to a Caesarean section. No specific treatment for mental disorder or mental illness was prescribed to S whilst in hospital and she was subsequently discharged after the operation. On her application for judicial review the Court of Appeal held that an unborn child was not a separate person from its mother and its need for medical assistance did not prevail over her right not to be forced to submit to an invasion of her body against her will, whether or not her own life or that of her unborn child depended on it, even if her decision might appear morally repugnant. It further held that merely because an individual's thinking process was unusual and contrary to the views of the overwhelming majority, that person could not be detained under the Mental Health Act unless the case fell within the prescribed conditions in that Act. Detailed guidance[25] to health authorities was given as to the procedure to be followed where a patient refuses surgery or invasive medical treatment. This guidance is not only applicable to cases where there is a *serious* doubt over a pregnant woman's capacity to accept or decline treatment, but more generally where there was a doubt over any patient's (pregnant or not) capacity to accept or decline treatment.

Further specific examples are as follows:

(i)   Caesarean section: *The Mental Health Trust, The Acute Trust and the Council v. DD*[26] in which a heavily pregnant woman wanted a home

---

21 [1994] 1 WLR 290.
22 [1995] 2 WLR 722.
23 [2000] Lloyds Rep Med 355.
24 [1998] 2 FLR 728
25 At paras 758, 759 and 760
26 [2014] EWHC 11 (COP).

birth with no social or health service involvement. The mother had borderline/mild learning disability and had a complicated medical history therefore making it a "high risk" pregnancy. The Court found that the mother's desire for a home birth was not only *"unwise"* in the circumstances it *"lacked the essential characteristic of discrimination which only comes when the relevant information is evaluated and weighed"*.[27] Accordingly it was lawful for the mother to be conveyed to hospital for a Caesarean section operation.

(ii)   Fear of needles: *Re MB (Medical Treatment)*[28] in which case the Court of Appeal found that the effect of a profound (albeit irrational) fear of needles was sufficient to amount to a lack of competence to consent to treatment.

(iii)   Anorexia:

    (a)   *A Local Authority v. E*:[29] the force-feeding of E was a proportionate interference with E's rights under Article 3 and 8 ECHR, in order to protect her right to life pursuant to Article 2 ECHR.

    (b)   This case is starkly and tragically contrasted to *NHS Trust v. L*[30] where the High Court found that "the terror of [L] gaining weight" led to the conclusion that in the particular circumstances "the slavish pursuit of life at any cost become unconscionable". This conclusion was supported by L's mother who had determined that force-feeding was not in L's interest and therefore it was unlawful to apply force-feeding to L. See also A NHS Foundation Trust v. X (by her Litigation Friend, the official solicitor)[31] referred to further below in section 8 of this chapter.

(iv)   Blood transfusion: *Nottingham NHS Trust v. RC*:[32] despite RC being an in-patient at a secure psychiatric hospital, the High Court assented to the Trust's request for a declaration that it was lawful to withhold treatment in the form of a blood transfusion in accordance with RC's wishes.

(v)   Amputation: *Heart of England NHS Trust v. JB*:[33] despite JB suffering from paranoid schizophrenia, the Trust had failed to establish that JB lacked capacity to consent/refuse treatment in the form of an amputation of a gangrenous foot (see also *Re C* above).

4   VOLUNTARY CONSENT

Consent to medical treatment is not valid unless it is given freely. Unreasonable pressure placed on the patient by the practitioner, or undue influence from a third party, may vitiate the consent given.

---

27 Para. 86.
28 [1997] 2 FLR 426.
29 [2012] EWHC 1639 (COP).
30 [2012] EWHC 1639 (COP).
31 (2014) 140 BMLR 41.
32 [2014] EWHC 1317 (COP).
33 [2014] EWHC 342 (COP).

The issue of pressure was considered in a prison setting by McCowan J in *Freeman v. The Home Office (No. 2)*.[34] The patient, who was serving a term of life imprisonment, claimed that since the prison's medical officer was in a position to influence his life in prison and his prospects of release, it was impossible as a matter of law for there to be free and voluntary consent to treatment by that doctor. The court rejected that contention but acknowledged there may be circumstances in which, as a matter of fact, the prisoner's will was overborne by the prison doctor where the latter has the power to influence the former's situation and hence *"the court must be alive to the risk that what might appear, on the face of it, to be real consent is not in fact so"*.

The issue of consent affected by undue influence arose in *Re T (Adult: Refusal of Treatment)*.[35] T, a woman who was 34 weeks pregnant, was injured in a car accident. She was taken to hospital where a Caesarean section was contemplated and the possibility of a blood transfusion was canvassed. T was informed that blood transfusions were not normally necessary and that there were other options. T's mother was a Jehovah's Witness and while T was not, she was persuaded to sign a form refusing consent to a transfusion. After the operation her condition deteriorated and she was admitted in a critical condition to intensive care under sedation. Following an emergency application to the High Court for a declaration that it would be lawful to do so, T's doctors gave her a blood transfusion. The Court of Appeal held that although an adult patient is entitled to refuse consent irrespective of the wisdom of that decision, for such a refusal to be effective her doctors had to be satisfied that at the time of refusal her will had not been overborne by another's influence and that her decision had been directed to the situation in which it had become relevant. In all the circumstances, including T's mental and physical state when she signed the form, the pressure exerted on her by her mother and the misleading response to her inquiry as to alternative treatment, her refusal to consent was not effective and the doctors were justified on the principle of necessity in treating her in accordance with their clinical judgement of her best interests.

5   INFORMED CONSENT

The patient must have some information in order to understand the nature of the treatment to which his consent is sought. If he is given some information and consents, that consent is real and is not necessarily vitiated by a failure to give full information.[36] Any cause of action the patient may have concerning the risks and implications of the treatment that were not explained to him lies in negligence, not in trespass.

As discussed in Chapter 6, the House of Lords held by a majority in the case of *Chester v. Afshar*[37] that the normal rule of causation of loss in tort is modified where a patient establishes a failure to warn of a risk associated with the proposed treatment where injury ultimately occurs, in circumstances where the patient would have refused consent to the treatment if he had been warned of that risk. Where the patient cannot establish that he would not have undergone the treatment at a later date, and suffered the same injury, the normal rules of causation would prevent recovery, on the ground that the practitioner's negligence in failing to warn was not causative of the injury.

---

34 [1984] QB 524.
35 [1993] Fam 95.
36 Although see below.
37 *Chester v. Afshar* [2004] UKHL 41, [2005] 1 AC 134.

However, in order to provide a remedy for breach of the practitioner's duty to inform, and to avoid the normal causation rule from rendering the duty useless, the House held that justice required a narrow modification of that rule so that it did not matter that the patient might have undergone the procedure at a later date. In those circumstances, the practitioner is liable for the injury sustained and its consequences.

Furthermore, a practitioner may not simply be liable where he fails to inform a patient of the significant risks of a medical procedure, but also where he fails to inform a patient of an alternative procedure with fewer or no associated risks. In *Birch v. University College London Hospital NHS Foundation Trust*,[38] the court considered the cases of *Sidaway*,[39] *Pearce*[40] and *Chester*,[41] as well as *Bolam*[42] and *Bolitho*,[43] and by logical extension, held that if there was a significant risk that would affect the judgement of a reasonable patient then, in normal circumstances, it was the responsibility of a doctor to inform that patient of that risk to enable the patient to determine for himself which course he should adopt.

Fully informed consent may therefore be absent unless the comparative risks of different procedures are explained, but whether the duty to inform of all relevant alternatives has been discharged will still very much turn on the facts of the individual case. In *Birch*, the most appropriate method of diagnosis for the patient's condition was by way of invasive catheter angiography to rule out a potentially life-threatening aneurysm. Unfortunately, non-negligent complications during that procedure resulted in a stroke, a risk that had been warned about when consent was obtained. The court accepted, however, that Mrs Birch would have chosen the alternative and non-invasive method of diagnosis by way of an MRI scan if she had been told of the comparative risks involved, and that she would have been better off even if the risk thereby was of a failure to diagnose an aneurysm as she did not in fact have an aneurysm and would not have had the stroke. As a result, although the defendant Trust was not negligent in deciding to perform the angiogram, the failure to discuss the comparative risks of alternative treatments with the patient rendered the Trust liable on the particular facts of that case as found by the court for the consequences of an invasive procedure, even though it was held to be an appropriate method of diagnosis.

The ratio in *Birch* was affirmed in *Meiklejohn v. St George's Healthcare NHS Trust*[44] in which the claimant claimed (in part) a breach of duty for a failure to obtain written consent and/or for a failure to inform her of alternative treatments for aplastic anaemia. This breach, it was argued, caused the claimant to consent to a course of treatment that resulted in unpleasant side effects. The Court of Appeal unanimously found that even if alternative treatments had been discussed, the clinician would have recommended the particular course of treatment undertaken. Furthermore that the claimant would have accepted that advice. It was noted that there was no authority for a duty to warn of possible alternative diagnoses not reasonably suspected.

Conversely in *Border v. Lewisham and Greenwich NHS Trust (formerly South London Healthcare NHS Trust)*,[45] the Court of Appeal reiterated the importance that not only do

---

38 [2008] EWHC 2237.
39 *Sidaway v. Board of Governors of the Bethlem Royal Hospital* [1984] QB 493, CA (Civ Div).
40 *Pearce v. United Bristol Healthcare NHS Trust* [1999] ECC 167, CA (Civ Div).
41 *Chester v. Afshar* [2004] UKHL 41, [2005] 1 AC 134.
42 *Bolam v. Friern Hospital Management Committee* [1957] 1 WLR 582, QBD.
43 *Bolitho (Deceased) v. City and Hackney HA* [1998] AC 232, HL.
44 [2013] EWHC 469 (QB).
45 [2015] EWCA Civ 8.

clinicians have to give the patient information on the comparative risks arising from a course of treatment, they should consider a patient's reasonably expressed wish for treatment.

In *Border* a doctor wanted to insert a cannula into the claimant's left arm. The claimant told the doctor not to as a previous procedure had rendered her susceptible to oedema. The doctor ignored the claimant and she developed oedema and disability in left arm. The county court judge dismissed her claim for medical negligence and found that despite the claimant not having given consent, the doctor was acting in accordance with standard practice in an emergency room. The Court of Appeal found that while it was established law that in a medical emergency, when the patient was incapable of giving consent, a doctor might proceed without consent provided that he was acting in the patient's best interests, on the evidence, it had not been such a case of medical emergency. The claimant had been in the emergency room, but she had been fully conscious and capable of giving or withholding her consent.

It is important to note that prior to the recent Supreme Court decision in *Montgomery* the test applied in cases of informed consent was by reference to *Bolam* and therefore, strictly, the test depended on whether the omission to inform more fully or inform at all was accepted as proper by a responsible body of medical opinion which could not be rejected as incapable of standing up to rational analysis (cf the speech of Lord Bridge in *Sidaway* and the approach to this issue by Lord Wolf MR in *Pearce v United Bristol Healthcare NHS Trust*[46]).

The application of the *Bolam* test in informed consent was based on a model of relationship between patient and doctor, of medical paternalism and the view of the patient being entirely dependent on information provided from the doctor (often dependent on what questions if any were posed by the patient). The first instance and appeal decisions in *Montgomery v Lanarkshire Health Authority*[47] provide a good example of this. Mrs Montgomery was a diabetic and was physically small. Moreover diabetic mothers often have larger babies. A particular risk was shoulder dystocia, which was a medical emergency if it were to occur. The Supreme Court found the risk of shoulder dystocia a 10% risk but the risk of a catastrophic injury arising from this was less than 0.1%. Mrs Montgomery was not warned of either risk. During delivery shoulder dystocia occurred. The delivery took 12 minutes during which the umbilical cord was wrapped around the baby's neck causing hypoxia and severe brain damage.

The agreed evidence before the court was that the claimant was anxious about the size of her baby and having a vaginal delivery. She had not, however, specifically asked about the risks associated with delivering her baby vaginally. The treating clinician decided not to inform Mrs Montgomery of the risks as "*the risks of a baby developing grave problems from dystocia was very small … if that condition was mentioned, then most women will actually say 'I'd rather have a caesarean section'… and it is not in the maternal interests to have caesarean sections*".[48]

At first instance and on appeal the courts rejected Mrs Montgomery's claim on the basis that a responsible body of medical opinion would not have advised Mrs Montgomery of the risks, partly because on the evidence it was found that she had not specifically asked about the risks associated with a vaginal delivery. Furthermore, it

---

46 [1999] ECC 167, CA (Civ Div).
47 [2015] UKSC 11.
48 Para 13 of the lead judgment of Lords Kerr and Reed.

was held on appeal that the relevant risk in this case was the very small risk of a grave adverse outcome and that this risk did not fall into that class of cases where notwithstanding the practice of a responsible body of medical practitioners the courts would say that no practitioner could reasonably omit to warn the patient. *Sidaway* was followed and the claim dismissed.

The Supreme Court accepted that the doctor's decision accorded with a responsible body of opinion. However, in a wholesale review of the law on informed consent and the factors relevant to the formulation of the correct test, it was held: "*patients are now widely regarded as persons holding rights rather than as passive recipients of the care of the medical profession. They are also widely treated as consumers exercising choices.*"[49] The fact that the treatment which could be offered by health professionals may depend on bureaucratic decisions and allocation of resources by non-medical professionals was also relevant. Social and legal developments in the accessibility of information, the importance of the autonomy of the individual were important and had been more recently (especially post *Chester v Afshar*[50]) reflected in professional medical practice. For example, the General Medical Council had in *Good Medical Practice* (2013) advised their members to "*Work in partnership with patients. Listen to and respond to, their concerns and preferences. Give patients the information they want or need in a way they can understand. Respect patients' right to reach decisions with you about their treatment and care.*" In this context the court noted that there was something unreal about placing the onus of asking questions upon a patient who may not know that there is anything to ask about.[51]

Lord Kerr and Lord Reed (with whom Lords Neuberger, Lord Clark and Lord Hodge agreed) observed that these developments "*point towards an approach to the law which, instead of treating patients in the hands of their doctors (and then being prone to sue their doctors in the event of a disappointing outcome), treats them so far as possible as adults who are capable of understanding that medical treatment is uncertain of success and may involve risks, accepting responsibility for the taking of risks affecting their own lives, and living with the consequences of their choices*".[52]

Within the framework of negligence "*this could be understood as a duty of care to avoid exposing a person to a risk of injury which she would otherwise have avoided, but it is also the counterpart of the patient's entitlement to decide whether or not to incur that risk*".[53] The court acknowledged that the patient's decision-making process may depend on all sorts of subjective matters for each patient, not solely medical considerations. A two part process was going on here in terms of the doctor's role: the first was an exercise of professional skill and judgment – to advise on the risks and pros and cons of one or another treatment or course of action. The second was the advisory obligation itself to discuss the risks and pros and cons of treatment or course of action which would then enable the patient to make an informed decision. "*The responsibility for determining the nature and extent of a person's rights rests with the courts, not with the medical professions.*"

It followed that the analysis of the law by the majority in *Sidaway* was unsatisfactory in so far as it treated the doctor's duty to advise as falling within the *Bolam* test and the Supreme Court concluded, in particular in light of the views of the House of Lords in

---

49 Lords Kerr and Reed (para 75 of the judgment in *Montgomery v Lanarkshire Health Board* [2015] UKSC 11.
50 [2004] UKHL 41, [2005] 1 AC 134.
51 Lords Kerr and Reed at para 58, citing Sedley LJ in *Wyatt v Curtis* [2003] EWCA Civ 1779.
52 Lords Kerr and Reed at para 81.
53 Lords Kerr and Reed at para 82.

Chester v Afshar: "*There is no reason to perpetuate the application of the Bolam test in this context any longer.*" The authoritative position on consent to medical treatment is thus set out at paragraph 87 by Lords Kerr and Reed:

> "*The correct position, in relation to the risks of injury involved in treatment, can now be seen to be substantially that adopted in Sidaway by Lord Scarman, and by Lord Woolf MR in Pearce, subject to the refinement made by the High Court of Australia in Rogers v Whitaker, which we have discussed at paras 77-73. An adult person of sound mind is entitled to decide which, if any, of the available forms of treatment to undergo, and her consent must be obtained before treatment interfering with her bodily integrity is undertaken. The doctor is therefore under a duty to take reasonable care to ensure that the patient is aware of any material risks involved in any recommended treatment, and of any reasonable alternative or variant treatments. The test of materiality is whether, in the circumstances of the particular case, a reasonable person in the patient's position would be likely to attach significance to the risk, or the doctor is or should reasonably be aware that the particular patient would be likely to attach significance to it.*"

Three important further points were made explicit:

(i)   Risk: "*the assessment of whether a risk is material cannot be reduced to percentages ... is likely to reflect a variety of factors besides its magnitude ... the nature of the risk, the effect ... on the life of the patient, the importance of the benefits ... of the treatment, alternatives available and the risks involved in those alternatives*".[54]

(ii)   Advisory role involves dialogue: "*the role will only be performed effectively if the information provided is comprehensible*" to ensure that the patient understands the seriousness of her condition, and the anticipated benefits and risks of proposed treatment and any reasonable alternatives.[55]

(iii)   Therapeutic exception: i.e. it would be seriously detrimental to the patient's health to disclose the risks. But this "therapeutic exception" should not be abused "*It is a limited exception to the general principle that the patient should make the decision whether to undergo a proposed course of treatment; it is not intended to subvert that principle by enabling the doctor to prevent a patient from making an informed choice where she is liable to make a choice which the doctor considers to be contrary to her best interests.*"[56]

It is apparent from paragraph 75 of the judgment that this approach to consent applies "*mutatis mutandis, to other healthcare providers*", not only doctors. The Supreme Court have therefore unequivocally confirmed the patient's right to autonomy in their consent to treatment. Per Lady Hale: "*Gone are the days when it was thought that on becoming pregnant, a woman lost, not only her capacity, but also her right to act as a genuinely autonomous human being.*"[57]

---

54 Lords Kerr and Reed at para 89.
55 Lords Kerr and Reed at para 90.
56 Lords Kerr and Reed at para 91.
57 Para 116.

6   FORM OF CONSENT

Formal written consent is not required for every treatment but in the case of extensive or invasive treatment, it is in the practitioner's interests to obtain consent in writing. Not only does such a document enable the parties to be clear on the consent given, but also express provision may be made for the situation where, for example, further surgery is found to be required whilst the patient is unconscious under anaesthetic.

Where consent is not given in writing, it may be given orally or may be inferred from conduct. Where it is given in writing, the form will usually state that the purpose and nature of the treatment has been explained to the patient. Such a form is not conclusive against the patient, merely evidence that he consented to the treatment in question.[58] By the same token, the fact that the form is not properly signed does not necessarily mean the patient did not properly consent.[59]

The current NHS standard consent forms can be found on the Department of Health website.[60] Four forms are currently available:

Consent form 1 - Patient agreement to investigation or treatment
Consent form 2 - Parental agreement to investigation or treatment for a child or young person
Consent form 3 - Patient/parental agreement to investigation or treatment (procedures where consciousness not impaired)
Consent form 4 - Form for adults who are unable to consent to investigation or treatment

Forms 1 and 2 contain express provision for further treatment where necessary: the wording in Form 1 is *"I understand that any procedure in addition to those described on this form will only be carried out if it is necessary to save my life or to prevent serious harm to my health"*. It is probable that the principle of necessity permits the practitioner to carry out the additional procedure in such circumstances without this express provision. Guidance to Trusts on amending consent forms to suit particular circumstances has also been published by the DoH,[61] and takes into account the judgment in the case of *Chester v. Afshar*,[62] and the Mental Capacity Act 2005.

7   PUBLISHED GUIDANCE:

The General Medical Council has produced a guide: "Consent: patients and doctors making decisions together", which came into effect on 2nd June 2008. The purpose of the guide is to expand upon the requirement in the GMC's "Good Medical Practice" (2006) that doctors must be satisfied they have the patient's consent or other valid authority before undertaking any examination or investigation, providing treatment or involving patients in teaching and research. The guide identifies the principles on

---

58 See *Chatterton v. Gerson* [1981] QB 432.
59 *Taylor v. Shropshire Health Authority* [1998] Lloyd's Rep Med 395. Cf *Williamson v. East London & City Health Authority* [1998] Lloyd's Rep Med 6, in which, on the facts, the absence of a signature on a form that had been amended to reflect more extensive surgery, indicated that the patient had not consented to that surgery.
60 https://www.gov.uk/government/publications?keywords=consent+forms&publication_filter_option =all&topics%5B%5D=all&departments%5B%5D=department-of-health&official_document_status=all&world_ locations%5B%5D=all&from_date=&to_date=.
61 www.gov.uk/government/publications/reference-guide-to-consent-for-examination-or-treatment-second-edition.
62 *Chester v. Afshar* [2004] UKHL 41, [2005] 1 AC 134, as discussed above.

which good clinical decisions should be based and sets out a framework for good practice in the areas of investigation and treatment, covering the various situations doctors may face in the course of their work.

The emphasis in the guide is on working in partnership with the patient or, if the patient cannot make a decision, with those close to the patient and with other members of the healthcare team. Detailed advice is given for situations such as where patients do not want to know about their condition or treatment (paras 13-17); discussing side effects, complications and other risks (paras 28-36), assessing the patient's capacity to decide (paras 71-74) and the scope of treatment in emergencies (para. 79). The guide also contains a legal annex summarising some of the cases and legislation on consent.

The Department of Health has also updated its 2001 "Reference guide to consent for examination or treatment", in 2009.[63] This is a particularly useful summary of the DoH's current view of *"English law concerning consent to physical interventions on patients – from major surgery and the administration or prescription of drugs to assistance with dressing"*, and applies to all health practitioners including students.

For particular reference to nursing and midwifery, the "Code"[64] published by the Nursing & Midwifery Council, as well as the (slightly more extensive) advice to its members on the issue of consent, published on their website,[65] should be considered. For dental professionals, the General Dental Council's guidance on consent can similarly be found on its website,[66] as a supplementary booklet to the GDC's core guidance for its members (namely, "Standards for dental professionals"[67]).

The GMC's "Good Medical Practice" explains that it provides guidance, not a statutory code, and that doctors must use their judgement to apply the principles to various situations they face and be prepared to explain and justify their decisions and actions. Notably, both "Good Medical Practice" and "Consent: patients and doctors", expressly state that *"Serious or persistent failure to follow this guidance will put your registration at risk"*, and the Nursing & Midwifery Council's "Code" notes that: *"Failure to comply with this Code may bring your fitness to practise into question and endanger your registration"*. In a similar vein, the DoH "Reference Guide to Consent" highlights not only the legal position, but also relevant guidance from regulatory bodies. The pertinent observation is therefore made, *"where the standards required by professional bodies are rising, it is likely that the legal standards will rise accordingly"*. Hence, in a clinical negligence action, a practitioner who failed to follow the guidance in these publications and cannot justify that departure, is likely to have a finding of negligence made against him.

---

63 www.gov.uk/government/publications/reference-guide-to-consent-for-examination-or-treatment-second-edition.
64 "The Code, Standards of conduct, performance and ethics for nurses and midwives", 2008, available online at the time of writing, at: www.nmc-uk.org/Documents/Standards/nmcTheCodeStandardsofConduct PerformanceAndEthicsForNursesAndMidwives_TextVersion.pdf. (The code has recently been revised with effect from 31st March 2015 and can be found at www.nmc-uk.org/The-Code.
65 Noted to have been last updated in April 2008, but still current and available on their website as at the time of writing, at: www.nmc-uk.org/Nurses-and-midwives/Advice-by-topic/A/Advice/Consent.
66 "Principles of Patient Consent", 20th May 2005, available online at the time of writing, on the GDC website, at: www.gdc-uk.org/Dentalprofessionals/Standards/Documents/PatientConsent%5B1%5D.pdf.
67 Published 20th May 2005, and available online at the GDC website, at: http://www.gdc-uk.org/Dentalprofessionals/Standards/Documents/Standards%20for%20the%20Dental%20Team.pdf. This guidance replaces that previously published in May 2005 and is effective in relation to claims relating to conduct after 30th September 2013.

8   THE MENTAL CAPACITY ACT 2005

The Mental Capacity Act 2005 ("the Act"), which came into force on 1st October 2007, placed the decision-making process for those unable to decide for themselves[68] onto a statutory footing.

The Act is now well established. The House of Lords Select Committee report published on 13th March 2014[69] highlights a growing concern at the Act's effectiveness at protecting vulnerable people: further discussion of which perhaps lies outside the scope of this book. The government responded to this report on 10th June 2014.[70]

The far-reaching nature of the Act is underlined by the first case involving the Act to reach the Supreme Court: *Aintree University NHS Foundation Trust v. James*.[71] This case is discussed below. *Aintree* confirmed that at the heart of the Act is the assessment of best interests:

> "*Nor is that Court concerned with the legality of NHS policy or guidelines for the provision of particular treatments. Its role is to decide whether a particular treatment is in the best interests of a patient who is incapable of making the decision for himself to determine whether treatment is in the best interests of someone who is incapable of making that decision himself.*"[72]

The office of the Court of Protection, replacing the office of the Supreme Court that had the same name, has comprehensive jurisdiction over the health, welfare and financial affairs of persons lacking capacity. The court has its own judges and procedural rules, the Court of Protection Rules 2007 and the Court of Protection (Amendment) Rules 2011. Part 21 of the Civil Procedure Rules[73] also reflects the provisions of the Act.

A Code of Practice, running to some 302 pages, was issued on 23rd April 2007 by the Lord Chancellor under ss. 42 and 43 of the Act. The Code gives practical guidance on a range of matters and has statutory force: by s. 42(4) all persons acting in a professional capacity (an expression that includes solicitors and counsel) in relation to a person who lacks capacity have a duty to observe its provisions. Whilst the Code is not a statute, the Supreme Court in *Aintree* confirmed that if the professional guidance published by the GMC and others came into conflict with the provisions of the Code, the provisions of the Code would prevail.[74]

Part 9 of the Court of Protection Rules 2007 deals with the commencement of proceedings. Practice Directions 9A-9H supplement Part 9. PD 9E sets out the procedure to follow where the application concerns serious medical treatment. Serious medical treatment cases must be heard by a judge of the court who has been nominated as such by virtue of s. 46(2)(a)–(c) of the Act (i.e. the President of the Court of Protection, the Chancellor or a judge of the High Court).

---

68 The Act has no general application to those under 16 years old: although if the incapacity is to stretch beyond 18 years old, ss. 2(5) and 18(3) of the Act permit the Court of Protection to make Orders in respect of that person.
69 http://www.publications.parliament.uk/pa/ld201314/ldselect/ldmentalcap/139/139.pdf.
70 https://www.gov.uk/government/uploads/system/uploads/attachment_data/file/318730/cm8884-valuing-every-voice.pdf.
71 [2013] UKSC 67.
72 *Aintree*, per Lady Hale, para. 18.
73 As amended.
74 *Aintree University NHS Foundation Trust v. James* [2013] UKSC 67, para. 27.

In the Rules and the Practice Directions, the person alleged to lack capacity is referred to as "P". The Practice Direction defines serious medical treatment as treatment that involves providing, withdrawing or withholding treatment in circumstances where:

(a)   in a case where a single treatment is being proposed, there is a fine balance between its benefits to P and the burdens and risks it is likely to entail for him;

(b)   in a case where there is a choice of treatments, a decision as to which one to use is finely balanced; or

(c)   the treatment, procedure or investigation proposed would be likely to involve serious consequences for P.[75]

"Serious consequences" are those which could have a serious impact on P, either from the effects of the treatment, procedure or investigation itself or its wider implications. This may include treatments, procedures or investigations which:

(a)   cause, or may cause, serious and prolonged pain, distress or side effects;

(b)   have potentially major consequences for P; or

(c)   have a serious impact on P's future life choices.[76]

Examples of serious medical treatment are given in para. 6 of the PD. Paragraph 5 provides that cases involving any of the following decisions should be regarded as serious medical treatment and should be brought to the court:

(a)   decisions about the proposed withholding or withdrawal of artificial nutrition and hydration from a person in a permanent vegetative state or a minimally conscious state;

(b)   cases involving organ or bone marrow donation by a person who lacks capacity to consent; and

(c)   cases involving non-therapeutic sterilisation of a person who lacks capacity to consent.

The teeth of the Mental Capacity Act 2005 lie at s. 15, the Court of Protection having statutory power to make declarations as to:

- whether a person has or lacks capacity to make a decision specified in the declaration;
- whether a person has or lacks capacity to make decisions on such matters as are described in the declaration;
- the lawfulness or otherwise of any act done, or yet to be done, in relation to that person. In this context "act" includes an omission and a course of conduct.

The determination itself of whether or not the person lacks capacity is neither an invasion into their private life that would engage Article 8 ECHR, nor does it inform the decision on whether the person has capacity.[77] The central role of the Court of Protection is stated thus in *Aintree*:

---

[75] Practice Direction E, para. 3.
[76] Ibid., para. 4.
[77] For a detailed discussion and analysis of the nature and scope of declarations under s. 15 of MCA 2005 see *YLA v. PM and MZ* [2013] EWHC 4020 (COP) per Parker J.

"nor is that Court concerned with the legality of NHS policy or guidelines for the provision of particular treatments. Its role is to decide whether a particular treatment is in the best interests of a patient who is incapable of making the decision for himself to determine whether treatment is in the best interests of someone who is incapable of making that decision himself."[78]

Five essential principles are identified in s. 1 of the 2005 Act that apply for the purposes of the Act:

"(1) *a person must be assumed to have capacity unless it is established that he lacks capacity;*

(2) *a person is not to be treated as unable to make a decision unless all practicable steps to help him to do so have been taken without success;*

(3) *a person is not to be treated as unable to make a decision merely because he makes an unwise decision;*

(4) *an act done, or decision made, under the Mental Capacity Act 2005 for or on behalf of a person who lacks capacity must be done, or made, in his best interests; and*

(5) *before the act is done, or the decision is made, regard must be had to whether the purpose for which it is needed can be as effectively achieved in a way that is less restrictive of the person's rights and freedom of action."*

Capacity is defined at s. 2. A person lacks capacity in relation to a matter if:

"at the material time he is unable to make a decision for himself in relation to the matter because of an impairment of, or a disturbance in the functioning of, the mind or brain."

The inability to "make decisions" is expanded at s. 3:

"For the purpose of section 2, a person is unable to make a decision for himself if he is unable:

(1) *to understand the information relevant to the decision;*

(2) *to retain that information;*

(3) *to use or weigh that information as part of the process of making the decision; or*

(4) *to communicate his decision (whether by talking, using sign language or any other means)."*

The role of the Court is to determine whether a treatment is in the best interests of the patient who is unable to make decisions for himself (as defined above). The potential conflict between the patient's wishes and feelings and an objective assessment of what was in the patient's best interests was explored in *Aintree* (both at the Court of Appeal and the Supreme Court).

The Court of Appeal rejected the argument that life should be preserved *at all costs*: preferring the question to be whether the treatment was indicated to bring a "therapeutic" benefit to the patient. Within this analysis lay the central question of

---

[78] *Aintree*, per Lady Hale, para. 18.

whether treatment was "futile" in the sense of whether the treatment had no prospect of curing or relieving the underlying disease or illness.

The Supreme Court, through Lady Hale, disagreed this analysis and that the test of a patient's wishes was solely objective, in a nuanced judgment that encapsulates the importance of this case, Lady Hale stated:

> *"Finally, insofar as Sir Alan Ward and Arden LJ were suggesting that the test of the patient's wishes and feelings was an objective one, what the reasonable patient would think, again I respectfully disagree. The purpose of the best interests test is to consider matters from the patient's point of view. That is not to say that his wishes must prevail, any more than those of a fully capable patient must prevail. We cannot always have what we want. Nor will it always be possible to ascertain what an incapable patient's wishes are. Even if it is possible to determine what his views were in the past, they might well have changed in the light of the stresses and strains of his current predicament. In this case, the highest it could be put was, as counsel had agreed, that 'It was likely that Mr James would want treatment up to the point where it became hopeless'. But insofar as it is possible to ascertain the patient's wishes and feelings, his beliefs and values or the things which were important to him, it is those which should be taken into account because they are a component in making the choice which is right for him as an individual human being.'*[79]

Put shortly in determining the best interests of a patient *"decision makers must look at his welfare in the widest sense, not just medical but social and psychological; they must consider what the outcome of that treatment for the patient is likely to be…"*[80]. An application of this in practice can be found in *A NHS Foundation Trust v. X (By her Litigation Friend, the official solicitor).*[81] P had suffered from anorexia nervosa for years in addition to being dependent on alcohol. A cycle of admission, weight gain whilst hospitalised, followed by binge drinking and weight loss on discharge had pertained for years. P had previously made it clear that she wished to refuse life-saving treatments with respect to her liver disease. The court considered that she had capacity in respect of her decision to refuse treatment for alcohol-related problems but lacked capacity in respect of her eating disorder. It was held that the common law, Article 2 ECHR and the Mental Capacity Act, s. 4(5) imposed an obligation to attach the highest priority to the preservation and sanctity of life. However, in considering the best interests test and the approach of Lady Hale in *Aintree* this was a case where the appropriate course was not to compel treatment. (This was the course of action sought by the treating clinicians who considered further treatment to be futile and unethical.)

The court will give weight to the view of treating clinicians such that if they decline to provide treatment on the basis of their clinical judgement, the court is unlikely to order such treatment. In *United Lincolnshire Hospital NHS Trust v. N (by her Litigation Friend, the official solicitor)*[82] the court considered whether further efforts should be made to provide artificial nutrition to a woman in her early 50s who was in a minimally aware state. All clinicians and the family concurred that no further efforts should be made to administer TPN (intravenous nutrition). The court was mindful of the strong presumption in favour of preservation of life per *Re M (adult patient) (minimally*

---

79 *Aintree*, per Lady Hale, para. 45.
80 *Aintree*, per Lady Hale, para. 39.
81 (2014) 140 BMLR 41.
82 [2014] EWCOP 16, [2014] COPLR 660.

conscious state: withdrawal of treatment),[83] however, the court would not order medical treatment to be provided if clinicians were unwilling to offer it on clinical grounds per the court of appeal in *AVS v. an NHS Foundation Trust*.[84] The court followed the reasoning in *Aintree* and concluded that on all the evidence the best interests of P would be served by withdrawing artificial nutrition and providing such palliative care as would be appropriate to ensure she suffered the least distress and retained the greatest dignity until her life ended.

For consideration of cases where treatment has or may be withdrawn see section 11 below.

9   MENTALLY DISORDERED PATIENTS

Consent to clinical treatment is required from a patient who suffers from a mental disorder in the same way as any other adult patient, unless (subject to certain exceptions) the treatment concerns the patient's mental disorder and is authorised under the Mental Health Act 1983. It is important to consider however that the mere fact of a person's mental illness does not mean that person lacks the ability to consent (see, for example, *St George's Healthcare NHS Trust v. S*[85]).

The 1983 Act has been significantly amended by the Mental Health Act 2007, effective from 1st April 2010. The 1983 Act's Code of Practice has also been rewritten to reflect the 2007 and more recent amendments and has very recently been updated. The changes to the Code of Practice from the previous edition are substantial. The Code of Practice not only sets out specific guidance on, for example, the appropriate use of restrictive interventions, particularly seclusion and long-term segregation, police powers and places of safety; but also five *"guiding principles"*. It is available on the government's website.[86] It is to come into force on 1st April 2015 subject to parliamentary approval.

It right to note at this stage that whilst the Mental Capacity Act 2005 is concerned solely with those that lack capacity and the determination of that capacity; the Mental Health Act 1983 concerns treatment of those with a mental disorder. The provisions for the determination of treatment and care under the Mental Health Act 1983 are therefore starkly different from the considerations under the Mental Capacity Act 2005 (although not exclusive from one another).

Part IV of the 1983 Act is concerned only with treatment of the patient's mental disorder and its provisions in relation to consent do *not* apply to treatment for other medical conditions, even if the patient lacks the capacity to consent to such treatment. In *Re C (Adult: Refusal of Medical Treatment)*[87] the 1983 Act did not apply because C's gangrenous foot was unrelated to his mental disorder. As discussed above, a person not suffering from mental disorder cannot be detained under the Act and treated because her thinking is bizarre and irrational and contrary to the views of the overwhelming majority of the community at large.[88]

---

83 [2011] EWHC 2443 (Fam), [2012] 1 WLR 1653.
84 [2011] 2 FLR 1.
85 See above.
86 https://www.gov.uk/government/publications/code-of-practice-mental-health-act-1983.
87 See above.
88 *See St Georges Healthcare NHS Trust v. S above.*

For the purposes of consent, the 1983 Act effectively divides treatment for mental disorder into seven categories:

(a)   s. 57: any surgical operation for destroying brain tissue or for destroying the functioning of brain tissue and such other forms of treatment as may be specified by regulations made by the Secretary of State for the purposes of s. 57;

(b)   s. 58: such forms of treatment as may be specified by regulations made by the Secretary of State for the purposes of s. 58 or the administration of medicine to a patient by any means (not being a form of treatment specified in s. 57 or in the regulations made under s. 58 or 58A) at any time during a period for which he is liable to be detained as a patient under Part IV if 3 months or more have elapsed since the first occasion in that period when medicine was administered to him by any means for his mental disorder;

(c)   s. 58A: electro-convulsive therapy and such other forms of treatment as may be specified in regulations made under that section by the appropriate national authority;

(d)   s. 62: urgent treatment;

(e)   s. 62A: treatment on recall of community patient or revocation of order;

(f)   s. 63: treatment not requiring consent, and

(g)   ss. 64A–K: treatment of community patients not recalled to hospital.

By s. 145(1) of the Act, medical treatment *"includes nursing, psychological intervention and specialist mental health habilitation, rehabilitation and care"*. Medical treatment in relation to mental disorder is *"medical treatment the purpose of which is to alleviate, or prevent a worsening of, the disorder or one or more of its symptoms or manifestations"* (s. 145(4)).

Section 57 applies to all patients (i.e. persons suffering or appearing to suffer from mental disorder, as defined in s. 145) whether or not they are liable to be detained, but treatment may not be given unless: (i) the patient consents to it, (ii) an appointed registered medical practitioner (RMP) (not being the responsible clinician, if there is one, or the person in charge of the treatment in question) and two other appointed persons certify that the patient is capable of understanding the nature, purpose and likely effects of the treatment in question and has consented to it, and (iii) the RMP certifies it is appropriate for the treatment to be given,[89] having first consulted with two other persons, one being a nurse and the other being neither a nurse nor an RMP, neither of whom is the responsible clinician, if there is one, or the person in charge of the treatment in question. Therefore treatment under s. 57 may not be given if the patient does not consent to it.

Section 58 applies only to persons who are liable to be detained in accordance with Part IV (subject to exceptions set out in s. 56(3))[90] and to community patients recalled to hospital under s. 17E. Treatment under s. 58 may not be given unless:

---

89 As further defined in s. 64(3).

90 The exceptions are: patients detained for an emergency application for admission for assessment under s. 4 but a second medical recommendation has not been given and received; temporary detention of an in-patient under s. 5; detention following remand to hospital by a court for report under s. 35; removal (by warrant or by a constable) to a place of safety under s. 135 or s. 136; detention pending admission to hospital under a hospital order under s. 37(4), and conditional discharge under s. 42(2), s. 73 or s. 74 without recall to hospital.

- the patient has consented to that treatment and either the approved clinician in charge of it or an appointed RMP has certified in writing that the patient is capable of understanding its nature, purpose and likely effects and has consented to it; or
  - where the patient has not consented, an appointed RMP (not being the responsible clinician or the approved clinician in charge of the treatment in question) has certified in writing that the patient is not capable of understanding the nature, purpose and likely effects of that treatment or being so capable has not consented to it but that it is appropriate for the treatment to be given (having first consulted with two other persons, one being a nurse and the other being neither a nurse nor an RMP, neither of whom is the responsible clinician, if there is one, or the person in charge of the treatment in question).

Where a detained patient did not consent to proposed treatment for the purposes of s. 58, on a judicial review of the clinicians' certificates the Court of Appeal held that the test to be applied is that the proposed treatment is both in the patient's best interests and medically necessary for the purposes of Article 3[91] of the Human Rights Convention. The standard of proof is not to be equated to the criminal standard: the question is whether the proposed treatment had been convincingly shown to be medically necessary; and it did not follow that the treatment could not be in the patient's best interests nor medically necessary merely because there was a responsible body of medical opinion to that effect.[92]

In *R (B) v. S,*[93] the court held that the express criteria in s. 58(3)(b) (that the treatment should be given, having regard to *"the likelihood of its alleviating or preventing a deterioration of his condition"*) should not be equated with the test of whether treatment is in the best interests of the patient, since the question will depend on wider considerations than the simple question of the efficacy of the treatment, such as whether an alternative and less invasive treatment will achieve the same result. (Under the 2007 amendments the criteria in s. 58(3)(b) is that *"it is appropriate for the treatment to be given"*. This is defined in s. 145(3) as meaning that the treatment is appropriate in that patient's case, taking into account the nature and degree of the mental disorder from which he is suffering and all other circumstances of his case). The court further held that treatment that satisfied the requirements of s. 58 of the 1983 Act, was in the best interests of the patient and was convincingly shown to be a medical necessity, would not infringe the claimant's rights under Articles 3, 8 and 14[94] of the Convention and that it was unnecessary to show that the treatment could only be justified if it was necessary to stop the patient causing harm to himself or others.

Section 58A (electro-convulsive therapy, etc.) also applies to persons who are not liable to be detained under the Act, are not community patients and have not attained 18 years of age. Detailed provisions as to consent by a consenting patient of any age and as to treatment for a patient who has not given consent are also set out in that section.

---

91 That is the "prohibition of torture and inhuman or degrading treatment or punishment".
92 *R (N) v. M and others* [2003] 1 WLR 562, applying *Herczegfalvy v. Austria* (1992) 15 EHRR 437.
93 [2006] 1 WLR 810, CA.
94 Article 3: *"prohibition of degrading treatment"*, Art. 8: *"private and family life"*, Art. 14: *"enjoyment of rights without discrimination"*.

By s. 60, a patient may, at any time before treatment under ss. 57–58A has been completed, withdraw his consent to that treatment, and those sections then apply to the uncompleted part of the treatment as if it were a separate form of treatment. If the patient ceases to be capable of understanding the nature, purpose and likely effects of the treatment, he is deemed to have withdrawn consent. On the other side of the coin, if the treatment was commenced without the patient's consent because he was certified as incapable of understanding its nature, purpose and likely effects and he becomes so capable before it is concluded, the certificate ceases to apply to the treatment and the sections apply again to the remainder of the treatment as if it were a separate form of treatment. Section 60 does not preclude the continuation of any treatment or of treatment under any plan pending compliance with ss. 57–58A if the approved clinician in charge of the treatment considers that the discontinuance of the treatment or discontinuance of treatment under the plan, would cause serious suffering to the patient.[95]

However, by s. 62 the provisions of ss. 57 and 58 do not apply in the case of urgent treatment, that is, any treatment which:

(a)   is immediately necessary to save the patient's life; or

(b)   (not being irreversible[96]) is immediately necessary to prevent a serious deterioration of his condition; or

(c)   (not being irreversible or hazardous[97]) is immediately necessary to alleviate serious suffering by the patient; or

(d)   (not being irreversible or hazardous) is immediately necessary and represents the minimum interference necessary to prevent the patient from behaving violently or being a danger to himself or to others.

Slightly more restrictive provisions apply to treatment under s. 58A.

Detailed provisions are inserted by the 2007 Act with regard to consent in the context of treatment under ss. 58 and 58A on the recall to hospital of a community patient (pursuant to s. 17E: "Power to recall to hospital", and s. 62A: "Treatment on recall of community patient or revocation of [a community treatment] order"), and with regard to the treatment of community patients not recalled to hospital (Part 4A, ss. 64A–64K).

A key provision in the 1983 Act is s. 63, which provides that:

> "*The consent of a patient shall* **not** *be required for any medical treatment given to him for the mental disorder from which he is suffering, not being a form of treatment to which section 57, 58 or 58A above applies, if the treatment is given by or under the direction of the approved clinician in charge of the treatment.*"

Under this section, treatment for the relevant mental disorder (other than as defined in ss. 57, 58 and 58A) may be given even if the patient positively refuses to consent.

In this context, "treatment" was given a wide interpretation before the statutory definition in s. 145 was widened by the 2007 Act. In *Re KB (Adult) (Mental patient:*

---

95 Section 62(2).
96 Treatment is irreversible if it has unfavourable irreversible physical or psychological consequences: s. 62(3).
97 Treatment is hazardous if it entails significant physical hazard: s. 62(3).

Medical Treatment),[98] force-feeding of an anorexic patient who refused to eat was authorised on the ground that it amounted to *"medical treatment given to [her] for the mental disorder from which [she] is suffering"* within s. 63. Feeding was not itself a treatment for her psychiatric disorder but it was held that since the disorder would become progressively more difficult to treat if the symptoms were exacerbated by the patient's refusal to eat, force-feeding was a part of the treatment of the disorder and was in any event necessary for an assessment of the underlying cause to be possible. This case is contrasted with the above case of *NHS Trust v. L*, substantially different on the facts and forced treatment being found as being not in L's best interests.

In *B v. Croydon Health Authority*,[99] a woman suffering from a psychopathic disorder, for which the only known treatment was psychoanalytic psychotherapy, was compulsorily detained under the 1983 Act. One of her symptoms was self harm and she stopped eating, causing her weight to fall to a dangerous level. The trial judge dismissed her claim for an injunction restraining the hospital from feeding her via a tube on the ground that such feeding constituted medical treatment for the purposes of s. 63. The Court of Appeal agreed, holding that s. 63 referred to treatment which, taken as a whole, was calculated to alleviate or prevent a deterioration of the patient's mental disorder and included a range of acts ancillary to the core treatment, including those which prevented the patient from harming herself or those which alleviated the symptoms of the disorder.

This construction of the definition of "treatment" in s. 145 is now reflected in s. 145(3), added by the 2007 Act.

Where a detained patient lacks the capacity to consent to proposed treatment other than for her mental disorder, the position is the same as in respect of non-detained patients.[100] In *NHS Trust v. C (Adult Patient: Medical Treatment)*,[101] a patient suffering from paranoid schizophrenia considered that a CT scan to investigate a potentially malignant kidney tumour was unnecessary and part of a plot against her. The court held that she lacked capacity in the sense that she was unable to use information and weigh it to arrive at a true decision and that a CT scan would be in her best interests. The court is entitled to arrive at such a conclusion by deciding between two competing schools of expert evidence.[102]

Where a patient is not subject to the provisions of the 1983 Act but has a mental disorder that renders her incompetent to make a treatment decision, the High Court no longer has power at common law to consent on behalf of the patient or otherwise approve the treatment, but does have an inherent jurisdiction to make a declaration that a proposed operation is in a patient's best interests. In *Re F (Mental Patient: Sterilisation)*,[103] the House of Lords accordingly upheld a declaration that the proposed sterilisation of an adult woman with the mental age of a small child was lawful as being in her best interests to avoid the risk of her becoming pregnant.

---

98 (1994) 19 BMLR 144, Ewbank J.
99 [1995] Fam 133, CA.
100 See above.
101 [2004] All ER (D) 175.
102 *An NHS Trust v. A (Adult Patient: Withdrawal of Medical Treatment)* [2005] All ER (D) 07 (CA).
103 [1990] 2 AC 1. The House held that that the *parens patriae* jurisdiction of the Queen over such of her subjects who are under such disability as to be unable to regulate their affairs had from time to time been delegated to judges of the High Court by Royal Warrant, but that the last such warrant had been revoked in 1960, possibly in the mistaken belief that the courts had been given all necessary powers under the Mental Health Act.

In *D v. An NHS Trust (Medical Treatment: Consent: Termination)*,[104] a pregnant woman suffering from severe schizophrenia was detained under the 1983 Act. Her doctors decided that termination of the pregnancy was necessary to prevent grave permanent injury to her physical or mental health and that she was incapable of making an informed decision about the termination. On those grounds the court held that the termination would be in her best interests and lawful. The court ruled that a termination carried out in accordance with the requirements of the Abortion Act 1967, in circumstances where a patient's best interests require it, is a legitimate and proportionate interference with her rights under Article 8(1) of the Convention,[105] being carried out for the protection of health under Article 8(2). It also held that where issues of capacity and best interests are clear and beyond doubt, an application to the court is not necessary and gave guidance where there is any such doubt.

10   CHILDREN

The law distinguishes between children who have capacity to give valid consent to treatment and those that do not. There is a statutory presumption that children aged 16 or over have the same capacity as adults to consent to medical treatment.[106] *Gillick v. West Norfolk and Wisbech Area Health Authority*[107] established that a child under 16 is capable of consenting to medical treatment provided that he or she has sufficient maturity to understand the implications of the treatment. The child must also understand consequences of refusing treatment.[108] Whether or not a child is "*Gillick* competent" is a question of fact that depends on an assessment of the child's mental and emotional age. The illness itself may reduce the child's capacity to make a competent decision[109] and a child whose understanding and capacity varies from day to day as a result of mental illness will not be regarded as having capacity.[110]

Where a child is "*Gillick* competent", he may consent to treatment even if the treatment is opposed by the child's parents. It must be noted that there is no *absolute* right to refuse medical treatment. However, if a child (being a person aged under 18) *refuses* treatment, either one of his parents,[111] or the court, may consent on his behalf in his (not the parents') best interests.[112] The court's power emanates from the exercise of its wardship jurisdiction, which has not been abrogated by the provisions of the Children Act 1989.[113]

The court's jurisdiction in determining what is in the "best interests" of the child is set out neatly in *Wyatt v. Portsmouth NHS Trust*.[114] The court's investigation must be a balancing act in which "all relevant factors are weighed"; arguably a much wider discretion than a "best interests" test under the Mental Capacity Act 2005. The court will have regard to the operational duty on health authorities to take preventative measures to protect an individual whose life was at risk (as to which see generally Chapter 5) pursuant to Article 2 of the ECHR and this would be balanced against the

---

104 [2004] 1 FLR 1110, Coleridge J.
105 That is: "*the right to respect for private and family life*".
106 Family Law Reform Act 1969, s. 8(1).
107 [1986] AC 112.
108 *Re E (A Minor) (Wardship: Medical Treatment)* [1993] 1 FLR 386.
109 *Re W (A Minor) (Medical Treatment: Court's Jurisdiction)* [1993] Fam 64.
110 *Re R (A Minor) (Wardship: Consent to Treatment)* [1992] Fam 11.
111 Consent is only required from one parent, even where the other parent opposes treatment.
112 *Re W (A Minor) (Medical Treatment: Court's Jurisdiction)* [1993] Fam 64.
113 *South Glamorgan County Council v. B and W* [1993] 1 FLR 574.
114 [2006] 1 FLR 554.

child's Article 8 rights. See in this respect *Re P (A child) sub nom AN NHS Foundation Hospital v. P*[115] where the court overrode the wishes of a 17-year-old child not to consent to life saving treatment after an overdose.

Where a child is not "*Gillick* competent", parental consent or the consent of the court is necessary, save in an emergency. The principles set out in s. 1 and s. 4 of the Mental Capacity Act 2005 apply in determining whether the child has capacity but, by s. 2(5), no power which a person ("D") may exercise under the Act in relation to a person who lacks capacity, or where D reasonably thinks that a person lacks capacity, is exercisable in relation to a person aged under 16.[116]

11   WITHDRAWAL OF TREATMENT

Adopting the principles identified in *Re F (Mental Patient: Sterilisation)*,[117] the House of Lords in *Airedale NHS Trust v. Bland*[118] decided it had jurisdiction to declare that it would not be unlawful for doctors to withdraw medical treatment from a patient who was permanently insensate. Anthony Bland, then aged 17, sustained catastrophic and irreversible brain damage in the Hillsborough football ground disaster on 15th April 1989 and was left in a condition known as a persistent vegetative state. Medical opinion was unanimous that there was no hope of improvement in his condition. The patient had not indicated his wishes if he should find himself in such a condition but his father's view was that he would not "*want to be left like that*". The hospital authority, with the concurrence of the patient's family and the consultant in charge of his case and the support of independent physicians, applied for declarations that all life-sustaining treatment and medical support measures could lawfully be terminated and that thereafter it was lawful not to furnish medical treatment.

The House of Lords upheld the declarations made by the judge, holding that since a large body of informed and responsible medical opinion was of the view that existence in the persistent vegetative state was not a benefit to the patient, the principle of the sanctity of life was not violated by ceasing to give medical treatment and care involving invasive manipulation of the patient's body, to which he had not consented and which conferred no benefit upon him. It held that the doctors responsible for the patient's treatment were not under a duty to continue such medical care and that, since the time had come when the patient had no further interest in being kept alive, the necessity to do so, created by his inability to make a choice, and the justification for the invasive care and treatment had gone, with the result that the omission to perform what had previously been a duty would no longer be unlawful.

However, it is not necessary for the patient to be in a permanent vegetative state for it to be declared lawful to withdraw treatment. In *Re D (Medical Treatment: Mentally Disabled Patient)*,[119] by reason of mental disability a patient was unable to consent or refuse kidney dialysis treatment or to cooperate with the frequent treatment except under general anaesthetic. On the basis of medical evidence that treatment of this patient was dangerous and impracticable, the court held that it was lawful not to impose it and required the doctors to provide such care as the patient would accept.

---

115 [2014] Fam Law 1247.
116 See above.
117 See above.
118 [1993] AC 789.
119 [1998] 2 FLR 22.

In *NHS Trust A v. M*,[120] it was decided that Article 2 ECHR[121] imposes a positive obligation on public authorities to give life-sustaining treatment in circumstances where, according to responsible medical opinion, such treatment is in the best interests of the patient, but does not impose an absolute obligation to treat if such treatment would be futile. A responsible medical decision to withdraw treatment on the basis that it was no longer in the patient's best interests, in circumstances in which death will result, does not amount to "deprivation of life" in breach of Article 2 because that phrase imports a deliberate act. Withdrawal of treatment is an omission to act that does not amount to an intentional deprivation of life, since the death of the patient is the result of the illness or injury from which he suffers. Hence Article 3[122] does not prohibit withdrawal of treatment in accordance with the best interests of the patient, and in any event requires him to be aware of the inhuman or degrading treatment experienced: it therefore does not apply to a patient in a permanent vegetative state who is insensate and has no comprehension of the treatment accorded him.[123]

The absence of any breach of Articles 2, 3 or 8 of the Convention where life-sustaining treatment was no longer in the patient's best interests, was further endorsed in the cases of *R (Burke) v. GMC*[124] and *Re OT*.[125] In the latter case, a hospital was granted orders and declarations allowing ventilation to be withdrawn for a seriously ill 9-month-old child (where further treatment was deemed likely to lead to further injury and death in any event); sanctioning palliative care instead which would allow the child to die with the least distress. That should be compared to the facts in the case of *Glass v. The United Kingdom*,[126] where treatment for a 12-year-old boy born with a severe neurological disability was in issue. During the course of his treatment a "Do Not Resuscitate" order was placed in his medical records without family consultation, and his family were informed that police would be in attendance to prevent the child being taken home, after they threatened to remove him. On one occasion, doctors were injured during a fracas when the child was resuscitated by a member of the family contrary to the hospital's treatment plan. When the child was eventually allowed to leave the hospital, with the warning to the family that he would not be readmitted, the child in fact improved with the aid of family care and his GP. The European Court of Human Rights held that the hospital had breached Article 8 of the Convention (*"right to private and family life"*) in overriding the wishes of the mother of a seriously ill child in such circumstances.

Unsurprisingly, the Court of Appeal has observed that if a NHS doctor were deliberately to bring about the death of a competent patient by withdrawing life-prolonging treatment contrary to that patient's wishes, Article 2 would plainly be infringed. In such circumstances a doctor would be left with no answer to a charge of murder.[127]

---

120 [2001] 1 Fam 348.
121 That is: *"protection of the right to life"*.
122 That is: *"prohibition of torture and inhuman or degrading treatment"*.
123 *NHS Trust A v. M*, at [49].
124 [2005] EWCA 1003.
125 [2009] EWHC 633 (Fam).
126 (61827/00) (ECHR) [2004] 1 FLR 1019.
127 *R (on the application of Burke) v. General Medical Council* [2005] EWCA Civ 1003, at [34] and [39]. The Court of Appeal pointed out that if English law permitted such conduct, it would violate this country's positive obligation to enforce Article 2.

12   GENERAL PRINCIPLES AND PRACTICAL CONSIDERATIONS

Early consideration of consent is always beneficial, as it may in fact avoid any need to deal with more difficult issues surrounding the quality of the actual treatment. To ensure consent is fully considered at the outset, the following summarised principles and factors should therefore be borne in mind.

Principles:

    (1)   No lawful intervention can occur where a competent adult refuses treatment.

    (2)   There is a presumption of capacity in the first instance; but it is a rebuttable presumption, where capacity is time and decision specific.

    (3)   Consent can be invalidated by inadequate information, acquiescence through limited understanding, undue influence, duress, or fraud.

    (4)   Consent is a continuous process. It may be withdrawn at any time, and the option to withdraw consent, or to seek a second opinion, should always be made available to the patient.

    (5)   The chain of causation may not be broken just because the patient cannot prove he wouldn't have had the treatment at a later date.

The following list of factors is not exhaustive, but should go some way to clarifying whether a tenable consent issue exists, and save time and costs in the long term:

    (a)   How did the need for treatment arise (e.g. emergency treatment/elective surgery GP referral)?

    (b)   The complexity of the condition and/or treatment.

    (c)   The aim of the treatment, and the patient's views or wishes, if any, concerning the available treatment options.

    (d)   The patient's purported understanding of the benefits and risks of the available treatment options.

    (e)   What discussions occurred with health professionals surrounding the treatment (including GP/nurses/hospital doctors)?

    (f)   If consent is documented, what did it cover (was the complication that occurred mentioned on the form or otherwise discussed, and if so, to what extent/were any consent documents appropriately amended to reflect the patient history and risks of treatment, etc.)?

    (g)   In what circumstances was consent taken (how far in advance of treatment/when and where and in whose presence)?

    (h)   The identity, experience, competence and qualifications of the health professional taking consent (and their ability to explain the matters involved).

    (i)   Was additional advice provided before or at the time consent was taken (concerning alternative treatment options and comparative risks/ancillary or emergency procedures that might be required as a result of the treatment/literature provided by way of leaflets)?

    (j)   Would the patient have had the treatment in any event (i.e. continued with the treatment in question if consent had been validly taken), or would the patient have refused the planned treatment?[128]

---

128 Relevant to causation in negligence but not in trespass; see above.

(k)   Did the patient, or whoever consented on the patient's behalf, have the capacity to consent at the time consent was taken (considering age/mental health/adverse influences/hearing, language or literacy difficulties)?

Chapter 8

LIABILITY FOR DEFECTIVE MEDICAL PRODUCTS

1   HISTORICAL PERSPECTIVE

This chapter aims to give a brief overview of UK product liability law as it relates to defective medicines and medical devices. After a summary of the historical development of the regulation of such products, it gives practical guidance as to the law and procedure relating to civil claims for injuries caused by defective medicines or medical devices.

At first glance there may not be a great deal of difference between the two, but in an age of increasing technological advancement, there are important divisions. Centuries ago medical devices such as syringes, pacemakers and prosthetics did not, of course, exist. Medical science was largely based around the development of new "medicines", initially natural. Therefore the establishment of a system for the regulation of the development and distribution of medicines has been somewhat piecemeal and haphazard and in relation to medical devices such a system is only very recent.

It took a snail in a ginger beer bottle and the disastrous effects of a new medicine to galvanise industry-wide change and better regulation. The combination of *Donoghue v. Stevenson*[1] and the thalidomide disaster of 1956–1961 led to recognition of a broad duty of care, increased regulation of the development and distribution of medicines and medical products and, ultimately, the Consumer Protection Act 1987 (CPA), which forms the basis of claims brought today for damage arising out of defective products.

2   DEVELOPMENT AND REGULATION OF MEDICINES

The modern definition of a medicinal product is contained in the European Council Directive 65/65 EEC, Article 1. It is defined as:

> *"Any substance or combination of substances that may be administered to human beings or animals with a view to making a medical diagnosis or to restoring, correcting or modifying physiological function in human beings or animals"*

and was ultimately adopted by the Medicines Act 1968, s. 130(1), which was passed following the report of the Committee on Safety of Drugs set up in 1963.

---

1 [1932] AC 562.

The development of medicines has revolved around issues of quality, efficacy and safety. Whilst it might be hoped that the latter two were always at the forefront of the developers' minds, that is not in fact the case. To a certain extent the quality of medicines has always been controlled. As far back as 1316 the Guild of Pepperers was subject to certain ordinances; there was a Royal Charter in 1607 for grocers, which included apothecaries and 10 years later there was a similar charter for apothecaries themselves. The College of Physicians was founded in 1518 and monitored the quality of medicinal products.

The 1540 Statute for Physicians and their Privileges created a right to appoint inspectors and to search apothecaries shops for faulty medicinal products, which were defined as medicines that were *"defective, corrupted and not meet nor convenient to be ministered in any medicines for the health of man's body"*. The General Medical Council was created by the Medical Act 1858 and one of its duties was to compile a pharmacopoeia, a list for standards of strength, purity and formulation of therapeutic agents, which led to the publication of the first British Pharmacopoeia in 1864.

Surprisingly, however, before the thalidomide disaster the efficacy and safety of new medicines was largely unregulated. In the early 1960s it was recognised that there was an inadequate statutory framework to regulate the development and distribution of new medicines, which led to creation of the Pearson Committee and subsequently the Medicines Act 1968, which for the first time in English law defined a *"medicinal product"* (s. 130(1)). The Medicines Act created a licensing authority, a medicines commission and various expert committees, namely the Committee on the Safety of Medicines, the Committee on the Review of Medicines, the Committee on Dental and Surgical Materials, the British Pharmacopeia Commission and the Veterinary Products Committee.

The Medicines Act also created a licensing authority within the Health and Agricultural Ministries, which has over the years become the Medicines and Healthcare Products Regulatory Agency (MHRA). The MHRA is responsible for assessing the safety, quality and efficacy of medicines and thereafter for authorising their sale or supply in the UK. It also oversees the bodies responsible for auditing medical device manufacturers and creating and monitoring post-marketing surveillance. The MHRA is also responsible for regulating clinical trials of medicines and medical devices, and compliance with statutory obligations.

Over the years the monitoring of the efficacy, quality and safety of medicinal products has developed into a wide array of Committees: the Paediatric Medicines Expert Advisory Group, the Biologists and Vaccines Expert Advisory Group, the Commission on Human Medicines, the Committee on the Safety of Devices and the Advisory Board on the Registration of Homeopathic Products, to name but a few.

3   THE DEVELOPMENT OF REGULATION OF MEDICAL DEVICES

There are three principal European Directives that control the design, development and distribution of medical devices. They are Directive 90/385 EEC on Active Implantable Medical Devices, Directive 93/42 EEC on Medical Devices and Directive 98/79 EEC on *In Vitro* Diagnostic Medical Devices.

The Directives define medical devices as:

"Any instrument, apparatus, appliance, material or other article, whether used alone or in combination, including the software necessary for its proper application intended by the manufacturer to be used for human beings for the purpose of:

- *Diagnosis, prevention, monitoring, treatment or alleviation of disease,*

- *Diagnosis, monitoring, treatment, alleviation or compensation for an injury or handicap,*

- *Investigation, replacement or modification or the anatomy of a physical process or*

- *Control of contraception."*

Those Directives led directly to the implementation of the Medical Devices Regulations 2002 (MDR) (SI 2002/618). There is no system of licensing of medical devices by way of an approved government agency, as there is for medicinal products. Medical devices must comply with the MDR, which set out certain essential requirements relating to the safety of the device in use. Once conformity is established the CE mark can be affixed, which means it is marketable throughout the EU.

The MDR deal with the regulation of Active Implantable Medical Devices (Part III), such as powered implants like pacemakers and *In Vitro* Medical Devices (Part IV), such as pregnancy tests, blood glucose monitoring or tests for transmittable disease. All other "General Medical Devices" are regulated by Part II of the MDR; those are everything else which is not a medicine but is used in the diagnosis and treatment of human disease, disorder and handicap. Items that were previously dealt with as medicines but are now regulated as medical devices are contact lens products, medicated dressings, surgical ligatures and sutures, and dental filling substances.

4 LIABILITY FOR A DEFECTIVE MEDICINAL PRODUCT OR MEDICAL DEVICE

The failure of the thalidomide litigation, *S v. Distillers (Biochemicals) Limited,*[2] a claim brought in negligence, finally persuaded government that the test of common law negligence first enunciated in *Donoghue v. Stevenson* was insufficient to compensate the victims of inadequate development and distribution of medicines and medical products.

The Medicines Act 1968 was born of out of the Pearson Committee on the Safety of Medicines, following the tragedy of thalidomide. But whilst the Act was aimed at better regulation of the development and distribution of such products, consumers were still left without remedy. It was not until the Consumer Protection Act in 1987 that the consumer finally received the protection from defective medicines and medical devices that was long overdue.

However, as will be seen below, this area of law is always striving to achieve a delicate balance between the interests of the unwitting consumer and the encouragement of medicinal and technological development. Therefore, although at first blush the

---

2 [1970] 1 WLR 114.

statutory framework appears straightforward, there are always likely to be significant difficulties in establishing a defect *and* that it caused damage.

5   CLAIMS IN NEGLIGENCE

Before considering claims brought under the CPA it is important to consider how the common law deals with claims for defective products. *Donoghue v. Stevenson* provided the perfect example of why the common law needed extending to create a general duty of care that existed beyond strict contractual obligations. The facts are well known, but worth repeating. A bottle of ginger beer was purchased in a café; the purchaser gave it to the plaintiff, who drank it. She was allegedly poisoned by a decomposed snail in the bottle. Because she had not purchased the ginger beer, the plaintiff had no contractual claim. She therefore sued in tort, which was at that time a novel course of action.

Prior to the House of Lords determination of the point, the plaintiff's lack of privity of contract barred an action. However, Lord Atkin, in one of the most important judgments ever handed down, created the "neighbour principle". In extending the manufacturer's duty beyond just the purchaser to the ultimate consumer, he said:

> *"A manufacturer of products which he sells in such a form as to show that he intends them to reach the ultimate consumer in the form in which they left him with no reasonable possibility of intermediate examination, and with the knowledge that the absence of reasonable care in the preparation or putting up of the products will result in an injury to the consumer's life or property, owes a duty to the consumer to take reasonable care."*

There is now no doubt that this principle applies not just to food and drink, and a vast array of defective products have formed the basis of successful causes of actions. Medicines and medical devices are also capable of founding claims in negligence although, as we will see below, such claims are fraught with difficulty.

Provided the relevant tests can be satisfied, anyone who has suffered physical harm as a result of a defective product can bring an action. Further, a successful claim can be brought against not just the manufacturer, but also against a distributor. A wholesaler must take reasonable care, for example, to check the safety of the products that are distributed. Therefore, if the distributor of syringes knew that a batch had been damaged in transit and yet went on to sell them, he would be liable for any injury caused as a result. Of course, in medical cases that can present a real problem; the items may well have been distributed by a person in this jurisdiction, but it is not always so straightforward to establish that the distributor knew or ought to have known of the defect. In those circumstances the claimant is left with the invidious task of bringing proceedings against a distant manufacturer.

The law is as yet unclear as to whether public bodies owe a common law duty to protect consumers from injury. In the *CJD Litigation*,[3] Morland J concluded that the Medical Research Council might be liable in negligence for continuing to promote research into and subsequent production of hormone products despite there being serious risks of injury. It is not clear whether, for example, the Commission on Human Medicines owes a duty to protect consumers from injury when considering whether to

---

3 [1996] 7 Med LR 309.

license a new drug under the Medicines Act 1968 but the possibility remains open. It is suggested by the authors of *Clerk & Lindsell on Torts* (21st edition at chapter 11-15) that:

> *"In practice, it is suggested that those whose function it is to inspect particular items for safety are likely to owe a duty, especially where danger to human life is involved but otherwise claimants face an uphill battle."*

There may well be public policy reasons why the courts should not intervene in such delicate decision-making processes, but the Administrative Court has shown a willingness to challenge decisions that involve the policy arena, and the Human Rights Act has fortified the common law when it comes to intervening in the decisions of the state affecting the lives of citizens. In *Smith v. Chief Constable of Sussex Police,*[4] an action at common law against police for failing to protect a victim of a serious assault who had alerted the police to the risk of assault by a former partner, Pill LJ said:

> *"I consider it unacceptable that a court, bound by S. 6 of the [HRA] 1998, should judge a case such as the present by different standards depending on whether or not the claim is specifically brought under the Convention. The decision whether a duty of care exists in a particular situation should in a common law claim require a consideration of Article 2 rights."*

Perhaps the greatest bar to cases in negligence arising out of medicinal products or medical devices is the need to prove fault. In general practice this is often not a problem; it is foreseeable that a snail in a ginger beer bottle will cause harm and the fact of a snail at the bottom of a ginger beer bottle can *only* be due to fault on the part of the manufacturer. In manufacturing defect cases, the consumer will usually be able to establish fault, unless the defect was not foreseeable or not reasonably avoidable. However, when considering medicines and medical devices it is likely to prove much harder to establish fault. These tend to be "design defect" cases, in which the product (for example, the drug thalidomide) is manufactured as designed but the defect only becomes known once the product is manufactured; hence foreseeability is hard to prove.

The claimant will have to prove that the manufacturer should have foreseen the defect by the time it was marketed; but if this is a new medicine or device, that may be very difficult to establish. Further, the claimant may well face an uphill battle if it is argued that the manufacturer was justified in taking foreseeable risks, if the potential benefits outweighed the foreseeable risks (see the development risks defence under the CPA, further, below).

When considering medicines or medical devices this is especially pertinent. The fact that an individual might react in a certain way to a medicine and that the manufacturer knew or ought to have known that such a reaction may occur in a particular individual will not, of itself, be sufficient to establish liability in negligence. For example, the fact that a particular drug causes a side-effect in one consumer (because of a rare allergy, perhaps) will not be sufficient of itself to establish negligence if the drug benefits society as a whole.

Therefore, if the manufacturer can show that the drug meets a real demand, is as safe as it can reasonably be made and any dangers are not out of proportion to the need that it satisfies, a claim in negligence is likely to fail.

---

4 [2008] EWCA Civ 39.

Of course, if the manufacturer knows (or ought reasonably to know) that a particular medicine or device does carry a risk with it, there is a duty to warn the consumer. Hence it is no coincidence that everything from toothpastes to painkillers comes with "the usual health warning". Therefore, for example, it was negligent not to warn a claimant that a breast implant was likely to rupture after installation (*Hollis v. Dow Corning Corporation*).[5] In the case of drugs and medical devices the duty to warn is especially pertinent; the duty may well be not just to warn the consumer of the product, but also the treating doctor or person prescribing the product.

In the normal course of events, the duty to warn only extends to hazards that are known (or ought reasonably to be known) when the product leaves the defendant's control. However, the duty to bring attention to risks that subsequently become known does exist, if there is a clear indication of a serious danger. Therefore, if a drug company discovered that there was an inherent risk in one of its products that created a danger of serious harm, there is a common law duty to attempt to recall it and advertise the fact.

The claimant, however, must prove that if the warning *had* been given, the product would not have been consumed. This is likely to prove a real causation headache for consumers, particularly if (as may well often the case) a warning has been ignored for years without incident. The claimant bears the burden of proving that the negligence was a substantial cause of the subsequent injury. In drug cases that might be difficult, particularly if the claimant was ill in any event; the claimant will have to prove that it was the drug that was a substantial cause of injury, as opposed to some constitutional condition.

Despite the duty to warn, however, the need to prove fault and causation will always make claims for injury as a result of defective medical products difficult to win in negligence. Further, of course, in this day and age most of the products that we use are not manufactured within this jurisdiction. Therefore, consumers relying on the common law on the "snail in bottle" principle are faced with having to track down and bring to court manufacturers in different jurisdictions, which of course poses its own set of problems.

6   THE CONSUMER PROTECTION ACT 1987 (CPA)

The array of problems that faced the plaintiffs in the thalidomide (and Opren) litigation, in having to prove fault and a common law liability, finally persuaded both the European Union and Parliament that more needed to be done to protect the right of the consumer. A useful summary of the development of the CPA can be found in Burton J's judgment in the Hepatitis C litigation, *A & Others v. National Blood Authority & Others*.[6]

---

5 [1996] 129 DLR (4th) 609.
6 [2001] 3 All ER 289.

7   THE EUROPEAN DIRECTIVE

The CPA was enacted as a result of the European Union Product Liability Directive 1985 (25th July 1985). The Directive had first been discussed in 1969/70 following the thalidomide disaster and subsequent failure of that litigation. Of course, at that stage the UK was not even a member of the EEC (as it then was) and the impending membership of various states was one of the reasons why the Directive was so long in the making, in addition to the very complex negotiations that took place. One of the obvious difficulties of agreeing the Directive was drawing the delicate balance between the rights of the consumer as against the fear of holding back the important development of technology. This finally distilled into the development risk defence that the Directive (and the CPA) provide; in fact that defence was largely due to the insistence of Margaret Thatcher's government in the late 1970s and early 1980s.

Burton J summarised the main purposes of the Directive (at para. 13 of his judgment) as follows:

(i)   its purpose was to increase consumer protection;

(ii)   it introduced an obligation on producers which was irrespective of fault, by way of objective or strict liability, but not absolute liability;

(iii)   that its aim was to render compensation of the injured consumer easier, by removing the concept of negligence as an element of liability and thus of the proof of liability;

(iv)   that it left an escape clause for products otherwise found pursuant to the Directive to be defective, if the producer could bring himself within what was described as a "development risks" defence.

The Directive is made up of 19 unnumbered recitals and a number of Articles. It is unnecessary to set those out here, because they in turn became enshrined into the CPA. However, it is essential to realise the primary importance of the Directive. In fact, s. 1(1) of the CPA stipulates that Part I of the Act shall *"have effect for the purpose of making such provision as is necessary in order to comply with the Product Liability Directive and shall be construed accordingly"*. The CPA came into force on 1st March 1988 and now, over 25 years later, it forms the basis for all claims arising out of defective products.

8   STRICT LIABILITY

The key section in the CPA is s. 2(1) which creates a strict liability for defective products. It states that:

> *"Subject to the following provisions of this Part, where any damage is caused wholly or partly by a defect in a product, every person to whom subsection (2) below applies shall be liable for the damage."*

Sections 2(2) and (3) impose liability on producers, those who hold themselves out as producers, importers and suppliers (see below for further definitions of each).

9   WHAT IS A PRODUCT?

A "product" is defined in s. 1(2) as *"any goods or electricity and...includes a product which is comprised in another product, whether by virtue of being a component part or a raw material or otherwise"*. "Goods" are given a very wide definition in s. 45 and include (but are not limited to) ships, aircraft and any substance including food or drugs; however, the CPA is limited to the provision of physical assets, and not services rendered or advice given.

10   WHAT IS A "DEFECT"?

A "defect" is defined in s. 3(1):

> *"there is a defect in a product...if the safety of the product is not such as persons generally are entitled to expect; and for those purposes 'safety' in relation to a product shall include safety with respect to products comprised in that product and safety in the context of risks of damage to property, as well as in the context of risks of death or personal injury.*

It is important to recognise that "defectiveness" does not demand an element of "fault". Section 3(2) demands that in determining whether there is a defect in a product *"all circumstances shall be taken into account"*. That means that the court will consider all aspects from the manufacture to use of the product, including marketing, any instructions and warnings that might reasonably have been given.

Of course, some products are inherently dangerous, of which drugs are a good example. Logic demands that there cannot be anything wrong with selling a dangerous product *per se*. However, if the product is not properly marketed and provided with the proper warnings as to safe use, liability might arise.

In considering medicines and medical devices it is important to recognise a difference between a manufacturing defect and a design defect. A defect in the manufacture of a product will almost certainly be caught by the Act; a pacemaker that fails due to a defect in the manufacturing process; a prosthetic limb that collapses due to a flaw in a connecting pin; a medicine that is stronger than advertised due to a defect in manufacture. However, establishing a *design* defect can be much more difficult. For example metal on metal hip prosthetics where metal debris from abrasion has subsequently caused injury. In these cases, the test will be closer to that in negligence. There has to be a balance between the risks of injury and the purpose for which the product is designed. An often used example is a chain saw, which is clearly dangerous and poses risks of injury to those that use it. However, it cannot be defective just because its *design* renders it dangerous. If sold without instruction, however, it may well fall foul of the CPA.

11   WHO IS A "PRODUCER" OR AN "IMPORTER"?

The definition of "producer" falls into three categories. First, the person who manufactured the goods, to include manufacturers of individual components as well as the whole product.

Secondly, *"In the case of a substance which has not been manufactured but has been won or abstracted, the person who abstracted it"*. Therefore, a person who mines a dangerous mineral or distils a dangerous herbal product could be a producer. However, this definition does not cover a farmer who grows dangerous produce.

That shortcoming is largely covered by the third definition, which deals with a product which has not been manufactured, won or abstracted but essential characteristics of which are attributable to an industrial or other process having been carried out (for example, in relation to agricultural produce). The person who carried out that process will be the relevant "producer". Therefore, whilst a farmer would not be liable for growing defective peas, those that processed them would be.

A person who "holds himself out as a producer" is defined in s. 2(2)(b) as: *"Any person putting his name on the product or using a trade mark or other distinguishing mark in relation to the product, has held himself out to be the producer of the product."*

An importer is defined in s. 2(2)(c) as: *"Any person who has imported the product into a Member State from a place outside the Member State in order, in the course of any business of his, to supply it to another."*

12   WHO IS A "SUPPLIER"?

A supplier is defined in s. 2(3):

> *"Subject as aforesaid, where any damage is caused wholly or partly by a defect in a product, any person who supplied the product (whether to the person who suffered the damage, to the producer of any product in which the product in question is comprised or to any other person) shall be liable for damage if:*
>
> *(a)   the person who suffered the damage requests the supplier to identify one or more of the persons (whether still in existence or not) to whom subsection (2) above applies in relation to the product (that is, producers, those holding themselves out as producers and importers);*
>
> *(b)   that request is made within a reasonable period after the damage occurs and at a time when it is not reasonably practicable for the person making the request to identify all those persons; and*
>
> *(c)   the supplier fails, within a reasonable period after receiving the request, either to comply with the request or to identify the person who supplied the product to him."*

This provision allows a consumer to establish a liability if the actual manufacturer or importer of the product cannot be traced and the supplier does not provide the details of the manufacturer or importer as requested by the consumer. As long as the request is made within a reasonable time, liability will attach and it is not necessary that the supplier actually supplied the claimant. Therefore, a chemist that sells a medicine to a parent whose child ingests it and is injured could be liable under the CPA for any defect. If the medicine did not have a suitable warning that it should not be taken by asthmatics (for example) and the child was injured for just that reason, the child can bring an action against the chemist, if there is a failure to provide a timeous response to a request for the details of the manufacturer or importer (or if those details are for some reason unknown).

However, as soon as the supplier provides the details requested, he will escape liability. Further, the supply must be in the course of business.

13   DEFENCES

A claim may well fail if a product is misused. However, each case will depend on its own facts and it will turn largely on the actions of the consumer; a claimant will have difficulty establishing a liability against the manufacturer of a sleeping pill if he takes an overdose and falls ill. However, a manufacturer may find it hard to resist a claim by a child who consumes medicine from a bottle that has a defective (or insufficient) child-proof top on the basis that the medicine was misused.

Thereafter, there are a set of statutory defences provided in s. 4. Section 4(1)(a) of the CPA provides a defence if the defect is due to compliance with any statutory obligation or European Union obligation. Therefore, if the "defect" was something that the manufacturer was bound to include, any claim will fail, the burden falling on the defendant to prove it.

Section 4(1)(b) provides a defence if the defendant *"did not at any time supply the product"*. This is likely to be very limited in application.

Section 4(1)(c) provides that suppliers cannot be sued unless the supply was in the course of business and producers have a defence if they can show that the goods were never produced for profit.

Section 4(1)(d) addresses subsequent defects and allows a defence if *"the defect did not exist in the product at the relevant time"*, that being when it left the manufacturer's or supplier's hands.

Section 4(1)(f) provides a defence to the manufacturer of a component if it can be shown that the defect complained of was due wholly to the design of the end product and that he has complied with instructions from the manufacturer of the end product.

The most controversial defence is the "development risks" defence in s. 4(1)(e). In fact, its inclusion in member states' legislation is made optional by the Directive and many do not include it. The section provides a defence if:

> *"the state of scientific and technical knowledge at the relevant time was not such that a producer of products of the same description as the product in question might be expected to have discovered the defect if it had existed in his products while they were under his control."*

It is clear that this defence substantially dilutes the test of strict liability and introduces an element of foreseeability that, it is suggested, the Directive did not envisage. It is particularly pertinent to claims brought under the CPA relating to medicines and medical devices, because a manufacturer can always say that the relevant defect was not known at the time that the product was supplied (the "relevant time") but only came to light at a later date. Whilst producers will be expected to keep abreast of scientific developments, they may well have a defence if the subsequent defect could not have been appreciated at the relevant time. It has to be questioned whether this defence really undermines the whole purpose of strict liability, especially in drug-related cases; would the thalidomide litigation have succeeded against a manufacturer or supplier armed with this defence?

14   LIMITATION

The CPA applies only to goods supplied after 1st March 1988. Claims for personal injury must be brought within 3 years, as must claims for damaged property (as opposed to the normal 6; see Limitation Act 1980, s. 11(4)). There is a long stop period of 10 years from when the product was supplied. Time will start to run from when the cause of action accrued or, if later, from the claimant's date of knowledge as defined in s. 14(1A) of the Limitation Act 1980. Section 33 of the Limitation Act applies to extend the time for personal injury claims to be commenced, but not to property claims; further s. 33 cannot override the 10-year long stop date.

15   VACCINE DAMAGE PAYMENTS ACT 1979 (VDPA)

Finally, there is a statutory scheme in place to compensate those that have suffered severe disablement from certain vaccinations. The scheme, created by the VDPA, provides compensation to those injured as a result of being vaccinated against diphtheria, tetanus, whooping cough, poliomyelitis, measles, rubella, tuberculosis, smallpox or other any disease as specified by the Secretary of State.

The applicant must establish to the satisfaction of the Secretary of State that he or she was "severely disabled" as a result of the vaccination. The disablement must be assessed as *at least* 60%. If so, there is a one-off payment of £100,000, which is without prejudice to any other claims that might be brought.

16   THE PIP BREAST IMPLANT SCANDAL

In March 2010 breast implants manufactured after 2001 by the French company Poly Implant Prosthèse (PIP) were banned in the UK by the MHRA. The ban followed the discovery that these implants had been filled with cheap industrial grade silicone rather than medical grade silicone. It is believed that the risk of rupture of these substandard implants is between 2-6 times that of standard implants.

PIP went into liquidation in 2011. Its founder and other executives were prosecuted for fraud and its founder was sentenced to 4 years in prison by a court in Marseille in 2013.

It is estimated that 47,000 women in the UK had PIP implants in the relevant period. 95% of these implants were provided by private clinics. Whilst the NHS and some of the private clinics agreed to remove but not replace the affected implants without charge, other private clinics would not unless it was deemed clinically necessary. Since the scandal erupted in 2010, medical opinion in relation to the necessity of removal has been divided. In the UK the official government advice is that there is no need to have PIP implants removed unless they rupture; this differs from the advice given in Sweden, Germany and France. The inconsistency of approach has left many women in a state of anxiety about whether to undergo further surgery and the NHS recognise that this anxiety in itself may be justification for removal of un-ruptured implants. Official expert reports commissioned by the UK and more recently the European Commission are in agreement that the substandard implants pose no particular health threat upon rupture.

Aside from asking serious questions about the regulation of the cosmetic surgery industry in the UK and Europe the scandal has prompted some creative thinking about the way in which claims in relation to defective medical devices can be pursued. In on-going group litigation in the High Court nearly 1,000 women are seeking damages from companies running private clinics for supplying PIP breast implants. These claims have been brought in contract on the basis that the implants were of unsatisfactory quality in breach of the implied term as to quality set out in s. 4(2) of the Supply of Goods and Services Act 1982. Other claims have been brought against the providers of credit cards used to pay for private procedures under the Consumer Credit Act 1974. The defendants in the group litigation have brought Part 20 claims against the UK supplier of the implants under s. 14(2) of the Sale of Goods Act 1979. At the time of writing this litigation is ongoing and has not been the subject of any reported judicial decision in terms of the merits.

Chapter 9

REGULATION OF CLINICAL DRUGS TRIALS

1   INTRODUCTION

This chapter deals with the regulation of clinical trials of drugs on volunteers and patients. This is an area that was thrown into public view by the events in March 2006 when six healthy male volunteers were given doses of a new test drug TGN 1412 as part of a clinical trial conducted by Parexel[1] at an independent clinical trials unit in leased space on the premises of Northwick Park and St Mark's Hospital, London.[2] The men suffered serious reactions including organ failure and necrosis. Pictures on TV and in the press showing their blackened fingers and toes highlighted the risks to those participating in trials. These events were reminiscent of Ellen Roche, a healthy 24-year-old volunteer who died during a study on acute asthma at Johns Hopkins University, Baltimore in 2001. The sort of important questions that are raised by such trials are:

- Whether it is appropriate for volunteers to be paid, and if so how much?[3]
- When does money cloud the judgement needed to evaluate risks realistically?[4]
- Does informed consent include the knowledge of possible severe injury or death however small the risk?
- When should a drug be tested on healthy volunteers rather than patients?
- What procedures should be adopted, e.g. staggering administration of doses?
- How much do the regulatory and ethical bodies have to rely on information from investigators or researchers and sponsors, which may be subject to publication bias?
- With increasing sophistication of molecular targeting using specific human receptors, how far can pre-human trials carried out on genetically modified rodents, really inform sponsors and subjects of the risks involved in the human trial?
- Should trials be registered and disclosed? Competitive disadvantage may result but a balance is required in the public interest between the protection of the subjects' privacy where that is possible and the need for clinicians to know about the effects of trials.

---

1 Parexel is a company that carries out drug trials on behalf of pharmaceutical and biotechnology companies.
2 See Suntharalingam, G. *et al.* (September 2006) "Cytokine Storm in a Phase 1 Trial of the Anti-CD28 Monoclonal Antibody TGN1412". *The New England Journal of Medicine* (10) 355:1018–1028, available at: www.nejm.org/doi/full/10.1056/NEJMoa063842; www.bmj.com/content/332/7543/677.
3 Goodyear, M.D.E. (2006) "Learning from the TGN1412 trial". BMJ 333:677–678.
4 Bramstedt, K.A. (June 2007) "Recruiting Healthy Volunteers for Research Participation via Internet Advertising". Clin Med Res 5(2):91–97.

The "Northwick Park" TGN 1412 incident involved a "first-in-man" Phase I trial. There are four phases of a clinical trial of a new drug:

(a) Phase I

This phase involves looking at whether a drug is safe, if it has any side-effects and the appropriate dosage to prescribe. Clinical researchers will often recruit a small number of healthy volunteers for Phase I research as was the case with the TGN 1412 trial.

(b) Phase II

This phase of the trial tests the new drug on a group of ill patients to see if it has any positive effects on their health. Phase II trials look intensely at safety issues.

(c) Phase III

These trials only take place when Phase I and II trials have suggested that a new drug may be beneficial to ill patients. Phase III tests the new drug in larger groups of ill patients, which is more representative of the patient population. This phase also compares the new treatment with the best known treatment available in the UK to help decide which treatment works better.

(d) Phase IV

Phase IV happens after a drug has been licensed. This involves the assessment of the long-term terms risks and benefits of the drug.

2   LEGAL FRAMEWORK

2.1   Declaration of Helsinki

The General Assembly of the World Medical Association met in Helsinki in 1996, resulting in the latest Declaration of Helsinki on Ethical Principles for Medical Research involving Human Subjects. Key values are expressed as follows:

> "The World Medical Association has developed the Declaration of Helsinki as a statement of ethical principles to provide guidance to physicians and other participants in medical research involving human subjects...In medical research on human subjects, consideration related to the well being of the human subject should take precedence over the interests of science and society."

> "Some research populations are vulnerable and need special protection. The particular needs of the economically and medically disadvantaged must be recognized. Special attention is also required for those who cannot give or refuse consent for themselves, for those who may be subject to giving consent under duress, for those who will not benefit personally from the research and for those for whom the research is combined with care."

> "The subjects must be volunteers and informed participants in the research project...Every precaution should be taken to respect the privacy of the subject, the confidentiality of the patient's information..."

Subjects should be informed of aims, methods, sources of funding, any possible conflicts of interest, institutional affiliations of the researcher, the anticipated benefits and potential risks of the study and the discomfort it may entail. Freely given informed consent should be taken, preferably in writing. If the patient is dependent on the research physician, an independent well-informed physician should obtain informed consent. If a patient is unable to give informed consent, a legal representative should be arranged to deal with this.

2.2   Clinical Trials Directives

In the light of the Helsinki Declaration, the European Commission produced the Clinical Trials Directive (2001/20/EC) to regulate clinical trials of medicines, including medicines under development in humans, across the European Community. Articles 2 and 3 incorporate the Helsinki principle quoted above.

On 8th April 2005 the Commission set out their objective:

> *"With regard to the protection of trial subjects and to ensure that unnecessary clinical trials will not be conducted, it is important to define principles whilst allowing the results of the trials to be documents for use at a later phase. To ensure that all experts and individuals involved in the design, initiation, conduct and recording of clinical trials apply the same standards of good clinical practice, principles and detailed guidelines of good clinical practice have to be defined."*

This Directive sets out the principles for the design, conduct and reporting of clinical trials; the requirements for authorisation of the manufacture or importation of products; and on documentation and inspectors of trials. Information must be recorded accurately whilst protecting the confidentiality of the subjects. Critically, investigators' brochures must be in a concise, simple, objective, balanced and non-promotional form that enables a clinician to understand it and make an unbiased risk-benefit assessment of the appropriateness of the proposed clinical trial. The potential conflict of interest between the investigator salesman and the consumer clinician is obvious. Drugs are notoriously expensive to develop and pharmaceutical companies will be tempted to limit information especially on risks and safety of subjects in order to surmount the hurdle of clinical trials before the drug can become an asset.

A further directive was announced by the Commission of the 8th May 2005, Directive 2005/28/EC, known as the Good Clinical Practice Directive (GCP). This Directive laid down principles and detailed guidelines for good clinical practice in order to protect subjects who volunteer for clinical trials.

Between 9th October 2009 and 8th January 2010, the European Commission ran a public consultation to assess the functioning of the 2001 Clinical Trials Directive seeking comments and responses to a range of questions. The Medicines Healthcare Products Regulatory Agency (MHRA) which is the regulatory body responsible for the enforcement of sanctions in clinical practice in the UK coordinated a UK government position, representing views of those affected, on the specific questions posed by the Commission. The response reflected complaints by academics that the Clinical Trials Directive has made the research environment significantly more difficult and bureaucratic and complaints of a lack of consistency between states in the EU, although the MHRA and Research Ethics Committees were working more closely together. The UK did not support a change to a centralised procedure for authorisation of multi-state trials but did support the formalisation in law of the Voluntary Harmonisation Procedure. Various elements of the legislation required clarification including the relationship between the regulator and ethics committees.

On 16th April 2014 the new Regulation EU No 536/2014 of the European Parliament and of the Council on clinical trials on medicinal products for human use ("the Clinical Trials Regulation") was adopted and published in the Official Journal on 27th May 2014. It repeals the 2001 Clinical Trials Directive.

The aim of the new Clinical Trials Directive is to create an environment that is favourable for conducting clinical trials and, in particular, to make it easier to conduct multinational clinical trials, i.e. conducted in more than one member state, in the EU.

The Regulation simplifies the current rules, including:

(a)   A streamlined application procedure via a single entry point - an EU portal and database, for all clinical trials conducted in Europe. Registration via the portal will be a prerequisite for the assessment of any application;

(b)   A single straightforward authorisation procedure for all clinical trials, allowing a faster, thorough assessment of an application by all member states concerned, and ensuring one single assessment outcome and authorisation per member state. The authorisation procedure allows the individual EU countries to determine the roles of the bodies in charge of the assessment, on the condition that the assessment is fully independent and based on the necessary expertise;

(c)   The extension of the tacit agreement principle to the whole authorisation process which will give sponsors and researchers, in particular subject matter experts (SMEs) and academics, more legal certainty;

(d)   Strengthened transparency for clinical trials data;

(e)   Simplified reporting procedures so that researchers no longer have to submit largely identical information on the clinical trial separately to various bodies and member states;

(f)   The possibility for the Commission to conduct controls in EU countries and third countries to make sure the rules are being properly supervised and enforced.

Finally, the new legislation will take the legal form of a Regulation. The introduction of a Regulation, as opposed to a Directive, means that its provisions will be directly effective in all member states. The Regulation will be binding in its entirety and automatically incorporated into the national laws for all EU member states. This will ensure that the rules for conducting clinical trials are identical throughout the EU. This is vital to ensure that member states, in authorising and supervising the conduct of a clinical trial, base themselves on identical rules.

Ethics committees will be involved in the assessment of clinical trials application. However, as with the current situation, their responsibilities and detailed composition will be determined independently by each EU country. It is intended that adopting this approach will allow the different traditions in the various member states to be respected.

The Regulations entered into force on 16th June 2014 but will apply no earlier than 28th May 2016. There are transitional provisions for applications during this period. Until May 2016, clinical trials performed in the European Union are required to be conducted in accordance with the 2001 Clinical Trials Directive. This Directive will be repealed on the day of entry into application of Regulation EU No 536/2014. The 2001 Directive however still applies 3 years from that day to:

(i)   clinical trials applications submitted before the entry into application (no earlier than 28th May 2016);

(ii)   clinical trials applications submitted within one year after the entry into application if the sponsor opted for the old system.

2.3   UK Regulation

The 2001 Clinical Trials Directive was implemented in the UK by the Medicines for Human Use (Clinical Trials) Regulations 2004 (SI 2004/1031), known as the principal regulations.

The principal regulations impose legal obligations on those conducting clinical trials. Conditions include:

- anyone taking part in a trial must have a full understanding of the objectives of the research and any risks and potential inconveniences they may experience when taking part. This information will be given to them at a meeting with a member of the research team;

- a point of contact must be provided so that patients can obtain more information about the trial.

Before a clinical trial of a new medicine can begin, all of the following need to be in place:

- the science the research is based on must be reviewed by experts;
- the researchers must secure funding;
- an organisation, such as a hospital or research institute, must agree to provide a home base for the trial;
- the MHRA needs to review and approve trials of a medicine and issue a clinical trial authorisation (CTA);
- a recognised ethics committee must review the trial and allow it to proceed.

The MHRA inspects sites where trials take place to make sure they are conducted in line with good clinical practice (an international quality standard).

The Good Clinical Practice Directive was implemented in the UK on 29th August 2006 when the Medicines for Human Use (Clinical Trials) Amendment Regulations 2006 (SI 2006/1928) came into force ("the Amendment Regulations").

Further offences were added to those covered by the principle regulations, widening the legislation in this area, and the duties of a sponsor of a clinical trial in the UK are now more onerous. The penalties for breach of the regulations remain the same as under the principle regulations which, following criminal prosecution on indictment by the MHRA, provides for a sentence of up to 2 years' imprisonment. The following are new offences:

(a)   breach of the sponsor's responsibility for the investigator's brochure;

(b)   breach of the requirement on a sponsor to report serious breaches of good clinical practice or the trial protocol; and

(c)   breach of requirements relating to the keeping of a trial master file and archiving.

The MHRA stated, by way of explanation:

"whilst the limited evidence available suggests that the majority of clinical trials conducted in the UK already broadly conform to agreed standards and principles of GCP, the introduction of regulations will make compliance mandatory and provide appropriate enforcement powers, which together are expected to further reduce the risks to patients without inhibiting high quality clinical trials."

The Medicines for Human Use (Clinical Trials) Amendment (No. 2) Regulations 2006 (SI 2006/2984) made further amendments allowing emergency treatment to be provided to incapacitated adults where a legal representative has not consented but procedures have been approved by an ethics committee.

The Medicines for Human Use (Clinical Trials) and Blood Safety and Quality (Amendment) Regulations 2008 (SI 2008/941) came into force on 1st May 2008 and made additional provisions relating to trials involving minors in emergency situations. Where the treatment to be given to a minor as part of the trial needs to be administered urgently, time may not allow for the written consent of a person with parental responsibility or a legal representative to be obtained first. The amendment allows minors to be entered into a trial prior to informed consent being obtained provided that:

(a)   having regard to the nature of the trial and the particular circumstances of the case, it is necessary to take action for the purpose of the trial as a matter of urgency; but

(b)   it is not reasonably practicable to obtain informed consent prior to entering the subject; and

(c)   the action to be taken is carried out in accordance with a procedure approved by the ethics committee.

The Amendment Regulations also update the definition of the Clinical Trials Directive and Directive 2001/83/EC respectively to take account of the subsequent amendment of those Directives by Community Regulations and also amends the definition of the Gene Therapy Advisory Committee (GTAC).

Suspected unexpected serious adverse reactions (SUSAR) must be reported, and since September 2010 must be reported online on the MHRA eSUSAR website.

The Medicines for Human Use (Miscellaneous Amendments) Regulations 2009 amended reg. 30 of the principal regulation. It allows urgent safety measures to be notified to the Ethics Committee and the MHRA "as soon as possible" rather than the usual restrictive 3 days during any period when a disease is pandemic and is a serious risk or potentially a serious risk to human health.

The Medicines for Human Use (Advanced Therapy Products and Miscellaneous Amendments) Regulations 2010 amends the principal regulation so that the procedures for giving an ethics committee opinion and for authorising clinical trials apply to trials involving tissue engineered products in the same way that they apply to trials involving gene therapy and somatic cell therapy.[5]

3   COMPENSATION

3.1   No Fault Compensation for Personal Injury

A Local Research Ethics Committee (LREC) is appointed by the Health Authority to provide independent advice to NHS bodies within its area on the ethics of research proposals. The trial proposal is considered by the LREC. On approval the proposal is considered further by the MHRA before it can commence. The Health Authority should take financial responsibility for members' acts and omissions in the course of performance of their duties as LREC members.

Ethics committees are responsible for considering provision for indemnity or compensation in the event of injury or death attributable to the clinical trial, and any insurance or indemnity to cover the liability of the investigator or sponsor. It is for the ethics committee to consider in each trial whether it is acceptable to seek consent without no-fault compensation, given the risks. As sponsors, pharmaceutical companies often offer a standard form of commitment about compensation. In effect, the commitment offers no-fault compensation in cases of personal injury resulting from clinical research. It excludes harm caused by the negligence of an NHS body, its staff or agents. It applies when the study is conducted according to the protocol, and the sponsor is notified and has control of any offer of compensation. Universities initiating similar studies may have clinical trials insurance that offers both negligence cover and no-fault compensation for personal injury arising from the design of the study. This insurance also normally excludes clinical negligence for which NHS bodies are liable. Ex gratia payments of up to £50,000 may be considered.

Compensation in clinical trials is governed by the EU Clinical Trials Directive implemented in the UK by the 2004 Regulations.

Neither this Directive nor the UK Regulations require no-fault compensation in clinical trials but the Association of British Pharmaceutical Industry Guidelines for medical experiments in non-patient human volunteers (March 1988) offer such a compensation scheme at the manufacturer's discretion. For example, Phase I trials are covered by the Guidelines for Medical Experiments in non-Patient Human Volunteers of March 1988 (as amended in May 1990).

3.2   Consumer Protection Act 1987 and Negligence

In the event that compensation under such an indemnity cannot be agreed, then the injured patient may seek redress either at common law in a claim for negligence or alternatively in relation to the defective product under the Consumer Protection Act 1987. Manufacturers are strictly liable, even if it is an NHS body or university, when a defect in a medicinal product causes harm, although where the product is at the very early stages of research the "development risks" defence under s. 4(1)(e) may arise. The case will usually turn on the issue of causation.

---

5 Amends regs. 15 and 19 of the 2004 Regulations.

The NHS Litigation Authority's risk pooling scheme covers NHS bodies' product liability. NHS bodies may ask to be indemnified if they are required to manufacture or supply products in circumstances that would make them liable. Pharmaceutical companies may provide a warranty when supplying products that will not be altered. Under the UK Regulations, investigational medicinal products have to be supplied and packaged according to Good Manufacturing Practice, reducing the risk of product liability. Under normal circumstances NHS indemnity would not apply unless there was a question whether the healthcare professional either knew or should reasonably have known that the drug or equipment was faulty but continued to use it.

In actions in negligence, apart from the issue of causation, the merits of the case are likely to depend on evidence related to the following questions:

(a)   Were the injuries identified as a possible side-effect in the written information provided to the person before the start of the trial?

(b)   Were the symptoms unexpected or was there information from previous animal or human trials of the drug suggesting that this may be a problem?

(c)   What was the detail of the protocol?

(d)   Was all of the relevant information disclosed to the Ethics Committee, MHRA or person participating in the trial?

(e)   Was the trial protocol followed by those performing the tests and how closely?

(f)   Was there some effect even when that protocol was wholly adhered to, which was incapable of being anticipated by the manufacturer?

3.3   NHS Indemnity

The NHS is not able to take out commercial insurance against non-negligence and therefore NHS indemnity does not offer no-fault compensation. In the case of negligent harm, healthcare professionals undertaking clinical trials on patients or volunteers in the course of their NHS employment are covered by NHS indemnity. Similarly, for a trial not involving medicines, the NHS body would take financial responsibility unless the trial were covered by such other indemnity as may have been agreed between the NHS body and those responsible for the trial.

NHS indemnity provides indemnity against clinical risk arising from negligence through the Clinical Negligence Scheme for Trusts (CNST). In this context clinical negligence is defined as "*a breach of duty of care by members of the health professions employed by NHS bodies*". If there is negligent harm NHS bodies will accept full financial liability. This means that any civil claim brought by a patient injured due to the alleged negligent act or omission of the researcher or those acting on their behalf will be settled by the employing organisation.

Negligent harm is covered by NHS indemnity for all healthy volunteers or patient clinical trials, whether they involve medicines or not, as long as there is NHS R&D management approval.

NHS indemnity applies to the senior investigator in the project and automatically covers any other colleagues under their direct supervision.

NHS bodies should ensure that they are informed of clinical trials in which their staff are taking part in their NHS employment and that these trials have the required Research Ethics Committee approval.

3.4   Commercial research

Researchers involved in commercial research have a duty to ensure that the commercial company sponsoring the study provides full indemnity cover. Companies should provide a document that adheres to the ABPI (Association of British Pharmaceutical Industries) format and provide indemnity cover from the Company to the Trust in the event of injury caused to a patient attributable to participation in the trial.

Whatever arrangements are in place must be communicated to potential research participants during the consent process and a full explanation should included in the patient information sheet.

Other independent sector sponsors of research involving patients, for example universities and medical research charities, may make arrangements to indemnify research subjects from non-negligent harm. Public funded bodies are unable to take out research insurance for commercial research, however, many offer assurances that they will consider claims for non-negligent harm arising from their trials.

3.5   Response to the Northwick Trials

The Northwick trials occurred before the Amendment Regulations came into force. The MHRA had originally approved those trials.[6] But the details of the trial, including such crucial facts as the dose, rate of drug administration, planned number of doses, intervals between doses, and even whether multiple doses were received by any volunteer, were initially kept confidential under UK law. The government commissioned an independent inquiry by an Expert Scientific Group (ESG). The ESG report, touching on the issues raised in the questions at the start of this chapter, was published in December 2006 making 22 recommendations. Examples are:

- all investigators involved should be fully trained;
- high-risk drugs should be identified;
- use of an alternative initial dose-setting assessment for certain novel agents;
- giving only one subject the active medicine on the first day;
- following this with "staggered dosing" as doses are increased;
- conducting high-risk studies at a hospital with intensive care facilities.

More recently, experts have lobbied for a "readability test" to be imposed by ethics committees. The University of Leeds commissioned research into the information provided to volunteers in the Northwick Park Trials.[7] Members of the public took up to an hour to find all of the answers to questions about key facts in the volunteer information provided, and with 6 of the 21 questions, at least 20% of participants did not understand the key facts at all. The actual volunteers involved reported to the

---

6 Suntharalingam, G. *et al.* (September 2006) "Sytokine Storm in a Phase 1 Trial of the Anti-CD28 Monoclonal Antibody TGN1412". *The New England Journal of Medicine* (10) 355:1018–1028.
7 Knapp, P., Raynor, D.K., Silcock, J. and Parkinson, B. (9 October 2008) "Performance-based readability testing of participant materials for a phase I trial: TGN1412".

media, after their trial ordeal, that they were only given about 10 minutes to review their consent forms and the drug information sheet before entering into the clinical trial. This is a form of "readability" testing and is currently applied to patient information leaflets inside medicine packs to ensure that they are clearly written and can be understood by the target audience as required by EU law. There is currently no such requirement for participant information provided to people about medicines within clinical trials, whether licensed or unlicensed.

Chapter 10

DISCLOSURE AND MEDICAL RECORDS

1   INTRODUCTION

Disclosure is one of the most important tools in clinical negligence claims, and it is vital that its principles are properly understood. The fundamental purpose of disclosure is to further the overriding objective by ensuring that parties to litigation are on "an equal footing". On a practical level, that means identifying and allowing the inspection of documents that not only assist but may also damage the prosecution or defence of a claim.

The meaning of "documents" is not restricted to paper or writing, but extends to anything upon which evidence or information is recorded in a manner intelligible to the senses or capable of being made intelligible by the use of equipment. This includes computer databases, microfilms used to keep records, video and audio tapes and discs.

Within the context of clinical negligence claims, the most important category of document is likely to be the claimant's medical records. They will provide the most contemporaneous record of the treatment given to a patient and will, in many cases, be the basis of expert opinion which will determine the outcome of the litigation. An early and objective scrutiny of medical records can save a lot of time and expense.

2   MEDICAL RECORDS

2.1   What are Medical Records?

Medical records can include documents such as operating notes, X-rays, MRI scans, paramedic notes, as well as GP records and correspondence between professionals. They can come from a wide variety of sources if an individual has been treated by a number of different hospitals or departments within the same hospital. Complete disclosure of an individual's medical records will reveal his past medical history and may identify both acts and omissions which can form the basis of a clinical negligence claim.

2.2   Who do the Medical Records Belong to?

The medical records do not belong to the patient: they belong to the compiler, which is usually the doctor or practitioner involved in the treatment. That does not mean that the owner can do with them as he sees fit. He has an absolute duty to do with the records only what is in the patient's best interests. He cannot disclose the records to a third party without the consent of the patient. The Data Protection Act 1998 (DPA) prevents unauthorised or inappropriate use of personal details, although disclosure that is required by an order of a court, or is necessary for legal proceedings or obtaining legal advice, is exempt from the non-disclosure provisions by s. 35 of the DPA.

The Access to Health Records Act 1990 establishes the right of access to medical records by the patient. Only in very rare circumstances can the owner refuse to disclose the documents, for example, where their disclosure would be detrimental to the patient.[1]

2.3   Obtaining Medical Records Outside of the Litigation Process?

Medical records can be obtained outwith the litigation process by any patient. The request should be made in writing and should be complied within 40 days of the receipt of the fee or request, whichever is later. If a patient has died, then the right of disclosure arises under s. 3(1)(f) of the Access to Health Records Act 1990, which provides that the medical records may be applied for by the personal representative of the deceased or *"any person who may have a claim arising out of the patient's death"*.

2.4   What is the Evidential Status of Medical Records?

Medical notes are admissible as hearsay evidence, but in *Denton Hall v. Fifield*[2] the Court of Appeal considered how disputes about the contents of medical notes should be dealt with. In that case the Court of Appeal stated that if there was an issue about the accurate recording of what an injured person had said, as documented in the medical records:

(i)   the party seeking to contradict a factually pleaded case on the basis of medical records or reports should indicate that intention in advance;

(ii)   the opposite party must then indicate the extent to which objection is taken to the accuracy of the records; and

(iii)   once the area of dispute is identified, the parties will have to decide whether the maker of the medical records will have to be called to prove their content.

2.5   Other Records Personal to Clinicians

In some cases a treating clinician may have personal records, e.g. emails or correspondence which relate to a particular patient and do not form part of the medical records of the patient. Generally such records will remain personal to the clinician. However, the court will order disclosure if this can be considered to be a proportionate response to a legitimate aim as required by Article 8 of the ECHR. In *R (on the application of Ali Izzet Nakash) v. Metropolitan Police Service and General Medical Council (Interested party)*,[3] the claimant had been accused of a sexual assault. He had been prosecuted and in the course of the criminal investigation the police (unlawfully) obtained a copy of an internet discussion with another doctor revealing that the claimant had been sexually aroused by the patient some weeks before the alleged assault. The claimant had been acquitted in the criminal court (the evidence had been ruled inadmissible). However, the GMC wanted to investigate the doctor's fitness to

---

1 *R v. Mid Glamorgan Family Health Services Authority Ex p Martin* [1995] 1 All ER 356.
2 [2006] EWCA Civ 169.
3 [2014] EWHC 3810 (Admin).

practise and had sought disclosure of the record from the police who consented to make the disclosure. The claimant brought judicial review proceedings against the police. The court performed the balancing exercise required by Article 8 and considered the material disclosable pursuant to s. 35A of the Medical Act 1983.

3   TIME OF DISCLOSURE

3.1   Pre-action

As noted above, a patient can at any time obtain copies of his medical notes pursuant to the Access to Health Records Act 1990.

Where clinical negligence proceedings are anticipated, the Clinical Negligence Protocol has, since it was put in place in April 1999, outlined a prescribed method for obtaining medical records. Any request should (a) provide sufficient information to alert the healthcare provider where an adverse outcome has been serious or had serious consequences and (b) be as specific as possible about the records which are required. Annex B to the Protocol sets out an approved Law Society and Department of Health form.

If the healthcare provider fails to provide the records within 40 days, the patient or their adviser can apply to the court for an order for pre-action disclosure. Such application can be made pursuant to s. 33 of the Senior Courts Act 1981 or s. 52 of the County Courts Act 1984. CPR Part 31.16 sets out the necessary procedure. The application must be supported by evidence, and be targeted at a respondent who is likely to be a party to the proceedings. The disclosure must be "desirable" in order to (i) dispose fairly of anticipated proceedings, (ii) assist the resolution of the dispute without proceedings, and (iii) save costs.

The general rule is that a court will award the person against whom the order is sought his costs of both the application and compliance with the order (CPR, r. 48.1(2)) although a different order may be made having regard to all the circumstances, including the extent to which it was reasonable for the person against whom the order was sought to oppose the application and whether the parties have complied with the pre-action protocol (CPR, r. 48.1(3)).

3.2   During the Course of Proceedings

Most clinical negligence claims will fall to be allocated to the multi-track. When this step is taken, the court will give directions for the management of the case and set a timetable for disclosure or fix a case management conference or pre-trial review at which the parties can make representations as to the appropriate directions (CPR, r. 29.2). If a court gives directions on its own initiative, the normal rule will be to direct "standard disclosure" (CPR PD 29.4.10), although the parties may agree in writing, or the court may direct, that disclosure or inspection or both shall take place in stages (CPR, r. 31.13). If a party is dissatisfied with the disclosure given, an application for specific disclosure can be made at any time.

The duty of disclosure continues until the proceedings are concluded (CPR, r. 31.11). So if documents to which that duty extends come into a party's notice at any time during the proceedings, every other party must be notified.

4   THE BASIC DUTY OF DISCLOSURE

Disclosure duties are set out at CPR Part 31. The CPR were designed to streamline the procedures for disclosure, limit the extent of disclosure and give the court control over that extent. It is a key part of the CPR that disclosure should be proportionate to the nature of the action.

Documents may be divided into the following categories:

(i)   documents within the possession of the parties which they rely on in support of their case;

(ii)   documents within the possession of the parties which undermine their case;

(iii)   documents which are relevant to the issues in the case, but do not support or undermine either side's case;

(iv)   documents which may lead to a train of inquiry which may enable a party to advance his own case, or damage that of his opponent.

The fact that a document is relevant is not determinative of the issue of disclosure. The ultimate test is whether disclosure and inspection is necessary for disposing fairly of the proceedings.[4]

"Standard disclosure" is the normal order in all fast and multi-track actions unless the court orders otherwise. This requires a party to disclose only the documents in his control on which he relies and those which either support or adversely affect his own or another party's case (i.e. categories (i) and (ii) above). The burden rests with each party to state which documents he has and, to this end, CPR, r. 31.7 states that he must carry out a "reasonable search".

The definition of "documents in a party's control" has been widened by the CPR to include documents which (a) are in, or have been in, a party's physical possession; (b) the party has a right to possession of , and (c) the party has a right to inspect or take copies of. Where a hospital with possession of a patient's medical records has within those records notes compiled by a privately instructed surgeon or anaesthetist, those notes would be deemed under the hospital's control, even though the hospital was not, strictly speaking, the owner.

Once disclosed, there is a duty to allow inspection. In practice, this often amounts to no more than the provision of photocopies of documents. If an inspecting party requests copy documents then, provided they undertake to pay reasonable copying costs, copies must be provided under CPR, r. 31.15 within 7 days. Actual, physical inspection of documents can be requested in circumstances where it is felt necessary to see the original document, or where there are a large number of documents and it is felt cost effective to see them before deciding which should be copied.

The standard way of providing disclosure is by way of a list. This should be supported by a declaration of compliance (a "disclosure statement"). The list must be in Form N265 and should be sub-divided into three categories, namely (i) documents in the

---

4 *Croft House Care Limited v. Durham County Council* [2010] EWHC 909 (TCC).

party's control where there is no objection to inspection, (ii) documents in the party's control where there is objection to inspection, and (iii) documents that were in the party's control but are no longer. Where a party objects to inspection, then they are required to set out the grounds of the objection.

A party to whom a document has been disclosed may use the document only for the purpose of the proceedings in which it is disclosed except where the document has been made public (e.g. if it has been read out in "open" court), if the court gives permission, or the party who discloses the document and the person to whom the document belongs agree (CPR, r. 31.22).

5 REASONS FOR WITHHOLDING INSPECTION

There are most commonly two reasons for withholding inspection of a document.

5.1 Where it is Disproportionate

Where a party considers that it would be disproportionate to the issues in a case to permit inspection of documents, he can state this in his disclosure statement. Relevant factors will include the number of documents, the nature and complexity of the proceedings, the ease and expense of retrieval of any document, and its likely significance.

5.2 Where Legal Professional Privilege is Claimed

There are a number of different types of privilege, but the most common is legal professional privilege. This takes two forms; "litigation privilege" and "legal advice privilege". Where it exists, it is absolute although it can be waived. The privilege belongs to the client, but it attaches both to what the client tells his lawyer and to what his lawyer advises his client. See generally *Three Rivers District Council v. Bank of England (No. 4).*[5]

The first category of legal professional privilege is "litigation privilege". This covers all documents brought into being for the purposes of existing or contemplated litigation. "Contemplated litigation" means litigation must be reasonably in prospect.[6] It covers communications between a solicitor or client and a non-professional agent or third party. In clinical negligence actions, litigation privilege would *not* cover an independent investigation report into perceived negligence if such report was instigated when there was no more than a possibility of litigation. It *would* cover a medical expert's review of the medical records once a claim had been formally initiated.

The second category is "legal advice privilege" which covers communications between lawyers and their clients (as opposed to third parties).

A court can stay proceedings if a claimant refuses to give consent to hospitals or doctors to disclose otherwise confidential matters.

---

5 [2005] 1 AC 610.
6 See *United States of America v. (1) Philip Morris Inc (2) BAT Investments Ltd* (No. 1) [2004] EWCA Civ 330.

6   SPECIFIC DISCLOSURE

If a party perceives that standard disclosure has been inadequate, he may make an application for specific disclosure pursuant to CPR, r. 31.12. Such order may compel a party to (a) disclose documents or classes of documents specified in the order, (b) carry out a search to the extent identified in the order, or (c) disclose any documents located as a result of that search.

Before a court orders specific disclosure, it must be satisfied that the documents are (or have been) in the control of the party and the documents sought are relevant. The court will base its decision on "all the circumstances of the case" and the overriding objective (CPR PD 31 5.4). There must be a proper basis for the application, and courts will not entertain "fishing" expeditions. Applications for specific disclosure should be supported by evidence and, if resisted, should be met by evidence in response.

7   DISCLOSURE AGAINST NON-PARTIES

This may be relevant in circumstances where a patient's records are held by a hospital in circumstances in which a clinical negligence claim is being pursued against a named medical practitioner.

Applications for disclosure against non-parties are made pursuant to s. 34 of the Senior Courts Act 1981 or s. 53 of the County Courts Act 1984, and CPR, r. 31.17. They can only be made *during* the course of proceedings.

The court may order a third party to disclose documents so long as the documents are likely to support the case of the applicant or adversely affect the case of another party *and* where disclosure is necessary to dispose fairly of the claim or save costs. The application must be supported by evidence.

Where a court is considering whether to make a costs order in favour or against a person who is not a party to the proceedings, that person must be added to the proceedings (for the purpose of costs only) and be given a reasonable opportunity to attend a hearing at which the court will consider the matter further (CPR, r. 48.2).

8   SANCTIONS

The formal sanctions where a party has failed to comply with his disclosure obligations are costs orders, unless orders, orders to strike out, debarring orders and, potentially, contempt proceedings. CPR, r. 31.23 provides that proceedings for contempt of court may be brought against a person if he makes, or causes to be made, a false disclosure statement without an honest belief in its truth. Proceedings may only be brought by the Attorney General or with the permission of the court.

Chapter 11

CASE MANAGEMENT AND EXPERT EVIDENCE

1   INTRODUCTION

A useful guide to the sort of directions that need to be considered for the case management of clinical negligence actions can be found in the model directions for clinical negligence cases before the Masters assigned to the clinical negligence list in the Queen's Bench Division at the Royal Courts of Justice. The most recent version was published in 2012 and can be found at www.hmrc.gov.uk. They are not part of any of the CPR Practice Directions, but can be found in this work at Appendix 2. The model directions themselves state that they are not to be followed slavishly, but they do provide a well thought out and practical basis for progressing clinical negligence actions. The most recent model directions include important changes to the directions relating to experts and their role in the preparation of agendas. References to the 4th published version of the model directions (2005) can be found in the previous edition of this book. There was a 2010 edition which was slightly altered in the 2012 version at Appendix 2. Where the new directions remain unchanged, the previous directions are repeated.

It is also important to note the recent update to CPR Part 53 relating to the Clinical Negligence Protocol, the most recent version is no. 79 which comes into force on 6th April 2015. The amended provision now states that any letter of claim sent to an NHS Trust or Independent Sector Treatment Centre should be copied to the NHSLA, who will now have 4 months within which to respond rather than 3. These changes implement recommendations in the Jackson Report and are aimed at encouraging the parties to settle before the issue of proceedings.

2   ALLOCATION

Most clinical negligence cases will be allocated to the multi-track at the allocation stage following service of allocation questionnaires.

3   MEDICAL NOTES

Ordinarily medical notes will have been obtained long before proceedings are issued (see Appendix 1), but it is still important that disclosure is dealt with in the case management directions. An order for disclosure is required to trigger the duty to search and the continuing duty to disclose under CPR, r. 31.11. The model directions put the onus of preserving medical records on the defendant, but the obligation to prepare the notes for litigation lies with the claimant's solicitors:

> ***"Preservation of Evidence***
> *The Defendant do retain and preserve safely the original clinical notes relating to the action pending the trial. The Defendant do give facilities for inspection by the Claimant, the Claimant's legal advisers and experts of the said original notes upon 7 days written notice to do so."*

Whilst not repeated in the 2010 version, the recent model directions maintain the previous direction's helpful guidance in the maintenance of records:

> *"Legible copies of the medical (and educational) records of the Claimant/Deceased/Claimant's Mother are to be placed in a separate paginated bundle at the earliest opportunity by the Claimant's Solicitors and kept up to date. All references to medical notes in any report are to be made by reference to the pages in that bundle.*
>
> *All reports coming into existence for the purpose of the case disclosed by any party are to be placed in a separate paginated bundle at the earliest opportunity by the Claimant's Solicitors and kept up to date. Upon reports being added to such bundle the Claimants are to serve a revised index to such bundle upon all other parties. All references to such reports in subsequent reports shall include a reference to the relevant pages in that bundle."*

And then as to disclosure:

> *"There be standard disclosure [on the preliminary issue][limited to quantum] by list by .... 2012. Any initial request for inspection or copy documents is to be made within 7 / 14 days of service of the lists."*

When working on cases with numerous files it assists if the file description (e.g. "File A, Medical Notes, St Mungo's Hospital") is put on a label on the top left hand side of the inside of the front flap so that it can be read when the file is open. It assists all parties if experts refer to the same pagination in their reports and have the same bundles when they come to their joint discussions.

4   SPLIT TRIAL

Early thought should be given to whether the case is suitable for a split trial. If liability is in issue and quantum will be very expensive and time consuming to assess, or cannot be assessed for some time to come pending the outcome of further treatment or maturing of the patient, then the case may be suitable for a split trial. It should be remembered, however, that, if the parties do wish to settle the claim at a later stage, it may be helpful or necessary to have a good idea as to the value of the claim. The fact that a split trial is ordered does not mean, therefore, that all work on quantum should cease. It may still be worth, for example, obtaining a care report so that the rough outline of the future needs is known.

If a split trial is ordered then it is important to specify what exactly is being ordered. It is very rare that a split trial on breach of duty alone will be required and generally an order that "There be a trial of liability alone" should be avoided for lack of clarity. The model directions suggest the following where a split trial is ordered:

> *"A preliminary issue shall be tried between the Claimant and the Defendant as to whether or not the Defendant is liable to the Claimant by reason of the matters alleged in the Particulars of Claim and, if so, whether or not any of the injuries pleaded were caused thereby; if any such injuries were so caused, the extent of the same."*

5 COSTS CASE MANAGEMENT CONFERENCE (CCMC)

For all cases issued after the end of April 2014 the first CMC will be listed as a Costs Case Management Conference (CCMC).[1] Pursuant to CPR, r. 3.13:

> *"Unless the court otherwise orders, all parties except litigants in person must file and exchange budgets as required by the rules or as the court otherwise directs. Each party must do so by the date specified in the notice served under rule 26.3(1) or, if no such date is specified, seven days before the first case management conference."*

The introduction of CCMCs and concurrent failure to appoint additional Masters has caused a significant backlog of clinical negligence cases in particular, proposals for dealing with this include a one-off release but this remains to be resolved.[2] The rules are specific about the failure to file a budget on time. CPR, r. 3.14 states:

> *"Unless the court otherwise orders, any party which fails to file a budget despite being required to do so will be treated as having filed a budget comprising only the applicable court fees."*

In *Mitchell v. News Group Newspapers Limited*[3] the Court of Appeal (against the backdrop of the words of Lord Dyson in the 18th Implementation Lecture in respect of the Jackson Reforms) made it clear that this rule would be strictly interpreted and enunciated the following principles concerning relief from sanctions where such a rule had been breached:

(i) Court will consider the reasons for the default – burden on party seeking relief

(ii) If there is a "good reason" for default court likely to decide relief should be granted

(iii) Good Reason: e.g. a "document not filed at court was because solicitor suffered from a debilitating illness or involved in an accident"

(iv) Later developments in the course of the litigation process are likely to be a good reason if they show that the period for compliance originally imposed was unreasonable, although the period seemed to be reasonable at the time and could not realistically have been the subject of an appeal

(v) Overlooking a deadline due to overwork or otherwise unlikely to be "good reason"

(vi) Likely to arise from circumstances outside the control of the party in default.

---

1 CPR, r. 3.12 and Practice Direction 3E.
2 www.judiciary.gov.uk/announcements/harbour-lecture-by-lord-justice-jackson-confronting-costs-management and www.judiciary.gov.uk/announcements/harbour-lecture-by-lord-justice-dyson-mr-confronting-costs-management.
3 [2014] 1 WLR 795, [2014] 2 All ER 430.

This triggered a plethora of anticipatory applications to the courts for extending deadlines for service of witness statements or expert evidence or the like which may previously have been dealt with by consent. That led in turn to the Civil Procedure Amendment (No 5) Rules 2014 which came into force on 5th June 2014. They amended CPR, r. 3.8 so that where the parties agreed in writing an extension of time for compliance with court orders this could be done up to a maximum of 28 days provided that any extension did not put at risk a hearing date. *Mitchell* also triggered a good deal of satellite litigation about when a breach was "trivial" or not thus requiring relief sanctions to proceed, which is beyond the scope of this work. Useful guidance can be found in the notes to this rule in the White Book.

The court will not at this stage have power to limit costs already incurred, nor should the rate of fee earner used to date be amenable to change (though narrative comments may sometimes be included in a case management order depending on the practice of the local court or master). However, with this in mind many parties will elect to front load their costs and avoid litigation until as ready as they can be, mindful of any limitation issues.

Parties are encouraged in the model directions to attend the first CCMC armed with a provisional view as to whether the case is one in which the periodical payment of damage might be appropriate. By this stage parties ought to have a clear case strategy and to have considered closely both the number and disciplines of any experts sought and be prepared to justify this position to the court. They should be able to identify whether the experts will be jointly instructed or not and preferably to have identified the experts by name and to have obtained an accurate estimate of the fees which the expert will charge in addition to being able to identify with accuracy costs already incurred. It is important that a realistic timetable is considered to allow for conferences with experts and for exchange of other expert evidence (in cases with multiple experts) or the completion of further treatment or rehabilitation, or a change in important circumstances such as accommodation. Thought should be given to whether simultaneous disclosure or sequential disclosure would be preferable which may depend on the pre-action position. If a further CMC is required and further consideration of expert or witness evidence to be had at that stage, it can assist if the order reflects that this is yet to be discussed or finalised. As to supplemental witness or expert evidence: Turner J gave this guidance in *Karbahri v. Ahmed*:[4]

> "In cases where there is a realistic possibility that there will be evidential developments between the dates upon which witness statements are to be served and the trial date, this ought to be anticipated in the orders of the court. In such cases the wisest course would be to seek to persuade the court to make two orders relating to the service of witness statements. The first would provide for a date which would give a realistic opportunity for all sides to comply with respect to matters which have arisen beforehand. A later backstop date could be ordered for the service of supplementary statements limited in content to matters which occurred, or were reasonably discoverable, only after the first date...I would expect the same to apply to expert reports" (emphasis added).

If parties do need an extension of time for a procedural step such as the exchange of witness evidence or expert evidence it is clear from *Hallam v. Baker*[5] that applications

---

4 [2013] EWHC 4042.
5 [2014] EWCA Civ 661, per Jackson LJ.

for extensions of time are not applications for relief and so one does not need therefore to satisfy the principles concerning relief enunciated in *Mitchell*. This is the case even if an application is made after the expiry of the period if the application is to be made pursuant to CPR, r. 3.1(2)(a). Jackson LJ said:

> "12. A variety of circumstances may arise in which one or other party (however diligent) may require a modest extension of time. Under rule 1.3 the parties have a duty to help the court in furthering the overriding objective. The overriding objective includes allotting an appropriate share of the court's resources to an individual case. Therefore legal representatives are not in breach of any duty to their client, when they agree to a reasonable extension of time which neither imperils future hearing dates nor otherwise disrupts the conduct of litigation. On the contrary, by avoiding the need for a contested application they are furthering the overriding objective and also saving costs for the benefit of their own client."

> "31. The Rule Committee has inserted a new sub-paragraph 1.1(2)(f) into the overriding objective. In my view this new provision (which was not one of my recommendations) does not require courts to refuse reasonable extensions of time which neither imperil hearing dates nor otherwise disrupt the proceedings."

Again, for further more detailed guidance on such procedural matters, the White Book ought to be consulted.

6   COSTS CAPPING

The rules regarding costs capping orders can now be found in CPR, rr. 3.19, 3.20 and 3.21 as well as Practice Direction 3F.

A costs capping order may be in respect of the whole litigation or any issues ordered to be tried separately, and this can be made at any stage of proceedings. When deciding if a capping order is required against all or any of the parties the court will consider if it is in the interests of justice to do so, if there is a substantial risk that without such an order costs will be disproportionality incurred and that said risk cannot be controlled by case management directions or a detailed costs assessment.[6] Costs capping is considered in greater detail in Chapter 13.

7   WITNESS STATEMENTS

In relation to experts as a whole, the model directions contain fairly standard directions for exchange of witness statements:

> "Signed and dated witness statements of fact in respect of breach of duty and causation [and quantum] shall be simultaneously exchanged by .... 2012. Civil Evidence Act notices are to be served by the same date. The witness statements of all concerned with the treatment and care of the claimant at the time of the matters alleged against the defendant shall be served under this paragraph.

> Signed and dated witness statements of fact in respect of quantum, condition and prognosis shall be served by .... 2012 (claimant) and .... 2012 (defendant). Civil Evidence Act notices are to be served by the same date."

---

6 CPR, r. 3.19(4) and (5).

The unusual departure from the idea that the court does not interfere with the parties' choice of witnesses is again confirmed in the most recent model directions:

> *"Evidence of all concerned with the treatment and care of the Claimant at the time of the matters alleged against the Defendant shall be disclosed in accordance with this paragraph."*

In *Wisniewski v. Central Manchester Health Authority*[7] the Court of Appeal criticised the defendant health authority for failing to call a doctor to give evidence on the grounds that he was abroad.

8   EXPERT EVIDENCE

At an early stage the parties and the court need to determine on which issues expert evidence should come from joint experts, and on which the parties should be permitted to call their own experts.

Where two or more parties wish to submit expert evidence on a particular issue, the court may give each party permission to produce its own expert evidence or, under the express powers of CPR, r. 35.7, it may direct that the evidence on that issue is to be given by one expert only. The introduction of the "single joint expert" has been a major innovation under the CPR. It has required a change of culture for all involved, legal advisers, experts and courts, but has become an established part of clinical negligence practice. Not all expert evidence is suited to single joint expert instruction, and there are practical problems that can arise. The courts have now, after some initial over-enthusiasm in some quarters for the use of single joint experts, come to realise that they are not always appropriate.

There is often some confusion over the concept of an expert agreed by a joint selection under the pre-action protocol (see Appendix 1) and a single joint expert under CPR, r. 35.7. They are not the same. Although a defendant may agree to the instruction of an expert under the pre-action protocol, that of itself does not convert the expert into a jointly instructed single expert. A claimant who obtains a report from an expert whose instruction has been agreed with a potential defendant under the pre-action protocol but then does not wish to rely on it may still claim privilege in the report and refuse to disclose it to the defendant, see *Carlson v. Townsend*.[8] *Carlson v. Townsend* was followed in the unreported case of *Sage v. Feiven*,[9] in which the claimant obtained a report from an orthopaedic surgeon at the pre-action stage, which was not disclosed. When proceedings were issued the defendant invited the District Judge to order a report from the same surgeon as a single joint expert, and the District Judge did so, on proportionality grounds. On appeal this decision was overturned on the grounds that privileged information would be disclosed to the defendant and the parties were required to instruct a new expert.

There are limits on the extent to which the court can require single joint experts to be appointed and still provide an adversarial trial of the issues. The Court of Appeal recognised the limits of using a single joint expert where liability is in issue in a clinical

---

7 [1998] PIQR.
8 [2001] EWCA Civ 511.
9 [2002] CLY 430.

negligence action in *Oxley v. Penwarden*.[10] In *Oxley* the judge at first instance had ordered the parties, against their joint wishes, to agree on a vascular surgeon to prepare a single joint expert report on causation, in default of which the court would appoint one. The Court of Appeal disapproved of the order and considered that it was necessary for each party to have an opportunity of investigating causation through an expert of their own choice and to have the opportunity to call that evidence at trial.

In *S (a Minor) v. Birmingham Health Authority*,[11] the judge had ordered a single joint expert to prepare opinion evidence on liability and causation in a clinical negligence claim. The claimant appealed on the basis that the issues to be covered in the expert's report were so important to the likely outcome of the case that the parties should be entitled to instruct an expert each. The Court of Appeal agreed. This is the line that the courts have followed subsequently and if the expert evidence is key to an issue in dispute then single joint expert evidence is not regarded as satisfactory. If the evidence relates to a matter that needs to be addressed but is not key to the real issue in the case then a single joint report is seen as the way to save time and costs. Where all that is in fact required is a reference for rates, for example of nursing care, average earnings or car expenses, then reference can be made to the PNBA annual publication *Facts and Figures*, an essential tool for any clinical negligence practitioner and one that is recognised by the courts.

The approach to single joint experts outlined above is to be found in the Queen's Bench Guide:

> *"In very many cases it is possible for the question of expert evidence to be dealt with by a single expert. Single experts are, for example, often appropriate to deal with questions of quantum in cases where primary issues are as to liability. Likewise, where expert evidence is required in order to acquaint the court with matters of expert fact, as opposed to opinion, a single expert will usually be appropriate. There remain, however, a body of cases where liability will turn upon expert opinion evidence and where it will be appropriate for the parties to instruct their own experts. For example, in cases where the issue for determination is as to whether a party acted in accordance with proper professional standards, it will often be of value to the court to hear the opinions of more than one expert as to the proper standard in order that the court becomes acquainted with the range of views existing upon the question and in order that the evidence can be tested in cross-examination."*

Although the court may limit the parties to producing expert evidence from a single joint expert, it will not itself instruct a single joint expert. It is the parties who instruct a single joint expert, although under CPR, r. 35.7(2)(a) and (b) if the parties cannot agree who to instruct the court may select the expert from a list prepared or identified by the parties, or direct some other means of selection. The model directions provide:

> *"Each party has permission to rely on the evidence of a single joint expert in the following fields: [state the disciplines; and identify the issues*]. The experts are to be instructed by ....2012 and the joint expert is to provide his report by ....2012. In case of difficulty, the parties have permission to restore before the Master.*
>
> *If the parties are unable to agree on the identity of the expert to be instructed, the parties are to restore the CMC before the Master. At such hearing the parties are*

---

10 [2001] Lloyd's Rep Med 347.
11 [2001] Lloyd's Rep Med 382.

> *to provide details of the CVs, availability and the estimated fee of the expert they propose and reasoned objections to any other proposed.*
>
> ** These words may be deleted where the issues do not have to be defined."*

The parties may be able to agree the terms of the instruction, and it is best if they can do so. If they cannot then under CPR, r. 35.8 each party may give instructions to the expert, but at the same time those instructions must be sent to the other instructing parties. It is not possible, therefore, for one party to give confidential or private instructions to a single joint expert that are kept from the other instructing party. If the parties are sending their own separate instructions to an expert it is nevertheless important that it is made plain to the expert by all parties that it is a joint instruction.

When giving permission for a single joint expert the court may give directions about the payment of the expert's fees and expenses, including placing a limit on the amount to be incurred and ordering the instructing parties to pay that amount into court in order to provide security for the cost of the expert. Unless the court makes a different order each of the parties is jointly and severally liable for the payment of a single joint expert appointed under CPR, r. 35.7, i.e. each party is liable for the whole fee.

The court may also make a direction under CPR, r. 35.8 as to any inspection, examination or experiments that the expert wishes to carry out. This express power is in addition to the court's general management powers. It will rarely be necessary in a personal injury action for the court to use these powers, but, for example, a claimant would not be able to thwart the instruction of a single joint expert by unreasonably refusing to undergo an examination or, for example, an MRI scan that the expert considered necessary.

Instructing single joint experts does not remove practical problems. No party can keep their powder dry by withholding material from the other parties but giving it to the single joint expert, as instructions to a single joint expert have to be disclosed to all parties. If the report of a single joint expert needs clarification then any party may put written questions to the expert under CPR Part 35.6. It is not possible, however, for one party to have a conference with a single joint expert without the other parties unless the other parties consent. In practice, joint conferences are difficult to arrange and tend not to happen. This issue was raised in *P (a child) v. Mid Kent Area Healthcare NHS Trust*,[12] a clinical negligence cerebral palsy case. A non-medical single joint expert had been appointed on quantum issues and the claimant wanted the expert to attend a conference with counsel in the absence of the other party. The Court of Appeal refused to allow the conference on the grounds that all contact with a single joint expert must be transparent and one party should not be permitted to test the evidence before trial without the involvement of the other party. However, some of the Court of Appeal's *obiter* comments in *P (a child) v. Mid Kent Area Healthcare NHS Trust* have not been followed. In particular the suggestion that usually there should be no need to amplify or test the report of a single joint expert at trial by cross-examination has not stopped joint experts being called where CPR, r. 35.6 questioning has been tried but there is still a need for oral amplification and explanation. The general view has reflected the comments of Colman J in *Voaden v. Champion, "The Baltic Surveyor"*[13] in relation to an order for a joint single expert on valuation:

---

12 [2002] 1 WLR 210.
13 [2001] Lloyd's Rep 739.

> *"Whereas there can be no doubt that the order for a single expert under CPR 35.7 was made with the interests of economy and proportionality in mind, the assumption that this important issue could be tried without that single expert being available in court for the purpose of explaining his views was, I have to say, misconceived. Certainly, in relation to trials in the Commercial Court and the Admiralty Court it will only be in cases where the sole expert is to report on discrete and substantially non-controversial matters, collateral to the main issues, that it should be assumed that the sole expert will not have to be present at the trial to explain the contents of his report. In any other case the absence of a sole expert may well prejudice the fair resolution of the expert issues in the light of all the other evidence before it."*

In *Austen v. Oxfordshire County Council*[14] on appeal it was ordered that a psychiatrist instructed as a single joint expert should give evidence at a disposal hearing because otherwise there could have been an injustice, reflecting the reasoning of Colman J in *The Baltic Surveyor*.

The appointment of a single joint expert does not remove or replace the role of the court as the decision-making tribunal on the issues before it. In *Coopers Payne Limited v. Southampton Containers Limited*[15] the Court of Appeal held that it was open to a court to make a considered choice between the evidence of a single joint expert and the evidence of a witness of fact where they were inconsistent, although they considered that it would be unusual to disregard the expert evidence. Certainly the court would have to provide good reasons in its judgment for doing so. In *Regan v. Chetwynd*,[16] the court agreed with a claimant that the single joint expert's accident reconstruction report should be treated with caution. In *Fuller v. Strum*,[17] a chancery judge preferred the evidence of fact to that of a handwriting expert as to whether a will was forged on the basis that the expert was doing no more than drawing inferences from the facts given to him. In *Layland v. Fairview New Homes plc*[18] a summary judgment entered by a district judge on the basis of a disputed single joint expert report (concerning the alleged reduction in value of a property located close to an incinerator) was overturned. It was held that submissions and cross-examination on the report should have been allowed. In plain terms, therefore, the respect to be paid to a single joint expert's report depends on the circumstances, but departure from an unchallenged single expert's report will need to be justified. In *Armstrong v. First York*,[19] the Court of Appeal held that where a trial judge had found that the claimants in a road traffic accident claim had been honest and reliable witnesses, he was entitled to find that it followed from that finding of honesty that there had been a flaw in the uncontroversial evidence of an expert, albeit that he could not identify the error, since there was always a possibility that an expert, particularly in a developing field, could have been wrong.

The extent to which a medico-legal expert should comment on apparent discrepancies between claimants' witness evidence and what they reportedly told both treating doctors and the medico-legal expert was considered in *Charnock & others v. Rowan & others*.[20] The defendant's expert in that case (Mr Shah) advanced no substantive reasons for disbelieving any individual accounts, confining himself to observing there were

---

14 [2002] All ER (D) 97.
15 [2003] All ER (D) 220.
16 15th December 2000 QB.
17 [2001] 98 LSG 45.
18 [2002] EWHC 1350.
19 [2005] EWCA Civ 277.
20 [2012] EWCA Civ 2.

some slight discrepancies. The Court of Appeal noted that, implicit in the trial judge's judgment, was a suggestion that it is the examining doctor's job to make out the case, if there is a case, for disbelieving a claimant's account of how he or she came to suffer injury, or of the injury he or she has suffered. Sir Stephen Sedley made the following *obiter* remarks about such a proposition:

> *"There are of course cases in which, for clinical or related reasons, the doctor is driven to advance such an opinion; but if it was intended here to suggest that the doctor's role is routinely that of a sleuth, I must record my respectful disagreement. Forensic medical practice has been disfigured in the past by practitioners who took on such a role; but it was to Mr Shah's credit that he confined his report to those divergences which emerged from his own interviews and from the records supplied to him and did not take on himself the task of deciding who was to be believed."[21]*

In *P French and Co Ltd v. Walton Street Trading Co Ltd*[22] the defendant's application to instruct its own expert 2 weeks before trial was refused, as the court determined that the key issue (namely whether or not the defendant had suffered a loss of profits) could be explored in cross-examination of the joint expert. It was pertinent in that case that the sums in dispute were limited and that the application was made so close to the trial date.

Where the instruction of single joint experts is not ordered the court may even be prepared to consider allowing a party more than one expert in a particular discipline where the circumstances warrant it, despite the contrary emphasis in CPR, r. 35.4. In *ES v. Chesterfield North Derbyshire Royal NHS Trust*,[23] a claimant in a clinical negligence action was faced with a number of witnesses of fact for the defendant who were themselves experts in the discipline in issue. The claimant had to overcome the *Bolam* hurdle and argued that there would not be a level playing field if the defendant could in effect call additional experts. The claim was worth over £1.5m and the issues were complex so additional expert evidence was proportionate to the size and nature of the claim, the Court of Appeal allowed the claimant to instruct and rely upon additional experts.

ES v. Chesterfield North Derbyshire Royal NHS Trust was however distinguished in *Beaumont v. Ministry of Defence*,[24] also a clinical negligence claim: in *ES* the claim was brought against two medical practitioners, in *Beaumont* it was against one. The court accepted that when the defendant gave evidence he would inevitably display and rely upon his experience and expertise, and that might carry weight with the trial judge. However, that would be so in most cases involving allegations of professional negligence. The defendant was not of such exceptional eminence or expertise as to justify a departure from the normal rule, and the circumstances of the case were not exceptional when compared to other actions of the same general nature.

---

21 [2012] EWCA Civ 2, at para. 9.
22 Unreported, 27th January 2012 (Judge Thornton QC)
23 [2003] EWCA Civ 1284.
24 [2009] EWHC 1258 (QB)

9 EXPERTS' DISCUSSIONS

The joint statements produced by experts are at the heart of any subsequent trial. Sometimes trials are derailed due to lack of care in the preparation of joint statements.

The power to order such discussions is found in CPR, r. 35.12. The model directions make the point that discussions between experts are not mandatory and the parties should consider, with their expert, whether there is likely to be any useful purpose in holding a discussion and should be prepared to agree that no discussion is in fact needed.

The discussions can be by telephone, they do not have to be meetings. The discussions can be ordered at any stage, but generally follow the exchange of experts' reports. The discussions are without prejudice and CPR, r. 35.12(4) expressly provides that the content of the discussion is not to be referred to unless the parties agree. This provision is designed to encourage compromise and candour under the without prejudice protection. The fact that a discussion cannot be referred to does not prevent the use of knowledge gained as a result of the discussion. Thus it may not be permissible to ask "Is it right that it took Professor Smith 3 hours to persuade you that he was right and you were wrong on this point at the joint meeting", but it would be permissible to ask an expert in cross-examination why they had expressed their original opinion and how they had come to the new view in the joint statement, with a view to bringing out the vacillation and indecision that was demonstrated at the meeting. Judges vary in the stricture with which the rule is applied, and even without any desire to bend the rules it is all too easy for one expert in cross-examination to say something such as "I believe Dr Jones had some difficulty in accepting this point when we met, but did eventually have to concede the point". Caution is still needed, therefore, about what is said in the course of discussions.

Even if the experts reach agreement, that agreement does not bind the parties unless they expressly agree to be bound. It can be difficult to hold an expert to an agreement at trial, and impossible to hold a party to an agreement unless they have effectively made an admission, in which case the provisions of CPR, r. 14.1(5) as to allowing a party to withdraw an admission apply. Very often the apparent unravelling of an agreement between experts at trial is in fact no more than the discovery that, despite appearances, they were never agreed in the first place. Conversely, although a party may not be strictly bound by an experts' agreement, there may be little the party can do to rescue a point once the experts' agreement has destroyed the evidential basis for it.

The product of the discussions between experts should be a joint statement for the court. CPR, r. 35.12(3) provides that such a statement should show:

(a)   those issues on which they agree; and

(b)   those issues on which they disagree and a summary of their reasons for disagreeing.

Some court orders require more from a joint statement. The model directions stipulate that:

"(a)   *The purpose of the discussions is to identify:*

> (i)   *The extent of the agreement between the experts;*
>
> (ii)   *The points of disagreement and short reasons for disagreement;*
>
> (iii)   *Action, if any, which may be taken to resolve the outstanding points of disagreement;*
>
> (iv)   *Any further material points not raised in the Agenda and the extent to which these issues are agreed."*

The discussions will be better structured, and the joint statement more helpful, if there is a proper agenda. As the legal advisers know the issues in the case it is helpful if the agenda is prepared by them, in discussion with the experts if need be. It should be possible to identify from the experts' reports the issues relevant to the trial that need to be discussed. Even if the order for discussions provides a timetable with a substantial gap between exchange of reports and holding of discussions it is worth tackling the issue of the agenda as soon as exchange has taken place. Very often the drawing up of the agenda is left too late and as a result the agenda is ill thought out, has not been the subject of proper consultation with experts, and is less likely to be agreed. The model directions emphasise the responsibility of claimants' solicitors and counsel to prepare the draft agenda jointly with the relevant expert. They go on to provide:

> *"(a)   Unless otherwise agreed by all parties' solicitors, after consulting with the experts, a draft Agenda which directs the experts to the remaining issues relevant to the experts' discipline, as identified in the statements of case shall be prepared jointly by the Claimant's solicitors and experts and sent to the Defendant's solicitors for comment at least 35 days before the agreed date for the experts' discussions;*
>
> (b)   *The use of agendas is not mandatory. Solicitors should consult with the experts to ensure that agendas are necessary and, if used, are reasonable in scope. The agenda should assist the experts and should not be in the form of leading questions or hostile in tone. An agenda must include a list of the outstanding issues in the preamble.*
>
> *[Note: The preamble should state: the Standard of proof: the Bolam test: remind the experts not to attempt to determine factual issues: remind them not to stray outside their field of expertise and indicate the form of the joint statement. It will also be helpful to provide a comprehensive list of the materials which each expert has seen, perhaps in the form of an agreed supplementary bundle (it is assumed that experts will have been provided with the medical notes bundle)]*
>
> (c)   *The Defendants shall within 21 days of receipt agree the Agenda, or propose amendments;*
>
> (d)   *Seven days thereafter all solicitors shall use their best endeavours to agree the Agenda. Points of disagreement should be on matters of real substance and not semantics or on matters the experts could resolve of their own accord at the discussion. In default of agreement, both versions shall be considered at the discussions. Agendas, when used, shall be provided to the experts not less than 7 days before the date fixed for discussions.*
>
> *[Where it has been impossible to agree a single agenda, it is of assistance to the experts if the second agenda is consecutively numbered to the first, i.e. if the first agenda has 16 questions in it, the second agenda is numbered from 17 onwards]*

> *Experts give their own opinions to assist the court and should attend discussions on the basis that they have full authority to sign the joint statement. The experts should not require the authorisation of solicitor or counsel before signing a joint statement.*
>
> *[**Note:** This does not affect Rule 35.12 which provides that where experts reach agreement on an issue during their discussions, the agreement shall not bind the parties unless the parties expressly agree to be bound by the agreement]."*

The experts are not bound by the agenda and they can and should discuss whatever relevant issues they see fit within the scope of their duties. They should not feel obliged to reach a consensus where in truth they differ. They will not be complying with their duty to the court, however, if they ignore the agenda provided to them and thus fail to assist the court with the issues that have been identified as relevant. It can help if the agenda provides some basic information. If there is an agreed chronology then that should be provided. If there is an agreed set of medical notes paginated in the way that will be used at trial then that should be provided so that references in the joint statement can be easily followed at trial. It can help to set out a brief summary of the duties of experts under CPR, r. 35.10 and PD 35, as well as the requirements for discussions under CPR, r. 35.12 and any order in the case for the joint discussion and the joint statement. If there are a lot of documents and reports it can help to provide a list of documents that the experts ought to have for their discussion, highlighting the ones that are new since they last considered the case. It is alarming how often experts respond that they had not seen a document at the time of their discussion when a query is raised.

Where there is a dispute between factual witnesses then it is sometimes sensible to remind the experts that it is not their role as experts to resolve such a dispute, and that factual disputes are a matter for the trial judge. It may be helpful to the trial judge, however, if the experts identify the material facts upon which findings of fact need to be made and upon which their opinions are dependent.

Any questions to the experts should be related to the issues and asked for the purpose of progressing agreement. Questions such as "Do you agree the claimant is lying?", or "Do you agree that the defence will lose?" are not acceptable. The model direction used by the masters assigned to clinical negligence cases at the Royal Courts of Justice suggests that as far as possible the questions should be in a form capable of being answered "yes" or "no", but this is not always possible and can actually lead to confusion if experts feel restrained from adding the qualifications to their answers that they would otherwise wish to.

The discussions are between the experts and not between the legal advisers and the experts. It is not appropriate for legal advisers to participate, although the experts may agree that certain points should be checked with the legal advisers as part of their discussion. Legal advisers should not attend the discussion unless the parties and experts agree. This can be a contentious point and there have been cases where one party has feared that there will be an inequality of arms between experts in the discussions. In *H v. Lambeth, Southwark and Lewisham Health Authority*,[25] the Court of Appeal refused to allow legal advisers to attend the discussion even where there was a

---

25 TLR 8.10.2001.

fear that one expert was more experienced than the other and might overawe him. The model directions provide that:

> *"Unless otherwise ordered by the court, or unless agreed by all parties, including the experts, neither the parties nor their legal representatives may attend such discussions. If the legal representatives do attend, they should not normally intervene in the discussion, except to answer questions put to them by the experts or to advise on the law; and the experts may if they so wish hold part of their discussions in the absence of the legal representatives."*

One idea that was raised by Lady Justice Hale in the case of *H v. Lambeth, Southwark and Lewisham Health Authority*, which has excited some judicial interest, particularly in complex multi-party cases, is that a moderator should be appointed to chair the discussions. Although this may involve some additional cost, in cases where there are numerous experts to coordinate and to bring into the discussions, the appointment of a neutral chair may prove to be more efficient than leaving the experts to their own, sometimes rather disorganised, devices. In one unreported case a retired Circuit Judge was appointed as a moderator, and the appointment was regarded as a success. Recorders or accredited mediators may be suitable alternatives.

Denied attendance at discussions, legal advisers sometimes ask for discussions to be taped. This is not so that the discussions can be referred to at trial, as this is not allowed without agreement under CPR, r. 35.12, but so that the parties can understand what happened at the discussion and how any changes of opinion were brought about. The objections to taping, however, are similar to the attendance of legal advisers at the discussion. It does not really encourage candid discussion. It is also of limited use. What does a party do with the tape of without prejudice discussions if they do not like what they hear?

The real problem is that it can be very disappointing for a party if "their" experts fold at a joint discussion, ruining their case, without any proper explanation. A large number of complaints to the General Medical Council arise from dissatisfaction arising from a change of opinion. The model directions now provide that:

> *"If an expert radically alters his or her opinion, the joint statement should include a note or addendum by that expert explaining the change of opinion."*

Such a note should at least identify cases where the experts thought they were changing their opinion, and make experts consider the matter carefully before doing so. If they do change their opinion the note will at least provide the party with some explanation as to why. It may be that the joint statement has proceeded on a different factual basis than the basis that one expert was proceeding on at the time of an earlier report. This provision should help identify whether the experts really are changing opinions or whether in truth they are setting out different views dependent on the findings of fact made by the court.

There is nothing wrong with experts changing their opinions in discussions and the court is not attempting to prevent it, only to ensure that any change is real and is thought through. In *Transco Plc v. Griggs*,[26] both parties' medical experts changed their minds following discussions. To the Court of Appeal an expert's willingness to change

---

26 [2003] EWCA Civ 564.

his opinion in the light of discussion with others, and the evidence as it develops, was seen as a strength rather than a weakness.

Conversely experts should be careful not to allow the joint statement to become like partisan pleadings. In *Igloo Regeneration (General Partner) Ltd v. Powell Williams Partnership*[27] the trial judge was critical of the parties (and the experts) for allowing an exchange of five addendum reports followed by two joint statements, the second of which was described as *"essentially a running debate on numerous points which is almost like a long and partly repetitive pleading"*. Obvious though it might seem, the trial judge expressed how unsatisfactory it was that the experts on either side had fallen out with each other.

What if a party wants to instruct a new expert when an instructed expert, who was supportive on an issue, concedes the point in the joint statement? That was the case in *Guntrip v. Cheney Coaches Ltd*[28] in which Lewison LJ made the following observations:

"The expert's overriding duty applies not only to the preparation of an initial report, but also to the preparation and agreement of a joint statement with an expert advising an opposing party as well as, of course, to evidence given orally in court. If at any time the expert can no longer support the case of the person who instructed him, it is his duty to say so. Indeed, if the expert forms that view it is far better that he says so sooner rather than later before the litigation costs escalate. It is partly because an expert's overriding duty is to the court that the court discourages expert shopping, particularly where a party has had a free choice of expert and has put forward an expert report as part of his case. He must adduce good reason for changing expert. The mere fact that his chosen expert has modified or even changed his views is not enough. The expert may have had good reason for changing his views. He may have been confronted with additional evidence as in Singh v CJ O'Shea & Co Limited [2009] EWHC 1251 (QB). His opposite number may have pointed out flaws in his initial report, especially in cases where reports have been exchanged rather than served sequentially. It is not possible to lay down hard and fast rules. Even if permission to change expert is refused, it is always open to a party to put to the other side's expert in cross-examination, if he is called, points raised by his new expert."

10   MEDICAL LITERATURE AND EXPERTS' DECLARATIONS

Clinical negligence claims can turn into a battle between experts each relying on a bundle of literatures which may or may not even be in the public domain. It is only fair that early notice is given of the literature upon which any expert intends to rely. In *Breeze v. Ahmad,*[29] the Court of Appeal overturned a decision and sent it back for re-hearing where literature was referred to by an expert without notice to the claimant. In doing so the Court of Appeal approved the direction to be found in the model directions that:

"Any unpublished literature upon which any expert witness proposes to rely shall be served at the same time as service of his statement together with a list of published literature. Any supplementary literature upon which any expert witness proposes to rely shall be notified to all other parties at least one month before trial. No expert witness shall rely upon any publications that have not been disclosed in

---

27 [2013] EWHC 1718 (TCC).
28 [2012] EWCA Civ 392 at para. 17.
29 [2005] EWCA Civ 223.

> *accordance with this direction without leave of the trial judge on such terms as to costs as he deems fit."*

In *Toth v. Jarman*,[30] the Court of Appeal indicated that a party who wished to call an expert with a potential conflict of interest should disclose details of that conflict at as early a stage in the proceedings as possible and the expert should include the information in the report or the accompanying CV. Many experts include a declaration in their report that they have no conflict of interest, and the Court of Appeal suggested that the rules committee consider extending the requirement for an expert's declaration to cover such matters. In the meantime, it is clearly good practice to ensure that such matters are included in any report. The model directions deal with this as follows:

> *"Experts shall, at the time of producing their report, produce a CV giving details of any employment or activity which raises a possible conflict of interest."*

It should be noted again that PD 35 now states that the following should be included as the experts' declaration:

> *"I confirm that I have made clear which facts and matters referred to in this report are within my own knowledge and which are not. Those that are within my own knowledge I confirm to be true. The opinions I have expressed represent my true and complete professional opinions on the matters to which they refer."*

11 TRIAL

The model directions give some suggestions for preparation of bundles and arrangements for trial (see Appendix 2). It can help in the preparation of a trial to agree a timetable for the calling of witnesses and experts, though this will not be binding in the absence of an unusually draconian court order. It is common practice now to call all the factual witnesses for both parties and then to call the experts of each discipline "back to back". Thus, for example the claimant's obstetrician followed by the defendant's obstetrician, then the claimant's paediatrician followed by the defendant's paediatrician and so on. It does not follow, however, that the experts need only attend for the time when they are timetabled. Their opinions may depend on the factual evidence and so it can be crucial that they attend to hear the factual evidence as well as to assist the legal teams in identifying and exploring the medical issues. As the Court of Appeal in *Vernon v. Bosley (No. 2)*[31] pointed out, however, it is important that the experts do not, by association, lose their independence by becoming part of "the camp" with whom they sit at trial.

Since the Jackson reforms were introduced on 1st April 2013 the court has the power at any stage of the proceedings to direct that any of the experts from like disciplines shall give their evidence concurrently, a practice that has been dubbed "hot-tubbing" in Australia where it has been in use for a while. The relevant provisions in relation to "hot-tubbing" are contained in paras 11.1 to 11.4 of Practice Direction 35.

The most recent directions contain a precedent order that should be adopted and provided by e-mail to the Master at least 2 days before the hearing.

---

30 [2006] EWCA Civ 1028.
31 [1999] QB 18.

Chapter 12

ALTERNATIVE DISPUTE RESOLUTION

1   INTRODUCTION

The courts now encourage dispute resolution by a number of means other than through the normal trial process. Together these methods are referred to as Alternative Dispute Resolution, or ADR. CPR Part 1.4 requires the court to further the overriding objective by active case management, which includes, under para. (2)(e), encouraging the parties to use an ADR procedure if the court considers that appropriate, and facilitating the use of such procedure.

Since May 2000 the NHSLA has been requiring solicitors representing NHS bodies in such claims to offer mediation in appropriate cases, and to provide clear reasons to the authority if a case is considered inappropriate, and in March 2001 the Lord Chancellor gave an "ADR Pledge" on behalf of all public bodies that ADR would be considered and used by public bodies in all suitable cases wherever the other party accepts it.

ADR procedures include:

- without prejudice discussions;
- round table conferences;
- early neutral evaluation ("ENE");
- arbitration; and
- mediation with an independent mediator.

In the clinical negligence field the methods most commonly adopted are without prejudice discussions, which commonly involve a round table conference, and mediation, involving a neutral facilitator to help the parties find a resolution to their dispute.

The model direction used by the Masters at the RCJ assigned to clinical negligence cases provide:

"Alternative Dispute Resolution

25.   At all stages the parties must consider whether the case is capable of resolution by ADR. Any party refusing to engage in ADR by   2012 [a date usually about 3 months before the trial window opens] shall, not less than 28 days before the commencement of the trial, serve a witness statement, without prejudice save as to costs, giving reasons for that refusal. Such witness statement must not be shown to the trial judge until the question of costs arises.

26.   Such means of ADR as shall be adopted shall be concluded not less than 35 days prior to the trial.

['ADR' includes 'round table' conferences, at which the parties attempt to define and narrow the issues in the case, including those to which expert evidence is directed; early neutral evaluation; mediation; and arbitration. The object is to try to reduce the number of cases settled 'at the door of the Court', which are wasteful both of costs and judicial time.]"

This form of order was approved by the Court of Appeal in *Halsey v. Milton Keynes General NHS Trust*,[1] and is sometimes referred to as an "Ungley Order", after Master Ungley who first coined it at the RCJ. The full current model directions (2012) used by the Masters assigned to clinical negligence claims at the RCJ are set out in Appendix 2.

A useful text on the subject of ADR, the Judicial College's Jackson *ADR Handbook*, received endorsement from the Court of Appeal in the recent case of *PGF II SA v. OMFS Co 1 Ltd*.[2] Briggs LJ concluded at para. 30 that the advice given in the *ADR Handbook* (2013) was sound:

"The ADR Handbook , first published in 2013, after the period relevant to these proceedings, sets out at length in para 11.56 the steps which a party faced with a request to engage in ADR, but which believes that it has reasonable grounds for refusing to participate at that stage, should consider in order to avoid a costs sanction. The advice includes: (a) not ignoring an offer to engage in ADR; (b) responding promptly in writing, giving clear and full reasons why ADR is not appropriate at the stage, based if possible on the Halsey guidelines; (c) raising with the opposing party any shortage of information or evidence believed to be an obstacle to successful ADR, together with consideration of how that shortage might be overcome; (d) not closing off ADR of any kind, and for all time, in case some other method than that proposed, or ADR at some later date, might prove to be worth pursuing. That advice may fairly be summarised as calling for constructive engagement in ADR rather than flat rejection, or silence."

And at para. 34:

*"In my judgment, the time has now come for this court firmly to endorse the advice given in para 11.56 of the ADR Handbook, **that silence in the face of an invitation to participate in ADR is, as a general rule, of itself unreasonable, regardless whether an outright refusal, or a refusal to engage in the type of ADR requested, or to do so at the time requested, might have been justified by the identification of reasonable grounds.** I put this forward as a general rather than invariable rule because it is possible that there may be rare cases where ADR is so obviously inappropriate that to characterise silence as unreasonable would be pure formalism. There may also be cases where the failure to respond at all was a result of some mistake in the office, leading to a failure to appreciate that the invitation had been made, but in such cases the onus would lie squarely on the recipient of the invitation to make that explanation good."* (emphasis added)

The Court went on to clarify at para. 51 that a failure to engage with ADR did not automatically disentitle the successful party to claim all of its costs:

"a finding of unreasonable conduct constituted by a refusal to accept an invitation to participate in ADR or, which is more serious in my view, a refusal even to engage in discussion about ADR, produces no automatic results in terms of a costs

1 [2004] EWCA Civ 576.
2 *PGF II SA v. OMFS Co 1 Ltd* [2013] EWCA 1288.

penalty. It is simply an aspect of the parties' conduct which needs to be addressed in a wider balancing exercise. It is plain both from the Halsey case [2004] 1 WLR 3002, itself and from Arden LJ's reference to the wide discretion arising from such conduct in SG v Hewitt [2013] 1 All ER 1118, that the proper response in any particular case may range between the disallowing of the whole, or only a modest part of, the otherwise successful party's costs."

2 ADVANTAGES OF ADR

Getting all the clients and their legal advisers together to discuss settlement, whether at a mediation or a round table discussion, can create a momentum towards a settlement that is acceptable to all parties. The preparation for the meeting will have focussed all parties' attention on the case at the same time, and will have helped all parties to "buy in" to the idea of settlement and the opportunity to bring the dispute to an end. As with mediations, a round table meeting can speed up the process of offer and counter-offer that might otherwise require weeks or months of correspondence, over which time costs will be increasing.

3 PREPARING FOR ADR MEETINGS

It will be normally be part of a solicitor's duty to advise his client, and especially a lay client, of the nature of the process of mediation (or other ADR meeting) and of the status of any agreement reached as a result.[3]

In clinical negligence actions considerable thought needs to be given to the psychology of settlement meetings, in particular discussions involving the claimant. This is so whether the meeting is in the form of a mediation or a without prejudice meeting of the parties without outside facilitation. In cases of PTSD or other vulnerability the need for preparation of the client will be more obvious, but in all cases clients will need to be educated in preparation for a without prejudice discussion.

The nature of without prejudice confidentiality will need to be explained. The principle that what is said without prejudice cannot be referred to in court is important, but so too is the fact that what is said cannot be "unsaid" and that the other side may use it to colour their view of the case or to stimulate other enquiries that could result in admissible evidence.

Explanations of matters such as funding, Part 36 offers and payments, provisional damages and interest will need to be given. The costs implications of settling and not settling should also be discussed.

Clients may sometimes need to be prepared for the task of making a decision to end litigation. That can be daunting when, for example, what is being decided is the funding to enable someone to provide for the rest of their life.

In some cases this preparation can take place by meeting the client for an hour just before the meeting with the other side. In many cases, however, it is better to arrange a preliminary meeting with the client in advance of the date of the round table

---

3 *Frost v. Wade Smith & Tofields* [2013] EWCA 1960.

discussion. It may be possible to be more objective in setting agreed parameters for settlement, and in agreeing the negotiating strategy in a meeting when the other side are not sitting in another room waiting to talk to you.

Such a meeting allows clients to take in the information at their own pace without feeling under pressure, and to go away and prepare themselves, and often their family, for the prospect of settlement. The client will then arrive for the meeting having had less of a sleepless night through worry of the unknown, and will feel more in control of the process and able to make sensible decisions as a result; it is important to bear in mind that this may be just another meeting for the lawyers and insurers, but an important once in a lifetime occasion for the claimant.

Negotiation preparation should include matters such as whether you want to make an opening offer and what your opening position will be, as well as where you are prepared to end up by way of a settlement.

It is often sensible to include the claimant in part of the face-to-face meetings with the representatives of the defendant, be they the NHSLA or insurers. Clients should, in particular, be asked whether they wish to have a say at the meeting. If need be they can be given gentle encouragement and reassurance about having their say. They can then begin to think about what it is they do want to say. Some claimants can be very powerful advocates in their own cause if given the opportunity to speak direct to defendants at a mediation or round table meeting. They can talk about feelings and concerns that they will not get to talk about when giving evidence and it can have not only a dramatic effect on the views of opponents but also a cathartic effect for the client. It is also possible by this means to give the defendant's representatives an indication of the quality of the evidence likely to be given by the claimant at trial.

A well-managed round table meeting can provide both sides with a welcome sense of having "had their day" and their "say" without the need for a trial. If you feel that such a discussion would be useful but needs to be moderated by the presence of a neutral party, then that is one of the roles that a mediator can fulfil.

4 PRESENCE OF DOCTORS

It is unusual for the doctors whose treatment is being questioned to be invited to a without prejudice meeting, although they are more often parties to mediation, particularly if the mediation is early on in the process before the parties have become entrenched in litigation.

In *Naylor v. Preston AHA*[4] Sir John Donaldson, the then Master of the Rolls and the son of a gynaecologist, referred to there being a Duty of Candour on doctors:

> *"I personally think that in professional negligence cases, and in particular in medical negligence cases, there is a duty of candour resting upon the professional man. This is recognised by the legal profession in their ethical rules requiring their members to refer the client to other advisers if it appears that the client has a valid claim for negligence. This also appears to be recognised by the Medical Defence Union, whose view is that 'the patient is entitled to a prompt, sympathetic and*

---

4 [1987] 1 WLR 958.

above all truthful account of what has occurred' (Journal of the MDU 1086 page2). It was also the view (admittedly obiter) of myself and Lord Justice Mustill, as expressed in our judgment in Lee v. South West Thames Regional Health Authority [1985] 1 WLR 845.850. In this context I was disturbed to be told during the argument of the present appeals that the view was held in some quarters that whilst the duty of candid disclosure, to which we there referred, might give rise to a contractual implied term and so benefit private fee-paying patients, it did not translate into a legal or equitable right for the benefit of NHS patients. This I would entirely repudiate. In my judgment, still admittedly and regretfully obiter, it is but one aspect of the general duty of care, arising out of the patient–medical practitioner or hospital authority relationship and gives rise to rights both in contract and in tort."

The GMC recognises this duty in its code of Good Medical Practice (2013) for doctors:

"55. You must be open and honest with patients if things go wrong. If a patient under your care has suffered harm or distress, you should:

a   put matters right (if that is possible)

b.   offer an apology

c.   explain fully and promptly what has happened and the likely short-term and long-term effects.

...

61. You must respond promptly, fully and honestly to complaints and apologise when appropriate. You must not allow a patient's complaint to adversely affect the care or treatment you provide or arrange."

The giving of an open and honest explanation at a round table meeting or a mediation can help both parties.

5   TIMING

The timing of both mediations and round table meetings can be important. The model directions for clinical negligence actions developed by the Queen's Bench Assigned Masters at the Royal Courts of Justice suggest that consideration should be given to ADR about 3 months before the start of the trial window. In some cases there may be a benefit in holding a round table conference earlier, as the prospects for settlement may be improved if the parties have not yet incurred large costs that could be saved by an early settlement.

Where liability is the real issue it may be sensible to hold a meeting once the evidence, including expert evidence on liability is disclosed. Where quantum is the real issue the point may come after exchange of schedules and counter-schedules. There can be real benefit in holding a meeting before the parties' positions have become entrenched by Part 36 offers.

6   ROUND TABLE CONFERENCES

Without prejudice discussions can vary from a quick telephone call, or chat outside the Case Management Conference (CMC), to a formal round table conference of all the parties arranged as part of the timetable to try and reach a compromise of the action.

Because there is no standard format for a round table conference it is important for the parties at the beginning of the meeting to be clear as to what form it will take. Confidentiality should be expressly stated and agreed, particularly if any potential witnesses in the case are present, together with the anticipated format and timetable for the meeting. The process can benefit from adopting many of the practices of a mediation, discussed below.

7   EARLY NEUTRAL EVALUATION

Early neutral evaluation (ENE) allows the parties to obtain a non-binding assessment of the merits of the case to assist them with their own risk assessment, permitting them to test the strength of their own view of the case in a non-binding way. The parties will agree the joint instruction of a neutral experienced counsel or solicitor to review the papers and express a non-binding opinion. If they wish to avoid the time and expense of a trial then the parties can agree that the opinion to be obtained will be binding.

The evaluator does not act as a judge but gives the parties an informed assessment of the likely view of a judge on the materials made available to him or her. But while a judge is constrained to decide the facts and apply the law, the evaluator can suggest solutions beyond the scope of the judicial process. The neutral evaluator can give an opinion on the likely result, which may be attractive to one of the parties, while suggesting a practical solution that may be more attractive to both. In addition to advising on the likely result of the dispute if litigated, an evaluator can suggest solutions that involve apologies, or undertakings as to future treatment or care, or provision for future employment, in a way that would not be available if the matter proceeded to litigation.

8   MEDIATION

8.1   What is Mediation?

Mediation means using an independent person, the mediator, to facilitate the process of resolving a dispute. The mediator does not act as a judge to determine the dispute nor make rulings, but assists the parties to explore the strengths and weaknesses of their cases and tries to find if there is a point at which the parties' needs and expectations can be brought together to form a settlement. In some cases a mediator will not be necessary and the parties will be able to reach agreement without independent help, but where that has not happened then experience shows that mediation does work.

CEDR, the Centre for Effective Dispute Resolution, one of the early providers of mediation services in the UK originally defined mediation as:

> *"A voluntary, non-binding, private dispute resolution process in which a neutral person helps the parties try to reach a negotiated settlement."*

In 2004, however, in the face of growing judicial pressure to encourage mediation, it revised its definition to read:

"Mediation is a flexible process conducted confidentially in which a neutral person actively assists parties in working towards a negotiated agreement of a dispute or difference, with the parties in ultimate control of the decision to settle and the terms of resolution."

On 22nd October 2004 the European Commission adopted a proposal for a new EU Directive to require member states to promote and encourage mediation, within an effective and fair legal system, as a means of dispute resolution. The European Commission identified that mediation offers a quicker, simpler and more cost-efficient way to solve disputes. It also identified that mediation allows for a wider range of interests of the parties to be taken into account, with a greater chance of reaching an agreement that will be voluntarily respected, whilst preserving a sustainable relationship where appropriate. The Commission believed that mediation holds *"an untapped potential as a dispute resolution method and as a means of providing access to justice for individuals and business"*. The UK is sufficiently advanced in its adoption of mediation that it would already be compliant with the proposed directive.

Mediation provides a quick, confidential and relatively cost effective way of resolving disputes without trial, where the parties remain in control of the process and where issues can be addressed that are outside the narrow scope of litigation. Thus matters such as apologies or undertakings as to future treatment or care provision can feature in mediation in a way that litigation cannot handle. These are matters that may be peripheral in the litigation process but can be of fundamental importance to a party, and if addressed can assist the process of settlement.

8.2   When to use Mediation

8.2.1   Types of dispute

Mediation can be used to settle any kind of dispute. Litigation does not even have to have been started. The more complex a dispute the more appropriate it is for mediation, as mediation can be a way of cutting through the web of issues to find an acceptable outcome that reflects the litigation risks. It can provide litigants with a feeling of closure, without risk of appeal, but also a feeling that they have "had their day" and "their say" without the cost, and risks, of trial.

Mediation has proved particularly fruitful in multi-party cases. In multi-defendant cases it can allow defendants to negotiate with each other with the claimant on hand to consider any joint approach that may result.

8.2.2 Timing

The timing of a mediation in the case management process can be important. An early mediation may fail if the parties are not in a proper position to assess the strengths and weaknesses of each other's cases. That point should be reached once exchange of witness statements, experts' reports and schedules has taken place. By then, however, a considerable amount of the cost that the process is intended to save will have been incurred. Finding the right time will depend on the particular circumstances of each case and the nature of the real issues between the parties.

In order to make the process work at an early stage parties may need to be prepared to make early disclosure of evidence to the other side. The model directions for clinical negligence actions developed by the Queen's Bench Assigned Masters at the Royal Courts of Justice suggest that consideration should be given to ADR about 3 months before the start of the trial window. In some cases there may be a benefit in holding a mediation earlier, as the prospects for settlement may be improved if the parties have not yet incurred large costs that could be saved by an early settlement.

Where liability is the real issue it may be sensible to hold a mediation once the evidence, including expert evidence on liability is disclosed. Where quantum is a real issue the point may come after exchange of schedules and counter-schedules. There can be real benefit in holding a mediation before the parties' positions have become entrenched by Part 36 offers or payments into court. In some cases the parties agree to hold a round table conference first but as a default position to hold a mediation if that conference has not produced a settlement.

8.3 Agreeing a Format

Before a mediation starts the parties enter into a mediation agreement. The agreement confirms that the parties have authority to settle their claims and that they will keep the discussions private and confidential, the whole process being without prejudice to any court proceedings unless and until agreement is reached, just like a without prejudice meeting between the parties.

Confidentiality is an important part of the process of mediation, so that parties can feel free to talk and to explore ideas for settlement. If need be the courts will enforce the duty of confidentiality by injunctive relief, as in *Venture Investment Placement Ltd v. Hall*,[5] in which HHJ Reid QC, sitting as a deputy judge of the Chancery Division, granted an injunction restraining a party from referring to any part of the discussions that took place during the mediation process, where that party had allegedly made statements to others concerning the mediation discussions.

A normal mediation will last a day. Some court sponsored schemes provide "short form" mediations that last 2 to 3 hours and are targeted at resolving smaller disputes by bringing the parties together before they meet at the door of the court for trial. A short form mediation does not permit the parties to explore issues in depth in the way that can be achieved in a whole day mediation. Given the cost that parties will incur to prepare for a mediation, it can often be a better investment to pay for a commercially provided mediator to devote more time to the dispute.

8.4 How to Set Up a Mediation

To set up a mediation the parties can go to one of the organisations offering mediators, such as CEDR, ADR Group, or In Place of Strife. Alternatively the parties can go direct to a mediator and book him or her, just as if booked as counsel for a court hearing.

Some mediation providers have taken the view in the past that what a mediator needs is mediation skills, rather than detailed expertise in the area of the dispute. Some mediators are so skilled and experienced that they can mediate a dispute in any area, but that should not be taken for granted. Some research should be undertaken into the background of proffered mediators to gauge their suitability. A thorough understanding of clinical negligence work will assist a mediator to bring the parties to

---

5 LTL 16/2/2005.

a settlement. The main mediator providers are increasingly appreciating that such specialism is what the market for mediators wants, and are reacting to market pressure by offering suitable personnel as mediators.

A suite of rooms is needed for the mediation (normally it helps to have at least three rooms, or one per party plus one large enough to hold all parties). Either the parties can make an arrangement to host the mediation, or if that is a problem then arrangements can be made with the mediator to find a convenient location. Hiring of space, whether via a mediation provider or direct, can work out to be a significant expense. If you do not have the facilities it is worth exploring options with all solicitors and counsel in the case, or with the parties. Bear in mind, however, that you may be in the rooms for quite some time and it is worth finding rooms that the parties can feel comfortable in.

The mediator will need to be provided with some background information about the dispute. Normally the equivalent of a CMC bundle will suffice. The parties will often be asked to provide brief written summaries of the case and of their positions to help the mediator and also to help focus discussions. These may be private briefings to the mediator, or exchanged with the other parties, or a combination of the two, as agreed between the parties and the mediator.

The mediator will normally hold telephone discussions with each side before the day fixed for the mediation in order to agree practical arrangements and also to begin understanding what the dispute is really about.

A schedule of costs to date and of prospective costs to trial should be prepared. This is for the purpose of assessing litigation risks and in case there is an opportunity to negotiate a costs inclusive deal. Sometimes the mediator will have asked for this information in advance. If not then the mediator is likely to ask for it on the day.

8.5 Costs of a Mediation

The parties need to agree the mediator's fees before the mediation. The fee will normally be a fixed fee to include the day set aside for the mediation and any reasonable pre-reading and liaison with the parties. An hourly rate may be agreed for any additional work. Ordinarily either one party agrees to pay the mediator's fees or they are divided equally between the parties and then can be the subject of costs recovery as costs in the case as appropriate (just like the costs of a without prejudice meeting), unless the parties agree otherwise. A typical costs provision in a mediation agreement would be:

> *"The parties agree to pay their own costs of the mediation unless otherwise agreed."*

The previous CEDR form of agreement was ambiguous as to this,[6] but it has now been clarified and brought into line with general practice. It is worth checking the costs provision, however, and making sure that it is clear. In order to ensure that it is clear that the costs of the mediation can be recovered as costs in the litigation it is advisable to use a form of wording such as:

---

6 *Nat West Bank v. Feeney*, SCCO No. 9 of 2007, 14th May 2007.

> *"The parties agree to pay their own costs of the mediation and those costs and the costs of the Mediator shall be costs in the case of the proceedings unless otherwise agreed."*

In general courts would regard as unreasonable a refusal to mediate save on terms that each party pays their own costs of the mediation in any event, particularly where there was an inequality of bargaining positions by reason of funding differences.

To ensure that costs are recoverable on an assessment it is advisable to consider the terms of the confidentiality clause in the mediation agreement, for example by adding the words below in square brackets:

> *"No party to this mediation shall make any reference to this mediation in court proceedings [save for the purposes of any assessment of costs or as ordered by the court]."*

8.6   On the Day

On the day of a mediation the mediator will usually meet the parties separately and finalise the agreement and any questions about the process that have not been sorted out in advance. The mediator will normally then start with a joint session in which each party will be invited to make a brief opening statement of their position for 5 or 10 minutes. The mediator will then hold private discussions with each party separately to explore each party's position before engaging in some shuttle diplomacy to explore the room for settlement. That process may go on until agreement is reached or the attempt is abandoned, but where the mediator thinks it appropriate the parties and their representatives may be brought back together to address issues with each other, or just the lawyers, or the clients, or the funders may be put together for discussions as the mediator thinks might best assist the process.

A mediator may well want to ask questions about the issues in the case, and to test whether the parties have given due consideration to them, but it is not the role of the mediator to go into the detail of a case in the manner in which it would be explored at trial. The mediator does not come to conclusions on the issues in the case and it is important to prepare clients for this approach in case they feel that the mediator is ignoring their case. The mediator's view of the issues will be far broader than a trial judge's and it is not the mediator who produces the settlement.

The mediator is there to help the parties come to their own settlement. It is the parties' dispute and it must be the parties' settlement. It is this aspect that is one of the benefits of mediation as it leaves the parties in control of the dispute whilst allowing the mediator to guide the process of settlement.

Standard learning has it that mediations begin with an opening phase where the process is established and then move on to an evaluation phase where the issues are explored and discussed, either in joint sessions or in private sessions with the mediator. Then comes a negotiation phase, often with the mediator operating a sort of shuttle diplomacy. Then finally comes a conclusion phase, when the parties are brought to an agreement and the terms are worked out and set down in writing. In truth these phases are not fixed periods and a mediation can ebb and flow with phases of evaluation interspersing phases of negotiation. One of the roles of a mediator is to keep this process going where otherwise the parties on their own would call it a day and give up.

If agreement is reached at the mediation then it will be set out in writing. The mediation agreement will normally provide that no agreement will be binding until it is in writing and signed by or on behalf of the parties. This is a sensible basis on which to agree to proceed in any form of ADR meeting. It allows parties to raise settlement proposals for discussion knowing that they will not be committed until an agreement is signed. The parties will be encouraged to draft the agreement themselves but the mediator will assist in the process.

Even if a dispute does not settle within the time set for the mediation, the mediator will normally follow up the dispute in the subsequent days to see if any outstanding matters can be agreed and a resolution reached to end the dispute. Experience indicates that many cases settle soon after the mediation.

8.7   Refusal to Mediate: Adverse Costs Orders

In February 2002 the Court of Appeal refused a successful defendant its costs because it had rejected mediation, despite being encouraged to mediate by the single Lord Justice who granted the claimant permission to appeal to the Court of Appeal. In giving judgment in *Dunnett v. Railtrack plc,*[7] Brooke LJ said:

> *"Skilled mediators are now able to achieve results satisfactory to both parties in many cases which are quite beyond the power of lawyers and courts to achieve. This court has knowledge of cases where intense feelings have arisen, for instance in relation to clinical negligence claims. But when the parties are brought together on neutral soil with a skilled mediator to help them resolve their differences, it may very well be that the mediator is able to achieve a result by which the parties shake hands at the end and feel that they had gone away having settled the dispute on terms with which they are happy to live. A mediator may be able to provide solutions which are beyond the powers of the court to provide."*

The decision in *Dunnett v. Railtrack plc* prompted an increase in the number of mediations for fear that an adverse costs order would be made against even a successful party if mediation was refused. The argument in favour of an adverse costs order against the party refusing mediation appeared even stronger in the case of public bodies who are subject to the ADR Pledge described above.

In May 2004, however, the Court of Appeal in *Halsey v. Milton Keynes General NHS Trust,*[8] reaffirmed the principle that a successful party would only normally be deprived of its costs for refusing mediation where the refusal was unreasonable. They held that the court had no power to compel parties to undertake mediation and that to require parties to mediate rather than litigate would be in breach of Article 6 of the European Convention on Human Rights. The court could, and should, encourage mediation, and unreasonable conduct in refusing to mediate could be reflected in an adverse costs order. The burden was on the unsuccessful party to show that the successful party had been acting unreasonably in refusing ADR:

---

7 [2002] 1 WLR 2434.
8 [2004] EWCA Civ 576.

"The burden should not be on the refusing party to satisfy the court that mediation had no reasonable prospect of success. As we have already stated, the fundamental question is whether it has been shown by the unsuccessful party that the successful party unreasonably refused to agree to mediation. The question whether there was a reasonable prospect that a mediation would have been successful is but one of a number of potentially relevant factors which may need to be considered in determining the answer to that fundamental question. Since the burden of proving an unreasonable refusal is on the unsuccessful party, we see no reason why the burden of proof should lie on the successful party to show that mediation did not have any reasonable prospect of success. In most cases it would not be possible for the successful party to prove that a mediation had no reasonable prospect of success. In our judgement, it would not be right to stigmatise as unreasonable a refusal by the successful party to agree to a mediation unless he showed that a mediation had no reasonable prospect of success. That would be to tip the scales too heavily against the right of the successful party to refuse a mediation and insist on an adjudication of the dispute by the court. It seems to us that a fairer balance is strike if the burden is placed on the unsuccessful party to show that there was a reasonable prospect that mediation would have been successful. This is not an unduly onerous burden to discharge: he does not have to prove that a mediation would in fact have succeeded. It is significantly easier for the unsuccessful party to prove that there was a reasonable prospect that a mediation would have succeeded than for the successful party to prove the contrary."

After *Halsey* some assumed that they no longer needed to bother about mediation or ADR. That is not the case. Parties have to behave reasonably against a background in which it is no longer considered reasonable to turn a blind eye to the benefits of mediation. In *Burchell v. Bullard*[9] Lord Justice Ward said:

"Halsey has made plain not only the high rate of a successful outcome being achieved by mediation but also its established importance as a track to a just result running parallel with that of the court system. Both have a proper part to play in the administration of justice. The court has given its stamp of approval to mediation and it is now the legal profession which must become fully aware of and acknowledge its value. The profession can no longer with impunity shrug aside reasonable requests to mediate. The parties cannot ignore a proper request to mediate simply because it was made before the claim was issued. With court fees escalating it may be folly to do so. I draw attention, moreover, to para 5.4 of the pre-action protocol for Construction and Engineering Disputes – which I doubt was at the forefront of the parties' minds – which expressly requires the parties to consider at a pre-action meeting whether some form of alternative dispute resolution procedure would be more suitable than litigation. These Defendants have escaped the imposition of a costs sanction in this case but Defendants in a like position in the future can expect little sympathy if they blithely battle on regardless of the alternatives."

As a general rule, silence in the face of an invitation to join in ADR will be treated as unreasonable conduct which will be reflected in costs.[10] In *Christian v. The Commissioner of Police for the Metropolis*,[11] Turner J reduced the wholly successful defendant's bill of costs by a third. The defendant had failed to give a full response in accordance with the Pre-Action Protocol and ignored numerous suggestions that the matter go to ADR or a settlement meeting. Although the defendant had been successful it was not possible to

---

9 [2005] EWCA Civ 358.
10 *PGF II SA v. OMFS Co 1 Ltd* [2013] EWCA 1288.
11 [2015] EWHC 371 (QB).

conclude that ADR would have useless. The defendant had failed without adequate (or adequately articulated) justification to engage in ADR which had a reasonable prospect of success. The appropriate response was to reduce the defendant's costs by a third. This case is a good example of the principles in *Halsey* put into practice together with the exercise of the court's discretion generally as to costs. A party who agrees to mediate but then takes an unreasonable position in the mediation has been held to be in the same position as a party who unreasonably refuses to mediate,[12] although the confidential nature of the process may in practice make it impossible to bring such conduct before the court.

8.8   Arbitration as an Alternative to Court Proceedings

It has long been the case that in building, shipping and some forms of commercial disputes, arbitration has been the preferred method of resolution. The advantages are perceived as lower cost, a faster process, greater procedural flexibility, and access to arbitrators who are experts in their field. These considerations allied to significant increases in court fees, the delays caused by the introduction of CCMCs, the failure to recruit more Masters to the Queen's Bench Division, the tightening of procedural rules and the amendments to the overriding objective have resulted in a newly established arbitration service designed to deal with higher value clinical negligence and personal injury claims known as the Personal Injury Claims Arbitration Service (PIcARB).[13] The service is available throughout England and Wales. The arbitrations are dealt with pursuant to the Arbitration Act 1996, early neutral evaluation is said to encourage earlier resolution of issues. The system avoids the need for court fees (though there is a modest commencement fee) and seeks to minimise expense by adopting an online e-filing service. The procedural rules adopted are the CPR but said to exclude the requirement for cost budgeting, the more draconian strike out provisions pursuant to *Mitchell* and the more recent amendments to the overriding objective. A panel of 14 personal injury and clinical negligence silks are available to conduct arbitrations which includes all interlocutory applications as well as trial. Costs normally follow the event. If a defendant wins he will recover costs capped at 80% of the value of the claim (partial QOCS). The scope for appeals is limited to errors of law or procedure pursuant to the 1996 Act. It remains to be seen what the take up of this service will be. However, the current backlog for obtaining court hearings for any purpose and the costs of litigating through the court system may incentivise some claimants and defendants to adopt this method of dispute resolution.

---

12 *Malmesbury v. Strutt & Parker* [2008] EWHC 424.
13 www.PIcARBS.co.uk.

Chapter 13

GROUP ACTIONS

1 INTRODUCTION

Mass production and mass consumption in the second half of the 20th century brought about a situation in which a single defective product or service might injure ever-increasing numbers of people. This phenomenon was not limited to the pharmaceutical industry but litigation over pharmaceutical products brought into sharp focus the deficiencies in manner in which courts were able to deal with multi-party claims. In England and Wales there was no procedural system for regulating class actions such as existed at federal and state level in the US and in several Commonwealth countries. Large scale cases were managed on an ad hoc basis using a variety of tools, such as the existing rules for representative actions, the selection of test cases and consolidation of numerous claims. In 1992, in the course of the Opren litigation, the Court of Appeal indicated that there might be a strong case for legislation to provide a jurisdictional structure for the collation and resolution of mass product liability claims.[1] That call was heeded when the Woolf Inquiry on civil justice reform turned to look at multi-party actions in the second phase of the Inquiry which considered types of litigation causing particular problems for the civil justice system. The Inquiry did so against the background of the benzodiazepine litigation in which 13,500 legal aid certificates were issued at a cost of over £28m and 5,000 sets of proceedings were started but no claimant was successful.[2] Unsurprisingly, Lord Woolf considered that the problems of cost and delay which the Inquiry had already identified were magnified in the context of group actions.

The Final Access to Justice Report in July 1996 pointed to the difficulty of using existing procedures and the disproportionate cost of multi-party actions. It also recorded the dissatisfaction of judges, practitioners and consumer representatives with the existing system. The Report recommended new procedures, designed to achieve the following objectives:

(i)   provide access to justice where large numbers of people have been affected by another's conduct, but individual loss is so small that it makes an individual action economically unviable;

(ii)   provide expeditious, effective and proportionate methods of resolving cases, where individual damages are large enough to justify individual action but where the number of claimants and the nature of the issues involved mean that the cases cannot be managed satisfactorily in accordance with normal procedure;

(iii)   achieve a balance between the normal rights of claimants and defendants, to pursue and defend cases individually, and the interests of a group of parties to litigate the action as a whole in an effective manner.

---

1 *Nash & Ors v. Eli Lilly & Co & Ors* [1993] 1 WLR 782 at 810.
2 Lord Chancellor's Department, *Hansard*, 16th February 1995.

Those recommendations led to the introduction in May 2000 of an amendment to CPR Part 19 and an accompanying practice direction dealing with group litigation.

2 GROUP LITIGATION ORDERS

CPR, r. 19.10 brought into existence the Group Litigation Order (GLO), which it defined as an order made under r. 19.11 to provide for the case management of claims which give rise to common or related issues of fact or law (the "GLO issues"). This was a departure from the concept of representative proceedings, in which the interests of the individual claimants had to be the same.[3]

Under r. 19.11 the court may make a GLO where there are or are likely to be a number of claims giving rise to the GLO issues. No attempt has been made to specify a minimum number of claims in respect of which a GLO might be made.

A list of all GLOs is kept in the office of the Senior Master of the Queen's Bench Division and is published on the Court Service website (www.justice.gov.uk/courts/rcj-rolls-building/queens-bench/group-litigation-orders). In addition the Law Society maintains an information service for multi-party actions, which includes details of the lead solicitors in the action.

From the list on the Court Service website, it can be seen that GLOs are made comparatively infrequently. As at December 2014 there were 85 recorded GLOs. Of these, seven were product liability claims in the medical field (drugs, hip replacements, breast implants, etc.) and four related to clinical negligence or wrongdoing (organ retention and treatment by a psychiatrist). Perusal of the list reveals immediately that the system has not worked to record all GLOs or at least to place them on the website. Neither the claims involving Rodney Ledward (gynaecologist) nor those brought against Melvyn Megitt (orthodontist), all of which were subject to GLOs, appear on the list. Doubtless there are other GLOs that have not been recorded.

3 APPLICATION FOR A GLO

A GLO can be applied for on behalf of claimants or a defendant or the court itself can make a GLO of its own initiative.[4] The application, which must be made in accordance with CPR Part 23, may be made either before or after the issue of any relevant individual claims.[5]

Before applying for a GLO, the Practice Direction suggests that the Law Society's service should be consulted by the solicitor acting for the proposed applicant.[6] Any solicitor acting for a claimant should consider seeking further information through groups such as AvMA or APIL. The Practice Direction also suggests that the claimants' solicitors might form a Solicitors' Group and choose one firm to take the lead in applying for the GLO. The need for the role of lead solicitor to be defined carefully in writing is emphasised. Although couched in advisory terms, it is difficult to see how a

---

3 CPR, r. 19.6.
4 CPR PD 19B, para. 4.
5 CPR PD 19B, para. 3.1.
6 CPR PD 19B, para. 2.1. See also the Queen's Bench Guide, para. 12.9.2.

group litigation could sensibly be run without a lead solicitor and that solicitor should therefore be chosen as early as possible.

Paragraph 2.3 of the Practice Direction requires the applicant to consider whether some other order might be preferable to a GLO. In particular, the applicant needs to consider whether the claims should be consolidated or whether the claim should be brought as a representative claim. The importance of consideration of alternative means of resolution is emphasised by the decision in *Hobson*, below.

Having overcome these hurdles and decided to apply for a GLO, the application has to be made to the correct court. For the QBD in London, this means the Senior Master. For the High Court outside London, the application is to the Presiding Judge of the circuit in which the relevant District Registry is situated. In the county court, the application must be made to the Designated Civil Judge for the relevant area. When applying, the applicant should request that the application be placed before the appropriate judge as soon as possible. This enables the judge to consider referring the application to the President of the QBD or Head of Civil Justice prior to the hearing of the application for the GLO.

The Practice Direction, para. 3.2, contains the detailed requirements for the contents of the application or the evidence in support of it, as follows:

(i)   a summary of the nature of the litigation;
(ii)   the number and nature of claims already issued;
(iii)   the number of parties likely to be involved;
(iv)   the GLO issues that are likely to arise in the litigation; and
(v)   whether there are any matters that distinguish smaller groups of claims within the wider group.

A GLO cannot be made in the Queen's Bench Division without the consent of the President of the QBD and in the county court requires the consent of the Head of Civil Justice.[7] If the court is minded to make the GLO, either before or after the hearing of the application, it will send to the President of the QBD or Head of Civil Justice a copy of the application notice, any relevant written evidence and a written statement as to why a GLO is considered desirable.[8]

Apart from those restrictions, the discretion is a broad one, but the court will be keen to see that the benefits to be derived from a GLO are likely to outweigh the extra costs which the GLO will tend to bring and that the GLO is really required. A GLO can also be used to assemble a series of cases which are relatively low in value but in which one achieves economies of scale. For example, the Poly Implant Prothèses (PIP) breast implant litigation, the claims have a modest value as individual personal injury claims but when there are potentially thousands of cases there are costs savings to be made.[9] A GLO thus also provides the benefit to claimants that where their case may be difficult to bring in isolation, it is not so if the case is one of tens or hundreds.

If the existing directions are adequate to deal with a series of cases a GLO may not be granted. Thus in *Smyth v. Bryn Alyn Community (Holdings) Ltd*[10] an attempt by non-lead

---

7 CPR PD 19B, para. 3.3.
8 CPR PD 19B, para. 3.4.
9 J Robins, Group Litigation orders – *"unity is strength"*, LexisNexis Personal Injury, Autumn 2014.
10 LTL 8.5.03, Stanley Burnton J, QBD.

claimants in the third tranche of the North Wales Children's Homes Litigation to obtain a GLO in respect of their claims was refused. The litigation had proceeded under a practice direction from the Lord Chief Justice. The first two tranches had been disposed of and the lead cases in the third tranche had been tried but were subject to appeal. The claimants argued that a GLO was required in order to facilitate third party disclosure and the timetabling of future trials. Both the Senior Master and, on appeal, the judge disagreed. The existing structure under the practice direction was adequate and a GLO could not be justified.

There was another failed application for a GLO in *Hobson & ors v. Ashton Morton Slack*,[11] where claimants brought claims against several firms of solicitors, a union and a claims handler in respect of deductions made from awards under the coal miners' COPD and VWF claims handling agreements. The claimants struggled to show a sufficient degree of affinity between the claims against the various defendants and had to accept that the cases were highly fact-sensitive. It was accordingly difficult to formulate precise GLO issues.[12] In addition, the judge was highly critical of the failure to give any serious thought to alternative means of adjudicating on the claims. He thought that at most two or three test cases would have resolved the legal issue at the heart of the dispute. He also expressed concern over funding. No consideration had been given to public funding and the claimants had instead been signed up on CFAs with a group ATE policy.[13] The situation was compounded by a lack of certainty as to the sufficiency of the ATE policy and its enforceability. Finally, the judge held that there was a gross imbalance between the likely costs and the sums to be recovered: claimants' estimated total costs of £350,000 plus the ATE premium of £472,500; damages in the region of £25,000. The GLO had to be rejected on any costs benefit approach.

In *Anslow v. Norton Aluminium Ltd*[14] the defendant opposed the making of a GLO in relation to claims for public nuisance arising out of the defendant's operation of an aluminium manufacturing plant. In addition to arguments relating to the merits of the claims, the communality of interest of the claimants and general cost-effectiveness, the defendant argued that a GLO would adversely affect its reputation and would encourage further litigation against it. These arguments all failed, the court pointing out that the defendant's reputation would be affected by the claims whether or not they were labelled as a GLO. The court did however give permission for the defendant to revisit the issue after service of the claimants' statements.

In the recent case of *Various v. Barking, Havering & Redbridge University Hospitals NHS Trust*15 there was an application for a GLO where there was not a unity of clinical issue. The claimant lawyers argued on behalf of patients that there were concerns about the unit due to a diverse set of claims in different areas of clinical practice rather than one discrete area. What the cases reflected in unity was not a single category of claim, therefore, but rather an absence of an appropriate risk avoidance culture. On that basis a GLO was not granted.

---

11 [2006] EWHC 1134 (QB), per Sir Michael Turner.
12 See also *Tew v. BOS (Shared Appreciation Mortgages) No. 1 Plc* [2010] EWHC 203 (Ch), where the key issue of fairness under the Unfair Terms in Consumer Contracts Regulations required consideration of the circumstances of individual claimants. Whilst the fairness issues could not therefore be framed as a GLO issue, it was appropriate to order a GLO and to deal with questions of fairness by taking lead cases within the GLO.
13 The judge noted in passing that the Legal Services Commission's Funding Code expressed a strong preference for using a test case approach to multi-party claims, which it considered to be the most cost-effective option.
14 Lawtel 28.9.10, per Flaux J, QBD.
15 (2014) (QB), 21 May 2014.

The *Hobson* case illustrates one real disadvantage of GLOs – the frontloading of costs. There is a risk that very large sums of money are spent determining the criteria for membership of the group and whether individuals might meet those criteria. Large numbers of individual claims would need to be issued, supported by medical evidence, and it might only be at the end of that process that it could be said for certain whether an individual case raised a GLO issue.[16] It is notable that in the *Hobson* case the claimants were put to the expense of formulating generic particulars of claim prior to the full hearing of the application for the GLO so that the ambit of the GLO issues could be considered. In some cases the initial costs might be reduced by reducing the claim form to the simplest of documents bearing the briefest of details.[17] Given the requirement for medical evidence, it is difficult to see how this could sensibly be done for clinical negligence claims.

The GLO issues identified at the time of the application for a GLO will almost certainly require refinement and variation as the litigation proceeds. However, as the result in *Hobson* makes clear, the process of attempting to define the GLO issues at the outset may well indicate the suitability of the litigation for a GLO. If it becomes apparent that the issues raised are factual and disparate and raise different considerations in relation to different defendants, it may be that attempting to establish a group litigation will merely waste time and money. It should also be noted that the court may wish to keep the suitability of a GLO under review. Thus in *Anslow v. Norton Aluminium Ltd* the defendant, which had unsuccessfully resisted the making of a GLO, was given liberty to apply after service of the claimant's individual statements if it could show that a GLO was not after all appropriate.

After a GLO has been made, a copy of the GLO should be supplied to the Law Society and to the Senior Master of the Queen's Bench Division.[18] The Rules are not specific as to whose job this is. Normally it would fall to the lead solicitor.

4 CONTENTS OF A GLO

The GLO should follow the form of PF19, adapted as necessary. In the High Court, the parties are encouraged to submit a draft of the order to the Senior Master prior to the hearing to ensure that all necessary provisions have been included.

The GLO must:

(i)   contain directions about the establishment of a Group Register on which the claims managed under the GLO will be entered;

(ii)   specify the GLO issues which will identify the claims to be managed as a group under the GLO;

(iii)   specify the court (the "management court") which will manage the claims on the Group Register.[19]

In addition the GLO may:

---

16 See the observations of Keith J in the MMR/MR litigation, *Sayers v. Smithkline Beecham plc* [2006] EWHC 3179 (QB) at para. 3.
17 See Lord Woolf in *Boake Allen Ltd & ors v. HMRC* [2007] 1 WLR 1386 at paras 30-33.
18 CPR PD 19B, para. 11. Their addresses are given in the Practice Direction as, respectively, 113 Chancery Lane, London WC2A 1PL and Royal Court of Justice, Strand, London WC2A 2LL.
19 Rule 19.11(2).

(i)   in relation to claims raising one or more GLO issue, direct their transfer to the management court, order their stay until further order and direct their entry onto the Group Register;

(ii)   direct that from a specified date claims which raise one or more GLO issue should be started in the management court and entered onto the Group Register;

(iii)   give directions for publicising the GLO.[20]

Once the GLO has been made and subject to the management court's power to order to the contrary, every claim entered on the Group Register will be automatically allocated or re-allocated to the multi-track.[21] Further, any case management directions given in any case entered on the Group Register otherwise than by the management court are set aside and any hearing date fixed otherwise than for the purposes of the group litigation will be vacated.[22]

As soon as is possible after the making of the GLO, a managing judge will be appointed, who will assume overall responsibility for the management of the claims and will generally hear the GLO issues.[23] The managing judge may be assisted by a master or district judge who might be appointed to deal with procedural matters. A costs judge might also be invited to attend case management hearings.

Specific provision is made for case management directions to be given by the management court.[24] Such directions might include directions:

(i)   varying the GLO issues;

(ii)   providing for one or more claims on the group register to proceed as test claims;

(iii)   appointing the solicitor to one or more parties to be the lead solicitor;

(iv)   specifying the details to be included in a statement of case in order to show that the criteria for entry of a claim onto the Group Register have been met;

(v)   specifying a date after which no claim might be added to the Group Register unless the court gives permission;

(vi)   for the entry of any particular claim meeting one or more of the GLO issues into the Group Register.

The practice direction contains further details as to the management court's case management powers.

(i)   Directions given at a case management hearing will bind all claims that are subsequently entered on the Group Register.[25]

(ii)   Any application to vary the terms of the GLO must be made to the management court.[26]

---

20 CPR, r. 19.11(3).
21 CPR PD 19B, para. 7(1).
22 CPR PD 19B, para. 7(2) and (3).
23 CPR PD 19B, para. 8.
24 CPR, r. 19.13.
25 CPR PD 19B, para. 12.1.
26 CPR PD 19B, para. 12.2.

(iii)   The management court may give directions as to how the costs of resolving common issues or the costs of test claims are to be borne or shared between the claimants.[27]

(iv)   The management court may order that after a specified date all claims raising one or more of the GLO issues are to be started in the management court.[28] Failure to comply with such an order would not be fatal to the claim, but it should be transferred to the management court and entered on the Group Register as soon as possible.[29]

(v)   Although the GLO would almost invariably require all claims raising a GLO issue to be transferred to the management court, where the management court is a county court and the claim is proceeding in the High Court, it is only the High Court that can order the transfer and direct that the details of the case be entered on the Group Register.[30] This provision appears to apply to cases pending in the High Court at the time of the GLO as well as cases issued in the High Court thereafter.

(vi)   A cut-off date might be specified, after which no claim may be added to the Group Register unless the management court gives permission.[31] Cut-off dates are an important tool to ensure the orderly conduct of the group litigation. However, they only control entry into the Group Register. They do not affect limitation and would not prevent a claimant from later seeking the court's permission to join the group litigation or indeed from simply pursuing an individual claim outside the group litigation. This last point was highlighted in *Taylor v. Nugent Care Society*,[32] in which it was held that the need to preserve the integrity of the group litigation did not justify the striking out of a claim which had been issued substantially after the cut-off date and in respect of which an application to join the group action had been refused.[33] The defendant's position could have been protected adequately by staying the claim until after the end of the group action, by requiring that the claimant be bound by the generic decisions in the group action or by limiting the defendant's costs liability to the costs for which it would have been liable had the claim been part of the group action.

(vii)   The management court might require the preparation and service of a group particulars of claim which would contain the general allegations relating to all the claims and a schedule specifying in relation to each individual claim which of the general allegations are relied upon and any specific facts relevant to the claimant.[34] Directions for a group particulars of claim should include provision as to whether and, if so, how the particulars should be verified.[35] The specific facts required to be set out in the schedule might be obtained by use of a questionnaire, the form of which should be approved by the management court. The completed questionnaire might then take the place of the schedule.[36]

---

27 CPR PD 19B, para. 12.4.
28 CPR PD 19B, para. 9.1.
29 CPR PD 19B, para. 9.2.
30 CPR PD 19B, para. 10.
31 CPR PD 19B, para. 13.
32 [2004] 1 WLR 1129, CA.
33 Note the rather different approach under the British Coal VWF Claims Handling Agreement, where a reduction in the period of the limitation amnesty was justified by the public interest in having the claims resolved in the shortest reasonable and practicable time: In the *Matter of British Coal VWF Group Litigation* [2009] EWHC 892 (Comm).
34 CPR PD 19B, para. 14.1.
35 CPR PD 19B, para. 14.2.
36 CPR PD 19B, para. 14.3.

(viii)   The management court may give directions as to the trial of the common issues and also for the trial of individual issues.[37] The common issues and test cases will normally be tried at the management court but individual issues may be tried at a more convenient court.[38]

In the Queen's Bench Division it is suggested that the case management directions are likely to direct that a group particulars of claim is served, that one claim proceed as a test claim and that a cut-off date be fixed.[39] Despite that suggestion, the rules allow considerable flexibility as to how the claim should proceed. The essential choice will be between the adoption of a number of test cases and an approach based on contesting generic issues. Which approach is appropriate will depend on the precise circumstances of the litigation and the nature of the issues requiring resolution.

If it is decided to proceed using lead claims, considerable effort needs to be made to find the cases that are the most representative and will result in sufficient issues being decided so as to dispose of the non-lead cases. This requires extensive negotiation between the representatives of the claimants and defendants and it frequently happens that each side is permitted to nominate half of the test cases. A sufficient number of lead cases should be selected to allow for those that might settle or be withdrawn prior to trial and consideration might be given to having a number of reserve cases ready to take their place. If a direction has been given for a claim to proceed as a test claim and that claim has settled, express provision has been made to allow the management court to substitute another claim from the Group Register.[40] In such a situation, orders made in the settled test claim will be binding on the substituted claim unless the court orders otherwise.

5   EFFECT OF A GLO

One of the most important consequences of a GLO is that where a judgment or order is made in a claim on the Group Register, the order binds all parties to all claims that are on the register at the time of the judgment or order. The order will usually also bite on parties to a claim which is entered onto the Register after the GLO, since the court has the power to give directions as to the extent to which latecomers are bound by previous judgments or orders.[41] It would be rare for the court not to exercise that power, particularly in relation to case management directions which are stated generally to bind later claims.[42]

Although a party adversely affected by an order or judgment may seek permission to appeal against it, this applies only where that party was on the Group Register at the time the order was made. A party to a claim which is entered on the Register after the order or judgment may not apply for it to be set aside, varied or stayed and may not appeal against it. He may however apply for an order that the judgment or order is not binding on him.[43]

---

37 CPR PD 19B, para. 15.1.
38 CPR PD 19B, para. 15.2.
39 Queen's Bench Guide, para. 13.7.11.
40 CPR, r. 19.15.
41 CPR, r. 19.12.
42 CPR PD 19B, para. 12.1.
43 CPR, r. 19.12(3).

In respect of disclosure, unless the court orders otherwise, a document relating to a GLO issue which has been disclosed by a party to a claim on the Group Register is treated as having been disclosed to all the parties to all claims on the register and all claims subsequently entered on the Register.[44]

6   THE GROUP REGISTER

The Group Register is established in accordance with the directions given in the GLO. Notwithstanding the terms of para. 6.5 of the Practice Direction to the effect that the Register should normally be kept and maintained by the management court (unless directed otherwise), the normal expectation is that the Register will be maintained by the lead solicitors for the claimants.[45]

As para. 6.1A of the Practice Direction makes clear, before a claim can be entered on the Group Register, it must have been issued individually and thus the issue fee must also have been paid.

Any party to a case may apply for its details to be entered on the Group Register but the order will not be made unless the case gives rise to at least one of the GLO issues.[46] The court may also refuse to add the case to the Register (or remove a case already on the Register) if it is not satisfied that the case can conveniently be managed with the other cases on the Register or if its entry on the Register would adversely affect the case management of the other cases.[47] As to the effect of rejecting a claim for inclusion on the Register and the manner in which a rejected claim might thereafter be managed, see *Taylor v. Nugent Care Society*, above.

The Practice Direction contains provisions relating to inspection of the Register. Where the Register is maintained by the court, access to the Register and supply of the relevant documents is regulated by CPR, rr. 5.4, 5.4B and 5.4C.[48] Where the Register is maintained by a solicitor, any person may inspect it during normal business hours and upon the giving of reasonable notice.[49] The solicitor may charge a fee, which is not to exceed the fee chargeable by the court.

The management court has power to remove a claim from the Group Register on the application of any party to that claim.[50] If the claim is removed, the court may give directions as to its further management.

7   COSTS

The CPR provisions regarding GLO costs can now be found at r. 46.6. This rule attempts to provide a framework for dealing with issues such as the liability of individual claimants to contribute to generic issues or test cases and how costs are split between the individual claims and the issues dealt with communally.

---

44 CPR, r. 19.12(4).
45 This expectation may be different in the Chancery Division.
46 CPR PD 19B, paras 6.2 and 6.3.
47 CPR PD 19B, para. 6.4.
48 CPR PD 19B, para. 6.6(1). Fees for copies are payable at the rate set out in the Civil Proceedings Fees Order 2004 (SI 2004/3121), Sch. 1, para. 4.
49 CPR PD 19B, para. 6.6(2).
50 CPR, r. 19.14.

Rule 46.6(2) differentiates between individual costs (incurred in relation to an individual claim on the Group Register) and common costs, which are the costs incurred in relation to the GLO issues, individual costs incurred in a test claim and the costs of the lead legal representative in administering the group litigation.

Where an order for common costs is made against a group litigant (a claimant or defendant to a claim on the Group Register) the default position is that each group litigant carries a several liability for an equal proportion of the common costs. It is, however, made clear that the court has a discretion to make a different order where appropriate.[51]

Rule 46.6(4) deals with the liabilities of losing group litigants to contribute to the costs incurred on their side. It provides a general rule that where a group litigant is the paying party, in addition to the costs which he is liable to pay to the receiving party, he will be liable to meet the individual costs of his claim and an equal proportion, together with all the other group litigants, of the common costs. However, an individual claimant who succeeds, despite the claimants having lost on the generic issues, may not have to contribute towards the costs of those issues: see *Owen v. Ministry of Defence*.[52] In that case the claimant, who had a straightforward clinical negligence claim for a missed diagnosis of post-traumatic stress disorder, became one of 15 test cases in group litigation against the MoD in relation to its systems for the prevention, detection and treatment of psychiatric illness caused by combat stress. The generic claim failed[53] but the claimant pursued successfully his individual claim. The MoD then claimed to set off the claimant's proportionate share of the generic costs against his entitlement to individual costs or damages. The judge declined to do so. The claimant would have succeeded in his action whether or not the generic issues had been litigated. He had little choice but to be involved in the group litigation, which resulted in a substantial delay in the resolution of his claim. Accordingly, it was not fair and just to order the set off.

In order to sort individual costs from common costs, when making an order for costs in relation to an application or hearing that dealt with both a GLO issue(s) and issues relevant only to individual claims, the court will direct the proportion of the costs relating respectively to common costs and individual costs.[54] Despite the apparently mandatory requirement to carry out this apportionment, the Practice Direction[55] makes provision for a costs judge to perform the task where the court has not.

The costs rules also make provision for latecomers and early leavers. A group litigant may be ordered to pay a contribution to common costs incurred before that litigant's individual claim was entered on the Group Register. If a claim is removed from the Group Register, the court may make an order for costs in that claim which includes a proportion of the common costs incurred up to the date on which the claim is removed. The position of early leavers (discontinuers and settlers) was considered in detail by the Court of Appeal in *Sayers & ors v. Merck etc.*[56] in which three sets of group litigation were considered together. The court noted that settlers were unlikely to cause much

---

51 CPR, r. 46.6(3).
52 [2006] EWHC 990 (QB), per Owen J.
53 [2003] EWHC 1134 (QB), per Owen J.
54 CPR, r. 46.6(5).
55 CPR PD 19B, para. 16.2.
56 [2002] 1 WLR 2274.

difficulty, since the settlement would make some provision for costs. In relation to discontinuers, the court considered that there should not be a rule that a discontinuing claimant should at the time of discontinuance have a crystallised inability to recover common costs and a potential liability for the defendants' common costs. The determination of these issues should await the trial of the common issues, following which the extent of each side's success in relation to the common issues would be known.[57]

This approach in respect of common costs was echoed by Morland J in the protracted costs litigation surrounding the multi-party holiday claim of *Giambrone v. JMC Holidays Ltd*,[58] when he stated that in almost all group litigation cases there should be no need for any detailed assessment of costs until the conclusion of the group litigation. At the same time he accepted that the claimants' solicitors were fully entitled to an adequate cash flow from the defendants once the general issue of liability had been admitted or determined in favour of the claimants or damages had been assessed or settled in individual claims or batches of claimants. The effect of the delay in assessment should be attenuated by agreement from the defendants' solicitors to pay interim sums on account of costs. If agreement could not be reached on interim payments, an application should be made to the nominated judge, who should be provided beforehand with a summarised schedule of costs together with a succinct skeleton of the issues and rival arguments. With that documentation, the judge might be able to determine the application on paper. If an oral hearing is required, it should be capable of being dealt with in less than an hour.

8 COSTS CAPPING

8.1 The Position Prior to the 2013 Amendments to Part 3 of the CPR

Rule 46.6 does not deal with costs capping but this is an issue of key importance in group actions, where defendants in particular will be anxious to see that the court exercises control over the costs of the action. The issue was first considered directly in a group action by Gage J in the Nationwide Organ Group Litigation.[59] Prior to the 2013 amendments to Part 3 of the CPR,[60] there was no express provision for a costs capping order, the power was found to exist by virtue of the general costs discretion under s. 51 of the Senior Courts Act 1981, the court's case management powers (CPR, r. 3.1), r. 44.3 dealing with the factors relevant to the exercise of the costs discretion and s. 6 of the costs practice direction. The Court of Appeal has since confirmed that this reasoning was correct.[61] The order made by Gage J in the Nationwide Organ Group Litigation (unopposed in principle by the claimants) was both retrospective and prospective, covering all costs (save for specific interlocutory costs) up to the end of trial. Costs spent by the claimants on generic issues prior to the cap were £1.45m. They had estimated costs of a further £1m but these costs were capped at £506,500 which

---

57 The order as varied by the Court of Appeal read as follows: *"If in any quarter a claimant discontinues his/her claim against any one or more of the defendants or it is dismissed by an order of the court whereby that claimant is ordered to pay such defendants' costs, then he/she will be liable for his/her individual costs incurred by such defendants up to the last day of that quarter; liability for common costs and disbursements to be determined following the trial of common issues, with permission to apply if such trial does not take place."*
58 [2002] EWHC 2932 (QB): a case in which no GLO or costs sharing order had been made.
59 *A B & ors v. Leeds Teaching Hospitals NHS Trust* [2003] EWHC 1034 (QB); [2003] Lloyd's Rep Med 355. Gage J sat with Senior Costs Judge Hurst at the hearing.
60 As introduced by the Civil Procedure (Amendment) Rules 2013 (SI 2013/262).
61 *King v. Telegraph Group* [2005] 1 WLR 2282 at para. 85.

represented solicitors' costs, experts' fees, counsels' fees and other disbursements but excluded VAT. The judge took account of the following matters:

(i)   proportionality;

(ii)   the costs cap should only relate to the costs incurred in relation to generic issues;

(iii)   a broad approach needed to be taken to the costs cap, it would be neither possible nor cost-effective for the court to go into minutiae;

(iv)   the claimants' costs should not be assessed solely on the basis of the sum for which the defendants' representatives had agreed to conduct the litigation nor on the basis of the agreement between the claimants and the LSC, although those figures might provide a guide to costs;

(v)   the global figure at which the costs were capped was based on an assumption as to the length of trial – if the trial were to last longer, an application to vary the capping order might be made;

(vi)   it was hoped that the global figure having been assessed, the order for costs at the conclusion of the trial would avoid the necessity for most, if not all, of the costs to be the subject of a detailed assessment;

(vii)   liberty was given to each party to apply to vary the order in the event of unforeseen and exceptional additional costs or in the event of an unforeseen event leading to a reduction in costs.

Perhaps the most remarkable feature of this decision is the extent to which it was intended that the cap should replace detailed assessment – an approach repeated by Senior Costs Judge Hurst in *Multiple Claimants v. TUI UK Ltd.*[62] In relation to the costs items within the cap, neither side can therefore rely on there being a future detailed assessment of costs at which to challenge the sums claimed up to the level of the cap.

The decision in *A B & ors* was followed by Hallett J in *Various Ledward Claimants v. Kent & Medway Health Authority and East Kent Hospitals NHS Trust.*[63] The parties had agreed the need for a cap and the fact that it should, to an extent, be retrospective. They had also agreed that there was no need for a cap on expert fees or other disbursements – this agreement was the subject of judicial criticism in light of the claimants' estimate of experts' charges at £172,000. Two of the lead claimants were funded under CFAs and both sides agreed that the cap would apply to base costs only. This left the court deciding on the consequences of the use of distant solicitors, the hours to be spent and the chargeable rates of solicitors and counsel.

Although the application in the *Ledward* claim was heard just 3 months prior to the start of a 6-week trial, the guidance from the Court of Appeal was that any application for a costs capping order should be made at an early stage in the litigation, so that a party does not find that he has overspent if a cap is ordered later on.[64] Any defendant planning on making an application for a costs capping order should also bear in mind the fact that the considerations of fairness and equality of arms under the overriding objective mean that costs capping orders will usually be mutual.[65]

---

62 Case no. HQ04X03737, 2005, SCCO.

63 [2003] EWHC 2551 (QB), in which Senior Costs Judge Hurst again sat with the judge.

64 Brooke LJ in *King v. Telegraph Group* above, at para. 80.

65 See Akenhead J in *Multiple Claimants v. Corby BC* [2008] EWHC 619 (TCC) referring to *Tierney v. News Group Newspapers Ltd* [2006] EWHC 3275.

A restrictive view of cost capping orders was taken by Coulson J in *Barr v. Biffa Waste Services (No. 2)*[66] in which it was pointed out that CPR, r. 44.18(5) and (6) required a restrictive approach and that their criteria were only likely to be satisfied in an exceptional case.[67] The judge held that a costs capping order would not be made if the risk of disproportionate costs could be controlled by case management or on detailed assessment of those costs. The judge also rejected the suggestion that the claimants' recoverable costs should be limited to the value of the indemnity under their ATE insurance policy.[68]

8.2   Position after the Amendments to the CPR in 2013

The more restrictive approach of Coulson J is consistent with the current approach pursuant to the amended rules which came into force in 2013. The rules regarding costs capping orders can now be found in CPR, rr. 3.19, 3.20 and 3.21 as well as Practice Direction 3F. Rule 3.19 provides:

> "*3.19(5) The court may at any stage of proceedings make a costs capping order against all or any of the parties, if –*
>
> *(a)   it is in the interests of justice to do so;*
>
> *(b)   there is a substantial risk that without such an order costs will be disproportionately incurred; and*
>
> *(c)   it is not satisfied that the risk in subparagraph (b) can be adequately controlled by –*
>
> > *(i)   case management directions or orders made under this Part; and*
> >
> > *(ii)   detailed assessment of costs.*"

A costs capping order may be in respect of the whole litigation or any issues ordered to be tried separately, and this can be made at any stage of proceedings. When deciding if a capping order is required against all or any of the parties the court will consider if it is in the interests of justice to do so, if there is a substantial risk that without such an order costs will be disproportionality incurred and that said risk cannot be controlled by case management directions or a detailed costs assessment.[69] When deciding whether to exercise its discretion, the court will take into consideration all the circumstances of the case and those set out at CPR, r. 3.19(5). For a working example of this under the similarly worded newly amended CPR see *Tidal Energy Limited v. Bank of Scotland Plc.*[70]

In this case Lady Justice Arden considered an application for a costs capping order in a case concerning the construction of a CHAPS transfer agreement. The respondent bank wanted to instruct leading counsel and a junior. The appellant wanted to limit its potential costs outlay on the appeal so that it would not have to bear the costs of the respondent instructing counsel. It sought to argue that the risk in 5(c) was the substantial risk that without a costs cap costs would be disproportionately incurred and that the only type of exercise within (c)(i) or (c)(ii) that can constitute adequate control is a mechanism for preventing costs being incurred in the first place (not preventing the instruction of leading counsel but effectively guaranteeing that the

---

66 [2009] EWHC 2444 (TCC).

67 See *Peacock v. MGN Ltd* [2009] EWHC 769 (QB) The relevant provision is now found in CPR, r. 3.19.

68 The court had earlier ordered disclosure of the ATE policy on the grounds that it had been referred to in claimants' witness statements, was relevant and not privileged: *Barr v. Biffa Waste Services Ltd* [2009] EWHC 1033 (TCC).

69 CPR, r. 3.19(4) and (5).

70 [2014] EWCA Civ 847.

appellant would not have to meet the cost of such instruction). Arden LJ did not think the argument was tenable. She said:

> *"Paragraph (c) uses advertise words 'the risk in subparagraph (b) can be adequately controlled'. In my judgment, it is clear that a mechanism may constitute adequate control if it neutralises or satisfactorily manages the risk. It may not be possible to eliminate a risk but only to manage it. But, to my mind, that must be the interpretation of the rule because otherwise a detailed assessment of costs could never or scarcely ever be a mechanism of control within 5(c). Moreover, as I see it that would reflect a policy decision which the drafter of 3.19 may reasonably have taken, namely that the court should not be troubled by satellite litigation, constituted by cost cap litigation if the long-standing system of assessing costs would provide an adequate mechanism."*

She made reference also to the case of *Eweida v. British Airways Plc*[71] noting that in that case concerning a protective costs order, the wording of CPR, r. 44.18(5)(c)(ii) mirrors that in r. 3.19(5)(ii) above. Regard must be had therefore to the mechanisms for controlling costs at the beginning (CCMC) and at the end of case (detailed assessment). She went on:[72]

> *"The decision that I have made does not mean that in another case a party may not be able to lead evidence from, let us say, a costs drafter that the cost judge could not adequately distinguish between costs reasonably incurred and costs unreasonably incurred, for instance, of very extensive and detailed litigation on a technical matter. In those situations then of course, looking at the case on its specific facts, the court may reach the view that 5(c)(ii) is not a bar to making a costs cap order."*

Therefore unless the pre-condition at r. 3.19(5) is fulfilled, a costs capping order is unlikely to be made. See, for example, *Daniel Hegglin v. (1) Persons unknown (2)Google Inc*[73] where the court considered that judicious use of a combination of costs case management and detailed assessment would meet concerns about disproportionate expenditure in a case whereby the second defendant's costs already incurred were £1.28m and their expected expenditure was £1.68m.

Once made, no variation can be made unless there has been a material and substantial change of circumstances or there is some other compelling reason to vary the order. Applications for costs orders must be made in accordance with Part 23 as must any application to vary the costs capping order.[74]

9 CONDITIONAL FEE AGREEMENTS

The use of CFAs in group litigation can be controversial. In *Multiple Claimants v. TUI* (see above), the Senior Costs Judge, Master Hurst, drew attention to the potential problem at para. 79 of his decision:[75]

---

71 [2009] EWCA Civ 1025 T.
72 Paragraph 13 of the judgment.
73 [2015] 1 Costs LO 65.
74 CPR, rr. 3.20 and 3.21.
75 The Civil Justice Council has since suggested that regulated contingency fees might be permitted in multi-party claims: "Improved Access to Justice – Funding Options & Proportionate Costs", June 2007.

"There is a very real danger that in litigation of this type, where many Claimants would not think it worth risking their own money in order to sue for very modest damages, the funding regime created by the Access to Justice Act 1999 has provided a vehicle for litigation to be conducted for the benefit of the lawyers by generating costs rather than for benefit of the clients. This is a criticism frequently levelled against the contingency fee system in the United States in respect of class actions."

That criticism notwithstanding, it is clear that CFAs are being used in many multi-party claims. Their use is far from straightforward. The difficulty of formulating a group CFA means that the CFAs are entered into on an individual basis. However, most standard forms of CFA provide for automatic termination if a GLO is made. Further, multi-party litigation (whether or not under a GLO) seldom provides a clear-cut result in terms of costs – test claims may be lost, generic issues may be decided against the claimants and these losses will be reflected in the orders for costs. Obtaining adequate ATE insurance cover is also highly problematic (see *Hobson*, above). Where a case is brought on a CFA with ATE insurance there is often a need to show over 60% prospects for the claimant before the claim can continue.

Standard form CFAs will apply to the costs of an individual claim but will not deal expressly with the cost of generic issues. In *Brown v. Russell Young & Co*[76] the claim settled pre-issue, before any GLO could be made and without a costs sharing agreement or order. Nonetheless, the wording of the CFA and the provisions of CPR, r. 36.13(1) were wide enough to enable the claimant to recover generic costs.

Post LASPO the abolishment of the recovery of ATE insurance premiums in most cases and the use of QOCS (qualified one way costs shifting) should meet some of the concerns expressed by Master Hurst in *Multiple Claimants v. TUI* (see above). Chapter 3 deals with funding of clinical negligence claims.

---

76 SCCO, 2006, ref. 53R/2005, Senior Costs Judge Hurst.

Chapter 14

INQUESTS

1   INTRODUCTION

The inquest is the final stage in the public law framework for handling death. For most deaths, the deceased's own doctor is able to diagnose and certify a natural cause of death, which can then be registered on the death certificate. Thus, fewer than half of all deaths are reported to a coroner.[1] In 2012, of 499,326 registered deaths, 227,721 were so reported. Reports come to coroners from a variety of sources. Police, prisons and others must report deaths in state detention. A registered medical practitioner who attends to a person in his last illness must sign a death certificate and deliver it to the registrar of births and deaths,[2] and the registrar must report a death to the coroner in a variety of particular cases or where there is a doubt.[3] Medical practitioners usually report a death directly to the coroner in cases of doubt or suspicion.[4]

A coroner must, in certain circumstances, conduct an investigation into the death of a person whose death is reported to him (see below under the heading, "duty to conduct an investigation"). Where appropriate the investigation will include an inquest; but this will not be so in all cases. Inquests were opened on 32,542 deaths reported in 2012.[5] This was only 14% of all deaths reported to coroners. It is important to understand that much of the work of the coroner is not done in court. Knowing this – and the fact that a senior coroner may have 3,000 to 5,000 deaths reported to him each year – should help you to get off on the right foot with your coroner.

2   STRUCTURE OF THE CORONER SYSTEM

Coroners' work is governed by the Coroners and Justice Act 2009, the Coroners (Inquests) Rules 2013 and the Coroners (Investigations) Regulations 2013.[6] These were brought fully into force on 25th July 2013. Before that date, inquests were governed by the Coroners Act 1988 and the Coroners Rules 1984 (SI 1984/552). While the 2013 changes brought about many improvements (especially in relation to disclosure, the coroner's investigatory powers and the structure of the coroner system), in some respects the 2013 changes merely recognised the way coroners already did their work (notably the recognition that the coroner carries out an investigation before holding an inquest).

---

1 The proportion has remained relatively steady at around 45% of all deaths in every year since 2002: *Coroners Statistics 2012*, MoJ Statistics Bulletin, 16th May 2013.
2 Births and Deaths Registration Act 1953, s. 22.
3 Registration of Births and Deaths Regulations 1987, reg. 41.
4 They are not currently under any obligation to do so, but there will in time be regulations under Chapter 2 of Part I of the 2009 Act, requiring medical practitioners to report a death to a senior coroner. These provisions – under the heading "Notification, Certification and Registration of Deaths" – are the legislative response to the findings of the Shipman Enquiry.
5 See fn. 1, p. 12.
6 In this chapter the 2009 Act is referred to as "the Act", and the 2013 Rules and Regulations respectively as "the Rules" and "the Regulations".

Certain of the cases decided under the 1988 Act and 1984 Rules dealt only with imperfections in those legislative provisions which have been corrected by the Act, the Rules and the Regulations. While those cases will cease to be of relevance, other cases decided before 2013 contain statements of general principle to which practitioners and coroners will continue to have regard.

The Act, as enacted, created (in effect) a new national coroner service under a Chief Coroner. The Act was substantially amended before it was implemented. The post of Chief Coroner survived[7] but the centralised system did not.[8] The coroner system's localism continues to be a noteworthy feature.

England and Wales is divided into 99 coroner areas.[9] For each area there is a senior coroner and several fee-paid, part-time "assistant coroners".[10] All new coroners must be legally qualified. Most coroners are assistant coroners. There are also a few full-time "area coroners", who work in busy coroner areas. The senior coroner, assistant coroners and area coroners for a coroner area are (informally) known as the "coroner team". Between them they must be available to perform their functions at any time of the day or night.[11]

Since 2013 the coroner has been a creature of statute. All coroners (apart from the Chief Coroner) are appointed by the local authority or authorities constituting the coroner area, with the consent of the Lord Chancellor and the Chief Coroner.[12] The local authority provides the coroner team with its staff. The local police authority may also provide coroner's officers. Coroners' salaries and expenses are met by the local authority, which also provides the coroner team with its premises.

The Chief Coroner has made inroads into the considerable variation in practice between coroner areas with a view to establishing a more consistent practice. He publishes helpful "law sheets" and guidance notes on his website.[13] Law sheets are intended to state the law conclusively and it appears to be the expectation that coroners will apply the law as there stated. Guidance notes are more tentative in tenor. The Chief Coroner also supervises the training which coroners must now undergo, and oversees appointments. Practitioners should check the Chief Coroner's guidance webpage often, as it seems that it will be expanded and updated frequently.

3   THE PURPOSE OF THE CORONER'S INVESTIGATION

3.1   The Statutory Questions

Section 5(1) of the Act provides that the purpose of a coroner's investigation is to ascertain:

---

7 HHJ Peter Thornton QC was appointed 22nd May 2012 and is the first Chief Coroner.

8 The principal loss being the right of an appeal to the Chief Coroner set out in s. 40, repealed by s. 33(1) of the Public Bodies Act 2011.

9 Coroners and Justice Act 2009 (Coroner Areas and Assistant Coroners) Transitional Order 2013; Coroners and Justice Act 2009 (Alteration of Coroner Areas) Order 2013.

10 Schedule 3 to the Act.

11 Regulations, reg. 4.

12 Schedule 23 to the Act.

13 www.judiciary.gov.uk/related-offices-and-bodies/office-chief-coroner/guidance-law-sheets.

(a)   who the deceased was;

(b)   how, when and where the deceased came by his or her death; and

(c)   the particulars (if any) required by the Births and Deaths Registration Act 1953 to be registered concerning the death.

The questions, "who, how, when and where" are sometimes called "the four statutory questions". Subject to the power to issue reports aimed at preventing future deaths (see below), the coroner, or the jury if there is one, may not express an opinion on any other matter: s. 5(3).

Where necessary in order to avoid a breach of any rights under the European Convention on Human Rights, the purpose set out in s. 5(1) includes the purpose of ascertaining in what circumstances the deceased came by his or her death: s. 5(2). See below under the heading, "Section 5(2) inquests".

After hearing the evidence, the coroner or the jury must make a determination as to these questions and, if particulars are required by the 1953 Act, make a finding as to those particulars: s. 10(1) of the Act.

3.2   What the Coroner's Investigation Cannot Achieve

In *R v. HM Coroner for Birmingham and Solihull ex p. Benton*[14] the High Court dealt with an application for judicial review of a coroner's decision to record an open verdict. The applicant was a mother grieving for her 2-year-old child, who had died in circumstances which potentially called into question the medical treatment he received. She put before the court medical evidence to the effect that her welfare required that a new inquest be directed, since without an inquiry into matters which the previous inquest had failed to explore, she would continue to suffer distress. Kay J said this:

> "It is of critical importance to recognize the true purpose of an inquest. Sadly, the public's perception of such purpose does not always match the reality, and those caught up in the process expect more of the process than it can, or is permitted, to deliver thereby adding to their distress."

It will frequently be the case that the family expects the coroner to determine whether there was fault on the part of named (or unnamed) individuals: the surgeon, the doctor, the hospital administrators, etc. Their hopes are inevitably to be dashed. They may be left with the perception that the whole exercise has been a cover-up or a "whitewash". Practitioners representing bereaved families at inquests must understand their expectations and advise them early and appropriately.

4   DUTY TO CONDUCT AN INVESTIGATION

By s. 1(1) and (2) of the Act, a senior coroner who is made aware that the body[15] of a deceased person is within his area must as soon as practicable conduct an investigation into the person's death if he has reason to suspect that:

---

14 [1997] 8 Med LR 362.

15 "Body" includes body parts: s. 48 of the Act

(a)   the deceased died a violent or unnatural death;

(b)   the cause of death is unknown; or

(c)   the deceased died while in custody or otherwise in state detention.

If he has reason to suspect any of these things, the coroner has no discretion: he must conduct an investigation. The coroner must himself decide whether he has reason to suspect. He cannot delegate this function to his officers or support staff: reg. 7. He must therefore be aware of all deaths reported to him.[16]

A post-mortem examination will normally be carried out which should occur as soon after the death of the deceased as is reasonably practicable.[17]

Unless the deceased died a violent or unnatural death or died in state detention, or the coroner thinks it is necessary to continue the investigation, the senior coroner[18] must discontinue the investigation if a post-mortem examination reveals the cause of death before the coroner has begun holding an inquest: s. 4(1) of the Act. Thus initial suspicions may be negated, making further investigation (and subsequent inquest) unnecessary.

5   CORONER'S INVESTIGATORY POWERS

The coroner now[19] has the power to give notice to any person to give evidence at an inquest, or to produce documents or written evidence in the course of his investigation.[20] Failure without reasonable excuse to comply with such a notice is an offence.[21] The Act gives a power to the Chief Coroner to authorise a senior coroner, in specified circumstances, to enter, search and seize,[22] but there are no plans to bring these provisions into force.

The coroner's power to require a person to disclose documents should be understood against the background of the inquisitorial nature of his task. Whereas in civil litigation the extent of disclosure can be defined and limited by the statements of case, nothing comparable exists in relation to the coroner's investigation.[23]

The public interest in the pursuit of a full and appropriately detailed inquest may outweigh an objection on public interest immunity grounds to the disclosure of a report into a death, particularly where the disclosure is to the coroner rather than to the public.[24] Unless otherwise stated, reports disclosed to the coroner are received on a

---

16 But an area coroner or assistant coroner can perform any of the functions of a senior coroner: para. 8, Sch. 3 to the Act, so it is sufficient for one of the "coroner team" to make the decision. Consequently it is not necessary for the Rules or the Regulations to cover delegation of functions from senior to assistant and area coroners.

17 Regulation 11.

18 Or the area coroner or assistant coroner: see fn. 15.

19 Until the 2013 reforms, the coroner could only obtain a witness summons by making an application to the High Court or the County Court.

20 Section 32 of and paras 1 and 2 of Sch. 5 to the Act.

21 Paragraphs 6-8 of Sch. 6 to the Act.

22 Ibid, paras 3-5.

23 *Assistant Deputy Coroner for Inner West London v. Channel 4 Television Corporation* [2007] EWHC 2513 (QB).

24 Chief Coroner's Law Sheet no. 3, which deals with the decision in *Worcestershire County Council and Worcestershire Safeguarding Children Board* [2013] EWHC 1711 (QB); see also para. 2(2) of Sch. 5 to the Act, which applies to coroners' investigations the general rules of law on PII.

confidential basis, for his eyes only. Whether there is onward disclosure to interested persons will be a matter for the coroner and will be regulated by rr. 12-16 of the Rules (see below under the heading "disclosure").

6   THE INQUEST

The final stage of the investigation is, if appropriate, the inquest. If he has not discontinued his investigation after the post-mortem, then as part of his investigation the coroner must hold an inquest: s. 6 of the Act. The inquest must be opened and held in public: r. 11.

An inquest, as the word suggests, is inquisitorial in nature. Inquests are not adversarial proceedings. Their purpose is to establish the facts and provide an explanation of a death. No interested person appearing before the coroner has a case to present. They may ask questions of witnesses, and this is often referred to as "cross-examination"; but such questions can only be directed at the s. 5(1) matters. The coroner must disallow questions which are irrelevant: r. 19(2).

By s. 10(2) of the Act the determination at the conclusion of the evidence at the inquest may not be framed in such a way as to appear to determine any question of criminal liability on the part of a named person; or civil liability. Thus the coroner or his jury may find that someone is criminally responsible for the death (which would be the implication of a finding of unlawful killing), but they cannot say who; and must not appear to determine any question of civil liability at all.

Until July 2013 this restriction was found only in the rules, and not in the statute. Now it is found in the statute, and not in the Rules or the Regulations. It thus appears that the Act intends to elevate and emphasise the restriction on establishing criminal or civil liability.

The reasons for this restriction have often been stated, for example by Lord Lane CJ in the early 1980s:[25]

> *"The inquest is a fact finding exercise and not a method of apportioning guilt. The procedure and rules of evidence which are suitable for one are unsuitable for the other. At an inquest there are no parties, there is no indictment, there is no prosecution and there is no defence."*

The rationale has always been that it would be unfair to everybody – interested parties, the coroner, the public and the person found guilty or liable – to require or permit the coroner to determine guilt or civil liability at an inquest. It might well make it more difficult for the coroner to answer the more limited questions set out in s. 5(1). And in any event, the state provides other forums for the determination of guilt or innocence, or civil liability.

The inquest must be completed within 6 months from the date on which the coroner is made aware of the death, or as soon as is reasonably practicable after that date: r. 8. If

---

25 *R v. South London Coroner ex p Thompson* (1982) 126 Sol Jo 625; see also Jamieson [1995] 1 QB 1.

an investigation is not concluded within 12 months the senior coroner must make a report to the Chief Coroner: s. 16(1)(a) of the Act.

7 SUMMONING A JURY

Section 7(1) and (2) of the Act provide that an inquest must be conducted by the coroner alone unless the coroner has reason to suspect:

(a) that the deceased died while in state detention *and* that either the death was a violent or unnatural one, or the cause of death is unknown;

(b) that the death resulted from an act or omission of a police officer in execution of his duty; or

(c) that the death was caused by a notifiable accident, poisoning or disease.[26]

If the coroner has reason to suspect any of these then he must hold his inquest with a jury. He can also hold the inquest with a jury if he considers there is sufficient reason to do so: s. 7(3).

It seems that juries will be convened less frequently than they were in the past, since the former provision in s. 8(3)(d) of the 1988 Act – that a jury must be convened where *"the death occurred in circumstances the continuance or possible recurrence of which is prejudicial to the health or safety of the public"* – is not reproduced in the Act.

In *Mohamed Al Fayed v. Deputy Coroner of the Queen's Household*[27] the court was concerned with s. 8(3)(d) but also considered that if the coroner was called upon to exercise his discretion as to the calling of a jury under the discretion given to him by what is now s. 7(3) then, whilst the views of the family were not determinative, they should be taken into account. Further, in exercising this discretion, the coroner ought to consider whether the facts of the case bear any resemblance to the types of situation covered by the mandatory provisions.

8 BASIC PROCEDURE AT AN INQUEST

8.1 Interested Persons

Any person who can satisfy the coroner that he is within s. 47 of the Act has a right to ask questions of witnesses at an inquest and to ask for disclosure from the coroner.

Section 47 includes the following persons: the deceased's spouse, civil partner, partner,[28] parent, child, brother, sister, grandparent, grandchild, child of a brother or sister, stepfather, stepmother, half-brother or half-sister; a personal representative of the deceased; a medical examiner exercising functions in relation to the death of the

---

26 This includes, for example, certain deaths at work; and see the Reporting of Injuries, Diseases and Dangerous Occurrences Regulations 2013. It will not necessarily include all deaths on the railway; see the Chief Coroner's Guidance no. 11.

27 [2007] EWHC 408 (Admin).

28 A person is the deceased's partner if the two of them (whether of different sexes or the same sex) were living as partners in an enduring relationship at the time of the deceased person's death: s. 47(7).

deceased; a beneficiary under a policy of insurance issued on the life of the deceased; the insurer who issued such a policy of insurance; a person who may by any act or omission have caused or contributed to the death of the deceased; a trade union representative (in an appropriate case, as defined); certain others unlikely to be relevant to readers of this chapter; and any other person whom the coroner thinks has a sufficient interest.

8.2 Disclosure

Disclosure to interested persons is dealt with by rr. 12-16 of the Rules. These apply to the disclosure of documents by the coroner during or after an investigation.[29] The investigation includes, but is not limited to, the inquest. Note that the coroner has powers to require a person to provide evidence and documents to him in the course of his investigation;[30] the question of whether those documents should be further disclosed to interested parties will fall to be decided under the Rules.

Rule 13(1) provides that, subject to the exceptions in r. 15, where an interested person asks for disclosure of a document[31] held by the coroner, the coroner must provide that document or a copy of that document, or make the document available for inspection by that person as soon as is reasonably practicable.

Rule 13(2) clarifies this by providing that it covers any post-mortem examination report; any other report that has been provided to the coroner during the course of the investigation; the recording of any inquest hearing held in public; and any other document which the coroner considers relevant to the inquest.

Disclosure may be in electronic form: r. 14(a). The coroner is entitled to disclose a redacted version of a document: r. 14(b). The coroner may not charge a fee for any document or copy document: r. 16.

The exceptions to r. 13 are important. They are contained in r. 15 and are as follows:

(a) there is a statutory or legal prohibition on disclosure;
(b) the consent of any author or copyright owner cannot reasonably be obtained;
(c) the request is unreasonable;
(d) the document relates to contemplated or commenced criminal proceedings; or
(e) the coroner considers the document irrelevant to the investigation – i.e. the coroner does not intend to rely on it at the inquest.

As to the first of these – the presence of a legal prohibition – the Chief Coroner's *Guidance to the 2009 Act* at [121], and his *Law Sheet no. 3* at [12], mention police reports as an example.[32] Such reports are intended to assist the coroner in understanding the issues and deciding which witnesses are to be called. They are not adduced in evidence because they are not primary evidence. It appears that certain reports

---

29 Rules, r. 12.
30 See above, section 6.
31 This includes *"any medium in which information of any description is recorded"*: r. 2, Rules. This will include, e.g., photographs and CCTV.
32 Referring to *R (Lagos) v. City of London Coroner* [2013] EWHC 423 (Admin).

obtained by the coroner in the course of his investigation are "for his eyes only". This may prove to be an area of friction between interested parties and witnesses. The Chief Coroner will, in due course, issue guidance on disclosure to interested persons.

As to the reasonableness of the request, in *R (Ahmed) v. HM Coroner South East & Cumbria*,[33] it was held that a coroner had been entitled not to disclose material prior to an inquest into the death of a 17-year-old girl when there was an ongoing criminal investigation. Although it would have been preferable for a degree of disclosure to have been made, it was a matter of discretion for the coroner. Here a blanket request had been made for all police material and the coroner replied that he could not disclose all the material but would consider more specific requests. No specific request was however made. The court commented that whilst a more liberal approach had developed towards disclosure in inquest cases and it was often advisable that there should be disclosure of material central to the inquest, it was a matter within the coroner's discretion. It would have been preferable, regardless of the lack of specificity of the requests, had the coroner chosen to disclose some of the key material, for example the statements of those witnesses he intended to call. There were real difficulties with disclosure, particularly when there was an ongoing criminal investigation, but there were circumstances in the instant case which would have made it preferable for a degree of disclosure to have taken place. It was held however that the coroner's decision could not be characterised as unreasonable, given the ongoing investigation and the opportunity provided to the family to request specific disclosure. It was clear from the nature and tenor of the correspondence that had a sensible request been made, the coroner would have given real consideration to releasing whatever specific material seemed appropriate.

Outside the Act, the Rules, the Regulations and the discretion of a coroner, representatives of interested persons should feel free to obtain what they can in advance of the inquest. That may consist of police or hospital notes, GP records, complaints procedure documentation, serious untoward incident reports by the relevant NHS trust, etc. It is helpful to establish contact with the coroner or the coroner's officer well in advance of the hearing of the inquest, to find out what material the coroner proposes to put before the jury (or himself), and to see what can be disclosed.

8.3   Pre-inquest Reviews

Coroners often hold a short hearing a few days or weeks prior to the resumed hearing in order to define the scope of the inquest, the order of witnesses, the time estimate for the hearing, and the like. A coroner may hold such a hearing at any time during the course of an investigation and before an inquest hearing: Rules, r. 6.

In *Brown v. HM Coroner for Norfolk*[34] the Chief Coroner gave guidance as to the conduct of such hearings, as follows:

- The coroner should provide to interested persons a written agenda in advance of the hearing. If appropriate he should express provisional views so that agreement or opposition can be given.

---

33 [2009] EWHC 1653 (Admin).
34 [2014] EWHC 187 (Admin).

- The agenda should include a list of interested persons, a proposed list of witnesses identifying those who may be called and those whose statements may be read, the issues to be considered at the inquest, the scope of the evidence, whether a jury will be required, whether Article 2 of the ECHR is engaged, any issues of disclosure, the date of the final hearing and any other relevant matters.
- In complex or difficult investigations the interested persons should be invited to respond in writing stating areas of agreement or disagreement.
- The coroner should ensure that interested persons, particularly those unrepresented, have sufficient disclosure of relevant statements and documents.

8.4   Oral Evidence

It is for the coroner to decide who will be called to give evidence, although he can be invited to call witnesses who might assist. All witnesses will be examined on oath or affirmation: r. 20.   The order of examination is, unless the coroner otherwise determines, as follows: first the coroner; then any interested person; and lastly any representative of the witness: r. 21. No witness shall be obliged to answer any question tending to incriminate himself: r. 22(1).   The coroner must give a self-incrimination warning where it appears that a witness has been asked a question tending to incriminate him: r. 21(2).

A coroner must allow any interested person who so requests, to examine any witness: r. 19(1). But a coroner must disallow any question put to the witness which the coroner considers irrelevant: r. 19(2).   Thus questioning which is not relevant to the s. 5(1) matters must be stopped: the coroner has no discretion.

Evidence may be given by video link (r. 17) and/or from behind a screen (r. 18).

8.5   Written Evidence and Hearsay

Written evidence may be admitted pursuant to r. 23. This is framed in exclusionary terms: written evidence in answer to the four statutory questions is *not* admissible unless the coroner is satisfied of one or more of the following four facts about it:

(a)   it is not possible for the maker of the written evidence to give evidence at the inquest hearing at all, or within a reasonable time;

(b)   there is a good and sufficient reason why the maker of the written evidence should not attend the inquest hearing;

(c)   there is a good and sufficient reason to believe that the maker of the written evidence will not attend the inquest hearing; or

(d)   the written evidence (including evidence in the form of admissions) is unlikely to be disputed.

Before admitting such evidence the coroner must announce at the inquest hearing that it is his intention so to do. He must inform the interested parties that they are entitled to object to the admission of the evidence and to see a copy of it: r. 23(2).

The Chief Coroner wishes to encourage coroners to admit written evidence wherever possible, as this can save money and court time, and avoid the inconvenience of witnesses being brought to court unnecessarily.[35]

It is hoped that the new rule will be an improvement on the previous provision, r. 37 of the 1988 Rules, which was worded in an obscure way.[36] Rule 23 does not appear to give interested parties any right to prevent the coroner from admitting hearsay evidence if he thinks fit, as the previous rule apparently did.

8.6 Submissions and Directions

Before giving his determination, or directing the jury as to theirs, the coroner will hear legal submissions from the interested persons (or their advocates). If he is sitting with a jury, this will be done in the jury's absence. Submissions to the coroner on the facts of who the deceased was or how, when and where he died, are prohibited: r. 27.[37] Interested persons (or their advocates) do not address the jury at all.

Coroners should approach their decision as to what conclusions to leave to the jury on the basis that it is for the jury to decide all matters of fact, but that they are entitled to consider whether a conclusion, if reached, would be perverse or unsafe and so refuse to leave such a verdict to the jury (*R (Ernest Bennett) (Appellant) v. HM Coroner for Inner South London (Respondent) & (1) Officers A & B (2) Commissioner of Police of the Metropolis (Interested Parties)*[38]). For definitive guidance on the decision whether to leave a conclusion to a jury, see the Chief Coroner's *Law Sheet no. 2*.

All facts to be found are found to the civil standard, with the limited exceptions of conclusions of unlawful killing and suicide, which require the criminal standard of proof to be satisfied.[39]

8.7 Conclusion of the Inquest

Rule 34 requires the coroner, or jury where there is one, to complete a form entitled "Record of an Inquest" (Form 2 in the Schedule to the Rules). A copy of Form 2 is reproduced at the end of this chapter. It is an important document since it is towards this document that the entire inquest is directed, and practitioners should familiarise themselves with it.

Form 2 incorporates guidance notes, which do not have statutory force, and which set out nine suggested short-form conclusions as follows:

(i)   accident or misadventure;
(ii)   alcohol/drug related;
(iii)   industrial disease;
(iv)   lawful/unlawful killing;
(v)   natural causes;

---

35 Chief Coroner's Guide to the Coroners and Justice Act 2009, para. 142.
36 *R ((1) Paul (2) Ritz Hotel Ltd) v. Assistant Deputy Coroner of Inner West London* [2007] EWCA Civ 1259.
37 Although *"submissions would be merely beating the wind unless they were founded on the facts of the instant inquiry"*: *R (Lin) v. Secretary of State for Transport* [2006] EWHC 2575 (Admin) at para. 56.
38 [2007] EWCA Civ 617.
39 For a helpful explanation of the reasons for this, see the City of London coroner's extempore judgment cited in *R (Lagos) v. City of London Coroner* [2013] EWHC 423 (Admin).

(vi)   open;
(vii)   road traffic collision;
(viii)   stillbirth;
(ix)   suicide.

Conclusions of "lack of care" or "neglect" are limited to those circumstances in which there is a *"gross failure to provide adequate nourishment or liquid, or provide or procure basic medical attention or shelter or warmth for someone in a dependent position (because of youth, age, illness or incarceration)"* and only in circumstances where the *"gross neglect was directly connected"* with the death. See *R v. North Humberside Coroner ex p Jamieson*[40] and the application of those principles in *R (Longfield Care Homes Ltd) v. HM Coroner for Blackburn*.[41] The deceased in that case had been a resident of a care home and suffered from dementia. A carer had opened the only unrestricted window and placed a large sofa in front of it. Some time later, the deceased climbed out and fractured her elbow and pelvis and then died 19 hours later. The post mortem suggested that the cause of death was pneumonia complicated by the trauma of the fall. In this case the Coroner had gone too far in his direction to the jury because he had focussed on the lack of a risk assessment and had therefore trespassed into the something which more accurately belonged to the law of negligence than that relating to inquests. A verdict of death by natural causes or accidental death would not have been adequate to record what the jury found and so this was a case appropriate for a narrative verdict (as to which see further below) but not a verdict of accidental death contributed to by lack of care.

With the advent of the Human Rights Act 1998, a verdict such as "right to life was breached contrary to Article 2 of the European Convention on Human Rights" might be an appropriate verdict (as acknowledged in *R (Middleton) v. West Somerset Coroner and another*[42]).

Narrative conclusions are now the norm even where the enhanced scope of the inquest under Article 2 is not engaged (see section 10.2 below). The High Court in *R (Longfield Care Homes Ltd) v. HM Coroner for Blackburn* specifically endorsed the use of a narrative verdict where the death resulted from a number of causes, stating that the comments of the Court of Appeal in *Middleton* *"are not restricted to verdicts in cases of death where the State may have had a hand and are of general application"*.

8.8   Prevention of Future Death Reports

If anything revealed by the coroner's investigation gives rise to *"a concern that circumstances creating a risk of other deaths will occur, or will continue to exist, in the future"*; and if, in the coroner's opinion, action should be taken about those circumstances; then the coroner must make a report to a person who he believes may have the power to take action, to take that action: para. 7 of Sch. 5 to the Act.

These reports are now known as Prevention of Future Death Reports or PFD reports. The 2009 Act makes them one of the coroner's key functions. Prior to 2013 the power to make a like report was located only in the 1984 Rules, and the coroner had a

---

40 [1995] 1 QB 1.
41 [2004] EWHC 2467.
42 [2004] 2 WLR 800 at 814.

discretion whether or not to make one. Now they are elevated from the Rules to the Act, and the coroner is under a duty to make one in the circumstances set out above.

The coroner must not make a PFD until he has considered all the documents, evidence and information that in his opinion are relevant to the investigation: reg. 28(3). Thus he may make a PFD before the conclusion of the inquest, although this will probably be unusual and in practice the coroner often seeks to be addressed by legal representatives.

It is to be noted that the prohibition in s. 5(3) of the Act on the coroner or jury expressing an opinion on any matter other than the s. 5(1) purposes, is expressly made subject to the power to issue a PFD.

The coroner must send a copy of the PFD report to the Chief Coroner, who publishes most of them on his website. The Chief Coroner will periodically issue a summary of all PFD reports he receives. His first report is available on his website.[43] The Chief Coroner has issued a form in which coroners should issue PFD reports (again, it is available on his website).

A person to whom a coroner makes a PFD report must give the coroner a written response to it: para. 7(2) of Sch. 5 to the Act. The response must be provided within 56 days of the PFD report: reg. 29(4). It must give details of action which that person proposes to take or has taken, or an explanation as to why no action is proposed: reg. 29(3).

9   *JAMIESON* INQUESTS

Until the coming into force of the Human Rights Act 1998 (HRA), *R v. North Humberside Coroner ex p Jamieson*[44] was the leading authority on the scope and function of inquests. The deceased, whilst serving a long custodial sentence, hanged himself in a cell. He was a known suicide risk. The coroner directed the jury not to return a verdict in which lack of care formed a part and the jury found that the deceased had killed himself by hanging. The applicant (the deceased's brother) challenged the coroner's direction.

The Court of Appeal held that an inquest was a fact-finding inquiry directed solely to establishing (what are now) the s. 5(1) matters (i.e. (1) the identity of the deceased, (2) how, (3) when and (4) where he came by his death). The Court held that "how" connoted "by what means" not "in what broad circumstances" the deceased came by his death. The task is not to ascertain how the deceased died, which might raise general and far-reaching issues, but "how the deceased came by his death": a more limited question directed to the means by which the deceased came by his death. It was held that it was not for the coroner or his jury to determine any question of civil or criminal liability, to appear to do so, or to impute blame.

---

43 www.judiciary.gov.uk/related-offices-and-bodies/office-chief-coroner.
44 [1995] 1 QB 1.

10 THE MODERN SCOPE AND FUNCTION OF AN INQUEST

The HRA 1998 has provided a useful platform for reviewing the traditional scope of an inquest and as a result changes have been brought about to the restrictive approach adopted in *Jamieson*. These changes have been codified in s. 5(2) of the Act, which is as follows:

> *"Where necessary in order to avoid a breach of any Convention rights (within the meaning of the Human Rights Act 1998), the purpose mentioned in subsection (1)(b) ['to ascertain...how, when and where the deceased came by his or her death'] is to be read as including the purpose of ascertaining in what circumstances the deceased came by his or her death."*

10.1 The Right to Life

Article 2 of the European Convention on Human Rights (ECHR) records the existence of a "right to life" and reads as follows:

> *"Article 2 – Right to life*
>
> *1. Everyone's right to life shall be protected by law. No one shall be deprived of his life intentionally save in the execution of a sentence of a court following his conviction of a crime for which this penalty is provided by law.*
>
> *2. Deprivation of life shall not be regarded as inflicted in contravention of this Article when it results from the use of force which is no more than absolutely necessary:*
>
> *(a)   in defence of any person from unlawful violence;*
> *(b)   in order to effect a lawful arrest or to prevent the escape of a person lawfully detained;*
> *(c)   in action lawfully taken for the purpose of quelling a riot or insurrection."*

The European Court of Human Rights (ECtHR) at Strasbourg has made it clear that Article 2 imposes on states signatory to the ECHR substantive obligations:

(i)   not to take life without justification; and
(ii) to establish a framework of laws, precautions, procedures and means of enforcement which will protect life.

Further, there is a "procedural" obligation:

(iii) to initiate an effective public investigation into a death in which it appears that one of the substantive obligations has been, or may have been, violated and it appears that agents of the state are, or may be, in some way implicated.

This chapter confines itself to the practical importance of Article 2 to inquests, and therefore does not deal directly with the line of ECtHR, UK and English authority on hospital liability for breaches of Article 2 (for which see *Rabone v. Pennine Care NHS*

Trust,[45] *Savage v. South Essex NHS Trust,*[46] *Savage v. South Essex NHS Trust (No. 2)*[47] and, more generally, *Powell v. UK*[48] considered in more detail in Chapter 5.

10.2   Article 2/Section 5(2) Inquests

In *R (Middleton) v. West Somerset Coroner and another*[49] the House of Lords addressed what the ECHR requires (by way of verdict/judgment/findings, etc.) of an investigation into a death involving a possible violation of Article 2 ECHR and whether the coroner system met those requirements. The case arose out of a death in custody. The House held that it was necessary to look back to the Coroners Act 1988 – the predecessor to the 2009 Act – in order to comply with the UK's ECHR obligations. The ECHR required a broader interpretation of the word "how" in the 1988 Act. "How" has to connote "by what means and in what circumstances". It was not expected that this would require a change of approach in those cases where a traditional short form verdict would be satisfactory, but that it would call for a change of approach in others. In the latter class of case it is for the coroner to decide how best to elicit the jury's conclusion on the central issue(s). It may be done by a narrative verdict or by answers to questions put by him. The prohibition in (what is now) s. 10(2) must not however be compromised.

Thus in cases where Article 2 is "engaged" (see below), the wider investigative test of "by what means and in what circumstances" a person came by their death is to be used in place of "how", and a conclusion on the central facts at issue should be expressed.

Inquests requiring the broader, *Middleton* definition of "how" came to be known as "*Middleton* inquests" or "Article 2 inquests". Today they could equally be called "Section 5(2) inquests". Although in *R (Smith) v. Secretary of State for Defence*[50] Lord Phillips SCJ expressed the view that there is not much practical difference between a *Middleton* and a *Jamieson* inquest, it is the experience of practitioners that the scope of the inquest – in terms of the lines of questioning that are permissible and the extent of the findings made – is wider at a s. 5(2) inquest.

10.3   Circumstances in which a Section 5(2) Inquest is Required

The Strasbourg jurisprudence on when the investigatory obligation under Article 2 is "engaged" has been subjected to detailed analysis by English courts (though English judges invariably say that they do not find the task easy): *R (Goodson) v. Bedfordshire and Luton Coroner;*[51] *R (Takoushis) v. Inner London Coroner;*[52] and *R (Humberstone) v. Legal Services Commission.*[53] Those cases can be reduced to the principles articulated by Smith LJ in the last-cited case at [58]:

> *"Article 2 imposes an obligation on the state to set up a judicial system which enables any allegation of possible involvement by a state agent in a death to be*

---

45 [2010] EWCA Civ 698.
46 [2008] UKHL 74.
47 [2010] EWHC 865.
48 (2000) 30 EHRR CD 362.
49 [2004] 2 WLR 800.
50 [2010] UKSC 29 at para. 78.
51 [2004] EWHC 2931.
52 [2006] 1 WLR 461.
53 [2010] EWCA Civ 1479.

investigated. That obligation may be satisfied in England by criminal or civil proceedings, an inquest and even disciplinary proceedings or any combination of those procedures. This obligation envisages the provision of a facility available to citizens and not an obligation proactively to instigate an investigation.

Only in limited circumstances will there be a specific obligation proactively to conduct an investigation – which might mean a duty to conduct a Middleton inquest. Those limited circumstances arise where the death occurs while the deceased is in the custody of the state or, in the context of allegations against hospital authorities, where the allegations are of a systemic nature such as the failure to provide suitable facilities or adequate staff or appropriate systems of operation. They do not include cases where the only allegations are of 'ordinary' medical negligence."

The conclusion seems to be drawn that in all cases where there is a death in an NHS hospital which may have been caused by a wrongful act, Article 2 is "engaged" in the sense that the state must have a system which provides for the practical and effective investigation of the facts and determination of civil liability. However, in the majority of cases concerning hospital deaths, the extent of the investigation is normally met by the variety of processes available and the traditional kind of inquest – i.e. a *Jamieson* inquest – will suffice.

There is nevertheless a class of clinical negligence case contemplated by the appeal courts in *Humberstone* and *Takoushis* in which the state's obligation to proactively conduct a more thorough investigation *is* engaged. These may be cases where concerns are raised about a genuine systemic failure (*Takoushis*; and see *Humberstone* at [70] to [71]), or where gross negligence is alleged (see *Takoushis* at [96], and *R (Khan) v. Secretary of State for Health*[54]), or where the deceased was detained under the Mental Health Act 1983 (given that sectioning engages the state's operational duty to protect life under Article 2: *Rabone v. Pennine Care NHS Trust*[55]). Although they are a subset of the class "cases concerning hospital deaths", and as such can be expected to be fewer in number, in *Humberstone* the Court of Appeal refused to describe them as "exceptional", preferring the term "limited".

10.4 Practical Consequences for Management of Inquests

As a result of s. 5(2), and depending upon the circumstances of death, there may well now be legal argument as to the scope of the inquest either at a pre-inquest review or at the beginning of the resumed hearing. Some coroners feel that the question of the scope of the inquest cannot be finally decided until the evidence starts to come out, and the scope of the inquest can therefore expand or contract as the inquest goes on. The practice of coroners varies in this regard, albeit coroners will tend to proceed with caution if there is the potential for a finding that the state failed to discharge its obligations under Article 2. The Chief Coroner may in due course issue guidance on the coroner's decision whether to conduct a s. 5(2) inquest.

In relation to the issue of summing up to a jury involving the application of Article 2, see *R (P) v. HM Coroner for the District of Avon*.[56] The deceased hanged herself in prison. The central factual issues at the inquest were whether she intended to kill herself, and

---

54 [2003] EWCA Civ 1129.
55 [2010] EWCA Civ 698.
56 [2009] EWCA Civ 1367.

whether the prison's management and care of her deserved criticism. The coroner summarised for the jury the three available verdicts: suicide, accident or narrative verdict. The jury returned a verdict of accidental death, but the coroner had not told them that they could append a brief narrative to their verdict, dealing with the second issue (management and care by the prison). The Court of Appeal held that this had rendered the summing up materially defective. The coroner's first task was "*to decide how best, in a particular case, to elicit the jury's conclusion on the central issue or issues*" (*Middleton*). There is a public interest in juries being given a clear opportunity to express their findings in narrative form. (The appeal was nevertheless dismissed: a report of the Prison Ombudsman substantially filled the lacuna left by the limited nature of the jury's verdict, and therefore rendered the totality of the investigative process compliant with Article 2. So no fresh inquest was needed.)

11   RECOVERY OF INQUEST COSTS IN SUBSEQUENT CLINICAL NEGLIGENCE ACTIONS

Are the claimant's costs of attending the inquest by counsel prior to the issue of proceedings in a clinical negligence claim recoverable in that claim? In *Roach and another v. Home Office*[57] Davies J, sitting with Master Wright, decided that there was no general rule that the costs of one set of proceedings are irrecoverable as costs of another. The inquest costs will however be scrutinised by the costs judge in the same way as the costs of the proceedings. So the costs judge will consider whether the work done on the inquest was relevant to the subsequent proceedings and whether the cost was proportionate.

In *(1) Stewart (2) Howard v. Medway NHS Trust*[58] the claimant succeeded in recovering the costs of the inquest. The court held that the purpose of the party incurring the costs should be examined, not the purpose of the action in which the costs were incurred. Costs of an inquest could be of, and incidental to, other actions. It was reasonable for the claimant to have sought to make submissions and cross-examine witnesses at the inquest and to have had an impact on the findings of fact made by the coroner's court. The claimant was accordingly entitled to the pre-issue costs of the inquest.

In *Jacqueline King v. Milton Keynes General NHS Trust*[59] Master Gordon-Saker reached the same conclusion save that the cost of work done to persuade the coroner to reach a particular verdict was not recoverable, nor was the attendance of the family's expert medical witness although the costs of his report on liability and causation was adjudged recoverable in principle. This may lead to some practical problems in terms of counsel's fees but does at least pave the way for recovery of the expert's fees in relation to the crucial paper report upon which much of counsel's preparation may rest.

---

57 [2009] EWHC 312 (QB).
58 LTL 20/09/2004.
59 LTL 13/05/2004.

12   PUBLIC FUNDING

Legal Help, consisting of advice and assistance about a legal problem not including representation or advocacy in proceedings, is available for inquests where the applicants qualify financially, and can be used to assist bereaved families in making written submissions to the coroner (for example, a list of questions they wish him or her to ask witnesses).

Section 51 of the Act would have amended Sch. 2 to the Access to Justice Act 1999 ("Community Legal Service: excluded cases") so as to bring advocacy at some inquests – mainly deaths in custody – within the scope of the legal aid scheme. But s. 51 (and indeed most of the Access to Justice Act 1999) was repealed by the Legal Aid, Sentencing and Punishment of Offenders Act 2012 (LASPO).

Civil legal aid is now available only in relation to those legal services described in Part 1 of Sch. 1 to LASPO. Paragraph 41 thereof describes civil legal services provided to an individual in relation to an inquest "under the Coroners Act 1988" into the death of a member of that individual's family. The services described do not include advocacy: Part 3 of Sch. 1. Even this limited help is subject to exclusions, such that no legal services may be provided (on legal aid) in relation to a claim in negligence, assault or battery. Further, the individual must satisfy the Legal Aid Agency that they satisfy the financial eligibility criteria.

Advocacy at an inquest can be funded by means of exceptional case funding pursuant to s. 10 of LASPO. The Lord Chancellor has issued guidance to the Legal Aid Agency in deciding whether to give exceptional case funding in relation to an inquest. Pursuant to this guidance, the LAA will be prepared to recommend to the Lord Chancellor that he should grant funding for representation at an inquest:

- where there is a "significant wider public interest" (as defined) in the applicant being legally represented at the inquest; or
- where *"funded representation for the family is likely to be necessary to enable the coroner to carry out an effective investigation into the death as required by Article 2 ECHR"*.

The case of *R (Sumaiya Patel) v. Lord Chancellor & Assistant Deputy Coroner for Inner West London*[60] concerned the "significant wider public interest" criterion. The claimant was a widow of one of the 7/7 bombers. The Lord Chancellor had refused her request for exceptional funding, but had granted funding for the families of the victims, on the basis that while there was a significant wider public interest in representation of the victims' families, there was no such public interest in representation of the bombers' families. Dismissing the claim, the Administrative Court held that the threshold for "significant wider public interest" was high. The claimant had not demonstrated that representation would produce any benefits for people other than her, let alone that any such benefits were "substantial".

As for Article 2, there are several reported cases involving challenges to decisions of the old Legal Services Commission to refuse to recommend funding of legal

---

60 [2010] EWHC 2220 (Admin).

representation at inquests. In *R (Humberstone) v. LSC*,[61] the Court of Appeal approved the (then) Lord Chancellor's guidance in principle but held that it had been applied in an unreasonable way. The deceased was a 10-year-old boy who had died of asthma. His mother was arrested and interviewed on suspicion of manslaughter by gross negligence. She alleged that NHS staff and systems had caused or contributed to her son's death. Those staff and institutions would be represented at the inquest, which was likely to be a *Middleton* inquest (see above). She was likely to have difficulty understanding proceedings. In those circumstances the Court of Appeal (like the Administrative Court below them) held that the Lord Chancellor's guidance compelled the grant of funding for legal representation.

The test for whether representation (i.e. advocacy) is "required by Article 2 ECHR" is whether there are exceptional circumstances, factual and/or legal complexity so that legal representation is needed at the inquest in order to ensure an effective investigation with the next of kin involved to an appropriate extent (*R (Khan) v. Secretary of State for Health*;[62] *R ((1) Jane Challender (2) Paulette Morris) v. Legal Services Commission*;[63] *R (Andrew Jones) v. Legal Services Commission*;[64] and *Humberstone* (see above).

---

61 [2010] EWCA Civ 1479.
62 [2003] EWCA Civ 1129.
63 [2004] EWHC 925 (Admin).
64 [2007] EWHC 2106 (Admin).

APPENDIX: FORM 2, SCHEDULE TO THE CORONERS (INQUEST) RULES 2013

Form 2

Record of an inquest

The following is the record of the inquest (including the statutory determination and, where required, findings)—

1. Name of the deceased (if known):

2. Medical cause of death:

3. How, when and where, and for investigations where section 5(2) of the Coroners and Justice Act 2009 applies, in what circumstances the deceased came by his or her death: (see note (ii))

4. Conclusion of the coroner/ jury as to the death: (see notes (i) and (ii):

5. Further particulars required by the Births and Deaths Registration Act 1953 to be registered concerning the death:

1.	2.	3.	4.	5.	6.
Date and place of death	Name and surname of deceased	Sex	Maiden surname of woman who has married	Date and place of birth	Occupation and usual address

Signature of coroner (and jurors):

NOTES:

(i) One of the following short-form conclusions may be adopted:—

I. accident or misadventure

II. alcohol / drug related

III. industrial disease

IV. lawful/ unlawful killing

V. natural causes

VI. open

VII. road traffic collision

VIII. stillbirth

IX. suicide

(ii) As an alternative, or in addition to one of the short-form conclusions listed under NOTE (i), the coroner or where applicable the jury, may make a brief narrative conclusion.

(iii) The standard of proof required for the short form conclusions of "unlawful killing" and "suicide" is the criminal standard of proof. For all other short-form conclusions and a narrative statement the standard of proof is the civil standard of proof.

Chapter 15

LIMITATION

In the field of clinical negligence limitation is a creature of statute governed by the Limitation Act 1980 as amended and unless otherwise stated, references in this chapter to section numbers are to that Act.

1   WHY HAVE LIMITATION OF ACTIONS?

Limitations on the time in which claims can be brought exist to ensure that claims are not too stale when they reach court and to give certainty to the parties – particularly the defendant and its insurers who will wish to be able to close their books on potential claims.

In *Robinson v. St Helens Metropolitan BC*[1] Sir Murray Stuart-Smith said: *"The Limitation Acts are designed to protect defendants from the injustice of having to fight stale claims especially when any witnesses the defendants might have been able to rely on are not available or have no recollection and there are no documents to assist the court in deciding what was done or not done and why."* He went on to say, in the context of a dyslexia claim against an education authority but potentially of relevance in a claim against a health authority: *"These cases are very time consuming to prepare and try and they inevitably divert resources from the education authority to defending the claim rather than teach."*

2   PERSONAL INJURY CLAIMS

A claim founded on tort where the damages do not consist of or include damages in respect of personal injuries (see below) must be brought within 6 years from the date on which the cause of action accrued – s. 2.

However, the period is both shortened and potentially lengthened in the case of *"any action for damages for negligence, nuisance or breach of duty (whether the duty exists by virtue of a contract or of provision made by or under a statute or independently of [either]) where the damages claimed by the claimant…consist of or include damages in respect of personal injuries"* – s. 11(1).

In this case the claim *"shall not be brought after the expiration of"*:[2]

> *"three years from the date on which the cause of action accrued or the date of knowledge (if later) of the person injured."*[3]

---

1 [2003] PIQR P128.
2 Section 11(3).
3 Section 11(4).

Personal injuries are defined in s. 38 as including *"any disease and any impairment of a person's physical or mental condition"*.

3   INTENTIONAL TORT OR BREACH OF DUTY?

In *Stubbings v. Webb*[4] the House of Lords held that s. 11 did not apply in the case of deliberate assault, as might occur for example in the absence of consent to medical treatment, as intentional trespass to the person is not an action for *"negligence, nuisance or breach of duty"*. This decision was overruled in *A v. Hoare*[5] on the basis that it was wrongly decided, putting all claims in tort in which damages for personal injuries are claimed on the same footing, and subject to s. 11 and not s. 2.

4   DOES EXPIRY OF THE LIMITATION PERIOD PREVENT A CLAIM BEING BROUGHT?

The Limitation Act provides the defendant with a defence which it may claim if it wishes to but if it does not then the claimant can pursue his claim. If not pleaded by the defendant, it is not a matter with which the court will be concerned. The Act does not mean that the bringing of an action after the time provided is prohibited.

A claimant can therefore start a valid action even if on the face of it the action is out of time. It used to be a common practice not to refer to limitation in the Particulars of Claim. If the limitation defence was raised in the defendant's statement of case, then the claimant could draft a Reply as necessary to raise all relevant issues.

The situation has changed under the Civil Procedure Rules. The use of the Pre-Action Protocols, with the Letter of Claim and the defendant's considered reply to the claim, should have identified whether or not limitation is to be seriously in issue. Thus it will often be necessary for a claimant to address limitation in the Particulars of Claim setting out matters relevant to ss. 11 and 14 and s. 33 (see below). If the issue of limitation is first raised in the defence then the claimant will need to serve a reply to raise those further matters.

5   WHEN TIME BEGINS TO RUN

By s. 11 a claim for personal injuries shall not be brought after the expiration of 3 years from:

  (i) the date on which the cause of action accrued; or
  (ii) the date of knowledge (if later) of the person injured.

6   ACCRUAL OF A CAUSE OF ACTION

A cause of action for damages for personal injury for breach of duty accrues when damage occurs, that is when there is injury or disease. Until damage is caused, the

---

4 [1993] AC 498.
5 [2008] UKHL 6.

cause of action is not complete. In the context of clinical negligence, establishing when damage occurred is not normally an issue. However there must be *"actionable injury"*, and *"while such damage need not be substantial it must be more than minimal"*.[6]

> *"[A]n injury without any symptoms at all because it cannot be seen or felt and which will not lead to some other event that is harmful has no consequences that will attract an award of damages."*[7]

> *"The fact that negligence has produced a physiological change that is neither visible nor symptomatic and which in no way impairs the bodily functions should not attract legal liability."*[8]

Given the circumstances in which clinical negligence occurs and the uncertainty of outcome even in the absence of negligence, the question that will frequently arise is not when did injury occur, but when did the claimant first have knowledge that damage had been sustained.

7   KNOWLEDGE UNDER SECTIONS 11 AND 14

The date of knowledge is defined by s. 14(1) as:

> *"the date on which the person concerned first had knowledge of the following facts:*
>
> *(a)   that the injury in question was significant; and*
>
> *(b)   that it was attributable in whole or in part to the act or omission which is alleged to constitute negligence, nuisance or breach of duty; and*
>
> *(c)   the identity of the defendant; and*
>
> *(d)   if it is alleged that the act or omission was that of a person other than the defendant, the identity of the person and the additional facts supporting the bringing of an action against the defendant;*
>
> *and knowledge that any acts or omissions did or did not, as a matter of law, involve negligence, nuisance or breach of duty is irrelevant."*

8   ONUS OF PROOF

Where a claim is issued more than 3 years after the cause of action accrued the onus of proving knowledge is on the claimant.[9]

9   "KNOWLEDGE"

Careful consideration needs to be given to what amounts to knowledge. In *Nash & Ors v. Eli Lilly & Co & Ors*,[10] the Court of Appeal declined to lay down a definition but said that:

---

6 *Rothwell v. Chemical & Insulating Co Ltd CA* [2006] EWCA Civ 19.

7 Lord Hope in *Johnston v. NEI International Combustion Ltd (the Rothwell case)* [2007] UKHL 39 at 47.

8 Lord Phillips CJ in *Rothwell* CA at 61.

9 *Nash & Others v. Eli Lilly & Co* [1993] 1 WLR 782 at 796H.

10 [1993] 1 WLR 782.

> *"knowledge is a condition of mind which imports a degree of certainty and that degree of certainty which is appropriate for this purpose is that which, for the particular claimant, may reasonably be regarded as sufficient to justify embarking upon the preliminaries to the making of a claim for compensation, such as taking legal advice."*

Appropriate knowledge has also been described as knowledge of the facts constituting the *essence of the complaint of negligence*.[11] However, the correct approach to this issue is not straightforward and *Nash* certainly now needs to be read in the context of the Supreme Court decision in *Ministry of Defence v. AB*.[12] Their Lordships (Phillips, Walker, Hale, Brown, Mance, Kerr and Wilson LJ) were split 4:3 on the question of what constituted knowledge for the purpose of s. 14(1). The Supreme Court noted that there was a *"distinction in principle between a claimant's knowledge (actual or constructive) that he has a real possibility of a claim...and the assembly by the claimant and his legal team, with the help of experts, of material justifying the commencement of proceedings with a reasonable prospect of success."* In that case, over 1,000 claimants, who had been exposed to thermonuclear tests in the South Pacific in the 1950s, had issued claim forms in 2005 believing that they had been exposed to harmful radiation which had caused illness. It was not until 2007 that they obtained expert evidence which confirmed that they had been exposed to radiation. They attempted to argue that their date of knowledge did not run until the receipt of expert evidence, but even then it was apparent that this evidence was insufficient to overcome causation and their claims were framed on the basis of a material increase in ill health (they were seeking to extend the *Fairchild* exception).

The lead majority judgment was from Lord Wilson who said *"it is a legal impossibility for a claimant to lack knowledge of attributability for the purpose of section 14(1) at a time after the date of issue of his claim. By that date he must in law have had knowledge of it"* this so, not least in light of the statement of truth to be appended to the pleadings. Wilson and Walker LJJ both specifically endorsed the comments of Lord Donaldson MR *in Halford v. Brookes*[13] to the effect that *"reasonable belief will normally suffice"* (that view having been previously endorsed by Judge LJ in *Sneizek v. Bundy (Letchworth) Limited*[14] and ultimately by the House of Lords in *Haward v. Fawcetts*.[15] Lord Wilson in AB said *"this court should reiterate endorsement for Lord Donaldson's proposition that a claimant is likely to have acquired knowledge of the facts specified in section 14 when he first came reasonably to believe them. I certainly accept that the basis of his belief plays a part in the inquiry...what I do not accept is that he lacks knowledge until he has the evidence with which to substantiate his belief in court"*.[16]

As for reasonable belief it must be held: (per Lord Donaldson in *Halford*, specifically endorsed in *MOD v. AB*) *"with sufficient confidence to justify embarking on the preliminaries to the issue of a writ, such as submitting a claim to the proposed defendant, taking legal and other advice and collecting evidence"*. Another way of expressing it was that the belief should be "reasoned" and "reasonable". So, where a claimant held a firm belief which was of sufficient certainty to justify the taking of preliminary steps for proceedings, by

---

11 *Haward v. Fawcetts* [2006] UKHL 9.
12 [2012]UKSC 9. See Lord Walker at para 47–48.
13 [1991] 1 WLR 428.
14 [2000] PIQR P213.
15 [2006] UKHL 9.
16 Paragraph 11 of the judgment in AB.

obtaining advice about making a claim for compensation, such a belief is knowledge within the meaning of s. 14 and the limitation period begins to run. However, the date on which the claimant first consulted an expert or a solicitor is not, on its own, likely to assist the court in determining whether by then he had the requisite knowledge. It is the confidence with which the claimant held the belief and to the substance which it carried prior to consulting the expert that will matter. Suspicion alone therefore is not normally enough.[17] An example of the application of this principle is *Preston v. BBH Solicitors*,[18] in which it was held that the limitation period ran not from the date on which the claimant was told he had pleural plaques (for which he could not claim as that condition did not amount to a compensatable injury) with a possibility that he had asbestosis (a compensatable injury) but from the date (3 years later) when it was confirmed to the claimant that he did indeed have asbestosis.

10   CONSTRUCTIVE KNOWLEDGE

In deciding whether the claimant had knowledge of the matters set out under s. 14(1), it is necessary to take into account not only the claimant's actual knowledge but also imputed or constructive knowledge. Section 14(3) provides:

> *"a person's knowledge includes knowledge which he might reasonably have been expected to acquire –*
> *(a)   from facts observable or ascertainable by him; or*
> *(b)   from facts ascertainable by him with the medical or other appropriate help of expert advice which it is reasonable for him to seek;*
> *but a person shall not be fixed with knowledge of a fact ascertainable only with the help of expert advice so long as he has taken all reasonable steps to obtain (and where appropriate to act on) that advice."*

The test has been said to be that of the reasonable man of moderate intelligence.[19] The test is objective and does not allow for consideration of a particular claimant's readiness to resort to litigation. In *AB* Lord Walker said:

> *"Taken together the unanimous decisions of the House of Lords in A v Hoare (on section 14(2)) and Adams v Bracknell Forest Borough Council [2005] 1 AC 76 (on section 14(3)) appear to me to mark a decisive shift away from a subjective approach on these issues. What was within a claimant's actual knowledge is undoubtedly a subjective question. But the notion that whether a claimant has knowledge depends both upon the information he has received and upon what he makes of it, (Nash v Eli Lilly & Co [1993] 1 WLR 782) can no longer be accepted, at any rate without a lot of qualification. The recent authorities recognise that the policy of the law is for the date of knowledge to be ascertained in the same way for all claimants, without regard to their personal characteristics, which can be taken into account at the later stage of exercising discretion under section 33 of the 1980 Act."[20]*

---

17 *Albonetti v. Wirral MBC LTL* 11/8/2006.
18 [2011] EWCA Civ 1429; at para. 39 the Court of Appeal said that the claimant "*could not have considered the injury sufficiently serious to justify his instituting proceedings and no knowledge should be imputed to him that he was already the victim of asbestos*". See also *Lloyd v. Hoey* [2011] EWCA Civ 1060.
19 *Nash & Ors v. Eli Lilly & Co & Ors* (see above).
20 *AB v. MOD*, per Lord Walker at para. 47.

Adams v. Bracknell Forest Borough Council[21] was a dyslexia claim. Lord Hoffmann said:

> *"I do not see how [a particular claimant's] character or intelligence can be relevant. In my opinion Section 14(3) requires one to assume that a person who is aware that he has suffered a personal injury, serious enough to be something about which he would go and see a solicitor if he knew he had a claim, will be sufficiently curious about the causes of the injury to seek whatever expert advice is appropriate."*

It was suggested in *Johnson v. Ministry of Defence*[22] that Lord Hoffmann must have meant that there was an assumption that a person who had suffered a significant injury would be sufficiently curious to seek advice *unless* there were reasons why a reasonable person in his position would not have done, such as that the claimant had become so used to the condition from which he suffered that a reasonable person would not be expected to be curious about its cause. In that case the claimant had worked in noisy environments between 1965 and 1979. He became aware of some hearing loss aged 61 in 2001. He did not consult a doctor until 2006 who told him when he asked if there was wax in his ears that there was no wax in his ears which appeared clear and told him any hearing loss was probably age related. In 2009 he obtained expert evidence which attributed his hearing loss to his previous work. He issued proceedings the following year. His claim was held to be statute barred. The Court of Appeal dismissed his appeal. The test in *Adams v. Bracknell* was hard to apply where the condition came on gradually. However, for good policy reasons the test was fairly demanding and a reasonable man in 2001 would have asked the GP an open question as to the likely cause of his hearing loss and the GP would have asked about his work history. His date of knowledge was assumed to be the end of 2002.

In the context of a clinical negligence claim, in *Forbes v. Wandsworth HA*[23] it was recognised that a patient who is not cured when he hoped to be might respond by saying *"Oh well, it is just one of those things. I expect the doctors did their best"* or he might decide to take a second opinion as lack of success might be because of want of care.

> *"I do not think that the person who adopts the first alternative can necessarily be said to be acting unreasonably. But he is in effect making a choice either consciously…or unconsciously. Can a person who has effectively made this choice many years later, and without any alteration of circumstances, change his mind and then seek advice which reveals that all along he had a claim? I think not. It seems to me that where, as here, the plaintiff expected or at least hoped that the operation would be successful and it manifestly was not, with the result that he sustained a major injury, a reasonable man of moderate intelligence, if he thought about the matter, would say that the lack of success was 'either just one of those things…or something may have gone wrong and there may have been a want of care. I do not know which but if I am ever to make a claim, I must find out'."*

Forbes was applied in *Whiston v. London Strategic Health Authority*,[24] in which the claimant developed cerebral palsy as a result of brain damage during his birth in 1974. Proceedings were not issued until 2006. At first instance it was accepted that, despite

---

21 [2005] 1 AC 76.
22 [2012] EWCA Civ 1505
23 [1997] QB 402 at 412D.
24 [2010] EWCA Civ 195.

the claimant's mother being a nurse and trained midwife, the circumstances of the claimant's birth were not discussed with him until 2005. In considering the defendant's appeal the Court of Appeal noted that the House of Lords had *"tightened up"* the requirements of constructive knowledge and accepted that *"the decision in Adams requires the court to expect a heightened degree of curiosity of the reasonable claimant than it would do absent section 33".*[25] The Court of Appeal held that a reasonable person in the claimant's position would have wanted to know about the circumstances which had given rise to his medical difficulties. Constructive knowledge was attributed from when the claimant was in his early twenties. One of the reasons why the court felt able to take a strict, or objective, view of constructive knowledge was because of the room for subjective factors in the exercise of discretion pursuant to s. 33, and on the facts of that case s. 11 was disapplied by the exercise of that discretion (see below). In *Platt v. BRB (Residuary) Ltd*,[26] another deafness case, the claimant did not fare so well applying the *Adams* test. He was held to have constructive knowledge when (having suffered for some years with tinnitus and reduction in his hearing) he was referred to an ENT specialist in 1997 who examined him and asked whether he had worked in a noisy environment and the claimant replied that he had. He did not ask and was not told that he was suffering from noise induced hearing loss. A reasonable man (applying *Adams*) would have done so. He subsequently issued proceedings in 2011 having realised when he read an article in 2010 that his hearing loss might have been noise induced. His s. 33 application failed.

11 "KNOWLEDGE THAT THE INJURY IN QUESTION WAS SIGNIFICANT"

The claimant must have knowledge that the injury in question was significant. Section 14(2) provides that:

> *"an injury is significant if the person whose date of knowledge is in question would reasonably have considered it sufficiently serious to justify his instituting proceedings for damages against a defendant who did not dispute liability and was able to satisfy a judgment."*

There was uncertainty as to whether there was scope for some subjective element in applying this test so that the personal characteristics of the claimant, whether pre-existing or consequent on the injury suffered, could be taken into account. That has been resolved by the House of Lords in *A v. Hoare*:[27]

> *"The material to which [the test under Section 14(2)] applies is generally 'subjective' in the sense that it is applied to what the claimant knows of his injury rather than the injury as it actually was. Even then, knowledge may have to be supplemented with imputed 'objective' knowledge under Section 14(3). But the test itself is an entirely impersonal standard; not whether the claimant himself would have considered the injury sufficiently serious to justify proceedings but whether he would 'reasonably' have done so. You ask what the claimant knew about the injury he had suffered, you add any knowledge about the injury which may be imputed to him under Sections 14(3) and you then ask whether a reasonable person with that knowledge would have considered the injury sufficiently serious to justify his*

---

25 [2010] EWCA Civ 195 at para. 59.
26 [2014] EWCA Civ 1401, [2015] PIQR P7.
27 [2008] UKHL 6.

instituting proceedings for damages against a defendant who did not dispute liability and was able to satisfy a judgment."[28]

As Lord Hoffmann pointed out:

"Judges should not have to grapple with the notion of the reasonable unintelligent person. Once you have ascertained what the claimant knew and what he should be treated as having known, the actual claimant drops out of the picture."[29]

Therefore there is a three-stage test:

(1) What did the claimant actually know about the injury?

(2) What should the claimant have known (under s. 14(3))?

(3) Would a reasonable person with all of that knowledge have considered the injury significant, i.e. sufficiently serious to justify instituting proceedings against a defendant who did not dispute liability and was able to satisfy a judgment?

12 "KNOWLEDGE THAT THE INJURY WAS ATTRIBUTABLE IN WHOLE OR IN PART TO THE ACT OR OMISSION WHICH IS ALLEGED TO CONSTITUTE NEGLIGENCE, NUISANCE OR BREACH OF DUTY"

"Knowledge that any acts or omissions did or did not as a matter of law involve negligence, nuisance or breach of duty is irrelevant" – s. 14(1). It is knowledge of the injury being attributable to the act or omission complained of, and the legal consequences of such act or omission, that is relevant.

The test is one of attributability not causation and "attributable" means *"capable of being attributed to"* in the sense of a real possibility.[30]

What is needed is knowledge of the essence of the act or omission to which the injury is attributable rather than knowledge of the details of how the case may subsequently be pleaded. For example, where a surgeon carried out a mastectomy during surgery because he considered he had found a pre-cancerous lump, time was held to run from the moment the claimant was told of the laboratory analysis, which was that the lump was benign, because she then had knowledge which enabled her to attribute her injury to the defendants' fault.[31] Whether liability could be established had still to be considered, but did not stop the clock running.

In *Bentley v. Bristol & Western HA*,[32] the first instance judge had held that the claimant did not have knowledge of attributability when, following a hip replacement operation, her sciatic nerve was damaged to her knowledge; she only had the requisite knowledge when she knew the operation had not been carried out properly and that there had probably been excessive traction on the nerve. The Court of Appeal in the subsequent case of *Broadley v. Guy Chapman & Co*[33] held that *Bentley* had been wrongly

---

28 Lord Hoffmann at 34.
29 At 35.
30 *Spargo v. North Essex DHA* [1997] PIQR P235.
31 *Dobbie v. Medway HA* [1994] 4 All ER 450.
32 [1991] 2 Med LR 359.
33 [1994] 4 All ER 439.

decided and that the knowledge needed for the purposes of s. 14 was *"that her injury had been caused by damage to the nerve resulting from something which (the treating surgeon) had done or not done in the course of the operation"*.

In *Jones v. Liverpool HA*,[34] the claimant had suffered injury following surgery in 1974 and knew, in 1997, that his condition was caused by damage to his femoral artery in 1974, that further operations had not cured his problems and that until after the third operation he had not been treated with anti-coagulants. However, until 1991, he did not know that his problems could have been prevented by immediate corrective surgery after the first operation and the administration of anti-coagulants. Nonetheless, he was held to have known the facts which constituted the essence of the complaint in 1977, and consequently at that time had knowledge for the purposes of s. 14(1).

In *Whiston v. London Strategic Health Authority*[35] the claimant, who suffered from cerebral palsy as a result of oxygen deprivation during his childbirth, had known that he had been delivered by forceps. He had not, however, known that a junior doctor had used the wrong forceps and persisted with them for more than half an hour before seeking assistance from a more experienced registrar who delivered the claimant in less than 5 minutes with different forceps. The claimant did not have actual knowledge of the facts which constituted the essence of the complaint, though he was found to have had constructive knowledge.

Godfrey v. Gloucestershire Royal Infirmary NHS Trust[36] concerned the birth of a severely disabled baby following pre-natal scans which should have revealed the abnormalities. Knowledge that *"the injury was attributable…to the [defendant's] act or omission"* was held to have been present from the birth, at which point it was known that there had been scans, that no indication had been given to the claimant of any abnormalities and that the child when born was very severely disabled. It was not necessary to await the results of a medico-legal investigation to have the requisite knowledge.

While attribution is established as soon as the act or omission complained of is capable of being attributed to the defendant in broad terms, it is necessary that the actual act or omission which causes the injury is known. In *Rowbottom v. Royal Masonic Hospital*[37] the claimant's case was that the amputation of his leg was the result of failure to administer antibiotics following a hip replacement operation. It was held, by a majority and accepting that it was a borderline case, that prior to the addendum to the medical report to that effect the claimant was under the erroneous belief that the cause of the infection was a failure to install a drain, and not the absence of antibiotics. The claimant did not know that his injuries were capable of being attributed to the omission, the failure to administer antibiotics, until the later date.

In *Martin v. Kaisary*[38] the claimant suffered a cardiac arrest and brain damage following an operation for prostate cancer as a result of internal bleeding. He believed that the cause of the bleeding had been the administration of the drug heparin and his subsequent monitoring. Subsequently he was informed that the bleeding was from the operation site itself and not because of the administration of the drug. It was held that

---

34 [1996] PIQR P251.
35 [2010] EWCA 195.
36 [2003] EWHC 549.
37 [2002] EWCA Civ 87.
38 [2005] EWHC 531.

the claimant had not been reasonably able to discover the cause of his ongoing conditions until that subsequent information was provided to him.

In *Spargo v. North Essex DHA*[39] the principles were summarised as follows:

(1)   The knowledge required is a broad knowledge of the essence of the causally relevant act or omission to which the injury is attributable.

(2)   Attributable in this context means "capable of being attributed to" in the sense of being a real possibility.

(3)   The claimant has the requisite knowledge when he knows enough to make it reasonable for him to begin to investigate whether or not he has a case against the defendant, or the claimant will have such knowledge when he firmly believes that his condition is capable of being attributed to an act or omission which he can identify (in broad terms).

(4)   But the claimant will not have the requisite knowledge if he thinks he knows the acts and omissions he should investigate but in fact is wrong – or if his knowledge of what the defendant did or did not do is so vague or general that he cannot fairly be expected to know what he should investigate – or if his state of mind is such that he thinks his condition is capable of being attributed to the act or omission alleged but is not sure about this and would need to check with an expert before he could be properly said to know that it was.

But it should be noted that it has been suggested that it may be unhelpful if "valiant attempts" at guidelines such as this are treated as if they were statutory texts. The words of the statute must be the starting point.[40]

13   "KNOWLEDGE OF THE IDENTITY OF THE DEFENDANT"

This does not normally give rise to difficulties in clinical negligence claims, but could do so for example in identifying the appropriate corporate entity in relation to private medical care.

The claimant will generally be fixed with constructive knowledge if the identity of the defendant, although not known to the claimant, should have been ascertained by his solicitors.[41] Date of knowledge could be postponed for as long as it reasonably took to make and complete the appropriate enquiries where the identity of the defendant had wrongly been stated by the defendant.[42]

14   WHEN DOES THE LIMITATION PERIOD EXPIRE?

Time starts to run the day after the cause of action accrues, and presumably also the day after the day of knowledge. Issuing proceedings stops the clock running. If an

---

39 See above.
40 See *Ministry of Defence and AB* [2012] EWCA Civ 1505 per Lord Walker at para. 68.
41 *Henderson v. Temple Pier Co Ltd* [1988] 3 All ER 324.
42 *Cressey v. Timm* [2006] PIQR P9 (employer's liability claim).

incident causing immediate injury occurs at some time on 16th April 2005, or that day is the date of knowledge, then the last day on which to issue is 16th April 2008.[43]

If the last day falls on a weekend or court holiday, then the limitation period does not expire until the end of the next day when the court offices are open.[44]

If although received by the court on 16th April 2008 the court delays issue, then the date of receipt is deemed to be the date of issue – CPR 7APD para. 5.1 – and the court stamp on the claim form held on the court file or on the letter which accompanied the claim form should record that date (para. 5.2).[45] Wisely perhaps para. 5.4 states:

> *"Parties proposing to start a claim which is approaching the expiry of the limitation period should recognise the potential importance of establishing the date the claim form was received by the court and should themselves make arrangements to record the date."*

However proceedings are not brought within the limitation period if the request to the court for the issue of the claim, submitted on the last possible day, had not been accompanied by the appropriate court fee.[46]

15   CAN THE PERIOD BE EXTENDED BY AGREEMENT, ETC.?

A defendant can agree not to rely on or otherwise to waive his right to protection bestowed by a limitation period. An agreement should be clear and ideally in writing.

Conduct might be enough to act as a waiver, so that an estoppel was established in *Lubovsky v. Snelling*[47] where an insurance company's representative agreed that negotiation should proceed *"on the basis of an admission of liability"*, and in *Hare v. PRs of Mailk*[48] where the defendant agreed to conduct negotiations with the claimant on the basis that both parties agreed that the case should proceed and neither should take a technical point against the other.

However, making a voluntary interim payment where liability was not in question is not sufficient to act as a waiver,[49] and the defendant's failure to respond to the claimant's written request for an extension of time is not sufficient, even though the claimant genuinely understood that the defendant's silence amounted to consent.[50]

16   THE COURT'S DISCRETION UNDER SECTION 33

The 3-year time limit under ss. 11 and 14 of the 1980 Act is subject to the discretion of the court under s. 33, to disapply them:

---

43 See for example *Marren v. Dawson Bentley* [1961] 2 QB 135.
44 *Pritam Kaur v. Russell & Sons* [1973] QB 336.
45 *St Helens MBC v. Barnes* [2007] PIQR P10.
46 *Page et al v. Hewletts Solicitors et al* [2013] EWHC 2845.
47 [1994] 1 KB 45.
48 [1980] 124 SJ 328.
49 *Deerness v. John R Keeble* [1983] 2 Lloyds LR 260.
50 *K Lokumal & Sons (London) Limited v. Lotte Shipping Co Pte Ltd* [1985] 2 Lloyds LR 28.

> *"if it appears to the court that it would be equitable to allow an action to proceed having regard to the degree to which:*
> *(a)   the provisions of section 11 prejudice the claimant or any person whom he represents; and*
> *(b)   any decision of the court under this sub-section would prejudice the defendant or any person whom he represents."*

The Law Reform Committee report resulting in the introduction of the discretion now to be found in s. 33 rejected the proposal that the court should have a general discretion to extend time in meritorious cases, but recommended that *"in a residual class of cases"* regarded as *"exceptional"* the court should have a discretion to weigh the hardship to the parties and allow the claim to proceed if it would be equitable to do so. However in *Firman v. Ellis*[51] the Court of Appeal rejected an interpretation of the resulting legislation on this basis.

It is clear that the court has a wide discretion to allow the claim to proceed in spite of it having been commenced outside the 3-year time limit.

It is under s. 33 that the subjective matters now excluded from consideration under the objective interpretation of s. 14 are relevant and may be decisive, normally as one of the matters to be taken into account in the exercise of the discretion under subsection (3)(a) as *"the reasons for…the delay on the part of the claimant"*.

The discretion applies only to claims which are time-barred by reason of the provisions of s. 11 or 11A – Consumer Protection Act claims – or s. 12 – Fatal Accident Act claims.

17   PREVIOUS PROCEEDINGS

The House of Lords in *Horton v. Sadler*[52] overruled its previous decision in *Walkley v. Precision Forgings Ltd*[53] and as a result s. 33 can be invoked even where the initial cause of action was commenced within the limitation period and it is now sought to pursue a second set of proceedings.

Attempts to argue that resurrecting personal injury claims struck out for procedural failures was an abuse of process have failed. Discretion under s. 33 can still be relied upon (see *Aktas v. Adepta: Dixie v. British Polythene Industries Plc*[54]).

18   CONSIDERATIONS IN EXERCISING THE DISCRETION

In applying the provisions of s. 33 the court has to weigh the prejudice to the claimant of being unable to pursue his claim against the defendant, against the prejudice to the defendant of having to defend the claim after the primary limitation period has expired.

---

51 [1978] QB 886.
52 [2006] 2 WLR 1346.
53 [1979] 1 WLR 606.
54 [2010] EWCA Civ 1170.

Section 33 requires the court to have regard to all the circumstances of the case and to pay particular regard to the matters set out in s. 33(3).

> *"In acting under this section the Court shall have regard to all the circumstances of the case and in particular to -*
>
> *(a)   the length of, and the reason for, the delay on the part of the claimant;*
>
> *(b)   the extent to which having regard to the delay, the evidence adduced or likely to be adduced by the claimant or the defendant is or is likely to be less cogent than if the action had been brought within the time allowed by section 11, by section 11A or (as the case may be) by section 12;*
>
> *(c)   the conduct of the defendant after the cause of action arose, including the extent (if any) to which he responded to requests reasonably made by the claimant for information or inspection for the purpose of ascertaining the facts which were or might be relevant to the claimant's cause of action against the defendant;*
>
> *(d)   the duration of any disability of the claimant arising after the date of the accrual of the cause of action;*
>
> *(e)   the extent to which the claimant acted promptly and reasonably once he knew whether or not the act or omission of the defendant, to which the injury was attributable, might be capable at that time of giving rise to an action for damages;*
>
> *(f)   the steps, if any, taken by the claimant to obtain medical, legal or other expert advice and the nature of any such advice he may have received."*

The matters set out in s. 33(3) are exemplary and are not definitive. The court's discretion is unfettered.

The issue of limitation should be determined prior to deciding the issue of liability. To rely on findings on liability to assess the cogency of evidence for the purpose of determining limitation would *"put the cart before the horse"*.[55] It was argued by defendant appellants in *Raggett v. Society of Jesus Trust 1929 for Roman Catholic Purposes and Preston Catholic College Governors*[56] that it was inappropriate for the first instance judge to have determined substantive findings of fact in relation to historical sexual abuse taking place prior to considering whether to exercise the s. 33 discretion. The Court of Appeal held that it was a matter for the judge to decide in which order to deal with issues in a judgment. It was found that when considering s. 33, the judge had not directed her attention to her findings as to the happening of the abuse but to the cogency of the evidence. There was no error of law.

Whilst there is a judicial reluctance to provide any guidelines which might unduly restrict the operation of the discretion within the statutory framework, some general principles can be ascertained. In many cases the prejudice to the claimant and the prejudice to the defendant will be equal and opposite. The stronger the claimant's case the greater the prejudice to him in the application of the limitation defence and the greater the prejudice to the defendant in its disapplication. Accordingly, the prejudice to the defendant resulting from the loss of the limitation defence will almost always be balanced by the prejudice to the claimant from the operation of the provision. On the other hand, if it is shown that the claim is a weak case which will involve the

---

55 *KR v. Bryn Alyn Community* [2003] EWCA Civ 85 at para. 74(vii).
56 [2010] EWHC Civ 1002.

defendants in substantial costs in defending it against an impecunious claimant there may be significant relevant prejudice to the defendants if the limitation provisions are disapplied. *Ministry of Defence v. AB & Others*[57] involved claims for personal injury said to have been caused by nuclear testing. It was found to be inequitable to exercise discretion under s. 33, primarily because the claims were so weak on causation.

Legally aided claimants pose a particular costs risk to defendants, as also may the litigant in person or the claimant on a conditional fee with no or insufficient insurance cover. There may also be arguments that had the claim been brought earlier and before the introduction of conditional fee agreements the defendant would not have been liable to pay the additional liabilities under a CFA.[58]

Under s. 33 what is of paramount importance is the effect of delay on the defendant's ability to defend.[59] But with the CPR, an added factor is proportionality. "*The question of proportionality is now important in the exercise of any discretion, none more so than under Section 33*" – *Robinson v. St Helens Metropolitan BC*, approved in *Adams v. Bracknell*.[60]

In *Davidson v. Aegis Defence Services et al*[61] the Court of Appeal approved the guidance of Smith LJ in *Cain v. Francis*[62] and described it as "*the guidance which will almost always be of most use to first instance judges who are asked to disapply the three year time limit in personal injury cases*":

> "*It seems to me that in the exercise of the discretion the basic question to be asked is whether it is fair and just in all the circumstances to expect the Defendant to meet this claim on the merits, notwithstanding the delay in commencement. The length of the delay will be important not so much for itself as to the effect it has had. To what extent has the Defendant been disadvantaged in his investigation of the claim and/or the assembly of evidence in respect of the issues of both liability and quantum? But it will also be important to consider the reasons for the delay. Thus there may be some unfairness to the Defendant due to the delay in issue, but the delay may have arisen for so excusable a reason that, looking at the matter in the round, on balance it is fair and just that the action should proceed. On the other hand, the balance may go in the opposite direction, partly because the delay has caused procedural disadvantage and unfairness to the Defendant and partly because of the reasons for the delay or its length are not good ones.*
>
> *Although the delay referred to in 33(3) is the delay after the expiry of the primary limitation period, it will always be relevant to consider when the Defendant knew that a claim was to be made against him and also the opportunities he has had to investigate the claim and to collect evidence (see Donovan v Gwentoys). If, as here, a Defendant has had early notification of a claim and every possible opportunity to investigate and to collect evidence, some delay after the expiry of three years will have had no prejudicial effect.*"

---

57 [2010] EWCA Civ 1317.
58 See for example *Smith v. MOD* [2005] EWHC 682.
59 *Hartley v. Birmingham City District Council* [1992] 1 WLR 968 at 980C, *KR v. Bryn Alyn Community (Holdings) Ltd* [2003] QB 1441 at para. 81.
60 See above.
61 [2013] EWCA Civ 1586.
62 [2008] EWCA Civ 1451 at para. 73.

19   ONUS UNDER SECTION 33

The burden of showing that it would be equitable to disapply the limitation period rests on the claimant. It is an "exceptional indulgence" to a claimant to be granted only where equity between the parties demands it[63] although according to Leveson LJ in *Kew v. Bettamix Ltd*[64] "exceptional indulgence" means:

> *"no more than an indulgence that represents an exception to the general rule that a claim should be brought within the primary limitation period. Inevitably that casts a burden on the claimant to demonstrate good reason to justify the exception...The discretion remains unfettered but its exercise requires justification the reasons for which are articulated by the judge's judgment."*

It is not however helpful to discern whether the burden on the claimant is a heavy or a light one. The extent of the burden will vary from case to case, every case is fact-specific and the court's discretion is broad and unfettered.[65]

20   SECTION 33(3)(A): THE LENGTH OF AND REASONS FOR THE DELAY

It is only the delay after the expiry of the limitation period that is relevant here. However, when considering *"all the circumstances of the case"* the court can include prejudice accruing within the limitation period.[66]

Where the delay is short, a claimant may well be allowed to proceed. So where proceedings were issued one day late, the solicitors having been instructed 6 weeks after the accident, the discretion was exercised in the claimant's (and her solicitors') favour[67] as also where the delay was 9 days[68] and where the delay was 5½ months.[69] In *Hartley*[70] it was said that:

> *"if there was a short delay, which was in no way due to the plaintiff, but to a slip on the part of her solicitors which did not affect in the smallest degree the ability of the Defendant to defend the case because there had been early notification of the claim, the exercise of the discretion in favour of the plaintiff would be justified even if the plaintiff, if not allowed to proceed, would have a cast-iron action against her solicitors."*

The test with regard to establishing the reasons for delay is subjective, but having established what the reasons were, the court goes on to consider whether in fact the reason was a good one, or whether the claimant is culpable or not.[71]

Not thinking it worthwhile to bring proceedings is unlikely to suffice as a good reason for delay. So if the claimant had knowledge of his injury and his right to sue but took a conscious decision not to take action on the basis that, although objectively a

---

63 *KR v. Bryn Alyn Community (Holdings) Ltd* [2003] QB 1441 at para. 74(ii).
64 [2007] PIQR P16 at para. 28.
65 *Sayers v. Chelwood* [2012] EWCA Civ 175.
66 *Donovan v. Gwentoys Ltd* [1990] 1 WLR 472; *Price v. United Engineering Steels Ltd* (CA 12.12.97).
67 *Hartley v. Birmingham City District Council* [1992] 1 WLR 968.
68 *Hendy v. Milton Keynes HA* [1992] 3 Med LR 114.
69 *Corbin v. Penfold Metallising Co Ltd* [2000] Lloyds Rep Med 247.
70 See above.
71 *Coad v. Cornwall HA* [1997] 1 WLR 189.

"significant injury" he thought it too mild a condition to justify action, that is unlikely to be an adequate reason for delay.[72]

While poor legal advice may be very relevant as an explanation for delay, failing to take legal advice as to whether a claim in law existed may result in the discretion not being exercised.[73] But the claimant who had done his best to obtain appropriate medical and legal advice, and for example having initially obtained adverse expert medical opinion only subsequently obtains supportive medical evidence, would suffer an injustice if deprived of the opportunity to bring proceedings where there was no significant prejudice to the defendants.[74]

In *AB & Ors v. The Nugent Care Society*[75] the Court of Appeal considered the impact of *A v. Hoare*[76] in exercising the s. 33 discretion in claims for negligence in historic sexual abuse cases. At first instance the judge found that the claimants had been sexually abused but that the claims were brought out of time as proceedings had been brought long after the expiry of the 3-year limitation period which ran from claimants' date of knowledge. The claimants appealed against the judge's refusal to exercise his discretion pursuant to s. 33. The Court of Appeal referred to *A v. Hoare* which found that:

> "the right place to consider the question whether the claimant, taking into account his psychological state in consequence of the injury, could reasonably have been expected to institute proceedings, is under section 33. This consideration was previously treated as relevant to knowledge and not to the exercise of the discretion: see Bryn Alyn[77] at [76]. At [49] Lord Hoffmann expressly treated this part of the reasoning in Bryn Alyn as wrong. As he put it, sub-section 3(a) requires the judge to give due weight to evidence that the claimant was for practical purposes disabled from commencing proceedings by the psychological injuries he had suffered."[78]

The Court of Appeal found that the first instance decision failed to consider the psychological factors on the claimants' knowledge of injury or their ability to issue proceedings in determining whether or not s. 33 should be exercised. The impact of delay on the evidence was also considered (see below). The case was remitted to the lower court for reconsideration of s. 33.

It is not possible to lay down clear guidelines as to what are acceptable reasons for delay and acceptable periods of delay. It is a matter of fact and degree in each individual case. Each case will depend on its own facts.

The reasons for the delay and its length have to be balanced against the effect the delay has on the cogency of the evidence (see below). A distinction can be drawn between a claim which requires consideration of treatment (or failure to treat) over a substantial period of time, perhaps years, where by the nature of the condition or circumstances

72 *Buckler v. Sheffield City Council* [2004] EWCA Civ 920 (a pleural plaque case prior to the HL decision in *Johnston v. NEI International* (see above)).
73 *Skerratt v. Linfax Ltd* [2003] EWCA Civ 695.
74 *Sniezek v. Bundy (Letchworth) Ltd* [2000] PIQR 213.
75 [2009] EWCA Civ 827.
76 [2008] UKHL 6.
77 *KR v. Bryn Alyn Community (Holdings) Ltd* [2003] QB 1441.
78 *AB & Ors v. Nugent Care Society* [2009] EWCA Civ 827, para. 16.

contemporaneous medical records are understandably sparse as opposed to an act or omission on a particular occasion.

Similarly, in cases where the evidence is largely to be found in copious medical records, long delays are less likely to persuade the court not to exercise its discretion.

21   SECTION 33(3)(B): THE EXTENT TO WHICH THE EVIDENCE IS LIKELY TO BE LESS COGENT

Where a defendant can establish a significant loss of evidential cogency, the action is seldom allowed to proceed. The loss of important witnesses, or a witness's loss of memory of relevant facts, or the loss of relevant documents during the period of delay will be highly relevant to establishing the defendant's prejudice.

A long delay may raise a presumption of prejudice.[79] However, the burden of proving such prejudice rests with the defendant[80] and therefore something more than vague or general assertions of prejudice will be required.

In *AB & Ors v. The Nugent Care Society*[81] the Court of Appeal considered appeals against a first instance decision to refuse to exercise the s. 33 discretion in claims for negligence in historic sexual abuse cases. At first instance the judge declined to exercise his discretion primarily because the claims dealt with systematic negligence taking place many years before and he considered that the defendant would be unduly prevented from having a fair trial. The Court of Appeal noted that it was no longer necessary for evidence to cover the whole system being operated in the relevant home over the period as the defendant could be vicariously responsible for the abuse rather than just liable for systematic negligence.

> "In our opinion the difficulties of establishing those matters can be overstated. On the claimant's side the fact of the abuse depends largely, if not entirely upon the evidence of the claimant and must be set against any evidence available to the defendant."

The case was remitted for reconsideration of s. 33.[82] In relation to the second claimant Irwin J exercised discretion pursuant to s. 33 finding that the delay was principally because of a strong desire to suppress or avoid the abuse suffered. The cogency of the evidence was not diminished to any great degree by the death of the alleged abuser. However, in relation to the fourth claimant there were discrepancies and conflicts in his account and a significant number of key witnesses for the defence had died. There was a real risk of injustice if the fourth claimant's claim were allowed to proceed.

If breach of duty does not gives rise to immediate significant injury or if there is a significant period between breach of duty and the date for actual or constructive knowledge, this period of time prior to the commencement of the limitation period is part of *"the circumstances of the case"* within s. 33 to which the court will have regard, but it is of less significance than the period of delay which the court is required to take

---

79 *Buck v. English Electric Co Ltd* [1977] 1 WLR 806.
80 *Burgin v. Sheffield City Council* [2005] EWCA 482.
81 [2009] EWCA Civ 827.
82 [2010] EWHC 1005 (QB).

into account under s. 33(3)(b). The claimant may therefore argue that recent delay has had no or little impact on the cogency of the evidence as the damage was done before the claimant started being dilatory, while the defendant may assert that the earlier passage of time resulted in massive difficulties in defending the action and therefore any additional problems caused by the claimant's recent delay are a serious matter, and the court will assess these matters along with all other factors in exercising its discretion.[83]

In *Whiston v. London Strategic Health Authority*[84] the claim was brought 32 years after the cause of action accrued. Some evidence had been destroyed, namely the CTG record, which may have exonerated the doctor alleged to have caused the brain injury by negligent delay. However, this was found to be only a small part of the evidence and it could not be said whether it would have assisted the defence case or not. Their Lordships found that it was equitable to allow the claim to proceed as a fair trial was still possible and the decision of the claimant's parents not to pursue a claim earlier should not be held against the claimant. An extreme example in a person injury claim where proceedings were commenced over 14 years out of time as a result of inordinate delay by a solicitor, is presented by a case from Northern Ireland, *McArdle v. Marmion*,[85] in which the court cautioned against approaching "*the matter with an air of ruminative dissonance whereby, suffused with indignation at the inordinate delay by a professional adviser, the court loses sight of the decision on fairness and justice*". The investigations at the time of the accident together with early notification of a possible claim meant that the delay had not diminished the opportunity of the defendant to defend itself.

22   SECTION 33(3)(C): THE CONDUCT OF THE DEFENDANT AFTER THE CAUSE OF ACTION AROSE

The conduct of the defendant or his insurers or legal representatives has no effect on the running of time but it is a very relevant factor which may influence the court in the exercise of its discretion. A defendant who is perceived to have impeded the claimant in obtaining evidence such as relevant documents, or to have made it difficult for him to interview potential witnesses, runs the real risk of losing the sympathy of the court. It is not just deliberate conduct which may be relevant; unintentional conduct having the same effect can be held against the defendant in the exercise of the court's discretion. It is a matter of degree in each case.

23   SECTION 33(3)(D): THE DURATION OF ANY DISABILITY OF THE CLAIMANT

This refers to a disability which arises after the date of the accrual of the cause of action (for disability at the commencement of the limitation period see below). In *Thomas v. Plaistow*[86] the debate as to whether the disability under this subsection which might have resulted in the claimant delaying is a legal disability arising from mental

---

83 *Collins v. SSBIS & Stena Line Irish Sea Ferries Ltd* [2014] EWCA Civ 717.
84 [2010] EWCA Civ 195.
85 [2013] NIQB 123.
86 [1997] PIQR P540.

incapacity, or whether it can also refer to physical disability was resolved by the Court of Appeal.

"Disability" for the purposes of s. 33(3)(d) refers only to the concept of a person under a disability by reason of mental disorder so as to be a patient within the meaning of the Mental Health Act 1983, or now a protected party under the Mental Capacity Act 2005. A disability not amounting to mental disorder or lack of capacity may still be relevant, although not under this subsection, in explaining the claimant's delay or generally as part of all the circumstances of the case.

24   SECTION 33(3)(E): THE EXTENT TO WHICH THE CLAIMANT ACTED PROMPTLY AND REASONABLY ONCE HE HAD "KNOWLEDGE"

Where the claimant had "knowledge" within the meaning of s. 14 but was ignorant of his legal rights he will not have been able to stop the limitation clock running, but his subsequent conduct may be relevant to the exercise of the discretion. Once he has personal knowledge the court will consider whether there was further delay, and if so, whether it was reasonable. The court is looking to the conduct of the claimant himself, rather than that of his solicitors.

25   SECTION 33(3)(F): THE STEPS TAKEN BY THE CLAIMANT TO OBTAIN MEDICAL, LEGAL OR OTHER EXPERT ADVICE

It is the claimant's conduct that is relevant, rather than that of his solicitors. The court has regard to the steps taken by the claimant to obtain medical, legal or other expert advice and the nature of the advice received. A failure to seek advice will lead the court to consider whether or not that failure was reasonable in the particular circumstances. The court is likely to be understanding where the claimant has sought advice and obtained negative advice, be it from his solicitor, barrister or other expert, provided the claimant has provided them with a full history and all relevant detail.[87]

Where the nature of the advice received is relevant, the defendant is entitled to know whether that advice was negative or not, although the claimant cannot be forced to waive privilege. However, that does not remove other elements of professional privilege. As a matter of practical reality, professional privilege is often waived and the full text of the advice disclosed.

26   SETTING ASIDE THE DISCRETION

There are circumstances in which the court might, at a later stage in the proceedings, set aside the exercise of the discretion. This might occur, for example, if on the hearing of the damages assessment documents came to light which indicated that facts were not as had been found in the preliminary issue on limitation.[88]

---

87 See for example *Smith v. Ministry of Defence* [2005] EWHC 682.
88 *Long v. Tolchard & Sons Ltd* (CA 23.11.99).

27   COSTS

If a claimant succeeds on a s. 33 application, but loses on issues as to date of knowledge, then he will not necessarily be entitled to all of his costs if the hearing is largely concerned with the issues on which the claimant loses.[89]

28   CLAIMS FOLLOWING DEATH

28.1   Law Reform (Miscellaneous Provisions) Act 1934 Claim

> *"If the person injured dies before the expiration of the period mentioned in subsection 4 above, the period applicable as respects the cause of action surviving for the benefit of his estate by virtue of section 1 of the Law Reform (Miscellaneous Provisions) Act 1934 shall be three years from –*
> *(a)   the date of death; or*
> *(b)   the date of the personal representative's knowledge;*
> *whichever is the later."* (s. 11(5))

Therefore a claim by the deceased's estate for a fatal injury must be brought within 3 years of the date of death or the date of knowledge of the personal representatives, and can only be brought if the deceased's own claim was not statute barred at the time of his death.

28.2   Fatal Accident Act 1976 Claim

Similar provisions apply to those in relation to an estate's claim. Section 12(1) provides that:

> *"An action under the Fatal Accidents Act 1976 shall not be brought if the death occurred when the person injured could no longer maintain an action and recover damages in respect of the injury (whether because of the time limit in this Act or in any other Act or for any other reason)."*

If the claim would have been barred at death by the provisions of s. 11, then no account is to be taken of the possibility of that time limit being disapplied under s. 33.

The time limit is set out under s. 12(2) where it is provided that:

> *"No such action shall be brought after the expiration of three years from –*
> *(a)   the date of death; or*
> *(b)   the date of knowledge of the person for whose benefit the action is brought;*
> *whichever is the later."*

Where there are several dependants, then the date of knowledge provision is to be provided separately to each one of them. If that results in one or more but not all of the dependants being outside the time limit, then the court shall direct that any person

---

89 *Kew v. Bettamix* [2007] PIQR P16.

outside that limit shall be excluded from those for whose benefit the action is brought – s. 13.

Section 28 applies and therefore time does not run against a dependant under a disability.

29   SECTION 33 AND CLAIMS FOLLOWING DEATH

Section 33(1) applies the discretion to disapply the limitation period to claims barred by s. 11 (Law Reform Act claims) and s. 12 (Fatal Accident Act claims). Section 33(4) provides that where the deceased died after expiry of his limitation period *"the court shall have regard in particular to the length of and the reasons for the delay on the part of the deceased"* and s. 33(5) provides that where the relevant date of knowledge is that of someone other than the deceased, then the considerations under s. 33(3) will be modified so that references to the claimant include references to any other person whose date of knowledge is relevant, such as the personal representatives .

30   DISABILITY

30.1   Who is under a Disability?

A person is under a disability *"while he is an infant or lacks capacity to conduct legal proceedings"* – s. 38(2).

A person lacks capacity in relation to a matter *"if at the material time he is unable to make a decision for himself in relation to the matter because of an impairment of, or a disturbance in the functioning of, the mind or brain"* – s. 2(1) of the Mental Capacity Act 2005.

30.2   The Effect of Disability

Section 28 provides, by application of subsection (1) and (6), in relation to claims affected by s. 11 (live claims and estate claims) or s. 12(2) (Fatal Accident Act claims), that:

> *"If on the date when any right of action accrued for which a period of limitation is prescribed by this Act, the person to whom it accrued was under a disability, the action may be brought at any time before the expiration of 3 years from the date when he ceased to be under a disability or died (whichever first occurred) notwithstanding that the period of limitation has expired."*

Therefore a child who suffers personal injuries has a 3-year period in which to bring a claim expiring when they reach the age of 21.

In relation to a person lacking mental capacity when they suffer personal injuries, the limitation period does not start to run until they cease to lack such capacity. If they never gain capacity, limitation never starts to run.

There is no long stop and no equivalent to s. 33 discretion during a period of disability. So in *Headford v. Bristol and District HA*[90] the Court of Appeal allowed an appeal against an order striking out a claim because of prejudice to the defendant when brought 28 years after the events complained of by a person under a disability.

If, however, the claimant has capacity at the time of injury, but loses capacity later then that does not suspend limitation. Similarly if a claimant without capacity at the outset regains capacity for a period then the limitation period is not suspended again when they lose capacity again. The subsequent mental capacity will, however, be relevant to an application under s. 33 by subsection 3(d) (*"the duration of any disability of the claimant arising after the date of the accrual of the cause of action"*).

---

90 [1995] 6 Med LR 1.

Chapter 16

DAMAGES

1 PERSONAL INJURY DAMAGES ARISING FROM CLINICAL NEGLIGENCE

The principles of assessment of damages for personal injury arising from clinical negligence are the same as those where the personal injury arises from some other cause. The key to clinical negligence claims is to value the damage that arises from the negligence as opposed to the damage that the underlying condition which was being treated would have caused in any event even without the negligence. This requires experts dealing with causation and condition and prognosis to deal with the hypothetical condition of the claimant had the negligence not occurred and to state expressly what extra, or new, damage resulted from the negligence. In clinical negligence cases the doctor does not warrant a cure and is only responsible for the effect of the negligence.

Case law on assessment of personal injury and clinical negligence damages is bedevilled by a lack of consistent definition and categorisation. In this chapter we give an overview of the process of assessment of damages. For this purpose we will adopt current practice and categorise the various potential heads of damages as follows:

(i) general damages (this will cover all heads of loss incapable of precise mathematical calculation, including pain, suffering and loss of amenity);

(ii) interest on general damages (this should be calculated separately to interest upon past financial losses and expenses as it is calculated differently);

(iii) past financial losses and expenses (commonly known as "special damages");

(iv) interest upon past financial losses and expenses;

(v) future financial losses and expenses.

2 GENERAL DAMAGES

This term is commonly used to describe the *pain, suffering and loss of amenity* (PSLA) that arises from an accident or clinical negligence. In fact, the term is also used to cover a variety of different awards that are incapable of precise calculation, including: handicap on the open labour market/loss of earnings capacity, loss of congenial employment and loss of leisure.

The starting point will be the Judicial College Guidelines. However, practitioners are required to look beyond these guidelines to a consideration of previously decided cases involving similar injuries from sources such as *Kemp & Kemp on Quantum, Current*

Law, *Lawtel*, *Personal Injury Quantum Reports*, *Clinical Risk* and *The Personal and Medical Injuries Law Letter*.

Assessing PSLA awards is as much art as science. It is good practice to include a narrative section at the beginning of the claimant's schedule summarising the claimant's injuries, current condition, prognosis and continuing disabilities. Although the CPR does not require it, the schedule can even include the amount that will be contended for PSLA at trial, or at least the bracket that will be contended for by reference to the JC guidelines. The counter-schedule can then do likewise.

2.1 Disadvantage on a Future Labour Market (*Smith v. Manchester* Awards)

In addition to any reduction in residual earning capacity that will be compensated for by an award of lost future earnings a claimant's residual earnings may be at risk in a future labour market. These are sometimes referred to as *Smith v. Manchester*[1] damages. Mrs Smith was still in employment with Manchester Corporation earning her pre-accident earnings. She was at risk of a loss in the event that she might need to enter the labour market at some time in the future with a disability that she would not otherwise have had but for the negligence of the defendant. This potential loss was compensated for by a lump sum award. In *Morgan v. UPS*[2] the Court of Appeal suggested that the phrase *Smith v. Manchester* damages should be reserved for those cases where the claimant is still in work, but confirmed that even those not in work were still entitled to compensation for this loss. The introduction of the explanatory notes to the 7th edition Ogden Tables (see below) provides a method of calculating future loss of earnings which takes into account the increased risk to employment of a disability. In practice if this methodology is adopted then *Smith v. Manchester* type awards for disadvantage on the open labour market are claimed less frequently than before. Indeed it is arguable that the statistical approach to the calculation of future loss of earnings as advocated by the Odgen Tables Working Party (first suggested in the Introduction to the 6th Edition of the Tables) renders free-standing awards for disadvantage on the open labour market redundant.

There will, however, still be plenty of cases where a claimant has suffered a permanent injury that does not give rise to any significant disability but *does* have the potential to disadvantage that claimant on the open labour market in the future. These cases will remain suitable for a *Smith v. Manchester* award.

There is a two-stage test to be applied in all such cases:

(i)   Is there a *substantial* or *real* risk that a claimant will lose his present job at some time before the estimated end of his working life?[3]

(ii)   If so, what is the present value of that risk, having regard to the degree of risk, the time when it may materialise, and the factors affecting the chances of getting a replacement job or an equally well-paid job?

Awards for disadvantage on a future labour market are generally based upon a claimant's current net earnings. In the general run of cases awards of between one and

---

1 *Smith v. Manchester Corporation* (1974) 17 KIR 1.
2 [2008] EWCA Civ 375.
3 *Moeliker v. Reyrolle & Co. Ltd* [1976] ICR 253.

24 months' net earnings can be expected depending upon the age of the claimant and the extent of the risks outlined above. More serious cases can result in higher awards.

A claim for an award for disadvantage on a future labour market should be pleaded in the Particulars of Claim, although there is no absolute bar to an award where such a claim is not specifically identified so long as the material facts are pleaded and the defendant is not prejudiced.[4]

In cases where there are many uncertainties and a calculation for loss of earnings cannot be made on a conventional multiplier/multiplicand basis for future losses the court may take a broad brush approach and make a lump sum award which encompasses loss of earnings and handicap on the open labour market. This is known as a *Blamire* award after *Blamire v. South Cumbria Health Authority*.[5] This approach lends itself well to claims where the claimant's income may have varied substantially in the future or where he was self-employed.

2.2 Loss of Congenial Employment

This award is applicable where, as a result of the injuries sustained, a claimant has lost a job that he loves. Awards ranging between £1,000 and £12,000 are common. *Kemp & Kemp* and *Current Law* are particularly helpful when seeking appropriate comparators. Sometimes defendants rely on the case of *Willbye v. Gibbons*[6] to suggest that awards should rarely exceed £5,000 citing the judgment of Kennedy LJ. However, the award in that case concerned a claimant who had not yet even embarked on her chosen career and on the right facts more substantial awards may reasonably be made. For example in *Davidson v. Leitch*[7] the claimant who had been a highly paid equities trader was awarded £6,500 under this head of loss in 2013 after an obstetric injury precluding work in this field.

2.3 Loss of Leisure

The claimant is entitled, in an appropriate case, to recover an award to compensate him for having to work longer hours to earn their pre-accident earnings.[8] However, there is no agreed methodology to account for loss of leisure. Suggestions that it should reflect the wage of the claimant introduce the anomaly of the banker's leisure being worth considerably more than the manual worker's. Where the additional hours are very burdensome, it is worth considering whether the claim can be run on a partial loss of earnings basis if the claimant can avoid doing the additional hours, but still keep his job.

2.4 Interest

Pursuant to s. 69 of the County Courts Act 1984 and s. 35A of the Senior Courts Act 1981 interest is recoverable upon all items of general damages at the rate of 2% per annum from the date of service of the claim form until judgment or sooner settlement

---

4 *Thorn v. PowerGen* [1997] PIQR Q71.
5 [1993] PIQR 1.
6 [2003] EWCA Civ 372.
7 [2013] EWHC 3092.
8 For examples, see *Kernohan v. Dartmouth* (unreported, 1964) CA No. 9, *Tindale v. Dowsett Engineering Construction Ltd* (unreported, 2nd December 1980) and *Collett v. Bean* [1999] CLY 1497.

of the claim. Awards of interest are at the discretion of the court and may be withheld, for example, where there has been unexplained or unreasonable delay.

3   SPECIAL DAMAGES (FINANCIAL LOSSES AND EXPENSES)

Pursuant to CPR PD16, para. 4.2, a claimant in any clinical negligence action must attach to his Particulars of Claim *"a schedule of details of any past and future expenses and losses which he/she claims"*. Equally, it is the duty of a defendant to any such action to respond by preparing a counter-schedule of such losses and expenses. Schedules and counter-schedules must be verified by a statement of truth under CPR Part 22 – failure to do so will render the document defective and open to an application to strike-out.

It is hard to overestimate the importance of preparing the schedule/counter-schedule properly. It is the primary tool for the quantification of the claimant's loss and expense or the defendant's arguments in response. It is a form of communication. It should demonstrate to the opposing party that your case on the quantification of damages is accurate, supported by evidence, and convincing. A well-drafted schedule/counter-schedule indicates a readiness to proceed to trial and will be the cornerstone of any settlement negotiations. If drafted carelessly, improperly or unrealistically, a schedule/counter-schedule can undermine the credibility of a party and provide a stumbling block to the settlement of a claim. Schedules should contain narrative explaining why a claim is being made in the way that it is set out. Counter-schedules likewise should be informative, setting out why and on what basis a claim is disputed or denied.

4   PREPARING FOR THE SCHEDULE

4.1   Witness Evidence

As with all aspects of civil litigation, preparation is the key. First, it will be necessary to obtain a detailed witness statement from the claimant that will act as a springboard from which most of the schedule can be drafted. This statement should deal chronologically with the following:

(i)   the claimant's family and social life, hobbies, health, work and ambitions before the facts forming the basis of the claim took place;

(ii)   where the claimant believes his life and work would have gone but for the defendant's negligence (the "but for" prediction);

(iii)   the injuries that have been sustained by the claimant and the impact that this has had upon his life;

(iv)   the losses and expenses that have been incurred and will continue to be incurred into the future.

Often, it will be necessary to obtain further witness statements from members of the claimant's family or work colleagues dealing with certain heads of loss. This is common in relation to care and assistance received by a claimant or those cases where promotion prospects are in issue. A diary will help the claimant and his relatives to recall dates and events when faced with the daunting task of preparing a witness statement.

4.2   Supporting Documentation/Paperwork

In addition to witness evidence, supporting documentation/paperwork is vital to the recoverability of the financial losses and expenses claimed. From the earliest opportunity, the claimant must be told to keep all receipts, invoices and wage slips, etc. that can be used in support of proving their losses and expenses. If need be they should be given a big brown envelope to put all their receipts in. They can then hand the envelope to the solicitor when they next meet in return for a new envelope for the next batch. Claimants should also be encouraged to keep a diary or spreadsheet of these items on a daily/weekly basis.

4.3   Medico-Legal Evidence

Practitioners must take great care in ensuring that the claims made in schedules and counter-schedules are supported by a medico-legal expert. Carefully drafted questions are frequently required under CPR Part 35. See Chapter 11 for further guidance on expert evidence

5   FORMAT OF THE SCHEDULE

Often, given the preliminary state of the evidence, it will be extremely difficult to provide anything other than a basic preliminary schedule upon issuing proceedings, containing limited detail and calculations. However, so far as possible, this basic schedule should highlight the potential heads of claim that will be investigated in due course once further evidence has been obtained.

As the claim proceeds and certainly well before trial, it will be necessary for a claimant to serve a full schedule. This should include a narrative of each head of claim, with references to the evidence in support and detailed calculations justifying the amount claimed. The style of this schedule is a matter for the individual drafting the schedule. There is no magic in a particular format. What is important is that it is accessible to the other side and to the court and "tells the story" in a way that can be understood. Reference to endless appendices without explanation of what they contain will not assist, though distracting calculations can usefully be assigned to appendices so long as that is adequately explained in the text.

A full schedule should include:

(1)   date of birth of the claimant;
(2)   date of incident/accident;
(3)   date of schedule;
(4)   assumed trial date;
(5)   age of the claimant at time of treatment/admission/operation(s)/ discharge from hospital/care/schedule/trial/normal and actual retirement, as appropriate;
(6)   position on liability – whether admitted/disputed;
(7)   medico-legal evidence obtained;
(8)   narrative of all losses and expenses incurred up to the date of trial, with a breakdown of how the sums claimed have been arrived at;

(9)   amount claimed for interest upon awards for PSLA, where appropriate, and for past losses and expenses up to the date of trial;

(10)   narrative of all future losses and expenses post date of trial, with a breakdown of how the sums claimed have been arrived at.

In more serious cases a schedule may also include:

(1)   a separate section at the beginning of the schedule/counter-schedule in which they deal with the multipliers that will be contended for in the claim;

(2)   a narrative of any general damages claimed (PSLA, *Smith v. Manchester*, etc.) along with the awards that will be contended for at trial.

6   BASIS OF ASSESSMENT

6.1   Past Losses and Expenses

Most losses and expenses will be easy to quantify by adding them up to the date of trial.

The standard of proof when dealing with the recoverability of these past damages is the balance of probabilities. In *Tutas v. East London Bus and Coach Company*[9] the defendant contested a claim for physiotherapy expenses of £513.50. The trial judge disallowed them because the claimant did not have evidence of having paid them (he had ultimately disclosed invoices relating to the treatment). The claimant appealed to the Court of Appeal McFarlane LJ who said: *"Rendering of reasonable evidence as to the requirement to pay from those who are seeking payment would, in my view, normally be sufficient, unless one party or the other is on notice of a need to look behind matters. These sorts of topics, particularly, I would suggest, at a level of payment such as this, are in everyday life, in relation to these matters, to be taken as read without requiring nitty gritty proof of the channel of payment."* In *McGinty v. Pipe*[10] 40 pence per mile was allowed for travel.

Practitioners will need to be alive to the following matters:

(i)   Has the claimant taken reasonable steps to mitigate his past losses and expenses? *(Sotiros Shipping Inc v. Sameiet Solholt)*[11]

(ii)   Has there been any lost opportunity on the part of the claimant as a result of his injuries (e.g. loss of promotion, chance of obtaining employment)?

(iii)   Are the damages claimed reasonably foreseeable?

6.2   Interest on Past Losses

Interest on special damages is calculated at half the special account rate on the total special damage claim commencing on the date of the accident and ending on the date

---

9 [2013] EWCA Civ 1380.

10 [2012] EWHC 506 (QB), the same rate was allowed in *Tagg v. Countess of Chester Hospital Foundation NHS Trust* [2007] EWHC 509 (QB).

11 [1983] 1 Lloyd's Rep; Sir John Donaldson MR stated: *"A plaintiff is under no duty to mitigate his loss, despite the habitual use by lawyers of the phrase 'duty to mitigate'. He is completely free to act as he judges to be in his best interests. On the other hand, a defendant is not liable for all losses suffered by the plaintiff in consequences of him so acting."* This statement of affairs was approved in the Privy Council case of *Geest v. Monica Lansiquot* [2002] UKPC 48.

of the trial/settlement assuming that the loss is continuous from the date of the accident: *Dexter v. Courtaulds Ltd.*[12] If the loss is incurred at the beginning of the period only then conventionally the full rate is used. The special account rate varies over time and the up-to-date rate and useful tables for calculating cumulative interest can be found in the PNBA's *Facts and Figures*.

6.3   The Incidence and Recovery of Social Security Benefits

Social Security benefit recovery is governed by the Social Security (Recovery of Benefits) Act 1997 and administered by the Compensation Recovery Unit (CRU). The function of the CRU is to ensure that the defendant repays the state for the social security benefits received by a claimant as a consequence of an injury the defendant has caused. At the same time the Act allows the defendant to offset these benefits against the claim for damages so as to guard against double recovery. The deductions are only made on a like for like basis. Hence, general damages and other items of general damage, e.g. loss of congenial employment, are ring fenced whereas loss of earnings, care and loss of mobility will be set off like for like. The relevant period over which the benefits "bite" against a claim, is 5 years (s. 17). Useful guidance on the operation of the Act can be found in s. 13 of PNBA's Facts and Figures. Further guidance can be found on the DWP website: www.gov.uk/government/organisations/department-for-work-pensions. The table below is taken from their website.

---

12 [1984] 1 WLR 372.

Type of claim affected	Deductible benefits
Compensation for loss of earnings	Disablement pension payable under s. 103 of the Social Security Contributions and Benefits 1992 Act (also known as Industrial Injuries Disablement Benefit)
	Employment and Support Allowance
	Incapacity Benefit
	Income support
	Invalidity Pension Allowance
	Jobseeker's Allowance
	Reduced Earnings Allowance
	Severe Disablement Allowance
	Sickness Benefits
	Statutory Sick Pay
	Unemployability Supplement
	Unemployment Benefit
Compensation for the cost of care incurred during the relevant period	Attendance Allowance
	Care Component of Disability Living Allowance
	Disablement pension increase for Constant Attendance Allowance
	Living Component of Personal Independence Payment (PIP L)
Compensation for loss of mobility during the relevant period	Mobility Allowance
	Mobility Component of Disability Living Allowance
	Mobility Component of Personal Independence Payment (PIP M)

The liability to make CRU payments arises on the making of the first compensation payment. An interim payment will trigger the liability. Interest is payable on the full amount of special damages *before* recoupment.[13] "Compensation" as defined by Sch. 2 to the 1997 Act does include interest, so an offset can be made against the interest payable on claims for loss of earnings, care or loss of mobility.[14] Benefits which are not included above fall to be assessed in line with common law principles,[15] e.g. housing benefit, council tax benefit and Independent Living Fund payments (though the latter is understood not to be accepting new applicants).

On 29th April 2013 the government introduced Universal Credit, which combines six key income related benefits (including housing and council tax benefit). This is being rolled out across the country (www.gov.uk/universal-credit/overview). From 10th June 2013 new applicants for care and mobility related benefits receive Personal Independence Payments. There is no equivalent for the lower rate care component of

---

13 *Wadey v. Surrey County Council* [2001] 1 WLR 820.
14 *Griffiths v. British Coal Corporation* [2001] 1 WLR 1493.
15 *Hodgson v. Trapp* [1989] AC 807.

DLA and the threshold for mobility related payments is higher. Chapter 17 deals with the management of awards and the interrelationship between this and Social Security Benefits.

6.4   Future Losses and Expenses

The assessment of future losses and expenses can be a much more difficult task. There is a crucial difference in approach between past and future losses. Whereas past events are determined on the balance of probabilities the future is assessed as a question of future possibilities and chances.

By way of example, where the medico-legal evidence concludes that there is a 20% risk of the claimant requiring future surgery costing £10,000, a claim will be recoverable in the sum of £2,000 (minus a discount for accelerated receipt). It does not matter that the prospects of requiring this surgery do not meet a threshold of 51%. It is a question of identifying the percentage chance and reflecting this in the damages award.

Specific examples of how this works within the context of a loss of earnings claim are provided by the cases of *Doyle v. Wallace*,[16] *Langford v. Hebran*,[17] and *Herring v. Ministry of Defence*.[18] In *Doyle*, the Court of Appeal upheld a decision of the trial judge to assess the claimant's loss of earnings on the basis of the mid-point between the salary of an administrative worker and the salary of a teacher. This decision had been based upon a finding that the claimant would have certainly achieved a position as an administrative employee and had a 50% chance of achieving the more prestigious role of a teacher.

6.5   Loss of Chance

It is important to point out that the loss of chance approach does not apply to cases where it is said non-negligent treatment would have given rise to a better outcome. That is a matter of *medical causation* as opposed to quantification of loss. In these cases the claimant must prove that, on the *balance of probabilities*, the treatment he should have received would have made a difference to his condition.[19] If the chances are 50% or less, damages will not be recoverable. Issues of medical causation are considered in more detail in Chapter 6.

When it comes to quantifying the value of future losses the courts have no such problems. The normal situation is where someone's career prospects have been damaged and the court has to reflect on the varying prospects for promotion or success to different levels. In those circumstances the courts apply a percentage prospect to the additional earnings that might have been achieved at different levels thus assessing not just a single chance, but many chances. This approach has been adopted, for example, in *Doyle v. Wallace*, where the claimant had a 50:50 chance of becoming a drama teacher rather than a clerk, in *Langford v. Hebran*, where the claimant had differing prospects of success at different levels as a kick-boxing instructor rather than a bricklayer, in *Clarke*

---

16 [1998] PIQR Q146.
17 [2001] EWCA Civ 361.
18 [2003] EWCA Civ 528.
19 See *Hotson v. East Berkshire Health Authority* [1987] AC 750, *Tahir v. Haringey Health Authority* [1998] Lloyd's Rep Med 104, *Hardaker v. Newcastle Health Authority* [2001] Lloyd's Rep Med 512 and *Gregg v. Scott* [2005] UKHL 2.

v. Maltby,[20] a case of a city solicitor, and in *Collett v. Smith and Middlesbrough Football & Athletics Co Ltd*,[21] a case of a promising young footballer.

6.6 One-off Items of Future Loss/Expense

The calculation of a one-off item of future loss/expense is relatively simple: the current day value of the item is taken and a discount is applied to account for the accelerated receipt of such damages.

Practitioners will need to be familiar with Ogden Table 27 when carrying out such calculations. By way of example, where the claimant will require surgery costing £10,000 in 10 years time, the claim for surgery costs will be:

£10,000 × 0.7812 = £7,812 [Ogden Table 27 – discount factor 10 years at 2.5% discount rate]

Returning to the theme of percentage chances, if the same claimant had a 50% chance of requiring surgery in 10 years time, the claim for surgery costs will be:

£10,000 × 0.7812 × 0.50 = £3,906

6.7 Ongoing Future Losses/Expenses – the Multiplicand and Multiplier

The starting point when calculating ongoing/recurring future losses and expenses is to calculate the *multiplicand*, namely the *annual* future loss that will be sustained (be it annual loss of earnings, annual care and assistance, annual treatment costs, etc.).

The multiplier is the annual figure by which the multiplicand is multiplied to reflect the length of time over which the loss is likely to be suffered, taking into account the statistical risk of population wide mortality and a rate of return. Ogden Tables 1–26 are used for this purpose. As things stand, the discount rate to be applied when assessing future losses/expenses is fixed at 2.5%.[22] The Court of Appeal has thus far ruled out any attempt to adjust the discount rate used for a lump sum so as to reflect the difference between price and earnings inflation because it would be inconsistent with the statutory deemed rate of return: *Cooke v. United Bristol Healthcare NHS Trust*.[23] However, the Guernsey Court of Appeal, unencumbered by that statutory rate because the Damages Act 1996 did not apply in that jurisdiction determined a discount rate for future losses at -1.5% for earnings related losses and 0.5% for non-earnings related future losses in *Helmot v. Simon* on 14th January 2010. The Privy Council has since upheld the approach taken by that court,[24] although it is plainly not of general application in this jurisdiction. The Lord Chancellor has announced that the discount rate set under the Damages Act will be reviewed; two consultation papers have already been prepared and now a panel of three experts has been convened to deal with the issues arising. The outcome is hoped for by the spring of 2015 though there is no fixed timetable. In cases which may be suitable for a periodical payments order consideration should be given at an early stage to whether the claim is suitable for a

---

20 [2010] EWCA Civ 1201.
21 [2009] EWCA Civ 583.
22 Set by the Lord Chancellor under s. 1 of the Damages Act 1996 on 25th June 2001.
23 [2004] 1 WLR 251.
24 [2012] UKPC 15

lump sum or a PPO. Expert advice will generally need to be sought. In *Gilliland v. McManus and Another*[25] the court considered whether pursuant to the similarly worded civil procedure rules in Northern Ireland, a PPO ought to be made in a case where there was likely to be a finding of contributory negligence and Gillen J held: "*A plaintiff's legal adviser may find that he will need a very good reason, probably backed by expert financial advice, for not having discussed in detail or commended such a provision to his client in clear terms. Solicitors or barristers should incline to caution and carefully consider obtaining such financial or actuarial advice, since they are neither permitted nor (usually) qualified to give such advice themselves.*" Tactically it may be worth calculating a schedule for the purpose of a JSM on a 0.0% discount rate basis for the purpose of comparison with a lump sum. The choice between PPO's and lump sums and the relevant factors to consider are dealt with in detail in Chapter 17.

7   LOSS OF EARNINGS

In most cases, it is the claimant's loss of earnings that form the most significant aspect of his losses and expenses. The first question that must be answered in each case is, but for the injuries sustained as a result of the clinical negligence, what would the claimant have received in earnings?

In preparing the claim for loss of earnings it is sensible to obtain the following key pieces of information:

- a reasonable spread of pre-accident/incident wage records (usually 3 months, but practitioners should check a wider spread if income fluctuates over the course of a year);
- in the absence of wage records, a letter from the claimant's employer or copies of bank statements proving payments should be obtained;
- practitioners should seek to obtain evidence confirming any pay rises that the claimant would have been entitled to or, at the very least, inflationary rises in pay. Similarly, evidence should be sought in support of any future promotions/career progressions;
- where the claimant is self-employed, copies of business accounts, tax returns and tax bills should be obtained;
- sometimes, it may be necessary to seek earning comparisons with working colleagues (where the claimant is employed) or similar trades (where self-employed).

In some complex cases, expert evidence may be required from an employment consultant dealing with the claimant's pre- and post-accident/incident earning capacity. This is particularly so when:

(i)   the claimant is a child or in the course of education, training or retraining;

(ii)   the claimant was young when the accident/negligence occurred, with much career development ahead of him;

(iii)   the claimant was a high-earning professional.

---

25 [2013] NIQB 127, para. 10 of the judgment.

In most cases, however, the courts are likely to be reluctant to permit the use of employment consultants, particularly when the parties have access to resources such as the Annual Survey of Hours and Earnings, recruitment publications and the internet.

Subject to the considerations outlined above, the assessment of past loss of earnings should be relatively straightforward. The assessment of future loss is a far more difficult proposition.

In the ordinary way it is necessary to calculate the annual loss of income (multiplicand), taking into account potential future increases in that income from promotion and/or bonuses. There is an increasing trend now of explicit deductions for the expenses of working for example travel to work, or even the costs of childcare. In *Davison v. Leitch*[26] Andrews J said *"Damages for personal injury are compensatory, and intended so far as money can to put the Claimant in the same financial position as if the injury had not happened…However, that principle is qualified to the extent that a deduction must be made for the expenses of earning the income that has been lost. In Dews v National Coal Board [1988] AC 1, Lord Griffiths said at page 14F that the tortfeasor is, subject to sums necessarily spent to earn the income, entitled to no credit for expenditure saved as a result of the injury."* Thus in that case the costs of childcare essential to permit the claimant to work were deducted from her loss of earnings claim.

When the multiplicand has been established the court will consider the correct multiplier to be applied. This is when practitioners turn to the Ogden Tables, the 7th edition being the most recent.

For future loss of earnings, it is first necessary to identify the correct table to use. This will depend on the gender of the claimant and the period of the loss. The most obvious claims will be to the projected date of retirement. Having established these factors, the correct table can be identified. For example:

(i)   Male; retirement age of 60 = Table 7;
(ii)   Female; retirement age of 65 = Table 10.

Having identified the correct table, the correct age at date of trial must be selected and a line traced across to the appropriate figure in the 2.5% column (see above). For example, 35-year-old claimant with gender and predicted retirement ages above:

(i)   Male; retirement age of 60 = Table 7 = multiplier of 18.27;
(ii)   Female; retirement age of 65 = Table 10 = multiplier of 20.84.

Having identified the conventional multiplier it is then necessary to consider the individual facts of each case to assess whether this multiplier should be reduced to take into account contingencies other than mortality, i.e. are there other non-incident related factors which are likely to have led to the claimant being unable to work to the projected retirement age?

A starting point for every practitioner will now be the precise mathematical approach first adopted in the 6th edition of the Ogden Tables and reiterated in the 7th edition.

---

26 [2013] EWHC 309245.

However, sight should not be lost that this is a starting point and each case will depend upon its own facts.

Tables A–D of the 7th edition provides sets of discount factors for general contingencies for alternative pension ages. They are divided into separate categories for educational attainment, for disability and for employment. The suggested definitions of those categories of contingency are:

(i) employed is defined as being employed, self-employed or on a government training scheme;

(ii) disabled is defined as a person with an illness or condition which lasts (or will last) for more than a year and which satisfies the Equality Act definition that the condition substantially limits the claimant's ability to carry out day-to-day activities and limit the type of work that can be done; and

(iii) educational attainment is split between degree or higher qualification ("D"); A level or O Level equivalent but not degree ("GE-A"); and CSE/GCSE below grade 1/C ("O").

Having identified the pre-injury and post-injury categories the claimant falls within, Tables A–D show what discount rates should be applied to the conventional multiplier to identify future loss of earnings.

It will be necessary to set out the detail of the multiplier being used within the Schedule of Loss. A tactical decision will need to be made on whether the approach of the 7th edition Ogden Tables is being adopted or whether there is good reason to withhold or adjust any deduction. For example in *Huntley v. Simmonds*[27] the multiplier was adjusted from employed to unemployed status, to have regard to the fact that the claimant had spells out of work and was regularly "paralytic" at weekends pre-accident. Whereas in *Fleet v. Fleet*[28] the court declined to apply the suggested discount factor from Table A which exceeded 20% because the claimant had a long history of employment with the same employer. The reduction was no more than 10%. The two first instance decisions of *Billett v. Ministry of Defence*[29] and *Reaney v. University Hospital of Staffordshire NHS Trust*[30] are examples of cases where the court was concerned with the difficulties inherent in a strict application of the multipliers in the Ogden Tables but they also demonstrate the complications that can ensue if one strays from the path marked out by the Tables. Both cases are the subject of pending appeals to the Court of Appeal at the time of writing. In *Reaney* the claimant aged 61 developed a rare inflammatory condition, transverse myelitis, which caused damage to her spinal cord and left her incontinent with little power in her lower limbs. Due to negligence, she developed pressure sores, osteomyelitis, flexion contractures and a hip dislocation massively increasing the care she required. The judge found her life expectancy to be another 10.75 years to age 78. There was an argument as to whether Table 2 (which included contingencies other than mortality) or Table 28 (multipliers for a fixed period) should be used. Foskett J after a review of a long line of authorities including *Royal Victoria Infirmary v. B*,[31] *Crofts v. Murton*[32] and *Whiten v. St George's Healthcare Trust*[33]

---

27 [2009] EWHC 405 (QB).
28 [2009] EWHC 3166 (QB).
29 [2014] EWHC 3060 (QB).
30 [2014] EWHC 3016 (QB).
31 [2002] EWCA Civ 348, [2002] PIQR Q10.

used Table 28 because the most significant factors affecting her life expectancy – immobility, weight and smoking, had been taken into account in reaching the predicted life expectancy. He considered the use of Table 2 would introduce additional and thus unfair discount.

In *Billett* the claimant was a soldier who suffered an injury at the age of 24. In spite of the injury he was assessed by the army as fit for deployment anywhere. The injury rendered his feet permanently sensitised to cold and they became painful when cold. This led to the judge deciding that he was disabled because he would have to avoid jobs that required him to work outdoors. The question was then how should one approach the differential in his earnings now that he was earning a comparable amount of money in a family HGV business (by choice). The judge held that he had three options (i) a lump sum on the basis of *Smith v. Manchester* or *Ward v. Allies & Morrison Architects*,[34] (ii) an award based on Ogden Tables A & B without adjustment or (iii) an award based on Ogden Tables A & B using an adjustment per para. 32 of the explanatory notes to the tables. He took option 3 noting that the claimant's disability was limited. He took the midpoint between a disabled and non-disabled multiplier noting "*there is little logic in this approach except that it gives a figure which appears to me to reflect fully the loss sustained by the Claimant but to do so in a way which does not obviously over state that loss*". This gave a favourable result for the claimant.[35]

Whichever approach is taken to multipliers, parties will expect a detailed breakdown of the calculation and it must be included within the schedule.

8   PENSION LOSS

If as a result of injury a claimant is forced to retire earlier than planned, a claim for pension loss may arise. The first factor to consider is the nature of the material pension policy: the method of calculation will depend on whether the pension would have been a defined benefit or defined contribution scheme. In either case it is critical to get details of the scheme and to seek details from the pension trustees or administrators of what the pension will be and what it would have been if the claimant had worked and/or earned as intended but for the clinical negligence.

If the scheme is a defined contribution scheme then the conventional method is to claim the value of the contributions plus up to 5% for the benefit of the funds being invested in a large pension fund. Evidence on investment returns can be obtained from the Barclays Equity Gilt Study and the Association of British Insurers (ABI).

If the scheme is a defined benefit scheme then the calculation will be based on the formula to be applied by the pension trustees using the most up-to-date pay scales for the claimant. The loss of annuity can be simply calculated comparing the "but for" provision with the actual/likely provision then using Tables 15–26 of the Ogden Tables depending on the normal retirement date of the particular claimant to identify the correct multiplier. If the claimant would have commuted his pension and a lump sum is payable in advance of the normal retirement date then the loss of the lump sum

---

32 (2008) 152(35) SJLB 31 QBD, per Cranston J.
33 [2012] Med LR 1.
34 [2012] EWCA Civ 1287, [2013] PIQR Q1.
35 For a detailed commentary and response to this case see the article by Victoria Wass [2015] JPIL Issue 1.

needs to be adjusted in accordance with *Longden v. British Coal Corporation*[36] to reflect that part of the lump sum which represents capitalisation of annuity which would have been received after normal retirement age. Thereafter a discount must be made for accelerated receipt in accordance with *Auty v. National Coal Board*.[37] Finally a discount is commonly applied to the pension loss overall for the adverse contingencies of life. In *Auty* the discount was 27% reflecting a period of 31 years to retirement. An overview of cases suggests as a rule of thumb approximately 1% per annum (though claimants should probably plead a lower discount depending on the facts). It is worth noting that if a discount for contingencies other than mortality has already been applied to earnings, *Auty* should not be applied to the pension, as this would be a double discount.

In cases where the amount is significant and the assessment complex it may be appropriate to appoint a forensic accountant or an appropriately qualified independent financial adviser to produce a calculation, perhaps on a joint basis to avoid unnecessary argument.

9 CARE AND ASSISTANCE

9.1 The Non-serious Case

Where the need for care is short lived or is not great, take a detailed witness statement from the claimant and the carers as to the nature of the care provided, the number of hours expended on that care and the period over which the care was provided. The number of hours can then be applied to a care rate taken from the PNBA publication *Facts & Figures*, a proportionate method of calculation that is quite acceptable to the courts in straightforward cases.

9.2 The Serious Case

Where the need for care is substantial and ongoing, a care expert will need to be instructed to assess present and future needs, and to quantify the commercial costs of care.

Ensure that the medical experts (e.g. orthopaedic consultant) can justify the extent of the care recommended by the care expert.

In the most serious cases the evidence of a nursing expert with knowledge of managing care regimes (e.g. night-time care for turning in bed to avoid sores), and of a care manager may be necessary. Where a case manager has already been appointed then their evidence will be treated as evidence of fact, see *Wright v. Sullivan*.[38] Where it will be difficult for the claimant to give evidence a "day in the life" video should be considered.

The award is to reflect the claimant's needs and not whether there will in fact be a future expense (see *Fitzgerald v. Ford*[39] and *Sowden v. Lodge*[40]), so it is not a defence that

---

36 [1995] PIQR Q48.
37 [1985] 1 All ER 930.
38 [2005] EWCA Civ 656.
39 [1996] PIQR P72.

due to contributory negligence the claimant will not be able to afford the recommended regime.

Defendants will argue that no claim can be made for the time in hospital visits which are the normal hospital visits arising from family affection, and not given for the purpose of providing services which the hospital did not provide (*Havenhand v. Jeffrey*[41]).

9.3 What Care is Recoverable?

The claimant is entitled to recover damages in respect of the fair and reasonable value of the care and domestic assistance which has been provided gratuitously by a family member or friend even though the claimant is under no liability to pay that carer. However, the following two criteria must be satisfied:

(i)   the claimant would not have required such care and assistance but for the accident; and

(ii)   the medical experts support the claim as being reasonably necessary as a result of the claimant's injuries.

Defendants have in the past frequently relied upon the case of *Mills v. British Rail Engineering Ltd*[42] to suggest that a claim for care is limited to cases involving only serious injuries requiring family care. However, Brooke LJ said in *Giambrone v. Sunworld Holidays Limited*:[43]

> "*I reject the contention that Mills presents binding authority for the proposition that such awards are reserved for 'very serious cases' [26]...care for a child with gastro-enteritis of the severity experienced by these children will know that they require care which goes distinctly beyond that which is part of the ordinary regime of family life...*"

If caring for a child with gastro-enteritis is recoverable care, we would suggest that the following elements of care and assistance are likely to find favour with courts:

(i)   physical nursing care and attendance, e.g. washing, dressing, undressing, brushing teeth/hair, changing bandages and administering medication;

(ii)   assistance with mobility such as assisting on/off WC, wheelchair, bath/shower, into/out of vehicle;

(iii)   taking the claimant to/from hospital appointments – including waiting time;

(iv)   cutting up food/assistance with eating;

(v)   offering emotional support and reassurance, particularly where there is a recognised psychological injury (*Evans v. Pontypridd Roofing Limited*[44]);

(vi)   attending a sick child (*Giambrone v. JMC Holidays*[45]);

---

40 [2004] EWCA Civ 1370.

41 24th February 1997, Kemp 13-005, CA.

42 [1993] PIQR P130, CA.

43 [2004] 2 All ER 891.

44 [2001] EWCA Civ 1657.

45 [2004] EWCA Civ 158.

(vii)   performing domestic chores like cleaning, cooking, washing, ironing and shopping;

(viii)   providing care and assistance to family members or friends which the claimant would otherwise have provided (*Lowe v. Guise*[46]);

(ix)   arguably, feeding and looking after pets and animals.

9.4   Quantification

If professionally provided, the value will be the reasonable cost to the date of assessment with an appropriate multiplier for future care depending upon need and life expectancy.

If gratuitously provided:

- loss of earnings if the carer reasonably gives up a job (*Moriarty v. McCarthy*[47]) although likely to be capped at the commercial rate ("*the ceiling principle*");

- the rates for gratuitous case in PNBA's *Facts & Figures* 2014/2015 will be the starting point generally speaking. In all but the most straightforward cases an aggregate rate may be sought by claimants and contested by defendants. Much will depend on the facts of the case and the time when care is provided and the extent of the care provided;

- discounted by 20% to 33% to reflect "family affection" and the fact that agency fees, tax and national insurance will not be paid. The rationale is partly tax and NI and partly the convenience of it being provided in the family home (see *Burns v. Davies*[48]);

- there is no conventional figure, but 25% "may be regarded as normal" (see *Evans v. Pontypridd Roofing Ltd*[49]);

- 24 hours a day may be reasonable although care is not provided and received every single minute of the day (see *Evans*);

- awards for unpaid care are special damages and carry interest (see *Roberts v. Johnstone*[50]).

If the care is provided by professionals:

- examples of local care rates and the extent of services provided is crucial;

- the judgment in *Whiten v. St George's Healthcare Trust*[51] provides a very good working example of the calculation of the cost of professional care and is essential reading;

- if the care regime has fallen below the standard to be expected the court *may* discount the cost of past professional care *Kristopher Loughlin (by his Litigation Friend) v. (1) Kenneth Dal Singh (2) Pama & Co Limited and (3) Churchill insurance company;*[52]

---

46 [2002] EWCA Civ 197.
47 [1987] 2 All ER 213.
48 [1999] Lloyd's Rep Med 215, QBD.
49 [2001] EWCA Civ 1657, CA.
50 [1988] 1 WLR 1247 at 1259.
51 [2012] Med LR 1.
52 [2013] EWHC 1641, QB.

- much will hinge on the cogency of the expert care evidence and the evidence of the case manager (in substantial claims) and the extent to which the care regime and/or accommodation and/or equipment are supported by expert medical opinion.

9.5   Local Authority Funded Care

The question of how to deal with future local authority or PCT funded care in the context of significant care claims and the duties of local authorities pursuant to the National Assistance Act 1948 has been a vexed one. Put simply, the issue arises when the claimant wants the freedom to choose the best care regime for himself without having to be dependent on the vagaries of publicly funded care but the defendant argues that there is a risk of double recovery and a failure to mitigate if the claimant is permitted to claim privately funded care but can still avail himself of publicly funded care, which the state has a duty to provide in certain circumstances.

In *Peters v. East Midlands SHA*[53] the Court of Appeal held that *"the test is not whether other care or treatment is reasonable but whether the care and treatment chosen and claimed for is reasonable...The test is whether the Claimant has made a reasonable choice"*. This will depend on the facts of the case. If the claimant is settled in local authority funded care and it is reasonable that this regime will continue (often topped up with some private care) then the claim for future care will give credit for the local authority funded care but the multiplier may be adjusted for the contingency that local authority funding might fail or reduce in the future (per *Crofton v. NHSLA*[54]).

However, if the claimant is reasonable in electing private funding over state funding (as will often be the case) then the claimant is free to do so and need not give credit for future publicly funded provision. In *Peters* the court determined the failure to mitigate argument in the claimant's favour because of the uncertainties in respect of availability and the quality of publicly funded provision, especially in the face of likely statutory changes to the rules which govern such provision and because it was right that the tortfeasor pay for the damage it had caused. It got over the potential double recovery point by what is now known as a *"Peters undertaking"*, i.e. an undertaking by the deputy appointed on behalf of the claimant who was a protected party, not to apply for publicly funded care in the future without informing the court and the defendants. However, the Senior Judge of the Court of Protection has made it clear that he does not consider it the function of his court to police such undertakings and anecdotally it seems that defendants are not consistently pursuing such undertakings. For good practical guidance on the complexities of NHS continuing care, joint NHS and local authority care and residential and domiciliary care see the second edition of *APIL's Guide to Catastrophic Injury Claims*[55] (although this must now be read in light of the staged implementation of the Care Act 2014. The Care Act 2014 is a substantial piece of legislation that deals with eligibility for and the assessment of care in addition to standards of care. It affects the approach to charging for residential and community care. Complex and detailed guidance on the Act and its implementation can be found in the Care and Support Statutory Guidance on the Care Act 2014 issued by the

---

53 [2009] 3 WLR 737 at para. 80.
54 [2007] EWCA Civ 71.
55 Grahame Aldous QC, Stuart McKechnie, Jeremy Ford and Terry Lee, *APIL Guide to Catastrophic Injury Claims*, 2nd edn.

Department of Health which runs to over 500 pages. Chapter 23 of that guidance deals with the transition to the new legal framework).[56]

10 AIDS AND EQUIPMENT

In the most serious cases it will be necessary to obtain expert evidence on the aids and equipment required by the claimant. Any claims will also need to be supported by medical evidence. If the claimant can show that there is a reasonable need for particular aids or equipment, then it is likely to be recovered. *Whiten v. St George's Healthcare Trust* (above) is a good example of this, especially in relation to items such as assistive technology.

In larger cases, the cost of maintaining and replacing equipment will be considered and costed by the care/rehabilitation expert. For smaller cases it is essential that the future cost of maintenance and repair are considered by the practitioner and those calculations for future costs are included within the schedule.

11 INCREASED HOUSEHOLD BILLS

If as a result of injury a claimant is not working and staying at home in periods he would ordinarily have been at work, he is entitled to claim the additional costs of heating his property in this period. Ordinarily, this will be proved by comparisons between pre- and post-injury utility bills. Again, if this loss is likely to continue, an appropriate multiplier will be required to quantify the future loss under this head.

12 ACCOMMODATION – *ROBERTS V. JOHNSTONE*

This needs to be considered whenever the medical evidence shows that there will be permanent and serious mobility problems requiring specialist accommodation.

The first step in any such case is to take a witness statement from the claimant in order to understand the extent of his problems around the home. If possible, a house visit should be made and photographs taken illustrating the difficulties that the claimant faces. Thereafter, the following is recommended:

(i)   instruct a care expert/occupational therapist to prepare a report on care and accommodation required;

(ii)   if adaptations to the existing accommodation are required, instruct a surveyor to cost the adaptations;

(iii)   if new accommodation is required, (a) instruct an architect experienced in disabled housing to establish the need to move to disabled housing (to identify special adaptations, equipment and cost) and (b) get a report from a local estate agent to report on the likely cost of suitable

---

56 See
www.gov.uk/government/uploads/system/uploads/attachment_data/file/366104/43380_23902777_Care_Act_Book.
pdf.

new property and (if applicable) the value of the claimant's existing accommodation.

If the existing property is to be adapted, the claim will be for the cost of adaptations. If the adaptations add to the capital value of the property then the claim will be for funding the amount of the capital added as if it were a purchase. The balance of the cost will then be claimed as a capital sum.

If a new property has to be acquired, the capital cost of the new accommodation will not be allowed. Indeed, if a court were to award the entire purchase price of a property, less the proceeds of the existing property, this would result in overcompensation as the capital value of the new property would remain intact on the claimant's death and amount to a windfall to his estate.

In order to deal with this situation, the court will award damages for the denial of interest on the additional capital that has to be spent to buy the new accommodation. This is calculated, pursuant to the decision in *Roberts v. Johnstone*[57] as follows:

Multiplicand

2.5% of the net additional capital cost of buying the accommodation

Multiplier

The multiplier for life

By way of example:

> *Male aged 45 buys a bungalow for £200,000 and sells his existing two-storey house for £150,000, the multiplicand is £50,000 (£200,000 - £150,000) × 2.5% = £1,250. The multiplier is 23.88 (Ogden Table 1). The capital award will be 23.88 × £1,250 = £29,850*

In a situation where a claimant needs to change from rental accommodation, an example calculation would be as follows:

> *Male aged 45 buys a bungalow for £200,000. He was, and but for the accident, would have remained, in rented accommodation, paying £75 per week, £3,900 per year in rent. The multiplicand is £200,000 × 2.5% = £5,000, less £3,900 = £1,100. The multiplier is 23.88 (Ogden Table 1). The capital award will be 23.88 × £1,100 = £26,268*

In addition to the *Roberts v. Johnstone* award, a claimant is entitled to claim for the one-off expenses of moving:

- stamp duty;
- estate agent's fees;
- removal costs;
- connection to utilities;
- carpets, curtains, decorations;

---

57 [1989] QB 878.

- professional fees of conveyancing, architect, construction.

Extra running costs, including heating, lighting, damage, wear and tear, increased insurance and increased council tax should all be converted into capital sums and added to the damages awarded. Attempts to circumnavigate the rule in *Roberts v. Johnstone* thus far, have all failed, save that it may be appropriate in some cases for alternative accommodation to be funded by way of rent especially if life expectancy is very limited. In *Ryan St George v. The Home Office*[58] suitable rented accommodation had been found and rental was included as part of the PPO. In that case Mackay J had commented that the course adopted in that case should have a more general application in other suitable cases. In *Aiden Oxborrow (by his father and litigation friend Rory Oxborrow) v. West Suffolk Hospitals NHS Trust*,[59] the claimant relied on criticism of *Roberts v. Johnstone* in *McGregor on Damages* (18th edn) in respect of the inequity of not permitting the claimant sufficient money with which to acquire the needed accommodation. In *McGregor*, one solution suggested was that the claimant should be given the full purchase price of the property but with a charge in favour of the defendant (whilst noting the potential impracticalities of this). Tugendhat J said at para. 47 *"it seems to me that there is considerable force in Mr Spencer's submissions. Roberts v Johnstone does not address the issue that arises in the present case. However, I recognize that that approach to the issue of accommodation is now so well established that a court, at least in the first instance, and especially on an interim application such as the present, should not depart from it…not proceed on the footing that the trial judge is likely to depart from it"*. In the event the application for an interim payment for accommodation in that case was made on the basis of the approach in *Cobham Hire Services Ltd v. Eeles*.[60]

12.1   Interim Applications to Fund Accommodation

Pursuant to CPR, r. 25.7(4) and (5) the court may make an interim payment for no more than a reasonable proportion of the likely amount of the final judgment taking into account contributory negligence and any set off or counter-claim. The introduction of Periodical Payments Orders in higher value cases complicates this assessment because it may not be clear at the interim stage which losses will be capitalised and which dealt with by way of a PPO. Seriously injured claimants will frequently seek an interim payment to fund accommodation sometimes long before the case is trial ready. The general rule is that the interlocutory judge should not make an interim payment which might fetter the discretion of the trial judge. The mechanism for determining the approach to the interim payment is found in the Court of Appeal case of *Cobham Hire Services Ltd v. Eeles* referred to above.[61] There are a number of cases which now demonstrate the application of the test see, for example, *FP v. Taunton & Somerset NHS Trust*,[62], *Kirby v. Ashford & St Peter's Hospital NHS Trust*,[63] *PZC v. Gloucestershire Hospitals NHS Trust*[64] and more recently the decision of Deborah Taylor in *Gould v. Peterborough & Stamford Hospitals NHS Foundation Trust*[65] who applied the test in *Eeles* accepting that a conservative *but realistic* view of the likely damages that would be awarded.

---

58 [2008] EWCA Civ 1068.
59 [2012] EWHC 1010 (QB).
60 [2009] EWCA Civ 204.
61 See in particular the judgment of Smith LJ at paras 42-45 which summarise the approach that the judge should take.
62 [2011] EWHC 3380.
63 [2011] EWHC 624.
64 [2011] EWHC 1775.
65 24.2.2015 Lawtel (QB).

13   COURT OF PROTECTION COSTS

Where a claimant is subject to the Court of Protection then the schedule will need to claim the costs that will be incurred in administering the award in the Court of Protection. The PNBA publication *Facts & Figures* provides some guidance as to how such calculations might be approached, but in any substantial claim it will be worth obtaining a professional quote for the likely costs that will be incurred. Difficult issues may arise if the claimant has borderline capacity or may regain capacity in the future. The judgment in *Kristopher Loughlin (by his Litigation Friend) v. (1) Kenneth Dal Singh (2) Pama & Co Limited and (3) Churchill insurance company*[66] is a good example of the exercise the court is required to perform in terms of the application of the test pursuant to the Mental Capacity Act 2005 in determining whether an individual has capacity. Where a claimant may regain capacity in the future but the costs of the Court of Protection were to be paid by a periodical payments order, the court could approve a Tomlin order which permitted the cessation of periodical payments for the period of capacity. However, the court did not have the power to make a "stop-start" PPO in *AA v. (1) CC (2) Motor Insurers' Bureau.*[67] In *Saulle v. Nouvet*[68] Andrew Edis QC commented to the effect that *if* the claimant needed the help and support presumed by the Mental Capacity Act 2005 to understand and process information and make decisions, then arguably this could found a claim for the expense of providing such support. However, this comment was *obiter*. In *Re HM (a child) sub nom SM v. HM (by the official solicitor)*[69] Judge Hazel Marshall QC sitting in the Court of Protection gave lengthy and considered guidance on the circumstances when the Court of Protection should authorise the creation of a trust of the assets of the person lacking capacity as a means of administering those assets, rather than the appointment of a deputy.

14   PERIODICAL PAYMENTS

Periodical payments orders are dealt with in Chapter 17, Managing Awards.

---

66 [2013] EWHC 1641 QB.
67[2013] EWHC 3679 QB.
68 [2007] EWHC 2902.
69 [2014] Med LR 40.

Chapter 17

MANAGING AWARDS

1   THE AWARD OPTIONS

In this chapter we will consider the potential adverse consequences of lump sum awards and how to avoid them using PPOs.

Historically all awards were for a lump sum. This altered in 2005. Now an award of damages in a clinical negligence case may be made in three ways:

    (1)   a lump sum;
    (2)   a mixture of a lump sum and a periodical payments order;
    (3)   a mixture of a lump sum and a structured settlement.

A provisional damages order may be added to any of the above awards. In reality, with the advent of periodical payments, structured settlements became less frequent and now are no longer readily available as a product on the financial market. Options (1) and (2) are therefore most often the viable options in practice.

Interim payments and interim periodical payments may be made during the course of the case.

2   LUMP SUM AWARDS

2.1   The Problems with Lump Sum Damages

Before 2005 damages for clinical negligence were awarded to patients who had suffered injury and loss as a result of the treating clinician's negligence in a single lump sum. The principle applied by the courts to assessment of the lump sum was that the damages were intended to compensate the injured party for the loss and expense he had suffered in the past and for that which he would suffer in future. The calculation of the lump sum was designed to take into account the effect of inflation on the damages and included interest to compensate the claimant for being kept out of his money over the years between the trial and the loss. However the lump sum for future loss caused problems for many claimants. How could they protect themselves against future inflation which exceeded the assumptions made? How could they be sure the lump sum would cover the expenses caused by the injuries if they lived longer than the experts in the case predicted? Would they fall into penury due to poor investment or inaccurate expert evidence as to their life expectancy?

Four financially disadvantageous consequences could arise out of the receipt of a lump sum by the claimant for future loss:

(1)   the claimant might lose his entitlement to means tested social security benefits; and

(2)   the income received by the claimant from investing the award might attract tax; and

(3)   the conventional lump sum to cover future loss or expense might run out before the claimant died; and

(4)   the claimant's investments might not live up to expectations.

In 1994 the Law Commission reported that the majority of claimants saved or invested their money and the likelihood of this increased with the size of the award.[1] But a substantial proportion of claimants did not save at all (17% in the band £20,000–£50,000 and 10% in the band £50,000–£100,000). This showed that many claimants would fall into penury. Additionally the most common method of investing was in simple Building Society or Bank accounts. The survey also showed that 33% of victims receiving awards of £20,000 or more took no investment advice at all.

Before 2005, from the lawyer's perspective, because personal injury damages were awarded in a single lump sum neither the claimant's nor the defendant's lawyers were interested in what the claimant did with the money unless they entered into a voluntary structured settlement (see below). Since 2005 that perspective has changed.

2.2   The Discount Rate

Any lump sum award for future earnings or care requires a multiplier to be adopted. The multiplier should be determined by a combination of the claimant's life expectancy and a discount for accelerated receipt reflecting an assumed rate of return on capital.

Pursuant to s. 1 of the Damages Act 1996, the Lord Chancellor has the power to set the discount rate. Since 25th June 2011, the discount rate has been set at 2.5%, the rationale being that this reflects the annual rate of return that could be generated if a lump sum were invested in index-linked government securities (ILGS).

For many years, a simple lump sum investment in ILGS has been recognised to generate nothing like a 2.5% annual return, and the Lord Chancellor has been put under considerable pressure to reduce the discount rate. If this was done, the NHS would have to pay out considerably larger settlements to victims of catastrophic clinical negligence.

Despite his promise three years ago to the Administrative Court to review the discount rate "as promptly as practicable", the Lord Chancellor has yet to make a decision on whether 2.5% remains the applicable rate. There have been two consultation papers to date and the Ministry of Justice, in September 2013 published its Personal Injury Discount Rate Research which was undertaken by Ipsos MORI Social Research Institute. One of its findings was that the lack of periodical payment orders (PPO) generally appears to be due to insurers driving claimants towards lump sum settlements. The reason for this is due to the insurer's unwillingness to transfer the inflation and risks associated with finding a future financial liability to themselves. The ongoing nature of PPOs also means that longer life will inevitably cost them more than a full and final lump sum settlement. A PPO also places an ongoing liability on the

---

1 See Law Com No. 225, para. 10.2.

insurance company's balance sheet which cannot be quantified and is therefore difficult to budget for. This would have the effect of reducing the company's value in the event of a sale and is therefore not to all insurance companies' appetites. Financial advisers see the benefit of a mixed approach – a lump sum to pay for the immediate needs (e.g. a house) and a PPO to cover on-going costs. Finally, claimants like a lump sum as it provides increased flexibility and a type of "final closure". The report suggests that a decrease in the discount rate may encourage insurers to use PPOs more often. That said, the NHSLA leans heavily in favour of PPOs. The research showed that 66% of all NHSLA claims (2011/12) were clinical related. Such claims have increased year on year by 6% since 2009.

In the summer of 2014 it was revealed that the Lord Chancellor had asked a panel of three experts to provide him with expert investment advice. It was anticipated the panel would report by the spring of 2015 but this has yet to occur.

2.3 Periodical Payments Orders (PPOs)

From April 2005 the courts have been empowered to make awards in personal injury cases which include an order that the defendant will make future periodical payments to the claimant. The power was created by s. 2 of the Damages Act 1996.[2]

2.4 Tax on Awards

The sums awarded for loss of earnings, past and future, are calculated net of tax and national insurance: see the Finance Act 2000 and Finance Act 2004 and *British Transport Commission v. Gourley*.[3] Likewise no tax is due on the interest which accrued before the claimant received the award whilst it was in the Court Special Investment Account.

After the receipt of the award the interest and capital gains earned on the damages whether from a simple interest earning account with a bank or from shares, trusts, commodities or any investment will be subject to income tax and capital gains tax.

2.5 Means Tested Benefits

If the claimant was receiving means tested benefits at the time of trial the receipt of a lump sum will reduce or abolish his entitlement to means tested social security benefits. Means tested benefits include income support (IS); state pension credit (PC); housing benefit (HB); council tax benefit and community charge benefit (CTB); income-related employment and support allowance (ESA); income-based jobseekers allowance (JSA); universal credit; guaranteed pension credit; working tax credit (WTC); child tax credit (CTC); funeral expenses (FE); maternity grants (MG); and cold weather payments (CWP).

The capital limits above which means tested benefits are lost depend on the claimant's age and on the benefit being claimed. The bands tend to change each year. At the time of writing, the general capital rules for claimants aged below pension age are:

(1)   The first £6,000 that a claimant has (and their partner if they have one) is disregarded, whatever its source.

---

2 Substituted by s. 100 of the Courts Act 2003.
3 [1956] AC 185.

(2) Any capital that a claimant has between £6,000 and £16,000 is treated as generating a 'tariff income' of £1.00 per week on every £250 (or part thereof) above the £6,000 level, and their 'income' means-tested benefit is reduced by a corresponding amount.

(3) If a claimant has capital in excess of £16,000 they will not be entitled to means-tested benefits.

If the claimant is 59 or under state pension age then the level of IS/ESA he will receive will also depend on his income. The calculation of the amount of IS/ESA to which a claimant is entitled is made by setting off his income, both actual and notional, against the aggregate of the "amount required to live". This "applicable amount" depends on various factors, including, the number of persons in the family, their ages and the family's more general circumstances. Income from any lump sum award will form part of the equation in assessing the claimant's IS/ESA.

However, if the claimant is aged over pension age, any income received from capital awarded as a result of a clinical negligence case will be disregarded when computing entitlement to all means tested benefits except those provided for under the NHS and Community Care Act 1990.

The Social Security Amendment (Personal Injury Payments) Regulations 2002 and the National Assistance (Assessment of Resources) (Amendment) (No. 2) Regulations 2002[4] provided that PPOs received by the claimant, whether the defendant was self-funded or purchased a structured settlement annuity, are ignored for the purposes of assessing income for means tested benefits.

2.6   Non-Means Tested Benefits

To qualify for non-means tested benefits such as disability living allowance (DLA) or personal independence payment (PIP) the claimant may need to be of a certain age, or to have made certain contributions to the state in the past or to have a certain disability. Receipt of a lump sum award does not affect these and receipt of a PPO has no effect on eligibility for these benefits but could affect domiciliary care (i.e. care provided in a person's home) which is considered further below.

Non-means tested benefits include: disability living allowance (DLA), personal independence payment (PIP), incapacity benefit (IB), contribution based employment and support allowance (ESA), contribution based jobseekers allowance (JSA), industrial injuries disablement benefit (IIDB), and carers allowance (CA).

2.7   State Funded Accommodation, Medical and Social Care

For certain disadvantaged applicants the state provides free accommodation, care and medical benefits through local authorities and the NHS. The interaction between the claimant's past receipt of these benefits and the quantum of his damages is dealt with earlier in this text in Chapter 16 on damages. The receipt of such benefits may have a direct effect on the quantum of the annual periodical payments sought, see *Sowden v. Lodge*[5] and *Walton v. Calderdale Healthcare NHS Trust*[6] and *Crofton v. NHSLA.*[7] However

---

4 Overturning the Court of Appeal decision in *Beattie v. Sec. of State for Social Security* [2001] 1 WLR 1404.
5 [2004] EWCA Civ 1370; [2005] 1 All ER 581.
6 [2005] QBD (Leeds) Silber J, 18 May, Lawtel.

since *Peters v. East Midlands Strategic HA*[8] the claimant has had the right to choose private care over local authority care and so the effect of such free benefits is less relevant. For a more detailed but practical appraisal of different types of local authority and NHS funding for care beyond standard social security benefits and consideration of their likely impact on the quantum of a case see *APIL's Guide to Catastrophic Injuries,*[9] although the interrelationship between benefits and PPOs must now be read in light of the implementation of the Care Act 2014. The Care Act 2014 has wide-ranging provisions relating to the general responsibilities of local authorities, the assessment of needs of those who may require social care, the power to charge fees and assess financial resources as well as consideration of care standards, the duties of the CQC and issues relating to the integration of healthcare services and research in health. For detailed and complex guidance on the Act and its phased implementation see the Care and Support Statutory Guidance issued under the Care Act by the Department of Health in October 2014.[10]

In cases where a PPO was an option prior to April 2015 care needed to be taken to research the position in the claimant's locality as to whether annual income from a PPO would be excluded from consideration when the local authority assesses any financial contribution towards domiciliary care pursuant to s. 29 of the National Assistance Act 1948. In *Crofton v. NHSLA* (above) the Court of Appeal gave close consideration to the Fairer Charging Guidance in relation to capital but did not consider income from a PPO. The position was that capital held under a PI trust or administered by the court was not to be taken into account in terms of a contribution to domiciliary care. However, there was a discretion in respect of income from a PPO. Therefore the practice varied from local authority to local authority. This did in some cases swing the pendulum back towards a lump sum. It is a factor that the claimant's independent financial adviser needed to take into account when advising on the form of award. Following the phased introduction of the Care Act 2014 the disparity between PPO and lump sum settlements has been removed and it is understood that local authorities will in future treat income from a PPO and capital from a lump sum in the same way.

3 THE CHOICE: LUMP SUM OR PERIODICAL PAYMENTS ORDER

To determine whether the claimant should receive a lump sum award alone or one mixed with a PPO the claimant's lawyers will need to consider the advantages and disadvantages of each type of award.

PPOs do not stand alone. They will always accompany a lump sum for pain, suffering and loss of amenity and past loss.

The advantages of a PPO over a traditional lump sum for future loss or expense are as follows:

---

7 [2007] 1 WLR 923.
8 [2008] EWHC 778; and [2009] EWCA Civ 145.
9 Grahame Aldous QC, Stuart McKechnie, Jeremy Ford and Terry Lee, *APIL's Guide to Catastrophic Injury Claims* (2nd edn, Jordan Publishing, 2014).
10 See www.gov.uk/government/uploads/system/uploads/attachment_data/file/366104/43380_23902777_Care_Act_Book. pdf.

(1) <u>Lifetime guarantee</u>: the payments will cover the claimant's future needs for life so that he will never run out of funds.

(2) <u>Tax free</u>: periodical payments are received tax free and will not affect the claimant's entitlement to means tested benefits.[11]

(3) <u>Bankruptcy</u>: if the claimant goes bankrupt the payments for care will continue and the claimant's debtors will not be able to enforce against the periodical payments.[12]

(4) <u>Inflation</u>: the periodical payments will increase each year in line with Retail Price Index (RPI) for inflation or ASHE 6115 for care. There are no ASHE indices for case management or deputies fees.

(5) <u>Security</u>: the source of the periodical payments is financially secure. Periodical payments and structured settlement annuities have been granted 100% protection under the Financial Services Compensation Scheme (FSCS) or are underwritten by the Secretary of State.[13] If the provider of the periodical payments or structured settlement becomes insolvent the FSCS or the government would ensure that the periodical payments would continue to be paid without deduction. No other investment vehicle has such protective guarantees.

(6) <u>Stepped payments</u>: the periodical payments may be constructed so that they vary in future to take into account anticipated changes in circumstances.

(7) <u>Investment risk</u>: the claimant takes no investment risks. These risks are carried by the defendant.

(8) <u>Vulnerability</u>: unscrupulous relatives and friends are less likely to be able to take advantage of the claimant who has PPO.

(9) <u>Inheritance</u>: PPOs can continue after the claimant's death for the benefit of his dependants.

The disadvantages of periodical payments are as follows:

(1) <u>Beneficiaries</u>: if the claimant dies early no money will go into his estate. The defendants will not profit unless the order makes specific provision for the payments to continue after death.[14]

(2) <u>Borrowing on the PPO</u>: the claimant cannot assign or mortgage the security of the periodical payments without the consent of the court.[15]

(3) <u>Inflexibility</u>: periodical payments are not flexible when unforeseen events occur after the trial. Stepped PPOs can be made but only in limited circumstances which are foreseeable at the time of trial. When unforeseen circumstances arise the claimant will not be able to vary the level of payments or to use the capital tied up in other ways. The claimant does not have control over his money and he cannot invest it to gain higher profits.

(4) <u>Tax and benefits advantages</u>: There is no guarantee that in hard times the government will continue to permit the tax and benefits advantages which PPOs presently enjoy.

---

11 See s. 329AA (1) of the Income and Corporation Taxes Act 1988 (now ss. 731–734 of the Income Tax (Trading and Other Income) Act 2005) and s. 100 of the Courts Act 2003.
12 See s. 101 of the Courts Act 2003.
13 In public sector self-funded cases.
14 There is power to do so in the CPR, r. 41.8(2).
15 See s. 2(6) of the Damages Act 1996.

(5)   Cost: in small and medium-sized claims (e.g. damages less than £500,000) the cost of administering the PPO may make it an unattractive option.

4   PERIODICAL PAYMENTS ORDERS

The Department for Constitutional Affairs published guidance on PPOs in 2005. It stated that the policy behind the introduction of PPOs was dissatisfaction with the lump sum method of compensating claimants. The criticisms of lump sums payment are set out above.

4.1   The Power

Courts have the power to make a PPO for damages for "future pecuniary loss" in clinical negligence and personal injury cases pursuant to s. 2(1) of the Damages Act 1996. The words "future expense" are not mentioned but the section does cover future pecuniary expenses, for instance care costs.

There is no power to make a PPO in relation to past loss and expense or damages for pain, suffering and loss of amenity. However, with the parties' consent the courts may make a PPO for any damages.[16]

This power applies to clinical negligence cases resulting in death as well.[17]

4.2   PPOs Generally

The decision whether or not to make a PPO is a matter for the discretion of the court. In every case the court is directed that it "shall consider whether to make" a PPO by s. 2(1)(b) of the Damages Act 1996. The court is required by the rules to provide the parties with an indication "as soon as practicable" whether a PPO will be more appropriate.[18] This may occur at a case management conference, a pre-trial review or even at the trial.

The courts may impose a PPO even if the parties do not consent. This is unlikely to occur if both parties do not want one because the factors leading to the order expressly takes into account the parties' views.[19]

If the claimant seeks or the defendant wants to give a PPO this should be pleaded. However, CPR, r. 41.5(1) is permissive. It provides that each party "may" state in its statement of case whether it considers that a PPO or a lump sum order is more appropriate. CPR, r. 41.5(2) and (3) grant the courts the power to order a party to set out its preference as to the structure of the award and to provide details. The best practice is for the parties to set out their position on whether the award should include periodical payments in their pleadings or the schedules.

---

16 Section 2(2) of the Damages Act 1996.
17 See s. 7 of the Damages Act 1996.
18 See CPR, r. 41.6.
19 See *Godbold v. Mahmood* [2005] EWHC 1002.

4.3 Factors Taken into Account

The courts will take into account all of the circumstances of the case when considering whether to make a PPO and the main factor is the claimant's need:

"in particular the form of award which best meets the claimant's needs."[20]

Further factors to be considered are:[21]

(1) any deduction for contributory negligence;
(2) the reasons for the claimant's preference;
(3) the nature of any financial advice received by the claimant; and
(4) the defendants preferred form of award and the reasons.

4.4 Expert Reports on PPOs

It is important for the claimant (but generally unnecessary for the defendant) to obtain award management advice from an expert if a PPO is being considered.[22] The claimant will also need investment advice if the case is worth more than £50,000. The advice should cover the reason why PPOs are necessary and whether they should be self-funded or funded by way of the purchase of a structured settlement annuity. The report should cover the effects of tax and loss of benefits on the potential lump sum award and should also contain a comparison to show what the claimant could achieve with a lump sum award if he invested it in (i) safe, or (ii) moderately safe or (iii) risky investments. There should also be an appraisal of whether the claimant wants to invest himself and whether he has the ability to do so.

4.5 Future Heads of Loss and Expense

The main heads of damage covered by periodical payments orders are future care, case management expenses, deputies' fees, anticipated large capital expenditure and loss of earnings and pension loss. A lump sum award for care will almost always be wrong. In the words of Lord Scarman in *Lim Poh Choo v. Camden and Islington AHA*:[23] *"There is only one certainty: the future will prove the award to be either too high or too low."*

4.6 Calculating Periodical Payments

There are two broad approaches to calculating the level of periodical payments: top down or bottom up. The top down approach is wrong in principle, the bottom up approach is right.

4.6.1 *The top-down approach*

This is used where the conventional lump sum valuation of the claim is agreed between the parties and the claimant wishes to take advice on PPOs. The parties agree

---

20 CPR, r. 41.7.
21 See Practice Direction 41B.
22 This was made clear by Waller LJ in *Thompstone v. Tameside* [2008] EWCA Civ 5; [2008] PIQR Q10. See also the Northern Irish case of *Gilliland v. McManus and Another* [2013] NIQB where Gillen J stated [10] *"A plaintiff's legal advisers may find that he will need a very good reason, probably backed by expert advice, for not having discussed in detail or commended such a provision to his client in clear terms. Solicitors or barristers should incline to caution and carefully consider obtaining such financial or actuarial advice, since they are neither permitted nor (usually) qualified to give such advice themselves."*
23 [1980] AC 174, 192.

the sums involved in principle subject to those investigations. A conditional compromise agreement may then be signed. The defendant agrees to hold open the agreed lump sum until the claimant has had time to investigate the possibility of obtaining a financially worthwhile periodical payment. The defendant also consents to suitable periodical payments being established, as long as the overall cost of the settlement is not in excess of the agreed amount. At a later stage if the claimant decides that periodical payments are appropriate and the defendant agrees to fund such periodical payments in a suitably secure manner the compromise can then be reflected in a suitable proposed order for the court's consideration.

No payment should be accepted nor judgment entered before the periodical payments are put in place. The consent order will set out that the defendant is to provide the agreed periodical payments for the benefit of the claimant.

If the defendant is insured, rather than being the NHSLA, the insurer then purchases an annuity for the claimant, using all or part of this lump sum figure as the premium. The price of the annuity will reflect the state of the annuity market at the time, and is unlikely to reflect the assumptions used for the Ogden Tables, so the resulting payments are unlikely to match the original assessment of annual needs.

The Department for Constitutional Affairs (DCA) criticised this approach in its Guidance on periodical payments, stating:

> "... the 'top-down' approach reflects the method of calculating lump sums and preserves many of the disadvantages attached to those payments."

This approach is rarely if ever used now because of these problems.

4.6.2   *The bottom-up approach*

The better and more usual method of considering periodical payments is to start by looking at what the claimant needs (or will lose) in future and to agree the annual figure and then to arrange the periodical payments to provide for that need or loss.

The DCA Guidance in respect of periodical payments stated:

> "Under the 'bottom-up' approach, the various heads of damages (loss of earnings/costs of care etc) are considered to estimate the annual needs of the claimant. The order for periodical payments then simply provides for the claimant to be paid the appropriate amounts for the duration of his or her need (usually life), escalating in line with the RPI unless the Court orders otherwise. This means that there is no need for speculative estimates or extended disputes about life expectancy, as payments will be based on the claimant's annual needs and will be payable for as long as necessary."

It may not be appropriate to provide for all of the claimant's future losses by way of periodical payments (for instance accommodation costs or DIY may not be included), because the claimant may wish the flexibility which a lump sum brings on those items.

4.7   Security for the PPO

The courts may only make a PPO if the court is satisfied that the continuity of the periodical payments is "reasonably secure".[24]

The DCA Guidance stated:

> *"31. It is clearly very important that any periodical payments ordered by the Court can be paid for the period specified in the order. Section 2(3) of the 1996 Act therefore requires a Court making an order for periodical payments to be satisfied that the continuity of payments under the order is reasonably secure."*

Suitable PPOs have to be paid for the claimant's lifetime or until retirement. Therefore, the court must be satisfied that the defendant can meet the terms of any PPO for the claimant's lifetime regardless of how long that may be. The DCA Guidance reflects the statute on when security can be assumed:

> *"32. In order that the Court does not have to give specific consideration to the future security of periodical payments in every individual case, section 2(4) provides that the continuity of payment can automatically be considered to be reasonably secure where:*
> *(a)   it is protected by a Ministerial guarantee under section 6 of the 1996 Act;*
> *(b)   it is protected by a scheme under section 213 of the Financial Services and Markets Act 2000, or*
> *(c)   the source of the payments is a government or health service body.*

> *What methods of funding does 2(4) cover?*

> *33. Section 2(4)(a) covers 'self-funded' payments made directly by public sector bodies where a Minister has specifically guaranteed those payments under section 6 of the 1996 Act. At present no such guarantees have been given, but it is possible for this to be done in a particular case or generally (for example in respect of non-departmental public bodies).*

> *34. Section 2(4)(b) covers payments which attract protection under the Financial Services Compensation Scheme (FSCS), i.e. payments made by authorised insurers. This covers both –*
> *(a)   'self-funded' payments that are to be made directly by a defendant's liability insurer (with the exception of aircraft and shipping insurance, see paragraph 37 below) to the claimant, and*
> *(b)   payments made by a life insurer under an annuity contract. The annuity may of course have been bought by the defendant, the defendant's insurer, a defence organisation etc. The annuity could either be bought in the name of the claimant or be held by the defendant with some or all of the income directed to the claimant as beneficial owner. This allows defendants the flexibility to adopt the funding approach that best suits them while ensuring that the claimant's needs are met.*

> *A detailed explanation of how these payments are protected under the Financial Services Compensation Scheme, including how the enhanced protection under section 4 of the 1996 Act works, is at Annex C.*

---

24 Section 2(3) of the Damages Act 1996.

35. <u>Section 2(4)(c)</u> covers payments made by government or health service bodies. The Damages (Government and Health Service Bodies) Order 2005 lists the bodies which are designated as government and health service bodies for this purpose. Designation under the Order removes the need for a Ministerial guarantee to be given under section 2(4)(a) or for the body to have to satisfy the Court on a case-by-case basis that the continuity of payments is reasonably secure."

The list changes year on year and lawyers must check the up-to-date position. General insurance companies and Life Offices in England and Wales are considered secure where they are covered by the Financial Services Compensation Scheme. Health service bodies (NHS trusts) in England are not presently covered (save for the NHSLA or the Department of Health) although in Wales they are. The answer for claims under the Clinical Negligence Scheme for Trusts (CNST) was found in *YM v. Gloucester Hospitals NHS Foundation Trust.*[25] In that case the NHSLA agreed to be named as the source of the payments because it had entered into agreements with NHS trusts that permitted it to take on this liability. Therefore funding was considered secure. There was a model order attached to the judgment in that case. However, this has now been superseded by the model order in *RH (a child by his mother and Litigation Friend LW v. University Hospitals Bristol NHS Foundation Trust (formerly United Bristol Healthcare NHS Trust)*[26] considered further below in section 4.9. For claims that arise under the Existing Liabilities Scheme (where the matters complained of took place after 1st April 1995) periodical payments are funded directly by the Department of Health and so are secure.

The following are not considered automatically secure: offshore insurers; insurers of aircraft and ships; Lloyd's underwriters; the MDU and the MPS; private defendants. For further guidance on this see *APIL's Guide to Catastrophic Injury Claims 2nd Edition.*[27]

The DCA Guidance sets out what should be done in claims against insecure defendants:

"39. This does not mean that Courts cannot order periodical payments against these defendants and insurance bodies [those that cannot be considered automatically secure]. They may be able to provide statutorily secure periodical payments by purchasing an appropriate annuity from a life office for the benefit of the claimant, thus attracting the full protection of the FSCS under section 4(1) and (2) of the 1996 Act (but see para 52 below). Alternatively, it is open to these bodies to satisfy the Court that they can offer a method of funding, other than one of those deemed secure under section 2(4), that is reasonably secure."

Therefore, it would seem that "insecure" defendants have two options:

- prove they can provide "adequately secure" periodical payments by a means other than under s. 2(4); or
- purchase a structured settlement annuity to meet the obligations in full.

Rule 41.9 is as follows:

---

25 [2006] EWHC 820.
26 [2013] PIQR P12.
27 Chapter 18.

> *"CONTINUITY OF PAYMENT (RULE 41.9)*
>
> *3. Before ordering an alternative method of funding under rule 41.9(1), the Court must be satisfied that the following criteria are met –*
>
> *(1)   that a method of funding provided for under section 2(4) of the 1996 Act is not possible or there are good reasons to justify an alternative method of funding;*
>
> *(2)   that the proposed method of funding can be maintained for the duration of the award or for the proposed duration of the method of funding; and*
>
> *(3)   that the proposed method of funding will meet the level of payment ordered by the Court."*

The court will consider whether or not the defendant is able to fund appropriate periodical payments by means provided for under s. 2(4), other than by self-funding.

In para. 41, the Guidance states:

> *"Where the defendant or liability insurer is not covered by section 2(4), they will have to purchase an appropriate annuity for the claimant, unless the Court has approved an alternative method of funding (but see para 52 below)."*

Paragraph 52 of the Guidance addresses the major issue of the suitability of such an annuity. It states:

> *"52. At present, all existing Index-Linked Government securities (ILGS) will have expired by 2035. So index-linked annuities are only guaranteed to escalate in line with RPI until that date. Annuity contracts therefore provide for escalation to switch to a Limited Price Index if in future (i.e. after 2035) it becomes impossible for the provider to match its liabilities with appropriate index-linked assets. The contract prescribes a maximum percentage inflation figure (at present typically 1– 5%) that will apply in these circumstances. The payments will still inflate by RPI if this is lower than the maximum figure at the time. If in future the annuity purchased does not provide the payments required to meet the terms of the order, then liability for meeting the shortfall remains with the liability insurer."*

In June 2005 there was a single provider of structured settlement annuities on a RPI-linked basis and this structured settlement annuity had two problems. The maximum premium the Life Office would accept in any one case was £1m; and the RPI-linking was limited if ILGS were not available post 2035. It still remains to be seen whether the market will resolve these concerns and the greater concerns raised by the effect of *Thompstone*[28] and the ASHE 6115 index. Annuities based on ASHE 6115 are needed.

It is hoped that new providers of structured settlement annuities will enter the market, offering fully RPI-linked structured settlement annuities with no maximum premium cap. In other words, annuities without a 2035 clause. Consequently, until new providers of fully RPI-linked structured settlement annuities enter the market, the courts are unlikely to order periodical payments in every case.

It is a matter for the defendant how it funds the PPO. The DCA Guidance states that:

> *"It is a matter for the defendant or his insurer to decide what form of funding to use to meet the terms of the order. Where the defendant or insurer is covered by*

---

28 *Thompstone v. Tameside* [2008] EWCA Civ 5.

section 2(4), they can choose to meet the order by purchasing an annuity or by self-funding, and it will not be necessary to identify a specific annuity policy at the time of the order. This is intended to give defendants and their insurers (who will carry the investment risk) maximum flexibility to choose whatever funding arrangements are most appropriate while ensuring the security of these arrangements. For example, a defendant may wish to self-fund for a short period until a change in market conditions or the availability of a new product on the market make it preferable to buy an annuity. Where the defendant or liability insurer is not covered by section 2(4), they will have to purchase an appropriate annuity for the claimant, unless the Court has approved an alternative method of funding (but see para 52 below).

There may be circumstances where the defendant wishes to fund periodical payments in a way that is not defined as reasonably secure under section 2(4). Examples may be where a large corporation wishes to self fund payments from its own resources; where the case involves the Motor Insurers' Bureau which is funded by the insurance industry; or if a new type of financial instrument that is not covered by section 2(4) comes onto the market. In any such case, the Court must of course be satisfied that the continuity of the payments is reasonably secure. Rule 41.9(2) and paragraph 3 of the Practice Direction set out the criteria which the Court must be satisfied are met before it can order periodical payments under an alternative method of funding. The alternative method must still meet the terms of the order made. Rule 41.9(3) provides that where the Court is satisfied of the security of an alternative method of funding, the order for periodical payments must specify the method of funding to be used.

Where the Court is not satisfied by the security of the proposed alternative method of funding, section 2(5)(a) of the 1996 Act allows it to order the party responsible for the payments to secure their continuity by using a method under section 2(4). Section 2(5)(b) and (c) allows the Court to make provision about funding by methods that aren't secure under section 2(4) (for example by requiring an annuity to be purchased before the order takes final effect)."

4.8 A PPO may not be Assigned or Charged

A claimant may not assign or charge his right to periodical payment without the approval of the court and any purported assignment or charge is void without approval.[29] That approval will only be granted if "special circumstances make it necessary". These words are not explained in the Act. The DCA guidance states:

"This is intended to avoid the possibility of claimants receiving less than the true value of the award as a result of their assigning their right to receive the payments in return for a lump sum.

Rule 41.10 requires the Court in considering whether to permit an assignment or charge to have regard to a number of factors set out in paragraph 4 of the Practice Direction. These comprise:
- *whether the capitalised value of the assignment or charge represents value for money;*
- *whether the assignment or charge is in the claimant's best interests, taking into account whether those interests can be met in some other way; and*

---

29 By s. 2(6) of the Damages Act 1996.

- *how the claimant will be financially supported following the assignment or charge.*

  These restrictions on claimants' ability to assign or charge the right to periodical payments do not affect their ability to borrow against their future income. Unsecured loans will thus be permissible, but not secured loans that put the claimant's right to receive payments at risk."

4.9   The Index of Increase for Inflation

All orders for periodical payments are *"treated as providing for the amounts of the payments to vary in accordance with the retail price index"*.[30] The RPI is calculated by the government and is a measure of the change in the general level of prices that are charged for a collection of goods and services bought by the majority of UK households. It is a shopping basket containing some 650 goods and services. The percentage change in the headline RPI is calculated monthly in relation to the percentage change over the previous 12 months. The Office for National Statistics reviews the components of the RPI once a year, to keep it as up to date as possible, reflecting changes in consumers' preferences and establishment of new products.

Section 2(9) gives the courts power to use an index other than RPI. If the claimant can prove that the loss or expense which he will suffer in future will increase at a rate above the RPI then a different index will be used. Any alternative index will need to be sufficiently clear, durable, and certain to satisfy the courts. The DCA guidance at para. 10 mentions the words *"exceptional circumstances"* to justify a departure from the RPI and relies on *Hansard*.[31] After the Court of Appeal decision in *Thompstone v. Tameside*[32] the concern was that inflation would ravage future care PPOs. However, in *RH (a child by his mother and Litigation Friend LW) v. University Hospitals Bristol NHS Foundation Trust (formerly United Bristol Healthcare NHS Trust)*[33] there had been a trial before Mackay J in 2007 as to whether any periodical payment should be varied by reference to the RPI pursuant to s. 2(8) or whether the order should contain a provision and if so what provision, modifying the effect of subsection (8) pursuant to s. 2(9). The outcome was that the periodical payments should be index linked (for care and case management) to ASHE 6115 because this would be the best available indicator of growth in the earnings of the type of carer employed by the claimant (who had cerebral palsy). The defendant appealed to the Court of Appeal who dismissed its appeals and permission had been granted to go to the House of Lords but the petition was withdrawn and the case referred back for the purpose of approving a model order by which NHSLA claims for care and case management were index linked using ASHE 6115 data at the 75th, 80th and 90th percentile of earnings (depending on the facts of the case). In 2010 the Office of National Statistics revised its occupational classifications and split ASHE 6115 into two subdivisions. (6145 for care workers and home carers and 6146 for senior care workers). They agreed to keep publishing ASHE 6115 but then changed their methodology for the calculation of the gross hourly rates so the formula in the model order could not be applied. The matter came before Mrs Justice Swift who devised a new model order with expert assistance and directed that this model order should be applicable in all cases (642 of them) unless specific reasoned objections were provided. The model order is appended to the judgment and should be applied as a

---

30 Section 2(8) of the Damages Act 1996.
31 (HL) 19.5.2005, vol. 648, col. 536–537.
32 *Thompstone v. Tameside* [2008] EWCA Civ 5.
33 [2013] PIQR P12.

blue print in all NHSLA cases. In non-NHSLA cases Mrs Justice Swift urged deputies to consider adopting the same approach (para. 38 of the judgment).

In *Olivia v. Mahmood (1) and Liverpool Victoria (2)* (Lawtel 22.8.13), Lewis J approved a PPO linked to the Brazilian Inflationary table IPCA 62 in circumstances where a 21-year-old Brazilian sustained devastating brain injuries in a road traffic accident. Other examples of different indexation (including that for loss of earnings) can be found in *Sarwar v. Ali and Another*[34] and *Whiten v. St George's Healthcare NHS Trust*.[35] There is no index in ASHE for case managers or deputies. The index for lawyers' fees could be used for the latter. The case law and practice (in terms of settlements) in relation to this issue is likely to evolve in years to come.

4.10   Stepped PPOs

Following the precise wording of CPR, r. 41.8(3) the court may only make an order for PPOs which vary upwards or downwards on a certain date.[36] The date of the variation and the amount of the new sum for loss of income or for care or medical expenses must be stated in the order.[37] This is poorly phrased as they should be capable of being stepped not only by reference to a date but also to an event, such as the death or incapacity of a carer.

There may be difficulties agreeing stepped or foreseeable variations in PPOs for care, for instance, when parental care may change to commercial care at some time in future. If the step up to commercial care is dependent on a parent becoming too old to care for the claimant that event may occur at an unknown time in future.

A stepped PPO may be sought by claimants for loss of earnings where promotion or advancement is likely to have occurred but for the accident. It also applies where care is to be provided by the family for a period and then later by commercial agencies. Stepped PPOs are inflexible once they are set.

4.11   Conditions to PPOs

In *Wallace v. Follett*,[38] the Court of Appeal attached conditions to a PPO in order to protect the insurers' position:

(1)   to require the claimant to undergo further medical examinations during the course of the PPO to establish the claimant's general health in order to obtain a quotation for the purchase costs of an annuity to fund the periodical payments;

(2)   upon a written request from the insurer the claimant had to provide confirmation from his GP or other medical adviser that he had been seen within the last year and was still alive.

---

34 [2007] EWHC 274 (QB): loss of earnings indexed to 90th percentile for male full-time employees.
35 [2011] EWHC 2066 (QB): loss of earnings indexed to ASHE gross annual pay for all male full-time employees in the UK.
36 See CPR, r. 41.8(3).
37 In current value terms.
38 [2013] EWCA Civ 146.

4.12 The Form of the Order

The order making the periodical payments award must specify:[39]

    (1) the annual amount awarded;
    (2) the breakdown of the annual sum awarded for:
        (a) loss of earnings, and
        (b) care and medical expenses, and
        (c) recurring or capital cost expenses;
    (3) the frequency of the payments;
    (4) the duration of the payments – for life or otherwise;[40]
    (5) the annual increase in the payment in line with the RPI or another index;
    (6) the date of the steps for variation and the amount of the variation;
    (7) the foreseeable capital costs provisions setting out the amounts allowed at current values and the triggering events;
    (8) the method of funding of the payments.[41]

Administrative aspects of the PPO must be addressed in the order: how the payments are to be made, to whom the payments are to be made, how the defendant is to be informed of the death of the claimant, etc. The model order in *RH (a child by his mother and Litigation Friend LW) v. University Hospitals Bristol NHS Foundation Trust (formerly United Bristol Healthcare NHS Trust)*[42] should be followed especially in NHSLA claims and should be considered in non-NHSLA claims.

5 PROVISIONAL DAMAGES OR VARIABLE PPOS

Variable PPOs are permitted where it is proved or admitted that there is a chance that at some definite or indefinite time in the future the claimant will (as a result of the matter complained of) develop some serious disease or serious deterioration, per articles 1(2)(f) and 2(a) of the Damages (Variation of Periodical Payments) Order 2005. On the flip side if there is a chance that the claimant will enjoy a significant improvement in his mental or physical condition the court may make a variable order (Article 2b of the 2005 Order). This innovation permits the inverse of a provisional payments order. In *AA v. (1) CC (2) Motor Insurers' Bureau*[43] Mrs Justice Swift declined an application for a "stop-start" PPO in a case where the evidence suggested that the claimant's capacity might fluctuate and so there might be periods where Court of Protection costs would not be incurred (which were themselves the subject of an agreed PPO at £11,000 p.a.). She considered that the 2005 Order was really intended to cater for cases where it was necessary for there to be a re-assessment of damages in the future. She said: *"I have concerns as to whether an order which is wholly suspended and then starts again would come within the ambit of order permitting variation."* By article 5 of the 2005 Order, permission of the court must be obtained to apply for a variation, unless the court has already otherwise ordered. Further, the variable order:

---

39 CPR, r. 41.8.
40 CPR, r. 41.8(2) envisages some orders continuing after the claimant's death for the benefit of the claimant's dependants.
41 See CPR, r. 41.9.
42 [2013] PIQR P12.
43 [2013] EWHC 3679 QB.

(i)   must specify the disease, deterioration or improvement;

(ii)   may specify a period in which an application to vary may be made;

(iii)   may specify more than one disease or type of deterioration and/or specify different applicable periods for each.

The pragmatic solution in the *AA* case was for the parties to agree a Tomlin order with a schedule embodying their agreement in relation to the periodical payments approved by the court.

A party can only apply once within the time specified but can make more applications to extend the time for an application to vary within the time specified (articles 6–7). The court and the parties must preserve the case papers for the duration of the order or any extension to it (article 8).

6   WILLS AND PPOS

CPR, r. 41.8(2) makes provision for PPOs to continue after the death of the claimant.

The obvious example is a PPO to cover loss of earnings where the death is likely to occur as a result of the tortfeasor's negligence. This rule covers a lost years' claim making provision for the claimant's dependants. Care will not come within this rule.

PPOs continuing after death are not free of tax: see s. 329AA(2)(a) of the ICTA 1988, now ss. 731–734 of the Income Tax (Trading and Other Income) Act 2005.

Unfortunately, whilst the DCA Guidance acknowledges the fact that the tax-freedom associated with the periodical payments dies with the claimant it fails to consider whether the PPO should only continue beyond the life of the claimant if the claimant dies of a medical condition related to the claim? Additionally given that the PPOs become taxable in the hands of the dependant, will the courts award the gross PPO after death?

The nature of the defendant's chosen method of funding the periodical payments is vital for post-death dependants. If the periodical payments are funded by a structured settlement annuity, then the future payments are considered an asset of the claimant's estate and may be subject to inheritance tax, prior to them then being paid to the dependant and being taxed for income. However, as a structured settlement annuity has a capital content, it is only the interest content of each payment that falls to be taxed. If the periodical payments are self-funded by the defendant, then there does not seem to be any asset to fall to be considered for inheritance tax, but there is also no capital content, so the entire periodical payment falls to be taxed not just an interest element. Expert advice will be needed on such issues.

7   THE COURT OF PROTECTION

The Court of Protection was established by the Mental Capacity Act 2005 which came into force on 1st October 2007. It is a superior court of record with the status of a High Court, based in London but sitting around the country.

Where damages are recovered by or on behalf of a protected party, the court will give directions for the management of the money recovered (CPR, r. 21.11, PD 8). Where the sum to be administered is £30,000 or more, unless there is already an attorney under a registered enduring power of attorney, the donee of a lasting power of attorney or a deputy appointed by the Court of Protection, the order approving the settlement will contain a direction to the litigation friend to apply to the Court of Protection for the appointment of a deputy, after which the fund will be dealt with as directed by the Court of Protection (CPD 10.2).

The Court of Protection has jurisdiction for the welfare, health, property and financial matters of persons deemed to lack capacity. It has the power to make declarations as to whether an individual has capacity to make a particular decision, and has the power to appoint deputies to make those decisions or call for reports from the Public Guardian, Court of Protection Visitor, local authority or NHS body.

8 INVESTMENT ADVICE ON MANAGING LUMP SUM AWARDS

The general rule is that if the claimant chooses to invest the award he will be liable to tax on the income received and capital gains tax on profitable disposals.

Claimants with capacity and their advisers need to consider investment before the personal injury award is made. Children or claimants unable to manage their financial affairs who are protected by the Public Guardianship Office (PGO), Public Trustee Office and the Court of Protection need to do so as well now that the PGO has got rid of all of its advisers. The challenge is how best to arrange the award and/or to place, manage and invest the sums which the claimant is likely to receive with a view to providing the claimant with financial security during the course of his future suffering. The objective is to minimise the claimant's tax liabilities and to maximise the state benefits available to the claimant. For minors and brain damaged claimants, the Public Guardianship Office, Public Trustee Office and Court of Protection oversee these issues but no longer have investment brokers or advisers.

In cases where the likely level of the personal injury award is greater than £30,000 the claimant's lawyers should advise the claimant to seek professional advice on the form of award and on investing. The advice should come from a suitably qualified and authorised adviser. This is particularly necessary since the courts are bound to consider whether a PPO should be made. (*Gilliland v. McManus and Another*). [44]

In all cases where the claimant is entitled to means tested benefits now, or may be entitled to such benefits in the future and the award is sufficient to affect such entitlement, the claimant should be advised that a Personal Injury Trust may be established to avoid losing such entitlement.

The Law Society has imposed regulations governing the conduct of investment business by solicitors. Claimant solicitors should refer to the Society's rules and regulations for details. Unless the claimant's solicitors' firm has a department specialising in investment and tax advice the personal injury lawyers dealing with the case should avoid giving investment advice. Some big PI firms have such departments.

---

[44] [2013] NIQB.

Whether the claimant's solicitor can actually suggest the name of an adviser without fully investigating the qualification and competence of such an adviser is a matter of professional ethics. The claimant's solicitor has a duty to enquire as to the costs of such advice for the purposes of reclaiming it from the defendants. A commission arrangement is not appropriate.

The adviser should be suitably qualified and authorised by the Financial Conduct Authority to give such advice. Authorisation for such may be checked at www.fca.org.uk/firms/systems-reporting/register/search.

There are conflicts of interest between the parties when providing joint instructions to an expert on award management and on investment strategy for personal injury awards. The defendants will seek to obtain the lowest cost for any annuity sought and the claimant will seek to obtain the highest annuity for the lump sum available. The claimant will seek the best vehicle to cover his expenses and reduce tax and loss of benefits, the defendant may seek the best vehicle for them to keep any investment profits over and above inflation over the years whilst only having to increase the annual periodical payments made to the claimant by RPI. The NHSLA did not support obtaining joint reports in the past, see Circular 97/C5 of 17th April 1997. In 1994 the Law Commission in their report no. 224 on Structured Settlements suggested that if a joint report was to be obtained the claimant should obtain independent advice on the joint report. We do not recommend them.

8.1 Expert Reports on Award Management and Investment

These reports have historically been difficult to understand and of little help. The key players are now focussing better on the service required.

The instructions to be given to the expert should be to advise the claimant as appropriate on:

(1) how to provide for the claimant's future losses and expenses caused by the injuries for the whole of his life;

(2) how to maximise the profits available from the claimant's award for damages and the use of the award;

(3) how to minimise the claimant's liability for tax;

(4) how to maximise the claimant's entitlement to state benefits;

(5) how to cope with foreseeable and unforeseeable changes in future;

(6) how to construct the award – lump sum or periodical payment order; if PPO:
- to ensure any PPO is reasonably secure;
- to lay out the form of any PPO;
- to ensure the index-linking for future increase of any PPO is sufficient;

(7) to deal with interim payments (PITs, etc.);

(8) whether a PPO beyond death is needed or appropriate;

(9) whether a structured settlement should be used.

The advice given must be understandable to a layman. To achieve these ends the advisers will need to consider periodical payments (both self-funded and provided by purchasing structured settlement annuities), trusts and a range of standard investments then compare and contrast and report back to the claimant. NHS trusts may be required to obtain "value for money" reports before agreeing to enter into structured settlements or PPOs which they would self fund.

Experts should be provided with a complete summary of the evidence and the schedules of loss and details of the claimant's present tax and benefits situation. The expert should also take into account any assets available to the claimant, other than the award of damages.

8.2   Fees

The fees for advice on the form or strategy for the forthcoming award, on periodical payments, a structured settlement, or on implementing a trust for a protected party should be recoverable. The NHSLA circular: "Structured Settlement and Value for Money Reports" 97/C5 (17th April 1997) contained text indicating that they accepted that claimant was entitled to obtain investment advice reports before settlement and that the NHSLA should pay the reasonable cost of such. Though this advice is now out of date, and PD40C, which stated that the costs of such investment advice were regarded as the costs of the litigation has now been revoked, the costs remain recoverable.

The costs of obtaining investment advice on how to place or invest lump sum awards is not recoverable: see *Eagle v. Chambers (No. 2)*.[45] This reasoning applies equally to investment broker's costs incurred by the Public Guardianship Office where the funds are administered by the Court of Protection which used to invest larger awards in a mixed basket of ILGS, investment funds and unit trusts and equities with some cash retained in the Special Investment Account.

These fees are to be distinguished from the Court of Protection's fees for administering the funds which are recoverable.

9   PERSONAL INJURY TRUSTS

If the claimant has regular payments which must be made to a third person, for instance to carers or to mortgage lenders and does not wish the income to be received though his hands and if the claimant can survive without the capital sum which is required to fund such payments being in his name, then a personal injury trust may be set up to hold the fund and to make the payments.

Setting up a personal injury trust (PIT) is a good way to maintain a claimant's entitlement to means tested state benefits and local authority support and care. Any award exceeding £6,000 may have adverse consequences for a claimant eligible for means tested benefits.

---

45 [2004] EWCA Civ 1033, [2004] 1 WLR 3081.

9.1   Procedure to set up a PIT

It is not necessary to have the trust set up before the settlement takes place, although it is preferable. There is now provision for a 52-week disregard period for the PIT to be set up after receipt of the award. It is important to note that the 52-week disregard begins upon the first payment received as a result of an injury. This could include ex gratis payments from employers, critical illness insurance payments or interim payments.

Consequently, if the claimant is unlikely to have brought their payment below the £6,000 level by 'reasonable' spending within 52 weeks or they are likely to receive a further payment within 52 weeks or the 52-week rule does not apply because they have had a previous payment and this payment will take their total capital to above the £6,000 or £16,000 level, the claimant may wish to set up a personal injury trust. This will prevent the claimant's personal injury payment causing their benefits to reduce/stop, as regulations state that payments derived from a personal injury are disregarded as capital when assessing entitlement to means-tested benefits for people aged under pension age, if they are held on trust.

Trustees must be appointed and a trust bank account set up. The purposes of the trust must be stated in the deed. A copy should be supplied to the relevant benefits agency.

The costs of setting up such a trust may be as low as £600 or as high as £1,500.

The PIT is the only legitimate means for a claimant with capacity to pass his capital to another legal entity designed to hold his capital for his absolute benefit. There are a number of different types of PITs, the type typically used for personal injury payments, is known as a Bare Trust. The only person who can benefit from this type of trust is the claimant as the creator of the trust.

The trust deed sets up the trust which is a separate legal entity that is the effective owner of the claimant's funds and is usually administered by a minimum of two trustees whom the claimant appoints. None of the trustees, unless of course the claimant appoints himself as one, can benefit from the fund. The trustees' primary responsibilities are to pay out the funds to the claimant or on his behalf when he requires.

The trustees must have a discretionary power to say no if the claimant requests a payout from the trust fund, otherwise the Benefits Agency may look on the arrangement as a sham and disallow any means tested benefits. Some claimants may not be too keen on handing over full discretion and this drawback has to be taken into consideration. The claimant may however retain the power to revoke or break the PIT at any time; the claimant may also be given the power to appoint and remove trustees.

9.2   PITs and State Benefits

If due to contributory negligence the claimant does not recover a sufficient award to ensure that he can support himself and pay for the care which he needs for life he may need to consider a PIT to maintain his entitlement to benefits.

The sum of the capital and income from the PIT are disregarded when assessing some of the claimant's means tested state benefits. So looking at income support, pursuant to para. 12 of Sch. 10 to the Income Support (General) Regulations 1987 as amended by the Social Security Amendment (Personal Injury Payments) Regulations 2002 (SI 2002/2442) the claimant's personal injury or clinical negligence damages which are tied up in a special needs trust are ignored. The Income Support Regulations in this area of the law were clarified in October 2002. They are fiendishly complicated.

Regulation 46(2) of the Income Support Regulations 1987 states:

> *"Calculation of capital*
> *46.—(1) For the purposes of Part II of the Act as it applies to income support, the capital of a claimant to be taken into account shall, subject to paragraph (2), be the whole of his capital calculated in accordance with this Part and any income treated as capital under regulations 24(2) and 48 (treatment of charitable or voluntary payments and income treated as capital).*
> *(2) There shall be disregarded from the calculation of a claimant's capital under paragraph (1) any capital, where applicable, specified in Schedule 10."*

Paragraph 12 of Sch. 10: "capital to be disregarded" says:

> *"12.—(1) Where the funds of a trust are derived from a payment made in consequence of any personal injury to the claimant the value of the trust fund and the value of the right to receive any payment under that trust, for a period of two years or such longer period as is reasonable in the circumstances beginning—*
> *(a) if, at the date of the payment the claimant or his partner is in receipt of an income-related benefit, on that date;*
> *(b) in any other case, on the date on which an income-related benefit is first payable to the claimant or his partner after the date of that payment,*
> *but, for the purposes of regulation 17, 18, 21, 44(5) and 71 and Schedules 4 and 5 (applicable amounts and modifications in respect of children and young persons) in calculating the capital of a child or young person there shall be no limit as to the period of disregard under this paragraph.*
> *(2) For the purposes of sub-paragraph (1) any reference to an income-related benefit shall be construed as if it included a reference to supplementary benefit."*

Income from personal injury trusts is disregarded by regulation 40(2) and Sch. 9. Regulation 40(2) states:

> *"Calculation of income other than earnings*
> *40.—(1) For the purposes of regulation 29 (calculation of income other than earnings) the income of a claimant which does not consist of earnings to be taken into account shall, subject to paragraphs (2) and (3), be his gross income and any capital treated as income under regulations 24(3), 41 and 44 (treatment of charitable and voluntary payments, capital treated as income and modifications in respect of children and young persons).*
> *(2) There shall be disregarded from the calculation of a claimant's gross income under paragraph (1), any sum, where applicable, specified in Schedule 9."*

Paragraph 15 of Sch. 9 to the Income Support Regulations states:

> *"Sums to be disregarded in the calculation of income other than earnings:*

> *"15. Except in the case of a person to whom section 23 of the Act (trade disputes) applies and for so long as it applies, subject to paragraphs 36 and 37, £5 of any charitable payment or of any voluntary payment made or due to be made (whether or not so made) at regular intervals other than a payment which is made by a person for the maintenance of any member of his family or his former partner or of his children; and, for the purposes of this paragraph, where a number of such charitable or voluntary payments fall to be taken into account in any one week they shall be treated as though they were on one such payment."*

Paragraph 15 was amended by SI 2002/2442 so that the words "voluntary payment" were altered to include a payment from a PIT and from a structured settlement and from a PPO.

However, other regulations govern other benefits and they are multifarious and confusing. The regulations governing local authority care provision (whether in a care home or the claimant's home) are of most concern. When determining whether care benefits are to be provided by a local authority the care part of the clinical negligence award and the income from it may not be disregarded either for income or capital. On the contrary it may be regarded as the claimant's capital or income.

The regulations state that for personal injury awards, the capital and any income generated from the capital and used for purposes *other than which the claimant's means tested benefits are paid for*, plus an additional £20 per week in income, are to be fully disregarded. This has been interpreted by some as meaning that all of the sums in the PIT are ignored for all means tested benefits but in fact it does not. Capital and income from that capital which is *"specifically identified by a Court to deal with the provision of care"* and is used for the same purposes as the means tested benefits (care) is *not* disregarded. Take for instance the care award in a large case. That will be taken into account for means tested benefits. Apparently these provisions have led to a postcode lottery about which authorities will and which will not provide care. The inadequacies in the regulations were highlighted in *Crofton v. NHSLA*.[46] See also *Sowden v. Lodge*,[47] *Walton v. Calderdale*[48] and *Tinsley v. Sarkar*.[49] This has changed since the introduction of the Care Act 2014. PITs cannot now be means tested for local authority and NHS funded care.

The government has indicated that it may consider means testing a whole range of currently non-means tested benefits. Therefore, the PIT could also afford an effective protection against possible future changes to the state benefit system.

Recipients of incapacity benefit, currently a non-means-tested benefit, will be affected by the government's new rules, which are an attempt to move people from incapacity benefit onto jobseeker's allowance, which is a means-tested benefit, as a way of getting people back into work. Any PIT established now should maintain the claimant's eligibility to means-tested benefits in the future and would act as an insurance against the capital being taken into account.

---

46 [2007] EWCA Civ 71.
47 [2005] 1 WLR 2129, CA.
48 [2005] EWHC 1053.
49 [2005] EWHC 192.

9.3 Tax and PITs

In the vast majority of cases, the taxation treatment of the PIT is the same as if the claimant had the funds in his own name during his lifetime. In other words, it is taxation neutral.

However, the type of trust may affect the tax treatment of income and capital gains and impact upon the level of inheritance tax incurred.

The taxation treatment of income and/or capital gains realised by a PIT will depend upon the type of trust used. PITs can be either Bare Trusts, or Interests in Possession, or Disabled Trusts or Discretionary Trusts. The taxation position of each is different. Specific taxation advice may be required in relation to the most suitable to be used in each case. It is important to note that settlement of sums in excess of the inheritance tax nil rate band which are put into a discretionary trust (where it is not to be considered a disabled trust) may give rise to a tax charge on the excess.

In some circumstances the PIT trustees may have to submit tax returns as well as the claimant, which may give rise to an additional administrative charge.

9.4 Payments by the Trust

As the trust begins to operate, larger payments and regular payments by the trustees should be made to third parties not to the claimant. The usual recipients are the group of carers and the case manager for the injured claimant. Payments may also be made for large one-off items like houses or cars. The trustees will sign cheques and make payments, which they will do subject to their discretion at the claimant's request.

Effectively, the capital from the trust fund can be spent on whatever the claimant wants but ensuring that he remains within the benefit rules and does not hold more than £3,000 of capital in his own personal bank account at any one time. If the claimant is married or living with someone, the capital limit applies per couple and is not an individual allowance. If a purchase of goods or services is required which would mean increasing the claimant's capital above the £3,000 limit, for example to buy a house, car or holiday, then the trustees make the purchases of the goods or services on the claimant's behalf directly from the providers using capital from the trust bank account.

Once the claimant's personal capital holding is below £3,000 the trust can provide irregular capital payments to the claimant to top up his personal holding. As long as the claimant's capital remains under £3,000, the claimant can apply these funds to any item.

Chapter 18

HEALTHCARE ASSOCIATED INFECTIONS

1   INTRODUCTION

A Healthcare Associated Infection (HCAI) is an infection starting after contact with healthcare provision. It is broader than the earlier term "hospital acquired infection", but covers the same territory. "Infection" in this context refers to a process of damage to the body from acquired bacteria. It thus means more than mere contact with bacteria, which may "colonise" and survive in the body without causing damage.[1] Colonisation by a variety of bacteria is common amongst the general population as well as in hospitals and evidence that a patient is "colonised" (as opposed to "infected") with a HAI will not usually found a claim against the relevant hospital.

HAIs are not a new phenomenon. However, in recent times, the prevalence of antibiotic resistant strains of HAIs has created a larger and more serious problem for healthcare providers, the best known examples of which are MRSA (Methicillin-resistant Staphylococcus aureus) and C. Difficile (Clostridium difficile).

Other factors contributing to the seriousness of the problem are increased amounts of international travel allowing organisms to be spread rapidly around the world,[2] the fact that due to advances in modern medicine people are living longer, invasive surgical procedures such as transplants are becoming more commonplace and people are often sicker (and so more susceptible to infection) when admitted to hospital.

In recent times press and public interest in HAIs has grown considerably. Reports of patients infected with "hospital superbugs" due to dirty hospitals have been frequently seen in the press. However, successful litigation arising from HAIs remains rare.

One of the primary difficulties is in proving causation of injury in cases where it is difficult for claimants to prove that they became infected due to the negligence of the relevant hospital rather than by some non-negligent means (i.e. because the infection was pre-existing in the patient or was brought in by their visitors).

---

1 For a fuller definition see Ayliffe, Lowbury, Geddes & Williams: *Control of Hospital Infection - A Practical Handbook 3rd Edition* (1992).
2 For example the spread of SARS (severe acute respiratory syndrome).

2   PROVING NEGLIGENCE

2.1   Breach of Duty: Common Law Negligence

In a claim at common law the *Bolam* test[3] applies meaning that the burden is on the claimant to show that the treatment received fell below an acceptable standard and would not have been supported by any reasonable or responsible body of medical practitioners in that field.

HAI cases can be separated into two categories. The first ("acquisition") covers cases where it is alleged that the standard of care received was substandard such that the patient contracted a HAI. The second ("treatment") covers cases in which the allegation is of a failure to diagnose a HAI or of negligent treatment of an infection once acquired.

2.1.1   Category 1: Acquisition: Negligence by hospital staff leading to an infection being acquired in hospital

This category can be subdivided further as follows:

(i)   breaches of infection control policies specific to the claimant's case; and

(ii)   failings in the hospital system leading to inadequate infection control generally.

Allegations under this heading might include:

(i)   failing to implement infection control measures (i.e. poor ward hygiene, failure to wash hands, etc.);

(ii)   failing to screen patients for infection (particularly in high risk areas such as: special care baby unit, transplant unit, burns unit, before high risk procedures or if the patient falls into a certain category (e.g. the old, the young, the immuno-compromised);

(iii)   failing to wait until the results of screening are known before carrying out surgical procedures;

(iv)   failing to isolate patients at risk of passing on infection. (It must be recognised however that in any given hospital there are likely to be a limited number of side rooms for isolation of patients. The fact that a given patient is placed next to a known carrier of MRSA, for example, is therefore not necessarily evidence of negligence);

(v)   exposing patients to the risk of infection in an ongoing outbreak. Unreasonable exposure during an outbreak might include such things as not closing wards or continuing to admit patients for elective non-urgent surgery.

2.1.2   Category 2: Treatment: Failure to diagnose or treat a HAI properly

Alleged breaches in this category might include:

(i)   delay in requesting, or obtaining, or acting on test results;

(ii)   delay in commencing effective treatment;

---

3 *Bolam v. Friern Hospital Management Committee* [1957] 1 WLR 582.

> (iii)   failing to detect that a strain of infection is resistant to a particular drug or treatment;
>
> (iv)   non-compliance with a Trust's Infection Control Policy on hygiene in terms of the nursing of infected patients;
>
> (v)   managing infections requiring complex treatment regimes (for example for MRSA) without involving a consultant medical microbiologist.

2.1.3   *Expert evidence*

In acquisition cases it is likely that evidence will be required from a microbiologist together possibly with expert evidence in the fields of disease control and nursing care. In treatment cases evidence of breach of duty will most likely be provided by an expert in the speciality responsible for the patient's treatment, but there will also in such cases be a need for additional microbiology expertise to support causation, as well as nursing and disease control evidence to show what should have been done.

2.1.4   *Disclosure*

In acquisition cases, unlike treatment cases, the patient's medical notes are likely to be of only limited assistance. In both types of cases there are a number of categories of documents that may be relevant and should be sought. These include:

> (i)   the minutes of the infection control committee (or equivalent) for around 6 months before and after the date of acquisition of the HAI;
>
> (ii)   lists of patients/wards affected by the particular infection and anonymised microbiology notes of such patients (to assist in identifying the strain of infection);[4]
>
> (iii)   the Trust's Infection Surveillance Programme;
>
> (iv)   the Trust's statistics on infection outbreaks;
>
> (v)   applicable policies and protocols regarding the wearing of gloves/disposable aprons/ward cleaning, aseptic techniques, ward closures, etc.;
>
> (vi)   infection control nurse/cross infection nurse notes;
>
> (vii)   communications to staff, patients and possibly the press about aspects of a particular outbreak of infection (e.g. ward closures);
>
> (viii)   documents from other enquiries (e.g. internal reviews, untoward incident reports and inquests).

2.1.5   *Other evidence*

Even more than in most clinical negligence claims factual lay evidence can play an extremely important part in HAI cases. Witness statements from the claimant, their visitors and possibly other patients can be vital in demonstrating breaches which would not otherwise be documented (for example evidence of lapses in ward hygiene, whether staff had, and made use of, facilities for basic hygiene practices such as hand washing, whether soiled bandages were left exposed, whether wounds were left open when they should have been closed, whether communal bathing was used for exposed wounds, and the level of cleanliness of wards and communal facilities).

---

4 Although even if a number of patients have the same strain a microbiologist might not be able to conclude that they infected the claimant as many people can carry the same strain of an infection.

2.1.6   *Causation*

In the context of clinical negligence this generally means: "was the defendant's breach of duty the cause of the adverse consequences complained of?" (see Chapter 6 above). For HAI cases demonstrating legal causation can be a very real stumbling block. In an acquisition case it will be necessary to show that the action/inaction complained of caused injury in a patient rather than that injury being caused by infection in some non-negligent way (e.g. already colonised with infection pre-admission or infected by visitors). In order to be successful in an acquisition case therefore the claimant must be able to demonstrate:

> (i)   that there was a breach, or breaches, of infection control;
> (ii)   that, on the balance of probabilities, the infection was contracted in hospital; and
> (iii)   that the breach or breaches caused the infection and the injury complained of.

An expert microbiologist is unlikely to be able to conclude on the balance of probabilities that the HAI from which the claimant is suffering was acquired in hospital unless at the very least they have evidence that the infection is of a type known to be prevalent in hospitals and that breach of duty on the part of the particular hospital can be shown. As screening for HAIs in elective surgery cases has become routine however it has become easier for experts, and lawyers, to establish the timing and place of acquisition of infection[5] and so prove legal causation in particular cases.

Treatment cases pose questions more akin to those relevant in traditional clinical negligence cases. The relevant causation question in those cases is whether treatment (or earlier treatment) on the balance of probabilities have avoided the injury complained of?

2.1.6.1 *Fairchild* and *Barker*

Following the decisions of the House of Lords in *Fairchild* and *Barker*[6] many claimant lawyers were hopeful that favourable comparison could be drawn between the negligent contraction of HAIs and negligent exposure to substances which lead to mesothelioma. If they were similar, could that mean that the traditional "but for" causation test applicable in HAI cases could be replaced with the less restrictive "made a material contribution to the risk of injury" test which applies in mesothelioma cases following *Fairchild* and *Barker*?

Although the policy reasons behind *Fairchild* have been used as support for modification of the law of causation in the clinical negligence arena by the House of Lords, in particular Lord Steyn, in *Chester v. Afshar*,[7] there has been no consideration of the principle in relation to HAIs by the higher courts. Lord Steyn, in *Chester v. Afshar*, at para. 23 of his judgment commented that: "*At the very least Fairchild shows that where*

---

5 For example in *Cope v. Bro Morganwyg*, unreported, the claimant did not have MRSA at the time of a pre-operative test. As she subsequently developed that infection following a hip-replacement operation the Trust conceded that she must have contracted it in hospital.
6 *Fairchild v. Glenhaven Funeral Services* [2002] UKHL 22 and *Barker v. Corus (UK) plc* [2006] UKHL 20.
7 [2004] UKHL 41.

---

justice and policy demand it a modification of causation principles is not beyond the wit of a modern court". In respect of HAI cases, however, such a modification has not come about in the years since *Fairchild* and *Barker* and so claimants will continue to need to prove liability using the ordinary principles of breach and causation.

2.2 Breach of Duty

2.2.1 *Control of Substances Hazardous to Health (COSHH) Regulations 2002*[8]

For a time attempts were made to frame cases involving HAIs under the COSHH Regulations ("the Regulations") in addition to negligence. There are obvious benefits if the Regulations apply, the main one being that unlike in negligence where the claimant has to be able to demonstrate that "but for" the defendant's negligence they would not have sustained injury, under the Regulations the burden will be on the defendant to demonstrate compliance with the obligations set out in the Regulations and to show that all reasonable practicable steps were taken to control exposure where exposure could not be avoided altogether.[9]

2.2.1.1 The Regulations

HAIs would seem to fall within the definition of substances covered by the Regulations. Regulation 2(1) defines "substances hazardous to health" as including "biological agents". A "biological agent" is defined as *"any micro-organism...which may cause infection"*. Furthermore MRSA (as a variety of staphylococcus aureus) is plainly covered by the Regulations as the approved classification of Biological Agents prepared by the Health and Safety Commission includes staphylococcus aureus as a biological agent to which the Regulations apply.[10]

Although the Regulations are primarily intended to protect employees, regulation 3(1) provides that: *"Where any duty is placed by these Regulations on an employer in respect of his employees, he shall, insofar as it reasonably practicable, be under a like duty in respect of any other person, whether at work or not, who may be affected by the work carried on by the employer."*

By regulation 6 there is a duty to *"make a suitable and sufficient assessment of the risks...and of the steps that need to be taken to meet the requirements of these Regulations"* and under regulation 7 there is a duty to prevent, or where this is not reasonably practicable, to adequately control exposure.

The Court of Appeal in *Dugmore v. Swansea NHS Trust*[11] found that the obligations imposed by the Regulations apply regardless of whether the defendants knew or ought reasonably to have foreseen that a substance to which an employee was exposed was a substance hazardous to health. Lady Justice Hale, held, at para. 22 of her judgment

---

8 The Regulations were subject to some amendment in 2003 (SI 2003/978) and 2004 (SI 2004/3386). No relevant amendments were made to the Regulations under consideration.
9 In his article, "Litigating Hospital Acquired MRSA as a Disease", Daniel Bennett identified four benefits of a claim under the Regulations as opposed to in negligence: (1) There is no foreseeability test, (2) The duties imposed are strict and purposive, (3) The burden of proving that the duties have been complied with is on the defendant and (4) The causation test is the "material increase in risk" test and not the "but for" test. See [2004] JPIL Issue 3/04.
10 See www.hse.gov.uk/pubns/misc208.pdf.
11 [2002] EWCA Civ 1689.

that: *"the duty in regulation 7(1) is an absolute one: to ensure that exposure is prevented or controlled"*.

There is, however, a defence contained in regulation 5(1)(c) which provides that: *"Where the risk to health is a risk to the health of a person to whom the substance is administered in the course of his medical treatment"* the Regulations will not apply.

Claimant lawyers have argued that the Regulations apply to patients, who will fall into the definition of *"any other person, whether at work or not, affected by the work of an employee"* and that HAIs are not substances administered in the course of medical treatment and therefore the Regulations apply. Those acting on behalf of defendants have argued that HAIs (in particular MRSA) are contracted as a result of administering treatment and therefore the Regulations do not apply.

2.2.1.2 *Ndri v. Moorfields*

After a period of some uncertainty *Ndri v. Moorfields Eye Hospital NHS Trust*[12] provided authority to the effect that the Regulations do not apply to HAIs. That case concerned a patient who lost the sight in one eye after a cornea graft at the defendant's hospital. The tissue used in the graft was infected with bacteria and the claimant alleged that had the tissue used been decontaminated with an antiseptic, in addition to antibiotics, the infection would have been stopped and she would not have lost her sight. The claimant's case was pleaded in negligence and under the Regulations.

Sir Douglas Brown found against the claimant in negligence as well as under the Regulations. As to the latter Sir Brown said at para. 43 of his judgment:

> *"It is clear, in my view, from the whole structure of the Regulations that patients in hospital are not to be included amongst the persons to be protected. 5.1(c) is perhaps not happily worded but it is clear enough to exclude patients. 'Administered' is not particularly apt to describe the transplanting of an organ, but is sufficiently wide to cover it. It effectively excludes from the Regulation patients treated in hospital to whom a substance is administered. It is, in my view, inconceivable that it was the intention of Parliament to impose absolute liability in the circumstances of this case, and that way of putting the claim fails as well."*

Sir Brown's reading of regulation 5(1)(c) may be awkward and somewhat artificial however the point, for the time being at least, is settled. The Health & Safety Executive (HSE), perhaps understandably, agree with his conclusions. They have stated that: *"the HSE do not generally deal with clinical matters as these are more appropriately dealt with elsewhere. One exception to this is where there are management failures or failures of systems of work and in such cases HSE do sometimes become involved"*.[13] On their website the HSE instead refer readers to guidance produced by the Department of Health on the control of infection in hospitals.[14]

---

12 [2006] EWHC 3652 (QB).

13 www.hse.gov.uk/biosafety/healthcare.htm.

14 (a) "Getting ahead of the curve", strategy document for combating infectious diseases 10.1.02 DoH; (b) "Winning Ways", strategy document following on from "Getting ahead of the curve" 5.12.03; (c) Department of Health strategic guidelines for implementation of control of infection measures 7.3.95.

2.2.2   *Regulation*

In 2003 the Department of Health published guidance for NHS trusts on infection control and how to reduce HAIs. In 2005 the Healthcare Commission reported that there was clear evidence of poor standards of cleanliness in a significant proportion of hospitals in England. In response in 2006, the government set a target for the NHS to halve rates of MRSA by mid-2008 and published the first code of practice for the NHS regarding HAIs in the same year.

While initially inspection and regulation in respect of HAIs was under the control of the Healthcare Commission, the Health and Social Care Act 2008 established the Care Quality Commission (CQC) as the regulator of all health and adult social care services from 1st April 2009. Registration with the CQC is required for all individuals, partnerships or organisations that carry out "regulated activities" as listed in Sch. 1 to the Health and Social Care Act 2008 (Regulated Activities) Regulations 2012.[15]

The CQC produced key guidance on compliance for those that they regulate in the form of their *Essential Standards of Quality and Safety Guide*. Although "cleanliness and infection control" is one of the 28 outcomes[16] set out in the guide the CQC is not required by the Health and Social Care Act to produce guidance about legislation governing the prevention or control of healthcare-associated infections. Instead their guidance simply refers the reader to *The Code of Practice for health and adult social care on the prevention and control of infections and related guidance* published by the Department of Health.

In April 2015 when the Health and Social Care Act 2008 (Regulated Activities) Regulations 2014 come into force the CQC's 16 "essential standards" are to be replaced by 11 new "fundamental standards":[17]

> (1)   Person centred care (regulation 4);
> (2)   Dignity and respect (regulation 5);
> (3)   Need for consent (regulation 6);
> (4)   Safe and appropriate care and treatment (regulation 7);
> (5)   Safeguarding service users from abuse (regulation 8);
> (6)   Meeting nutritional needs (regulation 9);
> (7)   Cleanliness and safety and suitability of premises and equipment (regulation 10);
> (8)   Receiving and reacting on complaints (regulation 11);
> (9)   Good governance (regulation 12);
> (10)   Sufficient suitably qualified, skilled and experienced staff (regulation 13);
> (11)   Fit and proper persons.

Regulations 10 and regulation 12 are likely to be of most relevance in HAI cases. Regulation 10 relates to all premises safe for the service user's home and requires hygiene appropriate for the circumstances *"in accordance with generally accepted*

---

15 The regulations that govern registration by the Care Quality Commission are the Health and Social Care Act 2008 (Regulated Activities) Regulations 2010 (as amended by the Health and Social Care Act 2008 (Regulated Activities) Regulations 2014) and the Care Quality Commission (Registration) Regulations 2009.
16 Outcome 8.
17 Plus two new regulations, on fit and proper person requirements for directors and a statutory duty of candour.

professional standards, practices and principle". Regulation 12 requires registered persons to provide care and treatment in a safe way for service users. Compliance includes at 12(2)(h) *"assessing the risk of, and preventing, detecting and controlling the spread of, infections, including those that are health care associated"*. By regulation 22 a registered person commits an offence if they fail to comply with a requirement of regulation 12 and such failure results in either avoidable harm (whether of a physical or psychological nature) to a service user or a service user being exposed to a significant risk of such harm occurring.

In the guidance document produced by CQC in July 2014 as part of the consultation process in advance of the new Regulations regulation 12(2)(h) is included however, as before, no guidance is provided and the reader is simply referred back to the Department of Health guidance.

The Department of Heath guidance lists ten criteria that are used to judge whether an NHS Trust is compliant with the Regulations. These are as follows:

(1) Systems to manage and monitor the prevention and control of infection. These systems use risk assessments and consider how susceptible service users are and any risks that their environment and other users may pose to them;

(2) Provide and maintain a clean and appropriate environment in managed premises that facilitates the prevention and control of infections;

(3) Provide suitable accurate information on infections to service users and their visitors;

(4) Provide suitable accurate information on infections to any person concerned with providing further support or nursing/medical care in a timely fashion;

(5) Ensure that people who have or develop an infection are identified promptly and receive the appropriate treatment and care to reduce the risk of passing on the infection to other people;

(6) Ensure that all staff and those employed to provide care in all settings are fully involved in the process of preventing and controlling infection;

(7) Provide or secure adequate isolation facilities;

(8) Secure adequate access to laboratory support as appropriate;

(9) Have and adhere to policies designed for the individual's care and provider organisations, that will help to prevent and control infections;

(10) Ensure, so far as is reasonably practicable, that care workers are free of and are protected from exposure to infections that can be caught at work and that all staff are suitably educated in the prevention and control of infection associated with the provision of health and social care.

In addition the National Institute for Health and Care Excellence (NICE) have produced a quality standard on "Infection Prevention and Control"[18] as well as guidelines on "Infection: Prevention and Control of Healthcare-associated Infections in Primary and Community Care",[19] "Infection Control",[20] "Surgical Site Infection"[21] and "Prevention and Control of Healthcare-associated Infections".[22]

---

18 NICE quality standard QS61 published April 2014.
19 NICE guidelines [CG139] Published date: March 2012 (reviewed and left unchanged in September 2014).
20 NICE clinical guideline 139 (2012).

2.3   Conclusions

As the prevalence and virulence of HAI has increased medical practices have not always kept pace. As a result it appeared that HAI would yield a significant number of claims. The fact that the number of such claims has remained low with few successful cases is testament to the particular difficulty in proving causation that HAI cases present.

Lawyers have sought to mitigate against the difficulties presented by such claims, however it seems that the two possible routes so far identified (a relaxation in the causation test as per *Fairchild* or bringing a claim under the COSHH Regulations) are not the solution to the problem.

The development of regulation, quality standards and other guidance in this area has required healthcare providers to have in place stricter policies and procedures to deal with HAIs. Pre-admission or pre-operative screening is becoming routine bringing obvious benefits to those seeking to prove when a patient contracted a HAI. With the growth in both awareness and regulation within the healthcare sector it may be that in the future even fewer claims will need to be brought. In the meantime the prospects of many claims can be improved by reference to specific breaches of policy and procedure within the relevant hospital or by reference to any failure to comply with the Department of Health Code or NICE guidelines. In a claim against a specific Trust it will undoubtedly be of assistance if they have attracted the attention of the CQC for failing to maintain appropriate standards of cleanliness and/or infection control.

21 NICE clinical guideline 74 (2008).
22 NICE public health guidance 36 (2011).

Chapter 19

THE REGULATION OF HUMAN TISSUE

1   BACKGROUND

The regulation and control of use of human tissue involves the delicate balance between the individual rights of self-determination, privacy and human dignity and the wider public interest in scientific advancement and information. In this chapter we consider how this balance is achieved in the UK under the Human Tissue Act 2004. The Human Tissue Act 2004 came into being in response to the Isaacs Report 2003[1] and public inquiries into the organ retention scandals at the Bristol Royal Infirmary and at the Royal Liverpool Children's Hospital (Alder Hey). Those scandals arose when the parents of deceased children discovered that organs and tissues had been retained without their knowledge or consent. The Isaacs Report then revealed the extent of the practice within the medical profession of storing and using human tissue and organs without proper consent.

2   THE HUMAN TISSUE ACT

The Act came into force in September 2006[2] and for the first time codified the circumstances in which human tissue, including organs, could be removed, used and stored by medical practitioners. The Act also provided regulation for DNA analysis and provided for criminal penalties for breaches of certain sections. The Act also set up systems of inspection and licensing for certain activities including: anatomical examinations, post-mortem examinations, removal, storage and use of bodies, and material from, deceased persons (excluding transplantation) and storage and use of tissue from the living and the dead. The Human Tissue Authority is an executive non-departmental public body sponsored by the health department it was established under the act to perform these functions (as to which see further below).

2.1   Part 1 – Consent

The first part of the Human Tissue Act sets out the fundamental principle that consent underpins the lawful storage and use of body parts, organs and tissue from the living or the deceased for a variety of health-related purposes.

The Act requires that consent be obtained from an "appropriate person" for the storage and use of "relevant material" from living persons and for the removal, storage and use of "relevant material" from deceased persons for "scheduled purposes". Consent

---

1 The Stationery Office, HM Inspector of Anatomy, 12th May 2003.
2 Replacing the Human Tissue Act 1961, the Anatomy Act 1984 and the Human Organ Transplants Act 1989.

to the removal of tissue from a living person is not regulated by the Human Tissue Act and remains a matter for the common law. DNA, once extracted from cellular material, also remains outside the Act.

The consent required is "appropriate consent". The Act sets out that persons entitled to give "appropriate consent" are as follows:

- **Living adults** - if they are competent only they are permitted to give consent;
- **Living children** - may consent if they are competent to do so.[3] A person who has parental responsibility for the child can consent on his/her behalf only if the child has not made a decision and: (1) is not competent to do so; or (2) chooses not to make that decision, although he or she is competent to do so;
- **Living adults who lack capacity** - by a person acting in what he or she reasonably believes to be in the best interests of the person lacking capacity (for the purposes of obtaining scientific or medical information about a living or deceased person which may be relevant to another person and transplantation[4]); and by other persons in a number of other limited circumstances;[5]
- **Tissue from the deceased – adults and Gillick competent children -** either (i) gave his/her consent before their death (ii) if no prior consent given then the consent of a nominated representative (iii) if the deceased has done neither (i) or (ii) before death then the consent of a qualifying relative (ranked in a hierarchy by the Act).[6]

Although "appropriate consent" is defined by the Act, the term "consent" remains undefined. Accordingly, the Act does not assist medical practitioners on a number of crucial issues, including answering questions such as:

- How much information is required to be provided to a patient before they can provide legally valid consent; and
- Does a patient have to give explicit consent or can it be inferred from their behaviour?

Clarification can, however, be found in the revised Consent Codes of Practice issued by the Human Tissue Authority (see below). The revised Codes came into force from July 2014.[7] The second edition of Code 1, which deals with consent, confirms that for consent to be valid it must be given voluntarily by an appropriately informed person with capacity. Patients should be told of any implications that research use of their sample may have, and whether the consent is specific or generic. They should be told whether their research samples will, or could, be used in the commercial sector

---

3 *Gillick v. West Norfolk and Wisbech Area Health Authority* [1985] 3 All ER 402 (HL).

4 See the Human Tissue Act (Persons who Lack Capacity to Consent and Transplants) Regulations 2006.

5 See the Medicines for Human Use (Clinical Trials) Regulations 2004 and the Mental Capacity Act 2005, ss. 30–34.

6 See *CM v. (1) Executor of the Estate of EJ (deceased) (2) HM Coroner for the Southern District of London* [2013] EWHC 1680 Fam where permission was given for tissue samples from the deceased to be taken for the benefit of a doctor who had tried to save her life even though her parents had not known of her death and there was no qualifying relative, a more distant relative could be regarded as a "friend of longstanding" within s. 27(4)(h) of the Human Tissue Act 2004 who had given consent.

7 There are nine Codes of Practice covering matters such as consent, donation of organs for transplantation, post-mortem examination, anatomical research and the like. The codes were revised in July 2014 pending a wholescale review scheduled for 2015. Full copies can be found on the HTA's website at www.hta.gov.uk/codes-practice.

including by commercial pharmaceutical companies.[8] The Code provides that for consent to be valid, the person should understand what the activity involves and, where appropriate, what the risks are. When seeking consent, healthcare professionals or other suitably experienced people should ensure that it is appropriate for the intended purpose.

Other terms defined in the Act are as follows:

"Relevant material" is defined as material other than gametes, i.e. eggs or sperm material, which consists of or includes human cells. Hair and nails from living persons are excluded, as are embryos outside the human body (which are already regulated by the Human Fertilisation and Embryology Act 1990). Cell lines and extracted DNA are also excluded.[9]

"Scheduled purposes" is also defined in the Act. There are two categories:

(i) purposes generally requiring consent where the material is from the living or the deceased (includes: anatomical examination, determining the cause of death, establishing after a person's death the efficacy of any drug or other treatment administered to him, obtaining scientific or medical information about a living or deceased person which may be relevant to any other person (including a future person), public display, research in connection with disorders, or the functioning, of the human body (Sch. 1, Part 1);

(ii) purposes requiring consent where the tissue is taken from a deceased person (includes: clinical audit, education or training relating to human health, performance assessment, public health monitoring, quality assurance, health-related education or training, performance assessment, public health monitoring and quality assurance) (Sch. 1, Part 2).

2.2 The Regulatory System - Parts 2 and 3 of the Act

2.2.1 *Offences under the Act*

The Act also incorporates a regulatory system to control a number of activities including several criminal offences related to the removal, storage and use of human tissue. The main offences are as follows:

(i) under s. 5 it is a criminal offence to carry out an activity (removal, storage or use of human tissue for a scheduled purpose) for which consent is required by section 1 without obtaining appropriate consent;

(ii) under s. 8 a tissue user is prohibited from obtaining tissue for one purpose and using it for another (except where the second purpose is a Sch. 1 purpose, medical treatment or tissue disposal and the original consent covers this activity);

---

8 The Human Tissue Authority also produces model consent forms see www.hta.gov.uk/guidance/model_consent_forms.cfm.

9 www.hta.gov.uk/policies/relevant-material-under-human-tissue-act-2004, the Human Tissue Authority provided guidance on defining and categorising "relevant material" revised in February 2014.

(iii)   s. 45 creates the offence of "DNA theft". This offence is committed by having human tissue, including hair, nail, and gametes, with the intention of its DNA being analysed without the "qualifying consent" of the person from whom the tissue came or of those close to them if they have died (medical diagnosis and treatment, criminal investigations, etc. are excluded).[10]

Penalties for these offences range from a fine to up to 3 years' imprisonment, or both.

2.3   The Human Tissue Authority and the Human Embryology Fertility Authority

The Human Tissue Authority (HTA) was established as the regulator under the Act and also as the body responsible for ensuring best practice and providing guidance on the operation and application of the Act. Initially the government had intended to create one Regulatory Authority for Tissues and Embryos (RATE), with responsibilities across the range of human tissues cells and blood, to replace the HTA together with the Human Fertilisation and Embryology Authority (HFEA) referred to further below and certain functions of the Medicines and Healthcare Products Regulatory Agency (MHRA). In November 2007, however, the decision was made that the HTA should continue in its role as regulator under the Act.

Accordingly the HTA remains the body responsible for issuing licences under the Act for activities as set out above. By reason of the Human Tissue (Quality and Safety for Human Application Regulations 2007 (implementing the EU Tissues and Cells Directive), the storage of tissues or cells intended for human application is now also regulated by the HTA. Under those Regulations procurement, testing, processing, distribution and import/export of human tissues and cells must be carried out under a HTA licence or under a third party agreement with a HTA licensed establishment.

The role and operation of the HTA came under scrutiny by the government once again. In July 2010 the Department of Health published a report entitled: "Liberating the NHS: report of the arm's length bodies review" (the "ALB review"). This report proposed, amongst other things, transferring the research regulatory functions of the HTA and the Human Fertilisation and Embryology Authority (HFEA) to a new single research regulator. The ALB review proposed that the non-research functions of the HTA and the HFEA were reassigned to the Care Quality Commission.

In January 2011 the Academy of Medical Sciences published a report (the "AMS report") in which it is recommended that a new Health Research Agency (HRA) is created in place of the HTA and other organisations.[11] The report was critical of over-regulation in this area, which it perceives as having a damaging effect on medical research within the UK. The report's authors considered that health research activities in the UK are being "seriously undermined" by "an overly complex regulatory and governance environment". This is evidenced, they say, by a fall in the UK's global share of patients in clinical trials and by "the increased time and costs of navigating the

---

10 "Qualifying consent" has a slightly different meaning to "appropriate consent" (the term for consent required for removal, storage and use of relevant material - see above). In essence, while the relatives able to give "appropriate consent" are arranged in a hierarchy there is no such hierarchy in respect of relatives able to give "qualifying consent".
11 Chapter 7, recommendations 11, 13 and 14 are of relevance to the HTA. See also the response of the HTA to these reports on their website www.hta.gov.uk.

UK's complex research approval processes". In addition to recommending moving towards the sort of system in place in Scotland, by the creation of a new Health Research Agency, the report also suggested amending the Act so as to exclude certain substances such as "plasma, semen, urine, faeces and saliva" from materials covered by the Act. As the HTA, in their response to the report point out, however, certain of these substances are excluded from regulation in any event.

In the event, the HTA remains the competent authority in the UK responsible for ensuring safety of human tissue and cells used for patient treatment in compliance with the European Union Tissue and Cells Directive 2004/23 EC (as amended in 2012 and implemented by the Human Tissue (Quality and Safety for Human Application) Regulations 2007). Further they are the relevant authority for the purpose of the European Union Organ Donation Directive 2010/45/EU and the implementing directive 2012/25/EU (implemented by the Quality and Safety of Organs Intended for Transplant Regulations 2012).[12]

There is however, some overlap with the Human Fertility Embryology Authority which is the UK's independent regulator of treatment using eggs and sperm and of treatment and research involving human embryos. The HFEA sets standards for and issues licences to centres pursuant to the Human Fertilisation and Embryology Act 1990 as amended. It has the power to determine whether sperm taken from a deceased man should be stored pending its decision on the expert of that sperm for subsequent use in assisted reproduction abroad.[13] Sperm banked at fertility units licensed by the HFEA is considered to be the property of the producer of it, but damage to it does not constitute personal injury.[14]

A small number of centres doing research that aims to develop stem cells for human application are licensed both by the HTA and the HFEA (in which cases joint inspections should be the norm). There is also overlap between the HFEA and the Care Quality Commission in that 30% of HFEA licensed centres are either outside the CQC's geographical remit or are private centres not requiring CQC registration. 20% of HFEA licensed centres are exempt from the requirement to register with the CQC (they provide IUI with partner or donor sperm or are storage only centres).

2.4 Guidance from the Medical Profession

A number of organisations from within the medical profession have provided guidance on the application and interpretation of the Human Tissue Act 2004 and on practical matters in light of the Act. Of particular note is the guidance provided by the Joint Committee on Medical Genetics in 2011[15] and by the British Medical Association's Medical Ethics Department.[16]

---

12 In December 2015 there will be an opt-out system for organ donation in Wales (see the Human Transplantation (Wales) Act 2013 and the accompanying code of practice).

13 *L v. HFEA and the Secretary of State for Health* [2008] EWHC 2149 Fam.

14 Though there was a cause of action in bailment for the loss of non-pecuniary benefits that banking the sperm had been intended to provide see *Yearworth & Ors v. North Bristol NHS Trust* [2009] EWCA Civ 37.

15 www.rcplondon.ac.uk/sites/default/files/consent_and_confidentiality_2011.pdf.

16 See www.bma.org.uk/ethics.

2.5 The Human Fertilisation And Embryology Act 1990 as Amended

The Human Fertilisation and Embryology Act 1990 was drafted following the publication of a White Paper: "Human Fertilisation and Embryology: A Framework for Legislation" in 1987. This cornerstone piece of legislation finally received Royal Assent on 1st November 1990. Critically, the 1990 Act provided for the establishment of the Human Fertilisation and Embryology Authority (HFEA), an executive, non-departmental public body, the first statutory body of its type in the world. With the creation of the HFEA, the 1990 Act ensured the regulation, through licensing, of: (i) the creation of human embryos outside the body and their use in treatment and research, (ii) the use of donated gametes and embryos and (iii) the storage of gametes and embryos.

The Act was substantially amended by the HFE Act 2008 which itself is divided into three sections, the first containing amendments to the 1990 Act, the second dealing with parenthood and the third deals with miscellaneous matters.
The key amendments to the 1990 Act were:

(1) ensuring that the creation and use of all human embryos outside the body - whatever the process used in their creation - are subject to regulation;

(2) a ban on selecting the sex of offspring for social reasons;

(3) requiring that clinics take account of "the welfare of the child" when providing fertility treatment (s. 13(5)) and removing the previous requirement that they also take account of the child's "need for a father";

(4) allowing for the recognition of both partners in a same-sex relationship as legal parents of children conceived through the use of donated sperm, eggs or embryos;

(5) enabling people in same-sex relationships and unmarried couples to apply for an order allowing for them to be treated as the parents of a child born using a surrogate;

(6) changing restrictions on the use of data collected by the HFEA to make it easier to conduct research using this information;

(7) provisions clarifying the scope of legitimate embryo research activities, including regulation of "human admixed embryos" (embryos combining both human and animal material).

The HFEA has a code of practice (the 8th edition), it was most recently updated in 2014 [17] and gives detailed guidance to all those working and in receipt of services in the fertility sector.

3 CONCLUSIONS

Since coming into force both the Human Fertilisation and Embryology Act 1990 and the Human Tissue Act 2004 have engaged the attention of the medical profession

---

[17] www.hfea.gov.uk/code.html.

rather more than the legal profession. So far as the medical profession is concerned there can be no doubt that the requirements in particular of the Human Tissue Act have imposed a considerable administrative burden as well as having a detrimental impact on medical research (if the conclusions of the AMS Report are to be believed). The government has made some alterations to the functions of the HTA but there remains an overlap between its function and those of the HFEA and between the latter and the CQC and the Medicines and Healthcare Products Regulatory Agency (MHRA) which regulates all medicines and medical devices.

For now the complex requirements of the Human Tissue Act and the extensive demands currently placed on medical practitioners may remain of relevance to clinical negligence cases where it can be shown that such requirements were not complied with. It is important to note, however, that despite creating a number of criminal offences, the Human Tissue Act does not create any civil remedy for non-consensual use of tissue and so the position remains as it was under the Human Tissue Act 1961, see *AB v. Teaching Hospital*.[18] Also of particular interest to clinical negligence lawyers may be cases where "appropriate consent" had been obtained for a medical procedure but where it was being alleged that the procedure was not carried out as suggested when consent was obtained, or was carried out negligently, or where information obtained was inappropriately handled or released.

The position under the HFEA is slightly different because many of the procedures involve actual treatment of a patient where the usual rules of negligence will apply. For examples of the types of incidents most commonly reported, see the Human Fertilisation and Embryology Authority report published in October 2014 entitled "Adverse Incidents in Fertility Clinics – Lessons to be Learned".[19]

Further information

www.hta.gov.uk
www.bma.org.uk/ethics
www.gov.uk/government/organisations/department-of-health

---

18 [2004] EWHC 644 (QB).
19 www.rcn.org.uk/development/nursing_communities/rcn_forums/midwifery_fertility_nursing/news_stories/adverse_incidents_in_fertility_clinics.

Chapter 20

GLOSSARY OF COMMON MEDICAL ABBREVIATIONS

°	Not Present or No abnormality (e.g. J° "No jaundice")
+/-	Uncertain/equivocal
+	Present or Noted
++	Present Significantly
+++	Present in Excess
#	Fracture
↑	Increasing, up
→	Constant, normal
↓	Decreasing, down
Δ	Diagnosis
Diff.Δ OR ΔΔ	Differential Diagnosis
=	Equivalent to
3	OK or satisfactory
1/7	One day
2/52	Two weeks
3/12	Three months
A or AJ	Ankle Jerk/Reflex
AAA	Abdominal Aortic Aneurysm
AAL	Anterior Axillary Line
ABG	Arterial Blood Gas
ACL	Anterior Clavicular Line OR Anterior Cruciate Ligament
A.d	As Directed
A/E	Air Entry to Lungs OR Accident & Emergency
AF	Atrial Fibrillation

AFB	Acid Fast Bacillus
AFP	Alpha-fetoprotein
AI/R	Aortic Incompetence/Regurgitation
AoR	Aortic Valve Replacement
AS	Abdominal System OR Aortic Stenosis
ATCH	Adrenocorticotrophic hormone
A/V	Anteverted
AXR	Abdominal X-Ray
bd/bid	Twice a Day
B or BJ	Biceps Jerk/Reflex
BCC	Basal Cell Carcinoma
BMI	Body Mass Index
BNO	Bowels Not Opened
BOR	Bowels Open Regularly
BP	Blood Pressure or British Pharmacopoeia
BPd	Diastolic Blood Pressure
BPs	Systolic Blood Pressure
BS	Breath Sounds or Bowel Sounds or Blood Sugar
C_2H_5OH	Alcohol
CA or Ca	Carcinoma Cancer
CABG/S or CAG/S	Coronary Artery (Bypass) Graft/Surgery
CFS	Chronic Fatigue Syndrome
CNS	Central Nervous System
C/o or C.o	Complains of
CO_2	Carbon Dioxide
COAD	Chronic Obstructive Airways Disease
COPD	Chronic Obstructive Pulmonary Disease Chronic Lung Disease
CPD	Cephalo-Pelvic Disproportion
CSF	Cerbro-Spinal Fluid
CT or CAT	Computerised Axial Tomography
CVA	Cerebrovascular Accident Stroke
CVS	Cardiovascular System
CX or Cx	Cervix OR Cervical Spine
CXR	Chest X-ray

D&V	Diarrhoea and Vomiting
D/H	Drug History
DIP, PIP	Dorsal/Proximal Interphalangeal Joints
DLE	Discoid Lupus Erythematosus
DNA	Did Not Attend
DOA	Dead On Arrival
DS	Disseminated (Multiple) Sclerosis
DU	Duodenal Ulcer
DVT	Deep Vein Thrombosis
DXT	Deep X-ray Treatment
Dx	Diagnosis
EAM	External Auditory Meatus
ECG	Electrocardiograph
ECT	Electro-Convulsive Therapy
EDC	Expected Date of Confinement
EDD	Expected Date of Delivery
EMU	Early Morning Specimen of Urine
ENG	Head Engaged (Baby)
ENT	Ear, Nose & Throat
ESR	Erythrocyte Sedimentation Rate
EtOH	Alcohol
FB	Finger's Breadth
FBC	Full Blood Count
FBG/S	Fasting Blood Glucose/Sugar
FBS	Foetal Blood Sampling
FD	Forceps Delivery
F/H or FH	Family History
FHH	Foetal Heart Heard
FHHR	Foetal Heart Heard/Regular
FHR	Foetal Heart Rate
FMF	Foetal Movements Felt
FROM	Full Range of Movement
FSE	Foetal Scalp Electrode
FSH	Family and Social History or Follicle-stimulating Hormone

FTD	Formal Thought Disorder
FTND	Full Term Normal Delivery
GA	General Anaesthetic
GCS	Glasgow Coma Scale
GFR	Glomerular filtration rate
GI or GIT	Gastro Intestinal/Tract
GORD	Gastro-Oesophageal Reflux Disease
GTT	Glucose Tolerance Test
GU or GUT or GUS	Genito Urinary/Tract/System
GU	Gastric Ulcer
GUM	Genito-Urinary Medicine
Hb	Haemoglobin
HH	Hiatus Hernia
HI	Head Injury
HNPU	Has Not Passed Urine
HPC	History of Presenting Complaint
HR	Heart Rate
HS	Heart Sounds
HT	Height
HVS	High Vaginal Swab
Hx	History (of Complaint)
IBS	Irritable Bowel Syndrome
ICS	Intercostal space
IGT or IGTN	In Growing Toenail
IJ	Interjugular vein
IM	Intramuscular
IMB	Intermenstrual Bleeding
ISQ	In Status Quo
IVP	Intravenous Pyelogram
Ix	Investigations
JVP	Jugular Venous Pressure
K or KJ	Knee Jerk/Reflex
KUB	Kidneys, Ureters, Bladder
LA	Local Anaesthetic

LFT	Liver Function Test
LIF	Left Iliac Fossa
LIH	Left Inguinal Hernia
LKKS	Liver, Kidney, Kidney, Spleen
LMP	Last Menstrual Period
LN	Lymph Node
LOA	Left Occiput Anterior
LOC	Loss of Consciousness
LOL	Left Occipitolateral
LOP	Left Occiput Posterior
LP	Lumbar Puncture
L/R/ IH	Left or Right Inguinal Hernia
LS	Lymph System
LSCS or LUSCS	Lower (Uterine) Segment Caesarean section
LUQ	Left Upper Quadrant
Mane	In the Morning
M&C (S)	Microscopy & Culture Sensitivity of Bacteria
MCL	Mid Clavicular Line
MCV	Mean Corpuscular Volume
ME	Myalgic Encephalomyelitis
MET/S	Metastases
MI	Myocardial Infarction OR Mitral Incompetence
Mitte or mite	Dispense this number of tablets
MRI	Magnetic Resonance Imaging
MS	Multiple Sclerosis OR Mitral Stenosis
MSE	Mental State Examination
MSS	Musculo-Skeletal System
MSU or MSUS	Mid-Stream Urine Sample
N&V	Nausea & Vomiting
NAD	Nothing Abnormal Discovered/Detected
NBI	No Bone Injury
NFR	Not For Resuscitation
Nocte	At Night
OA	Osteoarthritis

OC/COC	Oral Contraceptive/Combined Oral Contraceptive
OCT	Orthotopic Cardiac Transplant
o.d.	Once a Day
O/E or o.e	On Examination
OGD	Oesophago-gastro-duodenoscopy
om	In the Morning
OM (R/L)	Otitis Media
on	At Night
ORIF	Open Reduction and Internal Fixation (of fracture)
otc	Over the counter (bought medication)
P	Pulse
PCB	Post Coital Bleeding
PCC	Post Coital Contraception
PE	Pulmonary Embolism
PERLA	Pupils equal and reacting to light and accommodation
PF(R)	Peak Flow (Rate)
PH	Past history
PID	Pelvic Inflammatory Disease OR Prolapsed Intervertebral Disc
PM	Post mortem examination
PMH also PHx	Previous Medical History
PND	Paroxysmal Nocturnal Dyspnoea
PO	Per Orim (by mouth)
POP	Progesterone Only Pill OR Plaster of Paris
PPs	Peripheral pulses
PR	Per Rectum
PRN	As Required
PTCA	Percutaneous transluminal coronary angioplasty
PTSD	Post Traumatic Stress Disorder
PU	Peptic Ulcer OR Passed urine
PV	Per Vagina
PVD	Peripheral Vascular Disease
qds (or) qid	Four times a day
RA	Rheumatoid Arthritis
RBC	Red blood cell

RDS	Respiratory Distress Syndrome
RFT	Renal (Kidney) Function tests OR Respiratory Function tests
RIF	Right Iliac Fossa
RIH	Right Inguinal Hernia
RHC	Right Hypochordrium
ROL or ROP	Right occipito lateral/posterior
R (R)	Respiration (Rate)
RS	Respiratory System
RSI	Repetitive Strain Injury
RTA	Road Traffic Accident
RTI	Respiratory tract infection
RUQ	Right Upper Quadrant
Rx	Prescription or Treatment
S or SJ	Supinator (jerk /reflex)
S/B	Seen by
SBG	Serum Blood Glucose
S/D	Systolic/diastolic
SkXR	Skull X-ray
SLR	Straight Leg Raising
SMR	Submucosal Resection
SOA	Swelling of ankles
SOB	Short of Breath
SOL	Space Occupying Lesion
SOM	Secretary Otitis Media
SOS	In an Emergency
SR	Sinus rhythm
SROM	Spontaneous rupture of membranes
Stat	Immediately
STD	Sexually Transmitted Disease
STI	Sexually Transmitted Infection
SVC	Superior vena cava
SVD	Spontaneous Vertex/vaginal Delivery
SVT	Supra ventricular tachycardia
Sx	Symptoms

T or TJ	Triceps Jerk/Reflex
T (usually with a circle with a dot in the centre) Trachea Central	
Tá â	Temperature raised upwards or downwards
TATT	Tired all the Time
TB	Tuberculosis
TCI	To come in-date or fact that a person is due to be admitted to hospital
tds (or) tid	Three Times a Day
TFTs	Thyroid Function Test
TGH	To go home
THR	Total Hip Replacement
TIA	Transient Ischaemic Attack
TKR	Total Knee Replacement
TLC	Tender Loving Care
TM or Tm	Tympanic Membrane
Ts&As	Tonsillectomy and Adenoidectomy
TShR	Total Shoulder Replacement
TTO/A	To take home/away (medication)
TU(R)P	Transurethral (resection) of Prostate
U&Es	Urea and Electrolytes
UC	Ulcerative Colitis
URTI	Upper respiratory tract infection
USS	Ultra Sound Scan
UTI	Urinary Tract Infection
VE	Vaginal examination
VF	Ventricular Fibrillation
V/S/TOP	Vaginal suction termination of pregnancy
VT	Ventricular Tachycardia
WBC	White Blood Cell Count
Wt	Weight
XR	X-ray

Appendix 1

PRE-ACTION PROTOCOL FOR THE RESOLUTION OF CLINICAL DISPUTES

1 INTRODUCTION

1.1

This Protocol is intended to apply to all claims against hospitals, GPs, dentists and other healthcare providers (both NHS and private) which involve an injury that is alleged to be the result of clinical negligence. It is not intended to apply to claims covered by—

(a) the Pre-Action Protocol for Disease and Illness Claims;

(b) the Pre-Action Protocol for Personal Injury Claims;

(c) the Pre-Action Protocol for Low Value Personal Injury Claims in Road Traffic Accidents;

(d) the Pre-Action Protocol for Low Value Personal Injury (Employers' Liability and Public Liability) Claims; or

(e) Practice Direction 3D – Mesothelioma Claims

1.2

This Protocol is intended to be sufficiently broad-based and flexible to apply to all sectors of healthcare, both public and private. It also recognises that a claimant and a defendant, as patient and healthcare provider, may have an ongoing relationship.

1.3

It is important that each party to a clinical dispute has sufficient information and understanding of the other's perspective and case to be able to investigate a claim efficiently and, where appropriate, to resolve it. This Protocol encourages a cards-on-the-table approach when something has gone wrong with a claimant's treatment or the claimant is dissatisfied with that treatment and/or the outcome.

1.4

This Protocol is now regarded by the courts as setting the standard of normal reasonable pre-action conduct for the resolution of clinical disputes.

1.5

1.5.1 This Protocol sets out the conduct that prospective parties would normally be expected to follow prior to the commencement of any proceedings. It establishes a reasonable process and timetable for the exchange of information relevant to a dispute, sets out the standards for the content and quality of letters of claim and sets standards for the conduct of pre-action negotiations.

1.5.2 The timetable and the arrangements for disclosing documents and obtaining expert evidence may need to be varied to suit the circumstances of the case. Where one or more parties consider the detail of the Protocol is not appropriate to the case, and proceedings are subsequently issued, the court will expect an explanation as to why the Protocol has not been followed, or has been varied.

Early Issue

1.6

1.6.1 The Protocol provides for a defendant to be given four months to investigate and respond to a Letter of Claim before proceedings are served. If this is not possible, the claimant's solicitor should give as much notice of the intention to issue proceedings as is practicable. This Protocol does not alter the statutory time limits for starting court proceedings. If a claim is issued after the relevant statutory limitation period has expired, the defendant will be entitled to use that as a defence to the claim. If proceedings are started to comply with the statutory time limit before the parties have followed the procedures in this Protocol, the parties should apply to the court for a stay of the proceedings while they so comply.

1.6.2 The parties should also consider whether there is likely to be a dispute as to limitation should a claim be pursued.

Enforcement of the Protocol and sanctions

1.7

Where either party fails to comply with this Protocol, the court may impose sanctions. When deciding whether to do so, the court will look at whether the parties have complied in substance with the Protocol's relevant principles and requirements. It will also consider the effect any non-compliance has had on any other party. It is not likely to be concerned with minor or technical shortcomings (see paragraph 4.3 to 4.5 of the Practice Direction on Pre-Action Conduct and Protocols).

Litigants in Person

1.8

If a party to a claim does not seek professional advice from a solicitor they should still, in so far as is reasonably possible, comply with the terms of this Protocol. In this Protocol "solicitor" is intended to encompass reference to any suitably legally qualified person.

If a party to a claim becomes aware that another party is a litigant in person, they should send a copy of this Protocol to the litigant in person at the earliest opportunity.

2 THE AIMS OF THE PROTOCOL

2.1

The **general** aims of the Protocol are –

    (a) to maintain and/or restore the patient/healthcare provider relationship in an open and transparent way;

(b) to reduce delay and ensure that costs are proportionate; and

(c) to resolve as many disputes as possible without litigation.

2.2

The **specific** objectives are–

(a) to encourage openness, transparency and early communication of the perceived problem between patients and healthcare providers;

(b) to provide an opportunity for healthcare providers to identify whether notification of a notifiable safety incident has been, or should be, sent to the claimant in accordance with the duty of candour imposed by section 20 of the Health and Social Care Act 2008 (Regulated Activities) Regulations 2014;

(c) to ensure that sufficient medical and other information is disclosed promptly by both parties to enable each to understand the other's perspective and case, and to encourage early resolution or a narrowing of the issues in dispute;

(d) to provide an early opportunity for healthcare providers to identify cases where an investigation is required and to carry out that investigation promptly;

(e) to encourage healthcare providers to involve the *National Health Service Litigation Authority* (NHSLA) or their defence organisations or insurers at an early stage;

(f) to enable the parties to avoid litigation by agreeing a resolution of the dispute;

(g) to enable the parties to explore the use of mediation or to narrow the issues in dispute before proceedings are commenced;

(h) to enable parties to identify any issues that may require a separate or preliminary hearing, such as a dispute as to limitation;

(i) To support the efficient management of proceedings where litigation cannot be avoided;

(j) to discourage the prolonged pursuit of unmeritorious claims and the prolonged defence of meritorious claims;

(k) to promote the provision of medical or rehabilitation treatment to address the needs of the claimant at the earliest opportunity; and

(l) to encourage the defendant to make an early apology to the claimant if appropriate.

2.3

This Protocol does not—

(a) provide any detailed guidance to healthcare providers on clinical risk management or the adoption of risk management systems and procedures;

(b) provide any detailed guidance on which adverse outcomes should trigger an investigation; or

(c) recommend changes to the codes of conduct of professionals in healthcare.

3 THE PROTOCOL

3.1

An illustrative flowchart is attached at Annex A which shows each of the stages that the parties are expected to take before the commencement of proceedings.

Obtaining health records

3.2

Any request for records by the **claimant** should–

(a) **provide sufficient information** to alert the defendant where an adverse outcome has been serious or has had serious consequences or may constitute a notifiable safety incident;

(b) be as **specific as possible** about the records which are required for an initial investigation of the claim (including, for example, a continuous copy of the CTG trace in birth injury cases); and

(c) include a request for any relevant guidelines, analyses, protocols or policies and any documents created in relation to an adverse incident, notifiable safety incident or complaint.

3.3

Requests for copies of the claimant's clinical records should be made using the Law Society and Department of Health approved **standard forms** (enclosed at Annex B), adapted as necessary.

3.4

3.4.1 The copy records should be provided **within 40 days** of the request and for a cost not exceeding the charges permissible under the Access to Health Records Act 1990 and/or the Data Protection Act 1998. Payment may be required in advance by the healthcare provider.

3.4.2 The claimant may also make a request under the Freedom of Information Act 2000.

3.5

At the earliest opportunity, legible copies of the claimant's medical and other records should be placed in an indexed and paginated bundle by the claimant. This bundle should be kept up to date.

3.6

In the rare circumstances that the defendant is in difficulty in complying with the request within 40 days, the **problem should be explained** quickly and details given of what is being done to resolve it.

3.7

If the defendant fails to provide the health records or an explanation for any delay within 40 days, the claimant or their adviser can then apply to the court under rule 31.16 of the Civil Procedure Rules 1998 ('CPR') for an **order for pre-action disclosure**. The court has the power to impose costs sanctions for unreasonable delay in providing records.

3.8

If either the claimant or the defendant considers **additional health records are required from a third party**, in the first instance these should be requested by or through the claimant. Third party healthcare providers are expected to co-operate. Rule 31.17 of the CPR sets out the procedure for applying to the court for pre-action disclosure by third parties.

Rehabilitation

3.9

The claimant and the defendant shall both consider as early as possible whether the claimant has reasonable needs that could be met by rehabilitation treatment or other measures. They should also discuss how these needs might be addressed. An immediate needs assessment report prepared for the purposes of rehabilitation should not be used in the litigation except by consent.

(A copy of the Rehabilitation code can be found at: http:www.iua.co.uk/IUA_Member/Publications)

Letter of Notification

3.10

Annex C1 to this Protocol provides a **template for the recommended contents of a Letter of Notification**; the level of detail will need to be varied to suit the particular circumstances.

3.11

3.11.1 Following receipt and analysis of the records and, if appropriate, receipt of an initial supportive expert opinion, the claimant may wish to send a Letter of Notification to the defendant as soon as practicable.

3.11.2 The Letter of Notification should advise the defendant that this is a claim where a Letter of Claim is likely to be sent because a case as to breach of duty and/or causation has been identified. A copy of the Letter of Notification should also be sent to the NHSLA or, where known, other relevant medical defence organisation or indemnity provider.

3.12

3.12.1 On receipt of a Letter of Notification a defendant should—

(a) acknowledge the letter within 14 days of receipt;
(b) identify who will be dealing with the matter and to whom any Letter of Claim should be sent;
(c) consider whether to commence investigations and/or to obtain factual and expert evidence;
(d) consider whether any information could be passed to the claimant which might narrow the issues in dispute or lead to an early resolution of the claim; and
(e) forward a copy of the Letter of Notification to the NHSLA or other relevant medical defence organisation/indemnity provider.

3.12.2 The court may question any requests by the defendant for extension of time limits if a Letter of Notification was sent but did not prompt an initial investigation.

Letter of Claim

3.13

Annex C2 to this Protocol provides **a template for the recommended contents of a Letter of Claim**: the level of detail will need to be varied to suit the particular circumstances.

3.14

If, following the receipt and analysis of the records, and the receipt of any further advice (including from experts if necessary – see Section 4), the claimant decides that there are grounds for a claim, a letter of claim should be sent to the defendant as soon as practicable. Any letter of claim sent to an NHS Trust should be copied to the National Health Service Litigation Authority.

3.16

This letter should contain—

(a) a **clear summary of the facts** on which the claim is based, including the alleged adverse outcome, and the **main allegations of negligence**;
(b) a description of the **claimant's injuries**, and present condition and prognosis;
(c) an outline of the **financial loss** incurred by the claimant, with an indication of the heads of damage to be claimed and the scale of the loss, unless this is impracticable;
(d) confirmation of the method of funding and whether any funding arrangement was entered into before or after April 2013; and
(e) the discipline of any expert from whom evidence has already been obtained.

3.17

The Letter of Claim **should refer to any relevant documents**, including health records, and if possible enclose copies of any of those which will not already be in the potential defendant's possession, e.g. any relevant general practitioner records if the claimant's claim is against a hospital.

3.18

Sufficient information must be given to enable the defendant to **focus investigations** and to put an initial valuation on the claim.

3.19

Letters of Claim are **not** intended to have the same formal status as Particulars of Claim, nor should any sanctions necessarily apply if the Letter of Claim and any subsequent Particulars of Claim in the proceedings differ.

3.20

Proceedings should not be issued until after four months from the letter of claim.

In certain instances it may not be possible for the claimant to serve a Letter of Claim more than four months before the expiry of the limitation period. If, for any reason, proceedings are started before the parties have complied, they should seek to agree to apply to the court for an order to stay the proceedings whilst the parties take steps to comply.

3.21

The claimant may want to make an **offer to settle** the claim at this early stage by putting forward an offer in respect of liability and/or an amount of compensation in accordance with the legal and procedural requirements of CPR Part 36 (possibly including any costs incurred to date). If an offer to settle is made, generally this should be supported by a medical report which deals with the injuries, condition and prognosis, and by a schedule of loss and supporting documentation. The level of detail necessary will depend on the value of the claim. Medical reports may not be necessary where there is no significant continuing injury and a detailed schedule may not be necessary in a low value case.

Letter of Response

3.22

Attached at Annex C3 is a template for the suggested contents of the **Letter of Response**: the level of detail will need to be varied to suit the particular circumstances.

3.23

The defendant should **acknowledge** the Letter of Claim **within 14 days of receipt** and should identify who will be dealing with the matter.

3.24

The defendant should, **within four months** of the Letter of Claim, provide a **reasoned answer** in the form of a **Letter of Response** in which the defendant should—

> (a) if the **claim is admitted**, say so in clear terms;
> (b) if only **part of the claim is admitted**, make clear which issues of breach of duty and/or causation are admitted and which are denied and why;
> (c) state whether it is intended that any **admissions will be binding**;
> (d) if the **claim is denied**, include specific comments on the allegations of negligence and, if a synopsis or chronology of relevant events has been provided and is disputed, the defendant's version of those events;
> (e) if supportive expert evidence has been obtained, identify which disciplines of expert evidence have been relied upon and whether they relate to breach of duty and/or causation;
> (f) if known, state whether the defendant requires copies of any relevant medical records obtained by the claimant (to be supplied for a reasonable copying charge);
> (g) provide copies of any additional documents relied upon, e.g. an internal protocol;
> (h) if not indemnified by the NHS, supply details of the relevant indemnity insurer; and
> (i) inform the claimant of any other potential defendants to the claim.

3.25

3.25.1 If the defendant requires an extension of time for service of the Letter of Response, a request should be made as soon as the defendant becomes aware that it will be required and, in any event, within four months of the letter of claim.

3.25.2 The defendant should explain why any extension of time is necessary.

3.25.3 The claimant should adopt a reasonable approach to any request for an extension of time for provision of the reasoned answer.

3.26

If the claimant has made an offer to settle, the defendant should respond to that offer in the Letter of Response, preferably with reasons. The defendant may also make an offer to settle at this stage. Any offer made by the defendant should be made in accordance with the legal and procedural requirements of CPR Part 36 (possibly including any costs incurred to date). If an offer to settle is made, the defendant should provide sufficient medical or other evidence to allow the claimant to properly consider the offer. The level of detail necessary will depend on the value of the claim.

3.27

If the parties reach agreement on liability, or wish to explore the possibility of resolution with no admissions as to liability, but time is needed to resolve the value of the claim, they should aim to agree a reasonable period.

3.28

If the parties do not reach agreement on liability, they should discuss whether the claimant should start proceedings and whether the court might be invited to direct an early trial of a preliminary issue or of breach of duty and/or causation.

3.29

Following receipt of the Letter of Response, if the claimant is aware that there may be a delay of six months or more before the claimant decides if, when and how to proceed, the claimant should keep the defendant generally informed.

4 EXPERTS

4.1

In clinical negligence disputes separate **expert opinions** may be needed—

- on breach of duty;
- on causation;
- on the patient's condition and prognosis;
- to assist in valuing aspects of the claim.

4.2

It is recognised that in clinical negligence disputes, the parties and their advisers will require flexibility in their approach to expert evidence. The parties should co-operate when making decisions on appropriate medical specialisms, whether experts might be instructed jointly and whether any reports obtained pre-action might be shared.

4.3

Obtaining expert evidence will often be an expensive step and may take time, especially in specialised areas of medicine where there are limited numbers of suitable experts.

4.4

When considering what expert evidence may be required during the Protocol period, parties should be aware that the use of any expert reports obtained pre-action will only be permitted in proceedings with the express permission of the court.

5 ALTERNATIVE DISPUTE RESOLUTION

5.1

Litigation should be a last resort. As part of this Protocol, the parties should consider whether negotiation or some other form of alternative dispute resolution ('ADR') might enable them to resolve their dispute without commencing proceedings.

5.2

Some of the options for resolving disputes without commencing proceedings are—

(a) discussion and negotiation (which may or may not include making Part 36 Offers or providing an explanation and/or apology)
(b) mediation, a third party facilitating a resolution;
(c) arbitration, a third party deciding the dispute;
(d) early neutral evaluation, a third party giving an informed opinion on the dispute; and
(e) Ombudsmen schemes.

5.3

Information on mediation and other forms of ADR is available in the *Jackson ADR Handbook* (available from Oxford University Press) or at—

- http://www.civilmediation.justice.gov.uk/
- http://www.adviceguide.org.uk/england/law_e/law_legal_system_e/law_ta king_legal_action_e/alternatives_to_court.htm

5.4

If proceedings are issued, the parties may be required by the court to provide evidence that ADR has been considered. It is expressly recognised that no party can or should be forced to mediate or enter into any form of ADR, but a party's silence in response to an invitation to participate in ADR might be considered unreasonable by the court and could lead to the court ordering that party to pay additional court costs.

6 STOCKTAKE

6.1

6.1.1 Where a dispute has not been resolved after the parties have followed the procedure set out in this Protocol, the parties should review their positions before the claimant issues court proceedings.

6.1.2 If proceedings cannot be avoided, the parties should continue to co-operate and should seek to prepare a chronology of events which identifies the facts or issues that are agreed and those that remain in dispute. The parties should also seek to agree the necessary procedural directions for efficient case management during the proceedings.

ANNEX A: NB: At the time of publication the illustrative flowchart at Annex A was not available on the Justice website at http://www.justice.gov.uk/courts/procedure-rules/civil/pdf/preview/pre-action-protocol-amendments-6-april.pdf

ANNEX B: FORM FOR OBTAINING HEALTH RECORDS

Consent form
(Releasing health records under the Data Protection Act 1998)

About this form

In order to proceed with your claim, your solicitor may need to see your health records. Solicitors usually need to see all your records as they need to assess which parts are relevant to your case. (Past medical history is often relevant to a claim for compensation.) Also, if your claim goes ahead, the person you are making the claim against will ask for copies of important documents. Under court rules, they may see all your health records. So your solicitor needs to be familiar with all your records.

Part a – your, the health professionals' and your solicitor's or agent's details

Your full name:	
Your address:	
Date of birth:	
Date of incident:	
Solicitor's or agent's name and address:	
GP's name and address (and phone number if known):	
Name (and address if known) of the hospitals you went to in relation to this incident :	
If you have seen any other person or organisation about your injuries (for example, a physiotherapist) or have had any investigations (for example, x-rays) please provide details.	

Part b – your declaration and signature

Please see the 'Notes for the client' over the page before you sign this form.

To health professionals

I understand that filling in and signing this form gives you permission to give copies of all my GP records, and any hospital records relating to this incident, to my solicitor or agent whose details are given above.

Please give my solicitor or agent copies of my health records, in line with the Data Protection Act 1998, within 40 days.

Your signature:		Date:	/ /

Part c – your solicitor's or agent's declaration and signature

Please see the 'Notes for the solicitor or agent' over the page before you sign this form.

To health professionals

I have told my client the implications of giving me access to his or her health records. I confirm that I need the full records in this case. I enclose the authorised fee for getting access to records.

Solicitor's or agent's signature:		Date:	/ /

Notes for the client

Your health records contain information from almost all consultations you have had with health professionals. The information they contain usually includes:

- why you saw a health professional;
- details of clinical findings and diagnoses;
- any options for care and treatment the health professional discussed with you;
- the decisions made about your care and treatment, including evidence that you agreed; and
- details of action health professionals have taken and the outcomes.

By signing this form, you are agreeing to the health professional or hospital named on this form releasing copies of your health records to your solicitor or agent. During the process your records may be seen by people who are not health professionals, but they will keep the information confidential.

If you are making, or considering making, a legal claim against someone, your solicitor will need to see copies of all your GP records, and any hospital records made in connection with this incident, so he or she can see if there is anything in your records that may affect your claim. Once you start your claim, the court can order you to give copies of your health records to the solicitor of the person you are making a claim against so he or she can see if any of the information in your records can be used to defend his or her client.

If you decide to go ahead with your claim, your records may be passed to a number of people including:

- the expert who your solicitor or agent instructs to produce a medical report as evidence for the case;
- the person you are making a claim against and their solicitors;
- the insurance company for the person you are making a claim against;
- any insurance company or other organisation paying your legal costs; and
- any other person or company officially involved with the claim.

You do not have to give permission for your health records to be released but if you don't, the court may not let you go ahead with your claim and, in some circumstances, your solicitor may refuse to represent you.

If there is very sensitive information in the records, that is not connected to the claim, you should tell your solicitor. They will then consider whether this information needs to be revealed.

Notes for the solicitor or agent

Before you ask your client to fill in and sign this form you should explain that this will involve his or her full health records being released and how the information in them may be used. You should also tell your client to read the notes above.

If your client is not capable of giving his or her permission in this form, this form should be signed by:

- your client's litigation friend;
- someone who has enduring power of attorney to act for your client; or
- your client's receiver appointed by the Court of Protection.

When you send this form to the appropriate records controller please also enclose the authorised fees for getting access to records.

If you find out at any stage that the medical records contain information that the client does not know about (for example, being diagnosed with a serious illness), you should discuss this with the health professional who provided the records.

Unless your client agrees otherwise, you must use his or her health records only for the purpose for which the client signed this form (that is, making his or her claim). Under the Data Protection Act you have responsibilities relating to sensitive information. The entire health record should not be automatically revealed without the client's permission and you should not keep health records for any longer than you need them. You should return them to the client at the end of the claim if they want them. Otherwise, you are responsible for destroying them.

Notes for the medical records controller

This form shows your patient's permission for you to give copies of his or her full GP record, and any hospital records relating to this incident, to his or her solicitor or agent. You must give the solicitor or agent copies of these health records unless any of the exemptions set out in The Data Protection (Subject Access Modification) (Health) Order 2000 apply. The main exemptions are that you must not release information that:

- is likely to cause serious physical or mental harm to the patient or another person; or
- relates to someone who would normally need to give their permission (where that person is not a health professional who has cared for the patient).

Your patient's permission for you to release information is valid only if that patient understands the consequences of his or her records being released, and how the information will be used. The solicitor or agent named on this form must explain these issues to the patient. If you have any doubt about whether this has happened, contact the solicitor or agent, or your patient.

If your patient is not capable of giving his or her permission, this form should be signed by:

- a 'litigation friend' acting for your patient;
- someone with 'enduring power of attorney' to act for your patient; or
- a receiver appointed by the Court of Protection.

You may charge the usual fees authorised under the Data Protection Act for providing the records.

The BMA publishes detailed advice for doctors on giving access to health records, including the fees that you may charge. You can view that advice by visiting www.bma.org.uk/ap.nsf/Content/accesshealthrecords

This form is published by the Law Society and British Medical Association. (2nd edition, October 2004)

 BMA

 The Law Society

 Crystal Mark

ANNEX C: TEMPLATES FOR LETTERS OF NOTIFICATION, CLAIM AND RESPONSE

C1 Letter of Notification

To

Defendant

Dear Sirs

Letter of Notification

Re: [Claimant's Name, Address, DoB and NHS Number]

We have been instructed to act on behalf of [Claimant's name] in relation to treatment carried out/care provided at [name of hospital or treatment centre] by [name of clinician(s) if known] on [insert date(s)].

The purpose of this letter is to notify you that, although we are not yet in a position to serve a formal Letter of Claim, our initial investigations indicate that a case as to breach of duty and/or causation has been identified. We therefore invite you to commence your own investigation and draw your attention to the fact that failure to do may be taken into account when considering the reasonableness of any subsequent application for an extension of time for the Letter of Response.

Defendant

We understand that you are the correct defendant in respect of treatment provided by [name of clinician] at [hospital/surgery/treatment centre] on [date(s)]. If you do not agree, please provide us with any information you have that may assist us to identify the correct defendant. Failure to do so may result in costs sanctions should proceedings be issued.

Summary of Facts and Alleged Adverse Outcome

[Outline what is alleged to have happened and provide a chronology of events with details of relevant known treatment/care.]

Medical Records

[Provide index of records obtained and request for further records/information if required.]

Allegations of Negligence

[Brief outline of any alleged breach of duty and causal link with any damage suffered.]

Expert Evidence

[State whether expert evidence has been obtained or is awaited and, if so, the relevant discipline.]

Damage

[Brief outline of any injuries attributed to the alleged negligence and their functional impact.]

Funding

[If known, state method of funding and whether arrangement was entered into before or after April 2013.]

Rehabilitation

As a result of the allegedly negligent treatment, our client has injuries/needs that could be met by rehabilitation. We invite you to consider how this could be achieved.

Limitation

For the purposes of limitation, we calculate that any proceedings will need to be issued on or before [date].

Please acknowledge this letter by [insert date 14 days after deemed receipt] and confirm to whom any Letter of Claim should be sent. We enclose a duplicate of the letter for your insurer.

Recoverable Benefits

The claimant's National Insurance Number will be sent to you in a separate envelope.

We look forward to hearing from you.

Yours faithfully,

C2 Letter of Claim

To

Defendant

Dear Sirs

Letter of Claim

[Claimant's name] –v- [Defendant's Name]

We have been instructed to act on behalf of [Claimant's name] in relation to treatment carried out/care provided at [name of hospital or treatment centre] by [name of clinician(s) if known] on [insert date(s)]. Please let us know if you do not believe that you are the appropriate defendant or if you are aware of any other potential defendants.

Claimant's details

Full name, DoB, address, NHS Number.

Dates of allegedly negligent treatment

- include chronology based on medical records.

Events giving rise to the claim:

- an outline of what happened, including details of other relevant treatments to the client by other healthcare providers.

Allegation of negligence and causal link with injuries:

- an outline of the allegations or a more detailed list in a complex case;
- an outline of the causal link between allegations and the injuries complained of;
- A copy of any supportive expert evidence (optional).

The Client's injuries, condition and future prognosis

- A copy of any supportive expert report (optional);
- Suggestions for rehabilitation;
- The discipline of any expert evidence obtained or proposed.

Clinical records (if not previously provided)

We enclose an index of all the relevant records that we hold. We shall be happy to provide copies of these on payment of our photocopying charges.

We enclose a request for copies of the following records which we believe that you hold. We confirm that we shall be responsible for your reasonable copying charges. Failure to provide these records may result in costs sanctions if proceedings are issued.

The likely value of the claim

- an outline of the main heads of damage, or, in straightforward cases, the details of loss;
- Part 36 settlement offer (optional);
- suggestions for ADR.

Funding

[State method of funding and whether arrangement was entered into before or after April 2013.]

We enclose a further copy of this letter for you to pass to your insurer. We look forward to receiving an acknowledgment of this letter within 14 days and your Letter of Response within 4 months of the date on which this letter was received. We calculate the date for receipt of your Letter of Response to be [date].

Recoverable Benefits

The claimant's National Insurance Number will be sent to you in a separate envelope.

We look forward to hearing from you.

Yours faithfully

C3 Letter of Response

To

Claimant

Dear Sirs

Letter of Response

[Claimant's name] –v- [Defendant's Name]

We have been instructed to act on behalf of [defendant] in relation to treatment carried out/care provided to [claimant] at [name of hospital or treatment centre] by [name of clinician(s) if known] on [insert date(s)].

The defendant [conveys sympathy for the adverse outcome/would like to offer an apology/denies that there was an adverse outcome].

Parties

It is accepted that [defendant] had a duty of care towards [claimant] in respect of [details if required] treatment/care provided to [claimant] at [location] on [date(s)].

However, [defendant] is not responsible for [details] care/treatment provided to [claimant] at [location] on [date(s)] by [name of clinician if known].

Records

We hold the following records…

We require copies of the following records…

Failure to provide these records may result in costs sanctions if proceedings are issued.

Comments on events and/or chronology:

We [agree the chronology enclosed with the Letter of Claim] [enclose a revised chronology of events].

We enclose copies of relevant [records/Protocols/internal investigations] in respect of the treatment/care that [claimant] received.

Liability

In respect of the specific allegations raised by the claimant, the defendant [has obtained an expert opinion and] responds as follows:-

[each allegation should be addressed separately. The defendant should explain which (if any) of the allegations of breach of duty and/or causation are admitted and why. The defendant should also make clear which allegations are denied and why].

Next Steps

The defendant suggests…

[e.g. no prospect of success for the claimant, resolution without admissions of liability, ADR, settlement offer, rehabilitation].

Yours faithfully,

Appendix 2

MODEL DIRECTIONS

MODEL DIRECTIONS FOR CLINICAL NEGLIGENCE CASES (2012) - BEFORE MASTER ROBERTS AND MASTER COOK

Introductory note.

These are the Model Directions for use in the first Case Management Conference in clinical negligence cases before the Masters.

A draft order in Word format, adopting the Model Directions as necessary, is to be provided by e-mail to the Master at least 2 days before the hearing.

Parties are required to use the form of order at the end of this document – adapted as necessary. From April 2013 CPR Rule changes will require parties to take as their starting point any relevant Model or Standard Directions

The changes to the 2010 directions are to be found in paragraphs 4, 9, 10, 11, 19, 23, and 25. The changes are necessary but are not radical.

The e-mail addresses of the clinical negligence Masters are:

master.roberts@judiciary.gsi.gov.uk
master.cook@judiciary.gsi.gov.uk

The Model Directions allow the court and the parties to be flexible. For example, sequential exchange of quantum statements (say, with schedule and counter-schedule of loss) may be appropriate. The sequential exchange of expert evidence on breach of duty and causation may sometimes be appropriate.

It would be helpful if dates appeared in **bold** type.

Please note: Solicitors must ensure that the claimant is accurately described in the title to the order: e.g., "JOHN SMITH (a child and protected party by his mother and Litigation Friend, JOAN SMITH). It is never permissible to refer to such a claimant as "JOHN SMITH".

The order should make it clear that it is made pursuant to a Case Management Conference or an application or both.

Please note the role of experts in the preparation of Agendas.

THE MODEL DIRECTIONS

The annotations in italics are to assist the parties and are not part of the Model Directions and should not appear in the order.

A draft order – without the annotations – appears at the end of this document. Parties are requested to adopt this draft.

***

Allocation

1.   The case do remain on the Multi-track.

Allocation: The order states that "the case do remain on the Multi-track". Allocation may well have been dealt with before the CMC.

Preservation of Evidence

2.   The Defendant do retain and preserve safely the original clinical notes relating to the action pending the trial. The Defendant do give facilities for inspection by the Claimant, the Claimant's legal advisers and experts of the said original notes upon 7 days written notice to do so.

Maintenance of records and reports etc

3.   Legible copies of the medical (and educational) records of the Claimant / Deceased / Claimant's Mother are to be placed in a separate paginated bundle at the earliest opportunity by the Claimant's Solicitors and kept up to date. All references to medical notes in any report are to be made by reference to the pages in that bundle.

4.   The parties do retain all electronically stored documents relating to the claim.

Amendments

The following is suggested:

Permission to Claimant / Defendant to amend the Particulars of Claim / Defence in terms of the draft initialed by the Master [or the draft served on   / /12]; the Defendant to serve an amended Defence by   / /12. Costs of and occasioned by the amendments to be borne by (usually, the party seeking permission to amend). [Where no draft is available, but the form of the amendments is not contentious] (Party wishing to amend) to serve draft amended [Statement of Case] by / /12. If no objection to the draft amendments, response to be served by / /12, if objection is taken to the draft, permission to restore.

Judgment

The following is suggested:

There be judgment for the Claimant with damages to be assessed.

Or

There be judgment for the Claimant for ...% of the damages as are assessed (or agreed by the parties) as due on a full liability basis.

Split Trial

[An order "That there be a split trial" is inappropriate. The following is suggested.]

5.   A preliminary issue shall be tried between the Claimant and the Defendant as to whether or not the Defendant is liable to the Claimant by reason of the matters alleged in the Particulars of Claim and, if so, whether or not any of the injuries pleaded were caused thereby; if any such injuries were so caused, the extent of the same.

Disclosure

6.   There be standard disclosure [on the preliminary issue] [limited to quantum] by list by   2012. Any initial request for inspection or copy documents is to be made within 7/14 days of service of the lists.

Where there is a large number of documents all falling into a particular category, the disclosing party may list those documents as a category rather than individually. See: para 3.2 to Practice Direction 31A.

Factual Evidence

7.   Signed and dated witness statements of fact in respect of breach of duty and causation [and quantum] shall be simultaneously exchanged by   2012. Civil Evidence Act notices are to be served by the same date. The witness statements of all concerned with the treatment and care of the Claimant at the time of the matters alleged against the Defendant shall be served under this paragraph.

8.   Signed and dated witness statements of fact in respect of quantum, condition and prognosis shall be served by   2012 (Claimant) and   2012   (Defendant).   Civil Evidence Act notices are to be served by the same date.

Expert Evidence.
A.   Single Joint Experts.

9.   Each party has permission to rely on the evidence of a single joint expert in the following fields: *[state the disciplines; and identify the issues*].*   The experts are to be instructed by   2012 and the joint expert is to provide his/her report to the instructing parties by   2012.   In case of difficulty, the parties have permission to restore before the Master.

If the parties are unable to agree on the identity of the expert to be instructed, the parties are to restore the CMC before the Master. At such hearing the parties are to provide details of the CVs, availability and the estimated fee of the expert they propose and reasoned objections to any other proposed.

* These words may be deleted where the issues do not have to be defined.

B.   Separate Experts.

10.   In respect of breach of duty and causation, each party has permission to rely on the evidence of an expert in the following fields: *[state the disciplines; and the names of the experts where known];*   permission being given to call the said experts on matters remaining in issue.

The reports of the said experts are to be simultaneously exchanged by
              2012.

11.   In respect of quantum, condition and prognosis, each party (*[where there are several defendants]* the Defendants acting jointly, unless otherwise directed) has permission to rely on the evidence of an expert in the following fields: *[state the disciplines; and the name of the experts where known];* permission being given to call the said experts on matters remaining in issue.

The reports of the said experts are to be served by:

Claimant:	2012
Defendant(s):	2012

Literature and CVs

12.   Any unpublished literature upon which any expert witness proposes to rely shall be served at the same time as service of his report together with a list of published literature. Any supplementary literature upon which any expert witness proposes to rely shall be notified to all other parties at least one month before trial. No expert witness shall rely upon any publications that have not been disclosed in accordance with this direction without the permission of the trial judge on such terms as to costs as he deems fit.

13.   Experts shall, at the time of producing their reports, produce a CV giving details of any employment or activity which raises a possible conflict of interest.

Experts' Discussions

14.   **Unless otherwise agreed by all parties' solicitors, after consulting with the experts**, the experts of like discipline for the parties shall discuss the case on a without prejudice basis by   2012. *(Usually 8 weeks after the exchange of reports).*

Discussions between experts are not mandatory. The parties should consider, with their expert, whether there is likely to be any useful purpose in holding a discussion and should be prepared to agree that no discussion is in fact needed.

(a)   The purpose of the discussions is to identify:
      (i)   The extent of the agreement between the experts;
      (ii)   The points of disagreement and short reasons for disagreement;

(iii)   Action, if any, which may be taken to resolve the outstanding points of disagreement;

(iv)   Any further material points not raised in the Agenda and the extent to which these issues are agreed;

(b)   **Unless otherwise agreed by all parties' solicitors, after consulting with the experts,** a draft Agenda which directs the experts to the remaining issues relevant to the experts' discipline, as identified in the statements of case shall be prepared jointly by the Claimant's solicitors and experts and sent to the Defendant's solicitors for comment at least 35 days before the agreed date for the experts' discussions;

Claimants' solicitors and counsel should note the obligation to prepare the draft Agenda jointly with the relevant expert. Experts should note that it is part of their overriding duty to the court to ensure that the Agenda complies with the following direction.

The use of agendas is not mandatory. Solicitors should consult with the experts to ensure that agendas are necessary and, if used, are reasonable in scope. The agenda should assist the experts and should not be in the form of leading questions or hostile in tone. An agenda must include a list of the outstanding issues in the preamble.

[Note : The preamble should state: the standard of proof : the Bolam test : remind the experts not to attempt to determine factual issues : remind them not to stray outside their field of expertise and indicate the form of the joint statement. It will also be helpful to provide a comprehensive list of the materials which each expert has seen, perhaps in the form of an agreed supplementary bundle (it is assumed that experts will have been provided with the medical notes bundle)]

(c)   The Defendants shall within 21 days of receipt agree the Agenda, or propose amendments;

(d)   Seven days thereafter all solicitors shall use their best endeavours to agree the Agenda. Points of disagreement should be on matters of real substance and not semantics or on matters the experts could resolve of their own accord at the discussion. In default of agreement, both versions shall be considered at the discussions. Agendas, when used, shall be provided to the experts not less than 7 days before the date fixed for discussions.

[Where it has been impossible to agree a single agenda, it is of assistance to the experts if the second agenda is consecutively numbered to the first, i.e. if the first agenda has 16 questions in it, the second agenda is numbered from 17 onwards]

15.   **Unless otherwise ordered by the Court, or unless agreed by all parties, including the experts**, neither the parties nor their legal representatives may attend such discussions. If the legal representatives do attend, they should not normally intervene in the discussion, except to

answer questions put to them by the experts or to advise on the law; and the experts may if they so wish hold part of their discussions in the absence of the legal representatives.

16.   A signed joint statement shall be prepared by the experts dealing with (a) (i) – (iv) above. Individual copies of such statements shall be signed by the experts at the conclusion of the discussion, or as soon thereafter as practicable and provided to the parties' solicitors within **7 days** of the discussions.

17.   Experts give their own opinions to assist the court and should attend discussions on the basis that they have full authority to sign the joint statement. The experts should not require the authorisation of solicitor or counsel before signing a joint statement.

[**Note:** *This does not affect Rule 35.12 which provides that where experts reach agreement on an issue during their discussions, the agreement shall not bind the parties unless the parties expressly agree to be bound by the agreement*]

18.   If an expert radically alters his or her opinion, the joint statement should include a note or addendum by that expert explaining the change of opinion.

19.   Experts instructed by the parties in accordance with this and any subsequent Order shall be provided with a copy of the Order by the instructing party within 7 days after it is sealed, or at the time of instruction whichever is the later.

Schedules and periodical payments

20.   Claimant do serve a final Schedule of loss and damage costed to the date of trial by   2012.

21.   The Defendant do serve a Counter-Schedule by   2012.

22.   The parties do set out their respective positions on the periodical payment of damages in the Schedule and Counter-Schedule of loss. [or, The periodical payment of damages is not appropriate to this case.]

Periodical Payments. Parties should, at the first CMC, be prepared to give their provisional view as to whether the case is one in which the periodical payment of damages might be appropriate.

Schedules. Parties are encouraged to exchange Schedules in a form which enables the Counter schedule to be based on the Claimant's Schedule i.e. by delivering a disk with the hard copy, or by sending it as an e-mail attachment.]

Trial Directions

23.   The Claimant's Solicitors do by   2012 apply to Queen's Bench Judges' Listing in London / [the Listing Officer in the venue] for a listing appointment for a trial period for hearing within the trial window and give notice of the appointment to the Defendant. Pre-trial check lists to be filed as directed by Queen's Bench Judges' Listing.

Mode of trial: Judge alone; London; Category [Usually] B ; time estimate   days.

Trial window:

[Certified fit for High Court Judge if available].

Trial Directions

The Claimant will usually be directed to apply to the Queen's Bench Judges' Listing for a listing appointment no later than 6 weeks after the CMC.

The Queen's Bench Judges' Listing, in order to maintain the necessary degree of flexibility for listing, will give a 'trial period' rather than a fixed date, but, in order to accommodate the parties' need for certainty as to dates for experts to attend, will, if an approach is made closer to the beginning of the trial period, confirm the date for the trial to begin as the first day of the trial period.

The trial period will usually be directed to begin at least 2 clear months after the last event besides ADR – this is to allow for ADR.

In relatively modest claims (in term of quantum), the Master may direct:

> *"If the parties reach agreement upon breach of duty and causation, the parties are to immediately restore the case before the Master so that alternative directions on the assessment of damages may be considered."*

24.   Parties do agree the contents of the trial bundle and exchange skeleton arguments not less than 7 days before the hearing. Claimant to lodge the skeleton arguments and the Trial bundle under PD 39.3

Trial Bundles

Note: the object is to ensure that all the relevant material is provided at one time to the Clerk of the Lists to pass to the trial judge. The PD sets out both the contents of the bundle and the time when it must be lodged.

Alternative Dispute Resolution

25.   At all stages the parties must consider whether the case is capable of resolution by ADR. Any party refusing to engage in ADR by   2012 *[a date usually about 3 months before the trial window opens]* shall, not less than 28 days before the commencement of the trial, serve a witness statement, without prejudice save as to costs, giving reasons for that

refusal. Such witness statement must not be shown to the trial judge until the question of costs arises.

26.   Such means of ADR as shall be adopted shall be concluded not less than 35 days prior to the trial.

['ADR' includes 'round table' conferences, at which the parties attempt to define and narrow the issues in the case, including those to which expert evidence is directed; early neutral evaluation; mediation; and arbitration. The object is to try to reduce the number of cases settled 'at the door of the Court', which are wasteful both of costs and judicial time.]

Further CMC etc

27.   There be a further CMC on   2012 at   am/pm; Room E118/E112; time estimate 30 minutes. This hearing may be vacated by consent provided that all directions have been complied with; no further directions are required; and the Master is given reasonable notice.

28.   Permission to restore.

*[**Note**: A party may request the restoration of a CMC or application by letter or e-mail to the assigned Master. If possible the Master should be provided with an agreed list of dates to avoid. Where the application is urgent and the time estimate is no more than 30 minutes, the Master will endeavour to list a hearing at 10.00am as soon as possible. Applications estimated to take more than 30 minutes should be applied for as private room appointments in the usual way.]*
*[Both Masters are willing, in appropriate cases, to hear applications by telephone link, provided sufficient notice is given **directly to the Master concerned** and the relevant papers are provided in advance. E-mails are an acceptable means of communication, **provided that they are copied to all parties.**]*

[NOTE. :   The Court File in cases proceeding before the Masters will not routinely be placed before the Master. Parties wishing for it to be produced should notify the Case Management Section FIVE CLEAR DAYS in advance of the appointment. In all other cases parties should bring with them copies of any filed documents upon which they intend to rely.]

29.   Costs in case *[Or other costs order sought]*.

30.   Claimant to draw and file the order by   2012 and serve the Defendant (or Claimant to serve sealed order by   2012).

Dated the

DRAFT ORDER

See over

IN THE HIGH COURT OF JUSTICE   **Claim No. HQ012X0ZZZZ**

QUEEN'S BENCH DIVISION

MASTER [ROBERTS / COOK]

B E T W E E N

ABC

Claimant

And

DEF NHS TRUST

Defendant

ORDER

UPON a Case Management Conference

[AND UPON the Claimant's / Defendant's application issued on   2012]

AND UPON hearing solicitor/counsel for the Claimant and solicitor/counsel for the Defendant

IT IS ORDERED that

1.   The case do remain on the Multi-track.

2.   The Defendant do retain and preserve safely the original clinical notes relating to the claim pending the trial. The Defendant do give facilities for inspection by the Claimant, the Claimant's legal advisers and experts of the said original notes upon 7 days written notice to do so.

3.   Legible copies of the medical (and educational) records of the Claimant / Deceased / Claimant's Mother are to be placed in a separate paginated bundle at the earliest opportunity by the Claimant's Solicitors and kept up to date. All references to medical notes in any report are to be made by reference to the pages in that bundle.

4.   The parties do retain all electronically stored documents relating to the claim.

5.   A preliminary issue shall be tried between the Claimant and the Defendant as to whether or not the Defendant is liable to the Claimant by reason of the matters alleged in the Particulars of Claim and, if so, whether or not any of the injuries pleaded were caused thereby; if any such injuries were so caused, the extent of the same.

6.   There be standard disclosure [on the preliminary issue] [limited to quantum] by list by   2012. Any initial request for inspection or copy documents is to be made within 7/14 days of service of the lists.

7.   Signed and dated witness statements of fact in respect of breach of duty and causation [and quantum] shall be simultaneously exchanged by   2012. Civil Evidence Act notices are to be served by the same date. The witness statements of all concerned with the treatment and care of the Claimant at the time of the matters alleged against the Defendant shall be served under this paragraph.

8.   Signed and dated witness statements of fact in respect of quantum, condition and prognosis shall be served by   2012 (Claimant) and   2012 (Defendant).   Civil Evidence Act notices are to be served by the same date.

9.   Each party has permission to rely on the evidence of a single joint expert in the following fields: *[state the disciplines; and identify the issues]*. The experts are to be instructed by   2012 and the joint expert is to provide his report to the instructing parties by   2012. In case of difficulty, the parties have permission to restore before the Master.

10.   In respect of breach of duty and causation, each party has permission to rely on the evidence of an expert in the following fields: *[state the disciplines; and the names of the experts, where known]*;   permission being given to call the said experts on matters remaining in issue. The reports of the said experts are to be simultaneously exchanged by   2012.

11.   In respect of quantum, condition and prognosis, each party (*[where there are several defendants]* the Defendants acting jointly, unless otherwise directed) has permission to rely on the evidence of an expert in the following fields: *[state the disciplines; and the names of the experts, where known]*; permission being given to call the said experts on matters remaining in issue. The reports of the said experts are to be served by:

Claimant: 2012;   Defendant(s):   2012.

12.   Any unpublished literature upon which any expert witness proposes to rely shall be served at the same time as service of his report together with a list of published literature. Any supplementary literature upon which any expert witness proposes to rely shall be notified to all other parties at least one month before trial. No expert witness shall rely upon any publications

that have not been disclosed in accordance with this direction without the permission of the trial judge on such terms as to costs as he deems fit.

13.   Experts shall, at the time of producing their reports, produce a CV giving details of any employment or activity which raises a possible conflict of interest.

14.   **Unless otherwise agreed by all parties' solicitors, after consulting with the experts**, the experts of like discipline for the parties shall discuss the case on a without prejudice basis by   2012.

Discussions between experts are not mandatory. The parties should consider, with their expert, whether there is likely to be any useful purpose in holding a discussion and should be prepared to agree that no discussion is in fact needed.

(a)   The purpose of the discussions is to identify:
   (i)   The extent of the agreement between the experts;
   (ii)   The points of disagreement and short reasons for disagreement;
   (iii)   Action, if any, which may be taken to resolve the outstanding points of disagreement;
   (iv)   Any further material points not raised in the Agenda and the extent to which these issues are agreed;

(b)   **Unless otherwise agreed by all parties' solicitors, after consulting with the experts,** a draft Agenda which directs the experts to the remaining issues relevant to the experts' discipline, as identified in the statements of case shall be prepared jointly by the Claimant's solicitors and experts and sent to the Defendant's solicitors for comment at least 35 days before the agreed date for the experts' discussions;

The use of agendas is not mandatory. Solicitors should consult with the experts to ensure that agendas are necessary and, if used, are reasonable in scope. The agenda should assist the experts and should not be in the form of leading questions or hostile in tone. An agenda must include a list of the outstanding issues in the preamble.

(c)   The Defendants shall within 21 days of receipt agree the Agenda, or propose amendments;

(d)   Seven days thereafter all solicitors shall use their best endeavours to agree the Agenda. Points of disagreement should be on matters of real substance and not semantics or on matters the experts could resolve of their own accord at the discussion. In default of agreement, both versions shall be considered at the discussions. Agendas, when used, shall be provided to the experts not less than 7 days before the date fixed for discussions.

15.   **Unless otherwise ordered by the Court, or unless agreed by all parties, including the experts**, neither the parties nor their legal representatives may attend such discussions. If the legal representatives do attend, they should not normally intervene in the discussion, except to

answer questions put to them by the experts or to advise on the law; and the experts may if they so wish hold part of their discussions in the absence of the legal representatives.

16.   A signed joint statement shall be prepared by the experts dealing with (a) (i) – (iv) above. Individual copies of such statements shall be signed by the experts at the conclusion of the discussion, or as soon thereafter as practicable and provided to the parties' solicitors within **7 days** of the discussions.

17.   Experts give their own opinions to assist the court and should attend discussions on the basis that they have full authority to sign the joint statement. The experts should not require the authorisation of solicitor or counsel before signing a joint statement.

18.   If an expert radically alters his or her opinion, the joint statement should include a note or addendum by that expert explaining the change of opinion.

19.   Experts instructed by the parties in accordance with this and any subsequent Order shall be provided with a copy of the Order by the instructing party within 7 days after it is sealed, or at the time of instruction, whichever is the later.

20.   Claimant do serve a final Schedule of loss and damage costed to the date of trial by   2012.

21.   The Defendant do serve a Counter-Schedule by   2012.

22.   The parties do set out their respective positions on the periodical payment of damages in the Schedule and Counter-Schedule of loss.

23.   The Claimant's Solicitors do by   2012 apply to Queen's Bench Judges' Listing in London / [the Listing Officer in the venue] for a listing appointment for a trial period for hearing within the trial window and give notice of the appointment to the Defendant. Pre-trial check lists to be filed as directed by Queen's Bench Judges' Listing.

     Mode of trial: Judge alone; London; Category *[Usually]* B ; time estimate   days.
     Trial window:

     [Certified fit for High Court Judge if available].

24.   Parties do agree the contents of the trial bundle and exchange skeleton arguments not less than 7 days before the hearing. Claimant to lodge the skeleton arguments and the Trial bundle under PD 39.3

25.   At all stages the parties must consider whether the case is capable of resolution by ADR. Any party refusing to engage in ADR by   2012 *[a date usually about 3 months before the trial window opens]* shall, not less than 28 days before the commencement of the

trial, serve a witness statement, without prejudice save as to costs, giving reasons for that refusal. Such witness statement must not be shown to the trial judge until the question of costs arises.

26.   Such means of ADR as shall be adopted shall be concluded not less than 35 days prior to the trial.

27.   There be a further CMC on   2012 at   am/pm; Room E118/E112; time estimate 30 minutes. This hearing may be vacated by consent provided that all directions have been complied with; no further directions are required; and the Master is given reasonable notice.

28.   Permission to restore.

29.   Costs in case *[Or other costs order sought]*.

30.   Claimant to draw and file the order by   2012 and serve the Defendant (or Claimant to serve sealed order by   2012).
Dated the